My Life With The Pros

Bud Collins

My Life With The Pros

E. P. DUTTON   NEW YORK

Published in the United States by E. P. Dutton,
a division of NAL Penguin Inc.,
2 Park Avenue, New York, N.Y. 10016.

Published simultaneously in Canada by
Fitzhenry and Whiteside, Limited, Toronto.

Library of Congress Cataloging-in-Publication Data

Collins, Bud.
My life with the pros.

Includes index.
1. Tennis—History. I. Title.
GV992.C65 1989   796.342'09   88-28509
ISBN 0-525-24659-2

DESIGNED BY EARL TIDWELL

1 2 3 4 5 6 7 8 9 10

First Edition

For the fair Lulu,

> *who lovingly put up with her roommate's other love
> and pretended it was a sweet thing of value,
> even though she knew it was only a game,
> and he a case of arrested development.*

"If you're not having fun, then it isn't any fun."
    —Cecilia Martinez of San Francisco, who ranked as high
    as eleventh in the United States in 1968. She applied
    this credo to her job—tennis—and I second the
    notion.

Contents

Sixteen pages of illustrations follow page 176.

ACKNOWLEDGMENTS

Acknowledgments can be dangerous stuff. Suppose the acknowledgee doesn't care to be acknowledged? Or is even insulted to be thus associated with the acknowledger? Does the acknowledgee wonder: "Why did the bum do that? Did I take him to lunch once? Does he think I'll buy a book to see my name?"

To the suspicious, or unwilling, accessories hereto, whose names follow, and to whom I am grateful for one reason or another in helping make this possible, I say merely: Have your lawyer talk to my lawyer.

A lot of lucky things have happened to me, keeping me off the rolls of the meaningfully employed. One of them was the wandering eye of Tim Horgan. If Horgan, today an excellent columnist at the present *Boston Herald*, hadn't decided he could better himself in 1955 by leaving the now-defunct *Herald*, I, an office boy there, wouldn't have been offered his sportswriting job. Tim moved to the *Traveler*, and I inherited the boxing beat, the best of all sports to write, and thus had a remunerative means of staying in Boston, a place I'd wanted to live all along.

xi

(It was in boxing that I encountered that splendid, alas departed, rogue, promoter Sam Silverman, whose watchwords were: "Don't louse up a good story with the facts." Also Elliot ["Big Jumbo"] Price, a bookmaking kingpin, according to the front-page story in *The New York Times*, that reported his federal indictment. To those who offered condolences, Big Jumbo replied, "Are you shitting me? That's real class—to be indicted on page one of the *Times*.")

I've been very lucky in the people I've worked for and with on newspapers and TV. Tom Winship, managing editor of the *Boston Globe* until 1985, rescued me from the *Herald* in 1963 to write a sports column at his place where everyone has been kind and understanding, notably the present sports editor, Vince Doria. Tim Leland, who was the Sunday editor, suggested I write a travel column (entitling it "Anywhere") in 1977. That's been fun, and is still going. Presently Winship assigned me to write a general column on the op-ed page. It ran for a couple of years, allowing me to get shot at in Vietnam (only twice, disproving Vietcong marksmanship claims), among other things. Then the increase in tennis-TV travel, keeping me on the road more than half the time, brought me back to the sports department.

How can I repay the patience and guidance of my first producer-directors, Greg Harney at WGBH-TV in Boston, and Ted Nathanson at NBC? (Actually, my very first NBC producer on one show couldn't keep score in tennis, and told me to forget TV immediately, but that's another story.) Both were inestimable, as bosses and friends. Both have deservedly won a ton of awards, the prize-givers apparently overlooking/forgiving the fact that Harney and Nathanson put *me* on the air.

Huzzahs to fellow boothrats at NBC, unceasingly diligent and professional Dick Enberg, and droll, well-informed JoAnne Russell. Put together with the best of the TV sports commentators *and* an articulate woman who holds a Wimbledon title, Collins feels fortunate to be one-third of the ménage.

One NBC season, 1975, was all I had with an earlier partner, the late Dan Rowan, whose inimitable legacy is "Laugh-In." But it was wonderful to be on a mike with him, even if it was for one of NBC's most widely unwatched shows. Dan would be amused that the obits didn't mention his brief, but well-savored, career as tennis commentator. He loved the game, except for one afternoon in Mexico City. After the telecast we learned that a bomb threat had been ignored by the promoter. Envisioning what might have been a spectacular sign off, Dan angrily confronted the man, shouting, "Why didn't you clear the building?"

Obviously averse to the prospect of refunds, the promoter said bravely, "Well, we would have gone together. My family was in there, too."

A few hours later, Rowan smiled, "Blowing up on camera might have helped the ratings. It's the only way we'd get noticed."

Moreover, thanks to all my comrades in commentating (and possibly, irritating). Jack Barnaby, the old Harvard coach, was the first in 1963, and escaped after one show. Donald Dell (party of the first part in our Lip-and-the-Scalp combine, so named by Jack Kramer) was also my first regular sidekick, beginning in 1970 on PBS, and longest lasting. Kramer, an Einstein of tennis knowledge, was my first mikemate on commercial TV in 1968, on CBS. Cheers to the rest who carried me, in one way or another, on a variety of networks, syndications, local stations— some on vastly unseen productions that even they won't remember: Julie ("Doc") Anthony, Arthur Ashe, Tracy Austin, Bjorn Borg, Bill ("Tex") Bowrey, Vic Braden, Butch Buchholz, Mary Carillo, Rosie Casals, Don Criqui, Jimmy Crum, Frank Deford, Judy Dixon, Barbara Hunter Estep, Christine Marie Evert, Donna Floyd Fales, Stefano Flink, Bob Gallagher, Althea Gibson, Richard ("Pancho") Gonzalez, Mike Gorman, Seena Hamilton, Kathy Harter, Julie Heldman, Hillary Hilton, Ann Haydon Jones, Charlie Jones, Jim Karvellas, Nancy Chaffee Kiner, Billie Jean Moffitt King, Grace Lichtenstein, Chuck Lisberger, Barry MacKay, Don Meredith, Gardnar Mulloy, John Newcombe, Kim Prince, Marty Riessen, Gene Scott, Vic Seixas, Jim Simpson, Stan Smith, Billy Talbert, Virginia Wade, Anne White, Bob Wilson.

There were also doubles partners in tennis crime, saddled with me like camels, uncomplainingly and amazingly lugging me to unexpected victories: Janet Hopps Adkisson, Helene Chazan, Virginia ("Cannonball") Connolly, Jack Crawford, Sandy Cushman, Joanna Rowan, Ruth Jeffery Ryder, Lesley Visser.

Much gratitude also to Dick Marek, who took on this project, Amy Mintzer, who helped edit it, and good Jane Goode, who helped overcome my computer klutziness and got it floppied, or however they say it in the softworn world.

Thanks as well for support, whenever and wherever, to: Glenn Adamo, Russo Adamo (aka Russ Adams), Baker Adams, George Alexander, Muhammad Ali, Neil Amdur, Paul Annear, Phyllis Arscott, Dick Auerbach, Roberto Basche, Bob Beach, Big Judge and Siggy, Wendy Britton, Karla Cahalane, Z. Paul Callahan, Marty Carmichael, Margaret Carson, Ralph Chambers, Buffalo Bill-Joe Chazan, Gianni and Santa Mariana Clerici, Dick Cline, Filthy Phil Collyer, Laurie Colwin, Consuela Cotter, Doug Crawford, Nancy Curley, Bob Dailey, Dorothy Danzig, Charlie ("Rags Man") Davidson, Tweeds DeLuca, Harrison Dillard, Flossie Dunbar (widow of an early mentor, *Herald* columnist Bob Dunbar), Angelo Dundee, Judith Elian, Roy Emerson, Ed Fabricius, Omar Fareed, John Feinstein, Marilyn and Ed Fernberger, descendants of C. Nyles ("Fingers") Fortescue (founder of the science of netry), Neale Fraser, Andrea Gerlin, Evonne Goolagong, Tom Gorman, Will Grimsley, Cookie Annie Harney, Slew Hester, Ed Hickey, Mike Hills, Irwin the Icicle, Jessie Janjigian, Joan Hildebrand Jensen, Albert Kazis, Ethel Keeney, Gretchen Killius, Murf Klauber, Dorie Klissas, Rod Laver, Helen Lee, Larry Lieberman, Orso Lorge, Mike Lupica, George MacCall, Pauline McCance, Roy McKelvie, Geoff Mason, Jacqueline and Ed Miller, Caitlin Monahan, Charlie Moran, my uncle Studley (whose "Breakfast at Wimbledon" has been, from the beginning, a Fig Newton and a boilermaker), Carol Newsom, Gene Norris, Don Ohlmeyer, Lawrie Pignon, Dennis Ralston, Howard Reifsnyder, Bill Riordan, Tony Roche, Bob Rosen, Ken Rosewall, Jimmy Scalem, Ken Schanzer, Sam Schroeder, Peter Schwed, Ginny Seipt, Benny Sims, James A. Smith, Jr., Jeff Sparr, Seabury Stanton, Joe Steinfield, Fred ("Old Hacker") Stolle, Edythe Sullivan, Lee Templeton, Lance Tingay, Ted Tinling, Rino Tommasi, Ed Turville, Lefty Lou Ullman, Candy and Jimmy Van Alen, Kay and Michael Vickers, Arthur Watson, Michael Weisman, Death House Wogan, Helen and Big Z Zimman.

Not to forget: Peter Alfano, Vi Barnum, John Barrett, Michael Baz, Walter Bingham, Asher Birnbaum, W. Edward Boles, Sir Reginald Brace, Rita Mae Brown, Bill Buchanan, Mary Canfield, Jack Cola, Zu Collins, Big Red Crawford, Tweeds DeLuca, Palmer Faran, Belmar Gunderson, Greg Hemingway, Eddie

("Ace") Herr, Mike Holovak, Liz and David Kahn, Clif Keane, Edith Reublin Kennedy (the Onwentsia girl), Betsy Killius, Kristin Killius, R. J. Apple Lacy, Charles Liftman, Bob Malaga, Jane and Stan Malless, Captain Edythe McGoldrick, Sharon and Dan Monahan, C. J. Nock III, Dave O'Hara, Jim Passant, M. B. Rand, Eileen Reardon (Pedagogue of Pedal Nudistry), Coach Remer, Waldo Blubbo Riemenschneider, Ernie Roberts, Fran Rosa, John Russell, Sid Schwartz, Antonio Sciarappa, Dava Smith, Walter Tassera, John Weber.

As well as: The denizens of Suite 31-A (Dog Bailing, Bob Gagen, Ernie Hare, Norris Overly, Rusty Rundle, Fred Thomas, K. J. Tolley), and my Brandeis warriors (Bob Berlin, J. K. K. Cohen, Ethan Gluck, Jerry Hantman, Abbie Hoffman, Sam Karp, Michael London, Alan Lotterman, Jacques Loyseau, Paul McKinnon, David Nemiroff, Reuben Ordonez, Steve Reiner, Charlie Teller, Artie Zelman, Marty Zelnick).

And thanks to you, kind readers and viewers.

Prologue

Ilie didn't like the question.

"What's a nice Communist boy like you going to do with all this capitalistic prize money?" I moved the microphone toward his lips.

He scowled, mumbled something about not understanding, looked put upon. Nobody would ask him such a thing back home in Bucharest. But Ilie Nastase took the $7,200 check for winning the National Indoor title of 1970 at Salisbury, Maryland, accepting it in the spirit of socialism, and was well on his way to the first of several millions. He would become a darling of the U.S. IRS as well as the Romanian equivalent.

Betty Stove didn't like the questionable nickname.

"Don't call me Big Bad Betty on TV anymore!" the six-foot Dutchwoman suggested, punctuating the thought with an off-court version of an overhead smash. Grasping my right hand, she jerked me off the ground and flicked me over her shoulder. Whereupon I descended to a supine position on a Palm Springs sidewalk. Wham, bam, thank you, ma'am. I suggested that the

1

former Big Bad Betty probably wouldn't have to worry about that particular alliteration anymore.

But Betty's handiwork wasn't as tasty as that of Mike Higgins when I was writing about baseball. Higgins, the Red Sox general manager at the time, didn't like my appraisals of his stewardship, and pushed my face into a plate of beef Stroganoff. Bon apétit. A bon mot came from higher ground. Ted Williams, the .400 hitter, also didn't like something I'd written and decorated me with the ten-letter *c*-word. I think it was curmudgeon.

Jimmy Connors didn't like being questioned after a televized loss to Boris Becker in Chicago.

Brushing past the proffered mike, he blindsided me with his duffel bag stuffed with rackets. It wasn't Jimmy's first such expression of "no comment" in this direction. But how could I be mad at a guy who has given me so much to write and talk about for two decades?

Bjorn Borg didn't like the idea of questions that he felt might detract from what had just happened to him on that July afternoon at Wimbledon in 1981.

Deposed as champion after a run of five years and forty-one matches, Bjorn declined the usual immediate interview at the entryway to the All England clubhouse, just below the Royal Box. "Talk to the champion," was Borg's exit line, graciously leaving the air time entirely to his conqueror, John McEnroe.

Chris America didn't like climbing to the uppermost reaches of the Olympic Park stadium in Seoul, the NBC roost, to be questioned after her inexplicable defeat by Raffaela Reggi. It was *the* stunner as tennis returned to the Olympics in 1988 after a sixty-four-year absence.

But she did it, unswerving pro that Chrissie Evert is, withholding her tears until we were off the air.

I wonder if the ghost of Lev Richards, the guide I never met, is loitering around those places across the world to which he led me. I keep expecting to hear him say, "Never mind what they like or don't like. Just keep asking questions. It beats working, doesn't it?"

1

○

Sounds of
Delight

It was a siren song in a key of Jersey nasality.

Distinctive and alluring, and all but forgotten by now, it
crossed the country via air waves more than forty years ago,
pausing to touch some listeners arrayed on a fire escape in a
small Ohio town.

But it was softly sung, an overgrown whisper really, because this beguiling voice from the bulky Zenith portable radio
told us the speaker was very close to a tennis court at a mysterious place called Forest Hills where two men named Schroeder and Parker were playing for the championship of the United
States.

". . . Backhand return . . . Schroeder in behind his serve
. . . and makes the volley!" The voice rose automatically to
make itself heard amid a sudden explosion of applause. "Nice
low volley for Ted and he has a point for the set at 40–15."

As the clapping subsided, another voice, the umpire, confirmed: "40–15!"

We understood that well enough. After all, our own grandstand, a wide iron stairway at the rear of a graying sandstone

building, the local college gymnasium, oversaw the same sort of activity. Though considerably less prominent and proficient, they were the only games of tennis in town, and my only measure of this diversion. Wimbledon was an unknown name (it had been closed down, anyway, by World War II). Television existed only in the twenty-first century of the cartooned Buck Rogers. Sometimes I would sit alone atop the fire escape, high on a metal landing, a private sky box, captivated by the battle below between the two best players in town, a professor named Annear and a student from China named Wong. They played for themselves, but also for No. 1 in my mind—the crowd of one. If the duels of two Australians named Laver and Rosewall would one day be the most treasured in my mind, those of Annear and Wong kept their place as the first.

Played enthusiastically, if unremarkably, these games occupied a brief season of not much longer than ninety days, a summer on the college's four dirt courts. Free to the townies during the languid summer days when the college was closed, the courts were economy models, built the simplest way: scrape away the grass, water, roll, and line with lime. They were slow-drying, bumpy, backed by fences too close for the comfort of a baseliner's backswing.

Drab and dusty, the courts were nonetheless beloved. Addicted parishioners who communed there daily kept them in virtual nonstop use from the moment neighborhood roosters held roll call until the dusky, post-supper hour of the kids' game of kick-the-can on the unpaved street behind the south backstop.

Years beyond, in Plains, Georgia, interviewing a onetime First Hacker, Jimmy Carter, I could sense he had that same good earth feeling about a similar barren patch on which he'd learned tennis.

It was a rectangle cleared by his dad, Earl Carter, at the rear of their frame house on the outskirts of Plains. Traces, scars of Georgian red dirt not yet fully overcome by unruly grass, could still be seen a half-century later, and Jimmy Carter grinned wistfully as he said, "Every time I drive by the old house—I moved there when I was four—I always think about the tennis court there, between the house and the little store. It's not there anymore, of course, but to me it's still there. And I can envision me and my father playing."

Just why tennis was so popular—it no longer is—among the six hundred residents of that remote peanut-growing hamlet during the Depression isn't known. "I've never been able to explain it," Carter said. "But there were three other courts, and they were heavily used. The game was played seriously, not frivolously, and I was never able to beat my father."

The sounds remain clear to the former president. Carter can still hear the unmistakable *"Puh . . . puh . . . puh!"* of fuzzy rubber ball against racket strings of sheep's innards a lifetime ago, echoing through the backyard as his father competed with friends.

I can hear it, too, past and present. And future, God help me, because I'm a hopeless tennis degenerate. Unrepentant and unrecovered. Conditioned to want more before I knew or realized it, like a babe in a junkie's womb, I developed a habit. But at least it's one that supports me, not the other way around.

"Puh . . . puh . . . puh!"

An irresistible sound, it lured Rod Laver from his bed one starry, tropical Queensland night, maybe a couple of years after my radio-side vigil at the Ted Schroeder–Frankie Parker National final of 1942. A tyke he was. Innocent of any notions of the spectacular circumnavigation of the tennis world that was his destiny, removing him far from the Australian bush of childhood, Laver was drawn from the cocoon of sleep, unknowingly about to fly. To fly on a scrawny left wing that, on the grown man, would be sinewy, simian, and oppressive—carrying him to the championships of Australia, France, Britain, and the United States in 1962, and again in 1969. Stitched together they form a magnificent tapestry called the "Grand Slam."

His father, a cattle rancher, was playing with his older brothers on one of those crude country courts so many Aussies remember as though dreaming of paradise lost. Lighted dimly by bulbs strung from four posts, the court may have seemed a captivating gem in the rough to the fatefully awakened boy, a huge ruby descended like a meteor.

"It was antbed," Laver recalls the resourceful construction. "Lots of them on farms and ranches. Knock over some of those tall anthills and spread the red grit on a fairly level surface. That's the court many of us started on.

"I came out to watch them play in my pajamas. Bare feet. I was six or seven. I knew about the court, of course, but that night for some reason I was drawn by the sound, fascinated. A fellow named Charlie Hollis was staying with us, coaching my brothers. Instead of them sending me back to bed, Charlie said, 'Let's see Rod have a go.' "

Barefoot boy with cheeks of freckle was on his way to the Tennis Hall of Fame, pursuing that hypnotic sound—*"Puh . . . puh . . . puh!"*—with an effect few others, if any, have generated. Yet he was no more mesmerized than countless hackers and eavesdroppers beside the court, who have been as enriched as Laver by playing and watching.

Baseball is the crack of the bat on horsehide; tennis, the *puh!* of the strings on rubber.

It resounded clearly in our ears as we took a long-distance fix by radio on that early September afternoon in 1942. Maybe a half-dozen of us hunched around the radio on our fire-escape bleachers, romanced by the sounds of play, the applause, and the disembodied narrator. He said his name was Lev Richards, and we took his word for it. He talked about the aggressive twenty-one-year-old Stanford student, Ted Schroeder, thwarting the longtime ambitions of defensive specialist twenty-six-year-old Frankie Parker, and how both would undoubtedly be in their country's uniform before the next Nationals rolled around. Probably Richards mentioned the tough four-set struggle that Schroeder had survived in the third round against a Notre Dame student, Jimmy Evert. But that name wouldn't mean anything to me for another twenty-nine years, until Jimmy's sixteen-year-old daughter, Chris, returned the name Evert to a Forest Hills's scoreboard in tearing up the tournament.

While listening, we were watching the frolics of our fellow townies—initiating me to early tennis hero (and heroine) worship. Who was on the courts that Sunday afternoon? The regulars, probably. Like good and dutiful hackers, they were more concerned with their own strokes than those of the unseen Frankie Parker and Ted Schroeder. Possibly, handsome Eddie Finnigan was hacking away. An erstwhile basketball all-American who coached the college team, he was something of a faculty Tarzan, delighting in playing bare-chested. Or Howard Taylor, a slight, bespectacled fellow clinging doggedly to his relic, a Dayton Steel racket, with which he sliced balls—literally, and to the irritation of the balls' owners—with the steel strings. Infrequently introduced, new, snow-white balls stuck around a long time as used-gray. Less chic but still evident were the cheaper, long-wearing numbers in red, a color that preceded yellow by a half-century.

"Damns" and "Oh, hells," were thrown around, and even rackets, though with care. Even with the Depression over, times were still too hard for much "equipment abuse," that silly expression of today.

Most likely on view was my first No. 1, the town champ, Paul Annear, a sleek astronomy professor, along with his doubles partner, blocky Les Davis, whose five beautiful daughters were more highly admired than his attractive strokes. Maybe a blonde I always looked for, Phyll Arscott. Lovely and fresh, a goddess out of reach to a thirteen-year-old. But a merciful lady because she, a member of the Ohio State women's varsity, no less, would hit with me during slow hours, the occasional times I was allowed on court, feeding a latent appetite.

Insidiously I had been tuned to the wondrous detonations, the *"Puh . . . puh . . . puh!"* of abused tennis balls, as early in life as Jimmy Carter or Rod Laver without really noticing. They were my alarm clock in summer, among the first discernible noises of morning. Blending with the early vocals, a bass and contralto choir of cattle and mourning doves in a nearby barnyard, were the hooves of the milkman's horse and the clinking bottles. On his bike, Lewie the paperboy bumped over uneven slabs of sidewalk, hurling the Cleveland *Plain Dealer*— *"Fwaat!"*—onto our wooden porch. Prince, the springer spaniel, wheezed and pawed at the screen door. All this was sifted through the fully leafed apple tree that brushed and shuddered against my open bedroom window to incessant accompaniment of strings: *"Puh . . . puh . . . puh!"*

The reports of balls striking rackets and courts, and clanging against wire fences, the shuffle of sneakers, and the shrieks of the players—one of them my older sister, Mary, working on her sunrise service—traveled no more than fifty yards to imprint themselves on my brain. A skip across neighbor Pillars's backyard, then a careful meandering among the rows of Hannig's garden took me to the fire escape in under a minute—or, more often, to the gravel ball diamond on the other side of the courts.

Limited court time for little punks didn't dismay me. I enjoyed watching or playing, but only for a while. Sometimes, when we weren't playing ball, Dick Berr and I would take aging rackets our parents had used, warped brown clubs with broken and fraying strings, and knock a worn red ball back and forth on the sidewalk. But tennis, far from being a force in our lives, was a minor amusement of sweetly long summer days, ranking well behind hour after hour of baseball. We played baseball incessantly, chipping in to buy a "ninety-seven-cent smasher," and wrapping it with black tape to keep the ball in lopsided action after the cover came off. Cracked bats were nailed and taped.

Football grabbed us in autumn; basketball was taken illicitly by climbing that same fire escape and sneaking through a window into the gym; hockey materialized if the quarry froze. We swam in the quarries and the river, and sometimes Lake Erie, ten miles away, if my mother loaded up her '29 Chevy coupe with three or four of us. To get the necessities—a dime for a movie, a nickel for ice cream, pennies for candy, a buck or two set aside for a bike—we mowed lawns, shoveled snow, hustled newspaper and magazine routes.

In quieter times we made model airplanes, took piano lessons (under duress) from Mrs. Coates, planted gardens, read comic books (called "funny books"), and big little books. We listened to the radio: "The Lone Ranger" (". . . the thundering hoofbeats and a hearty 'Hi-yo, Silver!' "); "Jack Armstrong, the All-American Boy" ("Have you tried Wheaties . . . the best breakfast food in the land"); "Tom Mix" ("When it's roundup time in Texas . . .").

Or if we were sick, and stayed home from school, we could catch up on the soap operas: "Mert and Marge," "Mary Noble, Backstage Wife," "Ma Perkins," "Pepper Young's Family." People got killed on radio. But did they have affairs, abortions, drug problems? Maybe between the lines, not explicitly as in today's soaps. Those were not concepts with which we were familiar or could even identify, unlike my own teenage son, Rob. He does not agree that nobody on TV today is as funny as Charlie McCarthy and Edgar Bergen, Jack Benny, or Fred Allen were on those Sunday-night radio shows. Nor can he imagine that real people, not tapes, provided background laughter.

Tennis sometimes fitted into the secondary schedule along with bicycle rides ending at Manning's for milk shakes and sundaes, driving golf balls on the football field, and playing guns—neighborhood variations on the cowboys-and-Indians theme.

Near-at-hand Indians, the Cleveland variety of the American League, constantly infiltrated our conversations, dreams, and career aspirations. We followed their usually second-division movements admiringly, though not uncritically, by radio and the morning paper. As a treat, once or twice a season, we got to look them over in person at League Park, a journey of two hours by bus and streetcar deep into Cleveland's east side.

In season we were fans of the Cleveland Rams, a fumbling franchise in the National Football League; of the teams of the town's college, Baldwin-Wallace, and our province, Ohio State. We devoured the sports pages, but tennis was not a game we followed. Our newspapers were practically silent on the subject, except for the Nationals at Forest Hills. Then Lev Richards had our ears because we listened to anything sporting that came over the radio, persuading our parents to let us stay up late to relish Joe Louis knocking out somebody new and alien, a Max Schmeling or an Arturo Godoy.

As far as I can tell, Lev Richards, a nonprofessional broadcaster whose avocational voice was genial and informative, continued to describe what used to be called the Nationals— today the U.S. Open—through 1952. That September, my left ear close to a smaller portable radio, I heard his stroke-by-stroke account of American Gardnar Mulloy's annihilation by Frank Sedgman, the beginning of the Australian blight. It was the first of fourteen U.S. men's championships carried off down under over a stretch of twenty-two years.

I neither heard nor heard of Lev Richards again. Television had supplanted radio for the Nationals, but could never recreate the sense of elegance and mystery that his voice brought from the unimaginable pleasure dome, "Forest Hills."

Were they playing tennis on a wooded hillside? And he spoke of grass courts? Scanning the earthen courts before our eyes, who could picture a game of tennis on grass? The few hardy blades pushing through the surface of our courts were considered interlopers, to be plucked. Was it like the football field bordering our courts? Or golf greens at the club outside of town? What were the bounces like?

By 1952, when Lev Richards had left me forever, and I, Corporal Collins, was defending my country by serving in tennis combat alongside the commanding general (whenever he summoned me) at Camp Polk, Louisiana—as close as you could get to overseas without leaving the United States—I had visited Forest Hills. No Forest. No Hills. But honest-to-God grass courts were there, merely steps from a subway exit.

Just as my friends and I couldn't quite envision what Lev Richards was talking about—even though it was a game we thought we knew well enough—we didn't realize that our own game would shortly vanish like his voice. Within weeks a steam shovel had gouged our hearts and our good earth, creating a massive hole in the ground. As America moved to full war speed, nine months after Pearl Harbor, the courts gave way to a swimming pool, a necessity for a college abruptly entrusted with training future naval officers.

We were dispossessed. Our social hangout and clubhouse veranda, my sky box—the fire escape—was torn asunder in the abutment of the pool building to the gym.

Tennis was missing in action. Not many of the old gang reassembled at war's end at the new and forbiddingly black asphalt courts built on another campus location.

But we did have Lev Richards to transport us. For a few more Septembers he sang his siren song of a green and glorious place where bronzed Australians, Californians, and other exotics played like deities.

2

○

The Legman
Cometh

A life of watching games and avoiding labor attracts people to sportswriting. It's better than working. So is playing games for a living, only sportswriting is steadier.

It took me a while to find that out because playing the games, particularly baseball, seemed preferable until I was about fifteen, when the pitchers were beginning to develop a weapon to which I was developing an allergy: the curveball.

As a high school basketball player I had a 16-point average—per season. My early assumption that I'd play on the football team expired one raw November afternoon during a scrimmage when an ineffectual sophomore linebacker—me—was gored and trampled by the varsity fullback. At least I was maimed by a bull of some distinction, Chuck Gandee, who would go on to earn his keep with Ohio State and, for a while, the Chicago Cardinals. If you look closely you can see a cleat mark. But we all get stigmatized one way or another, and the coach, a kindly man aware that I'd been writing for the school paper, suggested gently, "You'd enjoy the game more in the press box. And it'd be safer."

Excellent advice. He assured me the squad could get along with one fewer linebacker, especially one weighing in at 120, and I was relieved—of uniform, hazardous duty, and anxiety.

But my first position in journalism, legman at the *Enterprise*, a local weekly, was the result not of advice or nepotism—but neighborism. Fortuitous propinquity, as Howard Cosell might say. We lived next door to Bob Pillars, the newspaper's owner-editor-publisher (also Linotypist, pressman, makeup chief, columnist, general reporter, job printing specialist, and romancer of Rosie, the nice lady who took want ads over the phone). His new legman wasn't equipped with the traditional pencil and notebook. Operative instruments were a broom and dustpan, and I used my legs to clean up the decrepit, uncleanable building, run errands, carry coffee to Pillars and his itinerant or moonlighting help, printers who drifted into town and then gave up on it.

The *Enterprise*, sagging in circulation, fortune, and its wood-and-tin structure, yet never in spirit, was little more than a long, high, noisy room with a couple of partitioned offices. Rumpled floorboards, imbedded with lead shavings and covered by ink-splotched paper, grimly and grimily resisted the determined efforts of the legman—literally an ink-stained wretch—to bring order.

But that was all right. The place looked, sounded, and smelled like a newspaper. Ink, coffee, boiling lead, cigarettes blended with the chatter of typewriters, the clack and clatter of Linotypes and presses, the screech of power saws and the clanging of an oversized phone bell that could be heard above it all. A community magnet, the *Enterprise* drew pols, press agents, tipsters, the kids who put out the high school and college papers, customers placing ads and ordering printing, hangers-on who loved to suck up the lively atmosphere of a newspaper, and Chuckie, a woodchuck tenanting the basement, periodic star of the editor's column. None of this insurance-office decor that deadens today's newspapers with their carpeted floors, for God's sake, and the zombied stillness of video display terminals.

It was a good place to be, to start, to take an ink transfusion. A few years later, I moved up from 25-cents-an-hour apprentice to bylined and salaried department head ($5 weekly, sports editor), an advance my uncle Studley described, "Well, you went from taking out the trash to writing it."

If my jock genes came from my father, those tainted with printer's ink came from my mother. The biological cocktail came out sportswriter. His genes were a little burned out when they got to me—not the desire to play games, but the ability. Worth Collins was the first four-letter man (football, basketball, baseball, track) in the annals of Wooster College, where he was an all-Ohio quarterback in 1912, a time when a 125-pounder could do that. While teaching and coaching he played semipro basketball and baseball, and is still remembered in Lorain, Ohio, for the winter of 1923 when "Pop" Collins's boys won the state high school basketball championship.

How many times did I hear the replay of the final triumph from my old man? Lorain beat Bellevue by a Pleistocene Age–sounding score, 15–14, on a last-second basket by a future fireman named Bep Farris. "We're a point behind but Bep is calmly dribbling all over the backcourt, freezing the ball for one last shot. Nobody could take the ball away from Bep. I'm watching the clock for him, and when it gets down to the end I shout, 'Let 'er go, Bep!' Cool as anything, Bep takes a two-handed set shot from the center of the floor, and it goes in as the gun goes off! The Bellevue crowd couldn't believe it. They thought they had the title. . . ."

That victory carried him to a better job, athletic director and one-man coaching staff for all sports, at tiny Baldwin-Wallace College in Berea, and a house on the campus—the frame house with rose garden and grape arbor near the tennis courts whose sounds I grew up with. A town of about five thousand then, Berea, surrounded by farmland to the southwest of Cleveland, had been known nationally for its quarries. The day of Berea sandstone was over, although the college buildings attested to its usefulness in construction, and a number of decorative grindstones were reminders of a once widely used local product. The quarries had filled with water, becoming excellent if perilous swimming holes, eventually recreational lakes set in a wooded park. It was, and is, though grown considerably, a pleasant college town, the streets of my neighborhood still canopied in spring and summer by old elms and maples.

My father entered my consciousness as a traveling salesman in farm equipment, long since fired by the college, as are all coaches who don't win enough. He believed that coaching was teaching kids to have fun at games, and wouldn't have dreamed of sending in a play. Once the game begins, he felt, it's up to the players. It's their game. Once, with that in mind, he convinced the Oberlin College football coach that the two coaches ought to leave their captains in charge of their games and go play golf. After eighteen holes, they would receive a final report from the players, like professors listening to a dissertation. However, the college presidents got wind of Dad's plan, and vetoed it.

He maintained ties with organized sports by officiating at high school and college games, and he took me along. But he was away during the week, selling corn pickers and manure spreaders. A sportswriter, or broadcaster, with manure spreaders in his background may have an edge.

Although we talked sports, watched games, played ball together, he wasn't a stage parent. He would have told all such animals that I constantly encountered in tennis, "Go play your own games, and let the kids play theirs."

Golf was his abiding passion—"God is just as much outdoors on a golf course on Sunday as in a church." His father, a Presbyterian missionary in Thailand, might not have agreed. But Grandfather Collins surely contributed to the inky side of my life. As one of his clerical duties, sometime before the turn of the century, he manned a printing press in Chiengmai, and hand-set and published the first Bible in the Lao dialect.

Dad had picked up a tennis racket two or three times in his life. When I imagined myself as a hotshot, No. 1 on the high school team, he asked for a game, and beat me. He was sixty and overweight, but the clever and competitive athlete still thrived within the short, stocky guy who could never rid himself of a paunch once he stopped coaching. "I thought you were supposed to be good at this game," he laughed after his chops, slices, and lobs had confused me.

Josephine Collins, my mother, wrote determinedly, compulsively, and rarely got into print—sometimes a feature for the local paper or a short story for a very small magazine, for which her largest check was ten dollars. She never acknowledged the pain of rejection slips. Writing may have been therapy for the ex-teacher who had been happiest as a schoolgirl in France. Her father, a French immigrant, sent her to his homeland for a time in her teens to learn the language and culture of a place she may have been better suited for than a small Ohio town.

She encouraged me when the high school paper held tryouts, and coached me as the editors, Joan Hildebrand and Bob Beach, took on a sports junkie who could fill their back page. My own athletic career didn't intrude on writing time, particularly the abortive fling at football, humanely terminated by Coach Spillman, as he laughingly put it, "in the interest of journalism."

Shortly, I was back amid the clamor of the *Enterprise*, a pro now, returned at sixteen to the scene of his grime. Laboriously scanning and jabbing the keyboard of a sclerotic Woodstock typewriter rather than poking about with a broom, I filled an eight-column page weekly instead of dustpans.

Engravings were too costly to allow much art. There were no ads on the page. The *Enterprise*, losing a death struggle for Berea's attention with the rival *News*, had all too few. That vast, sometimes intimidating page was mine—all mine—including a column (headed "Collins Comments") and whatever other news and features I batted out on the high school and college teams, bowling, horse shows, sandlot baseball and softball, church leagues. The paper came out Friday. Thursday morning deadline meant I stayed up all night Wednesday, writing copy, headlines, laying out the page. I was getting paid, or overpaid, five dollars a week to write about games; it was exhilarating. And I had exposure, a circulation of eleven hundred, some of whom noticed. Too, I had a smidgin of the power of the press. Not enough to disturb the balance of anything—although an impassioned column urging the board of education to grant a $100 raise to my savior-from-gridiron-mutilation, Coach Spillman, did get the desired result, and kept him from transferring his football intellect to another high school.

Bob Pillars sighed at my vendetta against the English language but was assured that one-eighth of his beloved newspaper would be accounted for. Even verbs appeared. Such verbs fledgling sportswriters—and some not so callow—use to illuminate the act of X defeating Y were used: bop, strangle, plow, gouge, whomp, romp, stomp, murder, destroy, rip, snip, trip, flip, slug, drill, kill.

You get the idea. Once a trashman . . .

3

○

Pilgrimage to Queens

The god called Kramer beckoned. Jack Kramer's handsome face on an August cover of *Time* magazine in 1947 was a powerful force, like one of those wartime posters of Uncle Sam declaring, "I want you!"

Kramer's portrait seemed to say it was time to seek out the mysterious Forest Hills that had been shaped in my consciousness by Lev Richards's words, spoken to me so softly and fetchingly over the radio each September since 1942. Having missed the diluted National singles conventions of 1944 and 1945 because of military duty, Kramer had won in 1946, and established himself as the paramount figure in the game, amateur or pro, by leading the U.S. seizure of the Davis Cup from Australia and then capturing the 1947 Wimbledon. At twenty-six the postwar strongman, he would be making one last concert appearance in the Forest Hills amphitheater before withdrawing to the wilderness of the pro caravan. His objective then would be to lift the crown from Bobby Riggs's unshrinkable head in their mano-a-mano series.

Following Kramer's star, my high school teammates, Gus Gehring and Al English, and I were traveling afar. Our pilgrimage to a fantasized shrine just off Continental Avenue in the New York borough of Queens seemed as tortuous, unendingly hot, and wayward as Ahab's wanderings, and in a conveyance as creaky as the *Pequod*. But the goal was worth it. Onetime Boston boxing emcee Freddy Russo would have expressed the essence in his distinctive rasp: "Collins is making his initial debut at the champeenships of the good old U.S.A.!"

Three men in an eight-cylinder tub, a '35 Ford, we drifted in an easterly direction from Cleveland through twenty-six hours of nonstop driving and nonsensical navigation that included misplacing the Pennsylvania Turnpike. But with the golden-haired image of Kramer imprinted on our minds, as on the *Time* cover, we somehow found and crossed the East River into the unpromising land of Queens.

Queens Boulevard, then as now, was garish, unfriendly, ominously thick in traffic, more cars and people within a few blocks than our entire hometown could muster. Yet no more than a few hundred yards off the boulevard, we found tranquillity, a sense of being on the threshold of revelation at the bowered wooden gate of the West Side Tennis Club.

It was dusk, the best time at Forest Hills, almost pastoral. Play was practically over for the day. We were directed to walk around the grounds to the ticket windows at the public gates. They were closed. But a man departing handed us his ticket stubs, and we hurried in. Sprinting up a steep concrete stairway, we burst through a portal and were stunned by a green flash. Dazzled, we beheld a strange and gorgeous meadow.

The sensation had been similar when, as a fourth grader hyped by anticipation, I ran headlong up drooping and echoing staircases to the upper deck of shabby League Park in Cleveland for my first big-league game. No grass had ever looked greener. But grass was the expected showground for baseball. No tennis court had ever looked like this one.

Yes, it was grass. Lev Richards hadn't made it up.

Two men in white were still playing to a congregation of perhaps two hundred. The minarets of the Forest Hills Inn and the groves of Forest Hills Gardens, the comfortable residential pocket in which the club nestles, stood confidently in the gloaming, sturdy defenders of the faith, gray against an azure evening. Laughter and the crystal-and-ice melodies of the terrace bar drifted from the distant clubhouse.

Forest Hills. It was, indeed, revelation to the weary, sticky pilgrims, a romantic encounter.

There is no romance to Forest Hills now. Smog and Queens press in. The Inn, no longer a stylish hotel, seems a decaying sentry. Fled to Flushing is the U.S. Open. Still, as night encroaches on the imitation-Tudor clubhouse, and those stony-orbed eagles peer from their stadium aerie like protective gargoyles, West Side quivers with the old sensations and mystique. You know that ghosts of championships past are afoot. It will be years, maybe decades, before Flushing Meadows has any ghosts of its own.

We sat where we pleased that September evening in 1947. Because the stadium was almost empty, the sound effects were tremendous, each stroke echoing like a gunshot.

How about Carver and Match as the leads in my "initial debut," the reward at the end of that rattletrapping drive to New York? Carver and Match? Thus these two guys racing the shadows were identified by the manually operated scoreboard atop the blue-and-yellow-striped marquee. Freddy Russo would have announced them as "last and final bout of the evening!" Now entertaining in the deserted horseshoe: Carver and Match.

No complaints. We were highly entertained. They hit the ball better than anyone we'd ever seen. Sam Match, a college boy good enough to win a national intercollegiate title, the doubles, for Rice, beat Alexander Carver, origins unknown.

Nearly thirty years after that, in Los Angeles, I chanced into a doubles game with Match, at the home of a friend. I asked him if he, too, recalled that meaningless engagement in the stadium that had taken on considerable importance to me. A personable stockbroker and nationally ranked senior at the time, Match said of course he did. It had been his first Forest Hills match, too. Sam's historic perspective was a shade off. I looked it up, and he had made his "initial debut" the year before, 1946.

Would I forsake him for an unforced error of a year? Not Sam Match, forever my initial debutant.

My pals, Gus and Al, and I stayed for two more days at the Nationals, sleeping at a hotel for retired fleas out on Long Island until the money and the weekend ran out. We did get to see the magnetic god who had pulled us there, Kramer, in a first-round shuffle past one Ed McGrath. Six rounds along, Jack would register his last amateur championship in a terrific five-set struggle with Frankie Parker, as described to us back in Ohio by Lev Richards.

Seven players, besides Match and Kramer, stuck in my neural mush. Two of them, Aussie Geoff Brown and American Bill Vogt, served harder and faster than I believed possible in stacking up ace after ace against each other.

John Newcombe, a rather large-serving Aussie himself, and I were discussing big servers in 1973, during his run to a second title at Forest Hills. "Ever hear of a guy named Geoff Brown?" Newk wondered.

I told him about my awed observation of the stringy Mr. Brown.

"Damned if he doesn't serve just about as fast now," Newk said, "and he's almost fifty. Only a skinny little guy, but what coordination—just whips that ball. Sheer strength isn't neces-sarily the clue to big serving."

A year after that, in Melbourne, I was introduced to an op-ponent in a friendly doubles. "This is Geoff Brown."

Oh? I knew he was none other when he whizzed a serve past my ineffectual flutter. Acing me was nothing spectacular, of course, but 125-pound Mr. Brown was, at fifty, definitely, and recklessly, over the speed limit for any age.

Jack Bromwich I'd heard of. But I wasn't prepared for his style, which made him seem as curious a specimen of Austra-lian fauna as a duckbilled platypus. Of all those tapped for the International Tennis Hall of Fame at Newport, Rhode Island, Brom—thrice a Forest Hills semifinalist, once a Wimbledon fi-nalist, twice an Australian champ—may have been the most distinctive. An oversized jaw and a deceptive lope added to the picture of a missing link from down under. Though nominally right-handed, he grafted a left-handed forehand onto the two-fisted stroke on the right. He volleyed left-handed. His serve, righty, was herky-jerky, the remainder of the two-handed woodchopping delivery he started out with. His racket, so loosely strung that seldom was heard the impact, directed disconcert-ingly placed strokes with uncanny accuracy. "You couldn't play serve-and-volley against Brom," says Don Budge, who began the original Grand Slam by beating Bromwich in the 1938 Australian final. "He'd pass you, or have you reaching for an impossibly angled low return. You had to work your way in carefully."

Francis Xavier Shields dwarfed them all in panache. As a darkly handsome throwback in long flannels, he seemed to have strode from a movie lot, a heartbreaking serve-breaker. Indeed he had done Hollywood time as a bit player in the movies—where his granddaughter, Brooke Shields, would make a name—and big player with lovely ladies. He was what he appeared, a swashbuckler of glowing personality, whose tragic flaw was alcoholism.

I didn't know all that then, nor that sixteen years previously, 1931, Frank Shields had been the only Wimbledon finalist not to show up for the final. An injured ankle forced him to default beforehand to Sidney Wood.

But how riveting he was, at thirty-seven, dashing about the grandstand court as coolly as his crony, Errol Flynn, dueling a villain. It took a long time for a collegian, Fred Kovaleskie, to subdue Shields: five sets and sixty-two games. There were no chairs to rest on in those more physically demanding days of the "play is continuous" rule. Each of the thirty-one times they changed ends, Shields paused to flamboyantly chug-a-lug a Coke, emptying the bottle in one motion. That's a lot of refreshment, and, a friend of Shields told me recently, "Frank also sipped a little something else that the Cokes chased."

It may have been a preservative because Shields was still playing the Nationals at forty-four.

Then there were a couple of nonentities: an American, Charlie Mattman, and an Indian, Man Mohan. They played a desperate match that neither seemed capable of winning. It was on a field court so we could stand next to them, getting the close-up sense of the caprices of grass—the skidding, low bounces (and nonbounces), wild spins, and caroms. A totally different game, altogether new and intriguing to us dirt-kickers.

I mustn't overlook an erotic teenage memory—our inspection, from a few feet away, of a well-chronicled derrière, one that had made a significant impression beyond the limit of tennis circles. Sometimes stuffed into a pair of scandalous lace panties fashioned by couturier Ted Tinling, this glorious bottom belonged to a Californian, Gertrude ("Gussy") Moran. We saw her only in training togs, pounding balls against a wooden wall fenced in for that purpose. Can't remember how well she hit the ball, but only that Gussy did more for T-shirt and shorts than Jack Kramer did for the serve-and-volley.

She was a peach, but the balls wouldn't resemble lemons for another quarter-century. Used tournament balls, basic white, were on sale, authentically smudged in green. I bought one to show the guys at home. A grass-stained tennis ball. A wonder of our earthen and asphalt world, something like a chunk from the White Cliffs of Dover.

That ball rested on a shelf in our dining room, among Mom's potted geraniums, to be talked about and admired, symbol of a journey to another realm. Our moon rock. Like a koala outside of its native habitat, however, the ball did not survive. Chlorophyll faded, disappeared. Its soul was gone, and the ball lay pale and dead on the shelf until I had to dispose of it.

4

○

Beantown, Ho!

On a beautiful, clear-brisk fall day—the kind New England leads the world in—I drove through the Berkshires, down Route 2, crossed the Massachusetts Avenue Bridge from Cambridge, and arrived in Boston, dragging my Ohio roots behind me.

Autumn of '54. Ken Rosewell was still a teenager. Billie Jean Moffitt (the future Mrs. King) was ten and dreaming of being a big-league ball player, which her kid brother, Randy, did become. Colette Evert was great with a great child she and her husband, Jimmy, would name Christine Marie three months hence. Jimmy Connors, just turned two, had begun using a sawed-off tennis racket like a broom, brushing at balls his grandmother rolled on the kitchen floor.

Bobby Riggs, winding up his tennis career, Part One, as one of the outcast touring pros, won the ragtag Boulevard Gardens Championships at Woodside, Long Island, for spare change, and was about to vanish behind the country club curtain as a golf hustler, waiting nearly two decades for Billie Jean to grow up. Then came Part Two as geriatric sex symbol and would-be woman beater. Another of the outcasts, Pancho Gonzalez, was beating the bush on one-night stands, giving a few lessons, and tinkering with a racing car.

Evonne Goolagong was chasing lizards with other tots in a far off Australian wheat town. Althea Gibson and Arthur Ashe weren't permitted to play tennis everywhere they would have liked because they were the wrong color. Big Bill Tilden had been dead for a year. Rod Laver joined the ranks of Australian high school dropouts at fifteen, opting for a career as a professional tennis amateur. The Davis Cup was in its most familiar residence, a vault in a Melbourne branch of the Bank of New South Wales. Maureen Connolly, possibly the greatest of all female players, accomplisher of the Grand Slam the previous year, failed to defend the Nationals's title at Forest Hills, her career finished at twenty-one by a highway accident. Bjorn Borg was nonexistent; my hair almost was.

Doing a reverse-Greeley, I had motored east to enter graduate school at Boston University. A career in flackery was what I vaguely had in mind in pursuing a degree at BU's school of public relations. I didn't know any better. Although I intended to return to Cleveland and a PR position waiting at a large hospital, the crossing of the Charles River amounted to the cutting of the Ohio cord.

After a harrowing graduation from Baldwin-Wallace, as uncertain as the Kennedy-Nixon election until the last returns came in, I set aside designs on a career sinecure as sportswriter to become friend-and-lobbyist as a press agent for Western Reserve University in Cleveland. Sports Information Director was the formal title. The trumpeting of the jockly causes of the Western Reserve (now Case Western Reserve) Red Cats in the usual college sports paid $3,300 annually, plus all the sweat sox I could cadge from the equipment room. They didn't go well with wing tips, however. It wasn't bad for openers out of college, particularly for a guy whose idea of a beautiful waterfall was a locker-room shower.

But, after wasting the taxpayers' money during a Korean War hitch, I decided to waste more by spending the GI Bill money on graduate school. Following the trail of my high school and college newspaper editor, Bob Beach, I enrolled at BU. This required a hard, impassioned PR job on my own behalf (which should have been worth a degree in itself), selling the dean on Collins as a repentant army veteran who had seen the errors of his undergraduate ways (and dearth of A's).

In the trunk of my '51 Ford were two of the best rackets money could buy, or so I thought. At twenty bucks apiece (with nylon strings), they were Jack Kramer model Wilsons made of wood, the only substance available for abuse by racket-throwers. I'd been partial to Wilsons since my childhood coveting of alluring rackets that were out of the financial question: top-of-the-line Ellsworth Vines and Alice Marble models, each bearing the namesake's picture and autograph. That's the trouble with today's split-shaft rackets: no room for a picture. Nor are the paint jobs nearly as imaginative as in the time of timber.

My first Don Budge was a model I proudly clutched for several years, pleased to have made roundabout contact with the renowned signatory by purchasing it from his brother, teaching pro Lloyd Budge. Lloyd was coaching Kenyon College, whom my college team played, and offered the enemy the same discount prices he gave his own kids. A Budge from a Budge was a heady bludgeon.

I stuck with Budges until the U.S. Army thoughtfully armed me with Kramers after I won the Camp Polk title, beating a colonel who was aged, but at least slow. This may have been lèse-majesté for a corporal, but it got me into a weekly doubles game with the commanding general, which gave me a bad case of the shakes when I bounced an overhead smash off his two-star head. But before I could snap to saluting attention on my knees, he barked, "It's all in the game, corporal. At ease."

Well before that, a sky-blue beauty, mystically entitled Onwentsia, had been the racket of my eye, the first I ever played a game with. A summertime loan from the girl-next-door, Onwentsia—only a silk-strung cheapie from Wilson's secondary line—captivated me as the sled, Rosebud, did Citizen Kane. Reluctantly returned on Labor Day, Onwentsia was never to be touched or seen again, perhaps fated, like Rosebud, to become kindling.

Along with the rackets in my luggage was a stack of *World Tennis* magazines that I'd been saving for a year. Pictures were the essence of the newly founded magazine, the only significant American publication devoted to the game. Photographed at play and work in private clubs and expensive resorts were amateurs, professional amateurs, and those rare birds, the professed (virtually phantom) professionals who flitted about on one-nighters.

Except for the pros, who played public arenas (usually to small gatherings), the game in 1954 happened mostly behind doors where the general public didn't stray in person or thought. Tennis had fallen behind the sporting times, conducted in a vacuum at the uppermost tournament level except for Wimbledon, Forest Hills, and a few other events. It was not really in vogue at any level. A secret sport.

Down at my level, where no tickets were sold, it was nonetheless a great delight, fun with some sweat shed, highly satisfying as it always has been and will be for hackers. The most exalted tournaments could disappear, and hackers would still thrive in their hackery.

Nevertheless, there were some of us who were fans, too, who subscribed to *World Tennis* to follow the upper crust of players along the world circuit. At times, the game seemed to be played only on those pages, in the photos and small print of the results across the globe gathered assiduously by the editor-publisher, Gladys Heldman. There wasn't much mention of it elsewhere, no television except for an hour or two of the Nationals at Forest Hills each September.

As a hacker and fan, I was aware that the secret sport got some respect in the Boston area. Maybe I would have an occasional chance to play on decent courts, I thought. Possibly I could slip off to the tournaments at those venerable bastions, the Casino at Newport, Rhode Island, or the Longwood Cricket Club in suburban Brookline, way stations of the world circuit, where the line, "Tennis, anyone?" didn't draw a derisive laugh.

It didn't occur to me that I would come any closer than a bleacher seat. But then, a few minutes after emerging from the Boylston Street subway stop, across Boston Common from Beacon Hill, I met the Boss—Ed Costello, who ran the sports department at the *Herald*.

5

○

Degenerate
Unveiled

The Boss seemed apologetic, even a little troubled, and I put on my grave, attentive look. After all, this nice middle-aged man, Ed Costello, had taken me in, anointed me sportswriter on a metropolitan daily, made it possible for me to remain in a city I'd fallen for, hard.

It was a warm June night in 1955, and we were discussing my assignments for the week ahead. Obviously he had an odious task for me, and was trying to break it easily. Up to now it had been fun, thanks to hitting it off with the Boss when I entered his *Herald* office in September.

My first week in the Bean had been a terrible letdown, filled with fears of surrender and retreat. With $110 monthly of GI Bill money plus a tuition scholarship for working as a Boston University sports information aide, I could just about make it through one year of graduate study. But the day after I arrived the scholarship fell through. I needed a job to stay, to afford college. It was suggested by BU's athletic director, Vic Stout, that I try the local papers. There were enough of them then:

26

seven dailies as well as the internationally circulated *Christian Science Monitor.*

The second sports editor I talked to was Costello at the *Herald,* a morning paper. Yes, he could use me Saturdays during the football season. Cover a high school game in the afternoon. Pay, five bucks. Answer phones in the office in the evening, taking the results of other games. Pay, five bucks. That meant $40 monthly for a while. Take out a loan, and maybe I could make it. But, after a couple of weeks, the Boss could see that I had more experience than the other college kids he'd hired for similar chores, and he put me to work as an office boy at ten bucks a night, sending me outside the building occasionally on assignments. I was saved financially. Then his lowest-ranking staffer moved to another paper, and he offered me that job when the school year ended. I was saved from ever working for a living again.

But on this June night Costello, the savior, was hesitant, as though he were talking to a child—in a way, he was—in a this-hurts-me-more-than-it-does-you tone of voice. The fact that the slender, fastidious, white-haired man stuttered didn't help. We talked of baseball. Boston was heated up, as only Boston can be over a baseball team. The Red Sox ("Sawks," in the regional vernacular), getting surprising mileage out of a ragbag shortstop named Billy Klaus, were in contention.

The conversation veered to Tony DeMarco, the Fistic Flower of Fleet Street (Collins vernacular, as I took over the boxing beat from my predecessor). Tony, a heavy-handed banger out of the Italian colony in the North End, had distressed his neighbors, and other townsfolk, by losing the world welterweight title in a brawl with Carmen Basilio, and was staying out of sight until his face resumed normal shades and contours.

So, what was the Boss planning for me? Did it involve mucking out stalls at Suffolk Downs to get a story out of some prominent horse trainer?

Almost as bad. "Well, uh . . . you know . . . as the new man . . . uh . . . there are certain things you have to do that nobody likes to do, but . . . uh . . . sometimes they have to be done. I promise," he was fatherly, "it won't happen often."

What was it? Donkey baseball? I'd once written about that perversion—softball played on donkeyback—for the *Enterprise.*

"I'd like . . . uh," he got it out, "I'd like you to go out to

Longwood for some women's tennis . . . uh—" He treated the words "women's tennis" as though he were an ayatollah considering women's rights.

"Longwood? Women's tennis?" I interrupted him.

He misinterpreted the interruption, and scowled. "I don't like a new man to question an assignment." I nodded, and he softened, probably because he'd been through this before with new men who got the rubbish details. "It's just something I have to ask you to do. We cover it because of Hazel. The College Girls Invitation and the Massachusetts Women's tournament. She's been running them for years."

"Hazel?"

"Hazel Wightman. Mrs. Wightman, please. I don't know if you know anything about tennis, but she'll tell you everything you need. It won't be too bad."

Bad? Hell, I thought he was doing me a favor. That's why I'd abruptly, impolitely interrupted him. I was pleased. To me Longwood Cricket Club was one of those magnetic names out of *World Tennis* magazine. I knew the first Davis Cup match had been played there, and it was a layover on the international tour, scene of the National Doubles Championships. The Boss didn't realize that he had a degenerate on his hands. In pointing me toward Longwood, a fountainhead of the game, with genuine living, growing grass courts, he was sending a pineapple addict to Hawaii, a country music freak to Nashville, a western films' buff to interview John Wayne.

I was too green to know it was a garbage run that went to one of the following: new man, staff screwup, old guy phasing out, or the resident lush. "Which one were you?" my daughter, Suzanna, has asked.

But, sensing his discomfort and apprehension, I responded blandly, "I don't mind, sir. I've heard of Longwood."

"We'll just want the scores and a couple of graphs," he instructed. "Say hello to Hazel for me."

I intended to, although at the appropriate moment I blew my lines because she turned out to be *the* Hazel Hotchkiss Wightman, and I wasn't ready for that. Nor for Hazel Wightman, who had donated the trophy, the Wightman Cup, for the female team rivalry between the United States and Great Britain. The woman who had won more U.S. championships than anybody before or since, beginning in 1909. And a double gold

medalist the last time tennis had been an Olympic sport, 1924.
But what was this certified historic personage doing here?
Weren't the famous sporting prizes memorials to somebody—
the Heisman Trophy, the Davis Cup, the Stanley Cup? I assumed that was the case with the Wightman Cup, yet this tiny,
snowy-haired person with authoritative pale blue eyes was undoubtedly in charge, alive, and Hazel.

"Mrs. Wightie, this is the reporter from the *Herald*," one
of the committeewomen ushered me up to Hazel.

"Oh, gosh," I said, "I thought you were dead."

Suddenly an avalanche of silence supplanted the low, discreet chatter of the Longwood veranda. People took furtive peeks
at the gauche intruder while appearing to studiously scan the
lime acres on which energetic young things scampered in pursuit of tennis balls.

"Well, I mean . . ." The Ohio rube in me was on the loose.
A hundred eyeballs seemed to bound against my back. It was
not the opening remark the Boss would have chosen to say hello
to the indomitable Mrs. Wightie, as she was called, undeniably
Lady Tennis. An upright, socially chosen Bostonian, she had
only a few years before ordered two Englishwomen, members
of the British Wightman team, to remove from their bodies,
and her sight, tennis dresses hemmed in colors. Of the radical
trim she had ahemmed, "We wear all white, don't we, ladies?"

The incident led Ted Tinling, the offending dressmaker, to
call her "Queen Canute, trying to hold back the tide of progress." To others, as well, Hazel indeed seemed imperious, regarding the game as her private preserve. Some referred to her
surreptitiously as the "Queen Mother." Even they conceded that
she cared deeply for the game, a tireless volunteer who gave
free lessons to youngsters in her garage and supervised many
tournaments.

Had my career in tennis concluded at the outset in unwit-
ting blasphemy of one of the icons? Was the queen unamused?

On the contrary. After what felt like a very long, puzzled
look, she got what I meant, and smiled. The veranda thawed
immediately. At sixty-five she was beginning a mellow stretch
that would last until her death two decades later. She became
a good, helpful friend.

I returned to the office salivating to play on those grass
courts. The Boss was appalled that the new man hadn't been.

He was also annoyed when he received a couple of phone calls thanking him for supplying a reporter who seemed interested. "Fellow from Longwood called to ask if I'd send you out again to cover the New England Juniors," he frowned. "Don't get the idea that we cover tennis on a regular basis, junior. There isn't that kind of interest."

The Boss knew his territory, and what the publisher, and his most influential readers, blue of blood and Ivy of diploma, expected. By national standards the *Herald* wasn't a very good newspaper. However, it waved as the quality rag in New England (outside of the *Christian Science Monitor*). Highly profitable, noted for its parsimonious management and conservative-Republican-Yankee voice in a Democratic-Irish-Catholic town, the *Herald* had taken over for the late *Transcript* (the late George Apley's breakfast reading) in local WASP nests.

The Red Sox were the sacred bulls, a regional religion, treated even more seriously—deliriously—by the *Herald*, possibly because they were mainstays of the paper's principal sources of wealth, its TV channel and radio station. Harvard sports got a big play. They did at the more proletarian *Globe*, too, because the publisher and editors were Harvard men. In an earlier time, nothing was bigger than The Boat Race, the Harvard-Yale rowing match on the Thames in Connecticut. So prominent was it that the *Globe*'s editor in chief, W. D. Sullivan, annually wrote the lead story. But one year, as deadline neared, no word came from Sullivan. What was wrong? Another of numerous reporters supplied the answer: Harvard old boy Sullivan was too broken up by the Yale victory, unable to write. Someone else was assigned to carry on for him.

Harvard against Yale in football was (and remains) The Game. But heavy emphasis on college sport, except for Boston College, laden with national schedules and aspirations, has subsided in the current crush of professional sport and proliferation of franchises.

If there were any tennis readers out there during the Boss's term, surely the *Herald* had a corner on them among its brahmins, preppies, clubbies, and stock marketeers. True, but not enough to matter much. The Boss could satisfy them with wire-service reports on Wimbledon and Forest Hills, and, he said, "by, basically, covering one tournament a year, the National Doubles at Longwood. There's some interest in that," he conceded. A unique international extravaganza, devoted solely to doubles, it preceded the National Singles at Forest Hills on the so-called amateur circuit. The tournament, since, unfortunately, fragmented and redistributed, had been a Boston fixture since 1917. It brought out the hard-core degenerates in varying numbers, never amounting to more than four thousand at a sitting in the wooden grandstands.

Otherwise he detected no agitation for an increase in space for tennis. Nor did he hear any tennis talk from his friends or sounding boards—waitresses, cabdrivers, everyday sports nuts— nothing that would induce him to believe that the secret sport was ready for exposure.

Anybody who wished to follow it more than casually was welcome to take daily summertime doses of Allison Danzig in *The New York Times* or Al Laney in the *New York Herald Tribune.* Those two critics, informed and polished, pretty much constituted American tennis journalism. Riding the eastern grass court circuit, the only tournaments in the United States that mattered, they spent six weeks in small, exclusive clubs between Philadelphia and Newport, and crossed the finish line covering the National Doubles in Boston and the National Singles at Forest Hills.

The Boss respected Danzig and Laney because they were top men in covering other sports, too. Danzig did football and Olympic stuff, Laney golf and features. He forgave them tennis, a game with which he was uncomfortable, played "by men in their underwear" uttering perverse cries such as "Love–40!" An invitation to an orgy?

He made it clear to staff photographer Russ Adams, since become the world's premier taker of tennis pictures, that he wasn't much interested in the male form during the National Doubles. Hazel Wightman, in whose direction the Boss did genuflect, understood. During any local tournament that drew outsiders, she housed and fed at least a dozen female competitors in her spacious domain near Longwood. For Adams's lenses she would have available the highest-ranking faces and figures, not necessarily champions. Hazel and Russ were aware that a little cheesecake was most likely to land a tennis photo in the *Herald.*

In his disdain for tennis, the Boss wasn't much different from his contemporaries who supervised the sports pages of

America's largest dailies. As a man growing up in the 1920s and 1930s, a time when tennis got more newspaper ink than even today, the Boss was among those afflicted by what I call the Tilden Turnoff. "What kind of a game can it be if the best player of all time was a fag?" was a comment I heard many times across my first fifteen years in Boston.

My belief is that the disgrace of Big Bill Tilden had a profoundly negative effect on the development of the game in America for a long time, perhaps two decades. Late in his life Tilden's homosexuality was highly publicized, revealed in seamy accounts of his trials for sexual offenses—dalliances with teenage boys—and subsequent jailings in 1947 and 1949. In today's more tolerant climate, Tilden, a champion as renowned during the 1920s as Babe Ruth or Red Grange, might be a talk-show hit in discussing his "deviance," and received with sympathy. But in his time of public loathing of such behavior, he was a mightily fallen idol, and his sport suffered.

No tennis player has ever had a stronger grip on the American public. During the 1920s, as amateur sport held sway, tremendous American nationalistic pride bolstered the defense of the Davis Cup, and the invincible Tilden was the defender during a half-dozen years of dominating the game. His nationally syndicated column, written by himself and carried by scores of newspapers, not only paid him fabulously (about $25,000) but further elevated Big Bill as a luminous figure, outspoken, aloof, condescending, yet a confident, smiling flag bearer. Does a McEnroe, Evert, Connors, or Navratilova exert that sort of appeal?

When, in 1928, the USTA (United States Tennis Association) felt Bill was too big, and tried to bring him down by banning him from the Davis Cup team, the result was an international furor, calmed only by his reinstatement. The team was in Paris, trying to regain the Cup, and the French were outraged at the thought that "Beeg Beel" would not play in the final for the United States, thus slowing ticket sales at the brand-new arena, Stade Roland Garros. U.S. ambassador Myron Herrick had to intercede to keep the peace, instigating State Department pressure on the USTA to put Tilden back in the lineup.

At the time of his first arrest, in 1947, Tilden, amazingly enough at fifty-four, was yet a drawing card with the pros. Imagine, then, the shock waves as this American hero was abruptly depicted as a depraved and very dirty old man, and consider the consequential downgrading of his game in numerous quarters as a "sissy" sport.

Coupled with the Tilden Turnoff was the shortsighted disinclination of the Badgers—tennis officials—to make the most of the post–World War II sports boom by heeding imaginative and progressive cries to mix pros and amateurs in a few open tournaments, as in golf. Instead, the amateur fiction was upheld. Tennis in America, dealt the dual blows of the Tilden scandal and insular, stuffy administration, receded, while other sports, professionalized, surged ahead, and caught the public eye and ear—thus the Boss's.

It was curious to me that golf and tennis, essentially born and bred in Victorian Britain, and nurtured in similar private club atmospheres, were so differently perceived by the American public. Dwight Eisenhower, pitching and putting on the White House lawn, and the charging, grinning Arnold Palmer gave golf a tremendous lift. Palmer was a pro, he televised splendidly, his earnings were news. Tennis had no one comparable. Golf clubs were more hospitable in receiving the press, and often encouraged reporters to play. The Boss was a golfer, but he wouldn't have been "caught dead in short pants," as he described male tennis costume, "chasing a ball."

His was a prevailing attitude, one with which I disagreed while accepting the way things were. To me, tennis was a wonderful game that could win a larger following if the press and TV—and the game's leaders—would give it a more thorough chance. But what of it? Tennis got my personal hackerly attention regularly, playing with cronies who had a reasonably balanced outlook: they were more interested in their own games than those of the top amateurs and pros. Whatever tennis assignments sporadically came my way I handled with relish, though no more so than anything else. The Boss no longer apologized for the odd tennis duties on my schedule. Instead he gave me a fishy look and said, "Enjoy it while you can, junior. You can't live on tennis or love."

6

○

Civilization
Lost

Once upon a grass-stained time, in the days I regard fondly (and
unfondly, too) as the Lost Civilization, the game was more or
less just that: a game. Even then, make no mistake, it was a
business also, ever since the All England clubbies charged admission for the kickoff Wimbledon in 1877.

But, like all professional sports, tennis became a *big* busi-
ness/game, with the emphasis on the former. Shakespeare might
have said of the Lost Civilization, "the playing's the thing,"
and been essentially right. Now he'd probably conclude, "Out,
damned sport!"—realizing that pure sport is only the tip of an
icebox filled with cold cash. Not merely the $50 million in prize
money for men and women throughout the 1988 season, but
also the more generous and incalculable sums from marketing,
endorsements, admissions, sponsorship, and TV rights.

Almost none of this kind of cash was waved near tennis
before Zero Hour, the year 1968, the dawn of open tournaments, which launched the finishing attack on the now Lost
Civilization. Where are we today? You could call ours the
tennis age of greed-and-games, the Lust-for-Loot Civilization.

Whatever, it commenced humbly enough on April 22, 1968, beside the sea at Bournemouth, England, in the form of the British Hard Court Championships, the first Open homogenizing pros and amateurs.

That introductory Open doomed the Lost Civilization just as surely as the barbarians' appearance signaled the beginning of the end for the Roman Empire, or the Pill made considerable inroads on chastity.

The Lost Civilization wasn't exactly chaste. Show me a true blue amateur in the upper reaches of any international competition and I'll find you a virgin hooker. Whitney Reed, a guy with the half-volleying touch of Xaviera Hollander is an unforgettable face from that time. It was a face that appeared at my apartment window, five stories above the street—not a cat burglar but a lion-headed guy.

"Heard you're having a do," he said as I opened the window and invited him in. He would have been just as happy to be handed a few beers over the sill for consumption on the fire escape.

Of course he could have walked up the stairs like everybody else who came to that party—a "do," as he called it—but everybody else's approach to anything was hardly Whitney Reed's.

Reed was hardly any American Badger's idea of who the No. 1 tennis player in the United States should be. He didn't look it; he didn't act it. But for 1961 he was it, the thirty-fifth in the line of succession that began with Harvard blue blood Dick Sears in 1885. Reed was a Californian who seemed a blood brother to James Dean in appearance, mumbling speech, and outlook. But he wasn't a rebel without a cause. His cause was to have a good old time all the time, part of which was playing tennis.

"Let's have a little do," he'd say. Any time of day would do, if he wasn't scheduled on the court—and sometimes even if he was.

"I think we're gonna be defaulted," worried Jack Frost, his partner for the National Doubles of 1961. "We're late for our match already, and I can't get Whitney to get dressed."

"For the match?" I said.

"Yeah, that, too."

"Well, where is he?"

Frost shrugged. "You see, Whitney has just fallen in love, and is exploring some of the possibilities in a car outside the clubhouse. I'm having difficulty getting his attention."

But Whitney diverted himself back to tennis again, and they won. What a team. Reed moved with all the grace of a gouty gorilla. Jack Frost made faces, snorted, and fell down a lot. They played extremely well in the process—sometimes together in doubles. Who remembers Frost and Reed as the No. 4 American team in 1961? Probably not even Frost and Reed.

I do. I cherish the recollections from that summer when they earned their ranking, mostly by zigzagging to the quarter-finals of the Nationals. Whitney insisted on playing an early-round match in a downpour that had shut down the rest of the tournament. His opponents, as well as partner Frost, weren't overjoyed to be playing on a grass court treacherous as ice, because they nearly broke their necks. But Reed wanted to give spectators, huddled on the Longwood clubhouse porch, "something to watch."

"They were nice to come, least we could do was play," he said. "Rain makes corn grow. It must be good for us humans, too." He was the only one who could stand up with assurance, but that was minor compared with the day in Jamaica when he dragged himself from a party at 11:00 A.M. in order to beat Roy Emerson and Neale Fraser, two of the great Aussies, in succession. Nobody could understand how Reed stood up at all, and the court was perfectly dry. It was Whitney who wasn't.

Between matches at the Doubles Reed crammed for his sex education course, and Frost went to the mattresses—specifically the mattress on my living room floor on which he camped for the week.

They were the last of the tennis bums. Whitney, twenty-nine, had the allure of a guru for those on the circuit in the late 1950s and early 1960s who felt that they were playing a game, not running a corporation. Although they competed as hard as they could, and took what they could get in handouts and perks, they thought it should be fun.

Can you imagine anything like this happening today? Whitney is playing against a highly regarded youngster out of St. Louis, Butch Buchholz, in the Newport Casino Invitational, one of the prime tourneys on the since embalmed grass-court circuit. It is match point against Buchholz, a teenager who will go on to more notable achievements than Reed as a pro. Buchholz serves. Fault. He serves again and the ball sails over the service line for a double fault. It's all over. Or is it? Reed has caught the ball, and throws it back to Buchholz with, "Come on, kid, try it again."

"What?" Buchholz is eloquent in the face of a gesture that confuses him because he has never experienced it before, and will not again.

"Aw, serve it again. We don't want to end on a double fault. That's no fun."

Dutifully, Buchholz accepts the reprieve, serves once more, acceptably, and they play out the point, which Reed wins. The match is over, definitely. Reed wins and has fun. Buchholz says he had fun, too: "Always, against Whitney."

Whitney also had fun when he lost because just playing was fun.

Free spirits haven't vanished altogether, but there aren't any Reedian bon vivants occupying No. 1 rankings or Davis Cup jobs.

To Whitney and his comrades, tennis bummery was a perfectly honorable and sensible dodge. He didn't make excuses for keeping body and merriment together through amateur tennis. At those dull, duty parties where the players were shown off to meet room-and-board obligations to their hosts, a leading question was always: "What do you do when you're not playing the circuit?"

The accepted answer was to name attendance at such-and-such college or employment in this-or-that job.

Whitney's reply: "I have a paper route."

It was games-playing fun, a free lunch in the better places for most players, a modest bank account for the very best—but no trust funds, well-compensated retinues, or lifetime security as enjoyed by the one-person conglomerates who hog the championships now. Margaret Court and Roy Emerson, the supremely athletic Aussies, made some nest-egg money during the 1960s and early 1970s as they set the records for major championship totals in singles and doubles—she sixty-two, he twenty-eight. How many millions would they rake in today?

But if there was no money to speak of—only nasty sportswriters like me spoke of it in print—the hours were better, the conditions healthier. Night and indoor play were virtually non-happenings. So was the bodily punishment of paving, which plagues America now as the tennis landscape becomes a gigantic green-topped parking lot.

Knees-and-spine-cushioning grass and clay were the prime battlegrounds. Aside from the red-earthy Italian and French championships, critical judgment focused on what happened at play in the fields of the Lord: luxuriant (though frequently unruly of bounce) turf. Particularly Wimbledon and Forest Hills. Wimbledon and the European clay court tourneys are the only survivors of the Lost Civilization, at least underfoot.

The rackets were wood; the togs and balls were white. As another survivor, Ohio-born Hall of Famer Billy Talbert, remembers it, "There were two rackets—the Wilson Jack Kramer or, for the Aussies and Europeans, the Dunlop Fort. You saw a few Slazengers in the hands of the foreigners and an occasional Spalding or Bancroft in America. There were two logos on the clothes —either the laurel wreath of Fred Perry or the crocodile of René Lacoste. We wore Converse shoes. That was pretty much it."

No hard-hearted, softwaring computer stalked the players, charting their every result and spitting out their place in the pecking order. Certainly rankings were made, had been since 1885, beginning in the United States. But they could be subjective, and based as much on court manner and popularity as performance. Nothing scientific. World rankings (top tens) were begun in 1914 by a British journalist named A. Wallis Myers, a figment of his judgment with the Wimbledon champs usually No. 1.

Rankings, now the computerized roll of merit on which tournament admission depends, were then passports to the good life, which meant room, board, transportation, a few bucks sub table, or portions thereof. Any kind of ranking was good for something. You could dine out on a sectional ranking—or a former ranking. Or an imagined ranking, like Dick Moody, an American circuit fixture in the mid-1960s, who sang for his supper. Moody was a fair player out of Utah who didn't win matches and moved better in dancing pumps than sneakers. But he entertained at tournament parties with his song-and-tap act, and that was enough to keep him afloat as a first-round loser during the summer season. His patter and persistence even got him into the Nationals at Forest Hills, where, if a computer had been lurking, only by purchasing a ticket could he have entered the gate.

But initiative, resourcefulness, and charm could take you a long way in the Lost Civilization, and provide more amusement than looking over your shoulder in fear of a malicious printout. Eduardo Zuleta, a compact, copper-hued character from Ecuador, was only a fair player, too, but he bore the additional credits of representing a strange-sounding, far-off country, and exuding a pleasing Latin manner. Also, somehow Eduardo could always come up with the ever-prized and always scarce Wimbledon tickets, a source of goodwill (and income) not to be underestimated.

Zuleta was an agreeable patsy, generally a first-round loser, but welcomed and offered hospitality wherever he went. He abused the system and his station only once, at Forest Hills in 1963. There, in his customary burial plot, the opening round, Eduardo had the temerity to cast off the shroud and win the first two sets and scramble to 5–5 in the third, two games from a stunning victory against the No. 1 seed, Chuck McKinley. As the Wimbledon champ, McKinley was a longed-for candidate to become the drought-buster, the first American male to win his country's title in eight years.

Panic was the operative mood of the Badgers who ran the tournament. "What the hell is Eduardo doing to us? Who let him in the tournament?"

The committeemen would have rallied gladly around whichever one of them had the presence to shoot Zuleta, pleading justifiable homicide. It wasn't necessary, nor did looks kill. Eduardo, who seldom played more than two sets, and never three, got tired. He came apart in the fourth set, and fell in the fifth like a good fellow, thereby not rubbing the Badgers too far the wrong way.

In those lost days, the players got on with it. No umpire would have put up with dawdling thirty seconds between points, a licit interval now. They kept moving. Even though tiebreakers weren't even on the horizon (cooking only in the brainpan of the deviser, Jimmy Van Alen) more games and activity were packed into less time than currently. Pancho Gonzalez and Charlie Pasarell used five hours, twelve minutes for their record five-set Wimbledon epic of 112 games in 1969 (the year before the tiebreaker came into general usage), while Ivan Lendl and Mats Wilander consumed four hours, forty-seven minutes for their U.S. Open final of 1987. Thank goodness Lendl and Wilander played two tiebreakers and only four sets, amounting to forty-two games.

But there were provisions for a ten-minute intermission after the second set for women, and third set for men, if either player requested it. Poor Zuleta. As well-wishers flocked to one of the cubicles set aside in the Forest Hills stadium for such sojourns to see what they could do to aid and cheer the losing McKinley, Zuleta was alone in his, soaked and clammy. Although the Badgers probably hoped Zuleta developed a case of pneumonia, such may have been prevented by the day's humanitarian, the unaging Gardnar Mulloy, who, at forty-eight, was playing in the senior singles, four years after his last appearance in the main event.

Mulloy stopped by Zuleta's cell to offer encouragement. Seeing that he had no change of clothing—"I don't expect to play more than three sets," Eduardo said—Gar stripped off his own. He handed everything but shoes over, then donned the Ecuadorian's sweat-saturated garb so that he could return to the clubhouse without streaking.

Greater love hath no man than when he lays down his own jock and shirt to comfort one of his fellows. They wore jocks then, not briefs, and fortunately for the tournament McKinley snapped back in his to deprive Zuleta of a golden moment of celebrity, a brief departure from destiny, first-round fodder.

Invariably middle-aged men were in charge of tournaments, deciding who got the handouts. Nobody could slink her way into their hearts quite like Patricia Stewart, a tall and well-nourished Hoosier. Hers were winning stats, though not on court. "I'm 38-26-36," she proclaimed with a smile, "numbers I much prefer to being number one in tennis."

No one let poor Patty starve as she made her rounds through the Lost Civilization.

7

○

Badgers and
Other Fauna

The game is elementary. Either the ball goes over the net or it doesn't, lands inside the rectangle or outside. The politics are hardly rectangular, but multisided and angled, at times so ridiculous and incomprehensible that no newspaper dares bore its readers with more than an occasional stab at the subject.

This much is elementary: Tennis is the Balkans of sport. Power shifts continually as wars flare among those who seek to exert control.

If you're old enough to remember Shirley Temple singing "Animal Crackers in My Soup," you're probably in, or close to, that age zone where Ilie Nastase lumped tennis officials at the time he came along: "Between sixty and dead." A sage observation from incorrigible Ilie in classifying the general mind-set of a quarter-century ago, even if unfair to some of those in charge, on court and off.

Animal crackers in an alphabet soup is today's stew—USTA, MTC, WIPTC, ITF, ATP, WITA, etc.—whose spooning I can bear to do only for a few moments as a primer. Currently there's hardly room for all the kinds of crackers: Badgers, Beavers, Vultures, Hares, Magpies, Owls. But there were only two in the bygone day of the Lost Civilization. Badgers and Hares. Management and labor. Officials and players.

Badgers ruled, absolutely, presuming divine right, although their badges of office seem to have been handed down from Saint Henry. That's Henry Jones, who proposed and presided over the baptismal Wimbledon in 1877. Doubly disreputable, Jones was a sportswriter and croquet player who inoculated the All England Croquet Club with the tennis virus, eventually causing an emendation of the nameplate to All England Lawn Tennis and Croquet Club.

As patron saint of the Badgers, administrative officials, and organizers, Henry Jones may have used a mallet as scepter, directing the athletic Hares through their paces. The Hares were powerless in the grasp of the Badgers, who had them by their cottontails. Male and female. They depended on the Badgers' kindnesses in the form of expense payments and other favors to get along because the Badgers owned the only game in any town.

Badgers, overwhelmingly male inhabitants of the tennis hierarchy ranging from national and international officers, committee and tournament personnel, take their name from conspicuous badges of office (and political achievement). Worn as decorations and battle ribbons almost since the beginning of tennis time, they festoon the lapels of suit coats, usually navy blue blazers. Blazered Badgers are ever anxious to let you know who they are by their badges: president of this or that club, association, or federation; chairman of whatever tournament or committee.

Badgers and Hares. That's all there were, for decades, within the established order of "amateur tennis." It was called that, with straight faces, by the Badgers—either pretty good actors or self-delusionists, guys who got their faces straightened and shirts stuffed, apparently, at group rates.

A half-century after Saint Henry counted the first offertory, the 1877 Wimbledon gate receipts, a new species, the Dingos, was identified in a freshly cropped-up thicket called "pro tennis." As wild dogs, the Dingos went their own nomadic and unorganized way, foraging for whatever they could find, which wasn't much, beyond the Badgers' citadels. Badgers said the Dingos were in reality a pack of rabid Hares that had gone astray, crazy for legitimate cash. Aside from putting out a NO DINGOS NEED APPLY sign at their tournaments, the Badgers, like everyone else, paid little attention to those outlaw creatures.

Times changed. The creatures of the kingdom multiplied, and the Badgers were shaken by a revolution that struck them like the overflow of Mount Vesuvius. Although not yet extinct, like Pompeians, the Badgers, nearly two thousand years later, felt a scorching and disestablishing flow all the same. Instead of lava, it was the hot breath of newcomers. Beavers (unionists) and Vultures (agents/lawyers/marketers) evolved at the eruption of open tennis in 1968 to begin melting the Badgers' nearly century-long dominance over the game itself. Male Beavers, the ATP (Association of Tennis Professionals), were soon followed by the female WITA (Women's International Tennis Association).

Once the lawyers attaché-cased the scene, I recalled the prophetic words of a Boston boxing promoter, Sam Silverman, regarding his own art: "When the lawyers showed up, we was in the hands of the Philistines." It's that way in every sport. Lawsuits and legal maneuvering have cluttered and clouded the soup from the moment attorneys got a whiff of the golden aroma wafting from tennis in 1968.

Open tennis, of course, meant letting in the Dingos. Until 1968 acknowledged professional tennis was on the outside, fenced beyond the accepted tournament structure, not really a sport with a defined schedule. Although an uncertain occupation supporting the few intrepid Dingos, it was preferred by that silent minority. They had shed the Badgers' shackles to find an acceptable living wherever they roamed on the perimeter, no longer kept Hares.

Badgers will always be with us. Who else would inhabit all those committees, and do the largely unpaid, and unthanked, work of tournament tennis—a function usually, and ungratefully, overlooked by the beneficiaries, the players. No other professional sport gets away with so much uncompensated labor.

But the Vultures and Beavers, though subtly and without the official stamp of leadership, became the guiding forces of the professional game. As the foremost tournaments were thoroughly professionalized, nobody was quarantined on the outside. In fact, there *was* no more outside. Backed by the union

Beavers and the agent Vultures, the Hares became muscularly independent. Dingos, as such, vanished.

In 1974 the Wise Old Owls, male persuasion, began hooting as a cooperative to try to provide administrative leadership under the banner of the MTC (Men's Tennis Council). An amalgam of Badgers, Hares/Beavers, and another new species, the Magpies (tournament directors), the Owls direct the Grand Prix circuit, earnestly trying to give direction and cut through the everyday chaos.

A year later, the female Owls, WIPTC (Women's International Professional Tennis Council) set up shop to oversee the Virginia Slims circuit. They were less noticeable since the women's game is smaller, and more orderly.

In a positive move toward professionalizing supervision of the professional games, No. 1 Owls—chief administrators Marshall Happer and Jane Brown, respectively—were eventually installed, characters as close to being commissioners as the game has known. Ever at odds with the agents, and at times the unionists, the Wise Old Owls strive admirably to maintain the game's integrity and keep the Vultures from carrying off the farm.

Tournament-directing and -promoting Magpies have taken over a Badgerly preserve. Tournaments weren't run for personal profit during the Lost Civilization, but open tennis offered that possibility. Screeching their wares, calling attention to the game, and attracting sponsors and underwriters, the Magpies asserted themselves, too. But they were odd creatures. Beneath the plumage they were sometimes Badgers, sometimes Vultures, occasionally Beavers.

Badgers as Magpies kept promotional control of the various national championships, to enrich their federations and associations, but frequently enlisted the marketing expertise of Vultures. For a time the unionist Beavers promoted their own tournaments. The ATP threatens to do so again, in 1990, despite historical evidence of a total lack of cooperation and responsibility by the leading men in advancing their own tournaments.

Vultures popped up as owners and/or promoters of so many tournaments that the properly alarmed Owls attempted to legislate against such conflicts of interest.

Perhaps the first pure Magpies of tournament tennis were the hard-working husband-wife lineup of Ed and Marilyn Fernberger in Philadelphia, and Bill Riordan in Salisbury, Maryland. Though distinctly un-Badgerly types, they had no personal profit motive. In founding the Philadelphia Indoor (now U.S. Pro Indoor) in 1962, during the amateur era, Ed and Marilyn sought to raise funds for youth tennis in the area. They're still at it, still successful.

Riordan worked on behalf of the USTA, resuscitating the National Indoor Championships in a strange yet successful move in 1964. Bill lifted the tournament from New York to Salisbury, where many more villagers attended. Alas, iconoclastic Bill is gone from the scene. But before he finished cutting an uproarious swath, the gregarious Riordan had promoted a number of items extremely well: his hometown, Jimmy Connors (whose manager he became), and himself. There undoubtedly was money to be made in the last two.

According to the charts, Badger No. 1 is president of the ITF (International Tennis Federation), followed in the pecking order by the presidents of the more than one hundred national federations constituting the ITF membership. Most important of these are the Big Four, proprietors of the major championships, the so-called Grand Slam opens: the USTA, the LTA (Lawn Tennis Association of Great Britain, of Wimbledon fame), the FFT (French Federation of Tennis), and TA (Tennis Australia). Sometimes, Biggest Badger is entitled to wear two badges. *Et voila!* You then have the clever Parisian pol Philippe Chatrier, head of both the ITF and FFT, whose vigorous campaign to return tennis to the Olympic Games after a sixty-four-year exile was rewarded in 1988.

Badgers, like the kings and court they had been prior to 1968, believed they ruled the Hares and kept the faith for the good of the game. It was both true and false. They were, and are, unpaid volunteers, most of them hackers themselves, impelled by a genuine infatuation with the game.

Without them there would be no structure, no organized tournament game, from the lowest age-group level, ten-year-olds, to the highest proficiency, the Grand Slam championships.

But as they rise in the political system, Badgers find remuneration in power and privilege that transcends money. Such perks as the best (Badger-displaying) seats at the best tournaments, and the expenses to get there, are among the rewards at the top. Not to overlook the opportunity to preside, within TV range, at presentations of trophies, and perhaps even deliver a deadening oration to victor, vanquished, and restive throng.

The acme of such oratory may have been delivered in 1972 by New Yorker Pete Davis. A Super Badger, one-time chairman of a once-prominent tournament at Southampton, Long Island, Davis was regularly on display at Davis Cup matches since his father, Dwight Davis, had donated the sterling bowl in 1900 for the worldwide team tourney. Handed the microphone at a final round presentation of the Cup, Davis said, "It's wonderful to be in Budapest. . . ."

Trouble was, Davis stood in downtown Bucharest, and the Romanian assemblage of 7,200 understood enough English to respond sufficiently in catcalls and boos and render the remainder of his speech unheard.

It is not clear whether that did as much for U.S.-Romanian relations as the Davis Cup final the year before in Charlotte, North Carolina. Nobody knows which Badger supplied the music for the Romanian national anthem to the band leader. But it was the wrong anthem, the capitalist ditty that was favored in Bucharest before communism became the governance of the land. Apologies were necessary, as well as a performance of the suitably Marxist tune the next day.

Ultimate Badgerville is the roost called the Royal Box at Wimbledon's Centre Court, the equivalent of Valhalla to a tennis official. Even the queen has been known to show up, every quarter-century or so, although HRH prefers racetracks and betting windows, and despises tennis. Most likely the duke of Kent, the president of the All England Lawn Tennis and Croquet Club (alias Wimbledon), and his lovely duchess are in attendance, along with assorted other azure corpuscular types—perhaps the disenfranchised king of Greece.

An invitation to sit in the same select precinct, along with the well-fixed All England Clubbies who run the biggest show in tennis, is apt to give an American Badger the Royal Box syndrome.

Few are able to resist it: The illusions of eminence are absorbed spiritually in the most direct way, emanating from the cushions on the wicker chairs. Only a very small minority are unchanged for the worse by the experience.

Different from all other Badgers are the All England Club

variety, set apart, in their own minds anyway, by Wimbledon's primogeniture. The badges of these gentlemen (and very few ladies), who conduct themselves in the manner of the best undertakers, are distinctive, miniature bow ties in club colors of mauve and green. The men take their duties with too much gravity ever to wear sports jackets at their sporting event. Sober business suits are the rule for those whose deportment leads you to believe they are about their Maker's business.

8

○

Revolt of
the Hares

Similar Badgerly preserves, though not so exalted in prestige as the Royal Box, are to be found at the principal court of the other major championships. Lunch, tea, and use of the bar in the elegant All England Club rooms are included with an invitation to the Royal Box. Badgers and their guests at the other three stadia in Paris, New York, and Melbourne, don't suffer either. The food is considered best, understandably, for Badgers and friends at Roland Garros in Paris.

A front-row TV set allows the royals to watch replays at Wimbledon. However warm the weather may be in London, protocol dictates that males in the Royal Box may go topless only if the duke of Kent mercifully removes his suit coat and rakishly bares his shirtsleeves. This has occurred but thrice in the last two decades.

One of the more Badgerly USTA presidents, Marvin Richmond, had a private TV set in the Flushing Meadows version of the regal enclave so that he could make sure CBS cameras were projecting his image to viewers at sufficiently frequent intervals.

So the Badgers have a very good time of it. Some of them have earned it, working their way up from supervising youth tournaments and giving themselves to administrative duty in regional and sectional associations. Others have skillfully politicked their way to the heights.

Probably the most adroit climber was an unassuming-looking Bostonian named Walter Elcock, who popped up as president of the USTA in 1971, then the ITF, with almost no background in the game, surely none at the grass roots. Nobody is quite sure how he pulled it off. But once in those lofty positions he got a positive rating simply because he did little harm.

Rare are those No. 1 Badgers such as USTA presidents Bob Kelleher in 1968 and Slew Hester a decade later, who were actually productive and progressive. Kelleher maneuvered U.S. approval of open tennis, killing off the Lost Civilization, and Hester uncoupled the U.S. Open from Forest Hills while building the National Tennis Center at Flushing Meadows.

Whatever good or bad they committed, the Badgers clearly exercised too much control over the Hares during the amateur era, and the transitionary early years of open tennis. Players played only where and when Badgers approved, and were allowed to make money only if Badgers looked the other way.

A few false starts were made in organizing the Hares, but eventually the ATP and WITA came into being, in 1972 and 1974, respectively. The players at last were able to protect themselves from arbitrary rulings and restrictions of the Badgers.

One of those fiats was issued in 1972 when the ITF banned WCT (World Championship Tennis), the men's pro troupe operated by Lamar Hunt, because Hunt sought a management fee in return for supplying his people. Included among the banned were the game's premier guys such as Rod Laver, Ken Rosewall, and defending Wimbledon champ John Newcombe. The ban lasted only until after Wimbledon, won by independent pro Stan Smith, because the USTA made it clear that such exclusion would never be countenanced by tournament organizers in America. No union would have permitted the ban in the first place, but there was no union then.

Twelve months later Wimbledon's Badgers were, unwittingly, the making of the union, the ATP, in an incident whose hero was the acerbic Yugoslav Nikki Pilic. The Pilic affair began casually when the No. 1 Yugoslav—the first acknowledged professional athlete of his country—decided he'd rather earn prize money in a tournament than take part in a Davis Cup match for the homeland the same week. Since it was a minor match, he obtained permission to skip from the Yugoslav Federation boss, an army general who happened to be an uncle of Pilic's wife.

However, when Yugoslavia, minus Pilic, lost that minor match to New Zealand, the reaction caused uncle to rue his decision and act outraged along with his fellow Badgers. But Pilic, startlingly refused to cry "uncle!" and went his own way anyway.

The Yugoslav Federation was quick to suspend him, even though at the time he was doing well in the French Open, where he reached the final. It was axiomatic in such a case that all other ITF members would honor the suspension until the Yugoslavs lifted it.

Next on Nikki's schedule was the Italian Open. While Italian Badgers are no less officious than their ITF lodge brothers, they are perhaps more complaisant and pragmatic. Declaring that communication was difficult between Rome and Belgrade, 450 miles distant, they said they hadn't heard about the Pilic suspension, and permitted Nikki, a definite ticket seller in the midst of a controversy, to play.

Wimbledon, ostensibly his next stop two weeks later, was another matter. Wimbledon was, as ever, sold out in advance. The Big W's Badgers, having barred their door to WCT the previous year, and hearing few outcries except from the Hares themselves, hung tough, along with the LTA, and refused Pilic's entry.

ATP, the fledgling union, spoke tough, too, threatening to walk unless Pilic was accepted. It was a perfect showdown to determine who was in charge of the players' destinies—they themselves or the Badgers.

Would the Hares dare strike the mother church? Nobody, certainly neither the Wimbledonians nor a patriotic British press, thought so. It wouldn't happen today, players unselfishly putting the welfare of all ahead of individual desires.

But pro tennis was genuinely a fraternity in the dawning days of open tennis, a band of frontiersmen whose most renowned names sensed that they had to lead, both off and on the job.

Could anybody believe that John Newcombe, champion in 1967, '70, '71, but caught in the WCT ban of 1972, would sit out a second successive Wimbledon on a principle? Or Stan Smith, the defending champion? Or four-time champion and still a contender, Laver?

But they did. Orchestrated by the ATP's executive director, Jack Kramer, and another founder, agent Donald Dell, union ringleaders Arthur Ashe, Stan Smith, and John Newcombe, fomented rebellion and got it.

Daring excommunication, seventy-nine members failed to show up for the weightiest occasion in their game. Virtually every prominent male name was missing.

Stiffed by the genuine players, the Wimbledon Badgers stiff-upper-lipped it, of course, supported by a press that became very establishment when workingmen blasphemed. Despite customary self-righteousness and attendance that stayed unusually high, the Badgers eventually knew they were beaten. While Pilic was hardly a favorite of his brethren, it was their stand on his behalf that established the ATP as a force and struck down— for good—absolute rule by the Badgers.

Although Pilic's suspension was lifted after Wimbledon, the USTA let it be known within the ITF that, as in the case of the WCT ban in 1972, there'd be no excluding the stars from America for such reasons. Names were needed to sell tickets there if not in London. How long could anybody else outside of Wimbledon—and perhaps even Wimbledon itself—defy the Hares? Nor did it warm Wimbledonians that their stonewalling on the Pilic affair resulted in a tarnished all-police state final, won by the Czech Jan Kodes over the Russian Alex Metreveli. Seemingly retreating to 1967, Wimbledon was once again a second-rate production in the first-ranked amphitheater.

Having won the right to play anywhere, regardless of Badgerly wishes, the ATP set about negotiating the steady rise of prize money and job (i.e., tournament) opportunities. Laver, in 1971, had been the first to hit the million-dollar mark in career prize money, but more than seventy were to follow, female and male.

The governing of the male game evolved to the MTC (Men's Tennis Council). The women had further to go to liberate themselves. Sexist as they come, Badgers exerted even tighter control over the females. Until 1971, when the Virginia Slims circuit was formed, most tournaments were traditionally coeducational. Women traditionally got the short end: expenses in the amateur days, and prize money after 1968.

Firebrand Billie Jean King, frequently suspended by the USTA for preaching women's rights and perpetrating acts of defiance, found an ally in Gladys Heldman, publisher of *World Tennis* magazine, then the most respected editorial voice of the entire game. Together they pushed for better treatment of the "little broads," as Heldman called them, and unionization.

Their declaration of independence was splitting from the men, except for the four majors. After a series of battles, none quite so dramatic as the Wimbledon boycott, and with Billie Jean and Gladys in the forefront, the WITA was organized.

Today the WITA does a better job at unifying its membership than the ATP. Still second fiddlers, even if well recognized and paid, the women display greater responsibility to the game that feeds them.

As serious money and interest began to touch tennis, agents were quick to follow the scent. First among the Vultures was Donald Dell, a lawyer who founded ProServ. Mark McCormack of Cleveland, an original among sports agents, concentrated his early attention on golf in the persons of clients Arnold Palmer, Jack Nicklaus, and Gary Player. McCormack's firm, IMG (International Management Group), had turned down Rod Laver's request to become a client in 1968. Unfamiliar with tennis, McCormack deemed, correctly, that it wasn't a public heartthrob.

But in 1969 he changed his mind, took Laver in, and began to woo tennis players avidly. Though Dell had a head start, McCormack did pull abreast. Together they became the dominant force, competing but sometimes coventuring, cleaning up everything that wasn't nailed down. Single-minded in sniffing out profit in a variety of areas, they became stronger than the unions, the Badgers, and the administrative bodies.

Not only representing and managing players, they did the same for various tournaments—owning some of them outright—and scooped up TV rights for many of them. They even produced their own TV coverage of some tournaments, and Dell—never denying his status as His Highest Conflict of Interest—appears on his productions as a commentator.

Agents exist in all sports, having materialized logically to represent, market, and protect athletes in a favorable economic

climate. But in no other sport have they moved in so thoroughly to cover all financial outlets. And in this freebooting
arena they have generally done well by their clients, whether
players or tournaments. Their constant activity has helped
the game grow and prosper. But too often their actions are
detrimental to the spirit and the health of the game, simply
because their interests are solely commercial. The care and
maintenance of a public trust like tennis requires soul and
devotion.

Agents have their useful role, undeniably, in a blend of
Hares, Badgers, Beavers, Vultures, and, I trust, Wise Old Owls
of the MTC and WIPTC. Having leaped, efficiently and ener-
getically, into the void created when tennis was declared open
and fully professional, the agents seized more than their share.
Perfectly natural. With strength in too many areas, however,
they have manipulated players and events unconscionably so
that tennis has sometimes been indistinguishable from professional wrassling.

When does the make-believe of exhibitions end and the real
thing (of authorized tournaments) begin? This can be difficult
to determine at a time when the leading players make more
money from agent-arranged recitals—money up front, no pressure to win—than the legitimate tournament circuit, and these
exhibitions aren't always clearly set forth as such to the confused public. Moreover, the exhibitions are generally played in
the same time period as legitimate tournaments.

When a player risks injury, exhaustion, and credibility in
exhibitions at the expense of the legitimate game, he is cheating himself, his profession, and the public. And there is too
much cheating.

The men are the chief offenders, although the women
aren't guiltless. Stars are playing fewer conventional tournaments because their exhibition opportunities have increased.
This is injurious to the legitimate game, the Grand Prix circuit
for men and the Virginia Slims circuit for women, on which
the stars make their reputations and enhance their exhibition
fees.

A problem of prosperity is that the one-time summer game
has expanded to a fifty-two-week tournament season. No definite off-season brings relief, as in most other sports. Until—if
ever—an eight- or nine-month major season can be established,

leaving room for exhibitions and recovery, the game will remain in a state of beguiling chaos.

Maybe it was never meant to be that Hares, Badgers, Vultures, Beavers, and Wise Old Owls would live in a state of harmony.

9

○

Sundown,
Fun Up

When the sun went down, the house lights went up and the parties began. Night tennis was something, an old campaigner named Al Stitt defined with a leer, "that we played up on the terrace courts." He meant Longwood Cricket Club's heaviest landscaped grass courts, most remote from the clubhouse. There were no lights.

But nobody was expected to have anything but a good time on the tournament circuit after sunset. Floodlit tennis did not exist in the Lost Civilization that was all but gone by 1970.

Blame it on Jimmy Van Alen, who had some weak-watted bulbs hoisted above the main court at the Newport Casino for his nonconformist pro tourney of 1965. Or on the folks at Longwood, who followed suit for the U.S. Pro in 1967. Soon after, the rest of America, and the world, fell in line. Alas, it was bound to come.

Night-and-day, day-and-night. Tennis went into overtime gear, becoming more puritanical than other sports, which confined services to either day or night. It was brutal on the parties. So was indoor tennis, also practically nonstop. Indoor tournaments wiped out the Caribbean circuit, a sunny refuge for those who felt they should continue to maintain themselves, well tanned and cared for, through tennis, during the cold winter months, and wished to do it in style in Jamaica or Puerto Rico.

Style vanished as big money appeared. Professionalization replaced fun and games, and the Civilization was doomed to be Lost. Now I feel like an archaeologist digging into a musty past. It wasn't so long ago, 1968, that the old order began to go out of order, but it seemed to be functioning all right, impervious to the cataclysm that was unimaginable when I first came into contact with it.

The rackets were wooden, and so was the thinking of the Badgers. Though any organized sport is an unreal world to itself, tennis may have been more so, yet that was part of its charm. Operating throughout the planet predominantly at small, private, restricted clubs, it was entertainment for the select few. The washed and initiated. An aura, unchanged from Victorian origins, was elitist, cool, controlled. In these hushed playgrounds of privilege where the combatants were referred to as Mr. and Miss amid cries of "Well played!" and restrained applause, the realities were often overlooked. It was very competitive, demanding, head-to-head conflict, but one in which the antagonists were expected to act like ladies and gentlemen at tea.

Even today, in the era of professionalism, this is unrealistically expected in some circles. Many still long for the sportsmanship, the moderate behavior, of the Lost Civilization, but it could be enforced then. Players were the playthings of the Badgers. One of the very Badgerly, the overseer of a Long Island fixture, admitted, "We don't want the game to be bigger or more popular. Tennis week at our club is a tradition, just as it is in other clubs on the Eastern grass-court circuit. We have tickets for some nonmembers in the gallery to help make expenses, and we put the players up, entertain and feed them.

"Why would we want to have professionals around? It would cost us too much, and they would be independent. Now we take care of [pay] a few of the regulars who have to maintain themselves through the game, but if we had to give prize money we would need a bigger enclosure. No thank you."

"It's too crowded now, too popular," I hear some people

say at Flushing Meadows. They long for the halcyon days of the National Singles at Forest Hills where, before the Open era, you could spread out in the stadium, or walk the grounds peacefully. Not that "too popular" means the masses have gravitated to tennis. But many more of the general public are aware, and willing to pay to attend. That's what professionalism brings: TV coverage, press attention, prize money—a new civilization.

Kept players had no choice but to be reasonably courtly to the Badgers. There was no appeal to suspensions for misbehavior. Earl Cochell, indulging in what the *Official USTA Yearbook* called "unbelievably unfortunate behavior" and "great discourtesy to the referee," became a nonperson after the Nationals of 1951.

He came into that tournament as the seventh-ranked American, but seemed to fall apart in a four-set fourth rounder against Gardnar Mulloy. Cochell, a twenty-nine-year-old right-hander, played some points left-handed, and once tried to climb the umpire's chair to borrow the microphone in order to scold spectators who didn't care for his act. During the intermission following the third set, customary in the pre-tiebreaker days, referee Ellsworth Davenport, an aged and revered Badger, walked over to the stadium dressing room to urge Cochell to calm down.

Cochell's McEnroevian response, predating McEnroe by a quarter-century: "Go shit in your hat!"

With no union, agents, or lawyers to protect him, Cochell, at the peak of his career, was summarily drummed out of the recognized game by the USTA. In effect, he was suspended forever, and expunged from the year-end 1951 rankings in which surely he had earned a prominent position. Gone, without a trace. Fortunately that couldn't happen today, but such was the authority exerted by the Badgers of the feudal Lost Civilization.

I had heard about Cochell, but was directly involved in another similar authoritarian case ten years later. This was the undeserved suspension of Dennis Ralston, barring him from Forest Hills in 1961. Ralston, today a coach at Southern Methodist University, a coach you'd like your kids to play for, did not have the most agreeable court demeanor in his youth. But he didn't merit the "Dennis the Menace" tag that some reporters hung on him either.

His sins were mild, measured against those of the present.

But perhaps, in the light of the time, he did warrant at least a public rebuke for cursing in a Davis Cup match against Mexico in Cleveland. A rebuke might have been merited, yes, but hardly a suspension keeping him out of the most meaningful tournament of the year, the National Singles. More shocking, the blow fell much later, after he and Chuck McKinley had won the National Doubles at Longwood, and were ready to head for Forest Hills.

Dennis departed Longwood with some business unfinished—the final of the Mixed Doubles, which was put off by rain. He and Darlene Hard were to oppose Aussies Margaret Court and Bob Mark. As chairman of that event (a nonbadge-wearing Badger-for-a-week), I was concerned about a proper completion. I made arrangements with the committee at Forest hills to have them play the final there. That was fine with the players but not, as it turned out, with prototypical USTA president George Barnes.

I journeyed to New York to see Barnes—not to argue against the unfair suspension, but to point out that Ralston's presence in the Mixed final was justified because the suspension ought not to be applied retroactively. Ralston had been in good standing during the National Doubles, and the Mixed was as intrinsic a part as the men's event, which he'd won. Only an act of God had delayed the final, and it was clear to me (and a lawyer I'd consulted) that Dennis was legally entitled to play that final. Especially with a national championship at stake. However, lawyers weren't standard equipment then. President Barnes gave my plea a quick brush, walking away from the conversation. The championship was defaulted to the Aussies, and Margaret Court had the easiest of her sixty-two major titles.

On two occasions I know of, players tried to organize strikes to better their status. Crawford Henry, a Georgian, planned a walkout at the National Doubles to protest what he and the rest called inadequate meals. But nobody walked. Billie Jean King, just beginning to flex her organizing muscles, was getting expense money herself at Forest Hills. But she was one of the few women who was taken care of. She urged the seeded players to strike the tournament unless all of them were treated equally. None budged. "They're afraid to buck the system," said outspoken Billie Jean.

The Great ATP Boycott of Wimbledon '73 was years in the

distance, and before formation of the union the players took what they could get. It all depended on their bargaining ability, or how badly their presence was desired. Although Billie Jean's husband, Larry King, was only a modest hacker, the National Clay Court tournament in Milwaukee lured her by giving both Kings air tickets and expenses. It was justified by putting Larry in the tournament, where he was immediately trounced.

Rod Laver, not much of a haggler, named "what I thought was a preposterous figure to play the National Indoor in New York in 1962, because I didn't want to go. A thousand bucks for the week, plus all expenses. I was shocked when they said to come along, and mad at myself. Mad for going to New York from Australia in the winter—and that I hadn't asked for more."

Good manners, charm, and pen strokes—the ability to write thank-you notes to hosts—counted as much as strokes on court for a high percentage of the players. Tournaments sold tickets on the strength of the elite entries, the internationalists, fairly recognizable names who traveled the globe and could make a living out of it. But the stars needed cannon fodder, and the bulk of the entries in American events were college kids tagging along for the fun of it, accepting whatever hospitality they could get from club members. The agreeable ones kept coming back year after year.

Tournament directors, always on the lookout for exotics to give the event a foreign flavor, were willing to slip them a few extra bucks. They didn't have to play too well as long as they added spice to pretournament publicity. Numerous engaging Latins of moderate ability subsisted on the circuit for a long time. Sometimes these arrangements backfired, as on a 1960 afternoon at Longwood where the tournament chairman, John Bottomley, sat on the spike of a dilemma.

Actually, he stood on tiptoe among the jolly throng on the clubhouse porch, alternately grimacing and grinning at the spectacle on the grass court below the party. During tournament week the porch is always awash in good feeling, but spirits were higher than usual because a couple of Longwood members, an ex-Harvard captain, Ned Weld, and a Harvard undergraduate, Paul Sullivan, were giving a very hard time to the No. 6 foreigners, Mexicans Tonio Palafox and Joaquín Reyes.

Normally those clubbies allowed into the tournament to fill out the draw were out of their league, first-round pushovers for visiting luminaries. The days of New Englanders as national factors were long past. But Weld and Sullivan were capable. Inspired by the well-fueled cheering, they were on the verge of winning the opening-round match in the fifth set, and Chairman Bottomley, caught up in the fervor, suddenly frowned, "Why am I clapping? We gave Palafox and Reyes plane tickets from Mexico City and a week in a good hotel. Sure I'm glad Weld and Sullivan are doing so well, but I can come out here and see them any day. Why are they persecuting a couple of our attractions?"

As the locals won, to uproarious hurrahs, Bottomley grunted, "I hope the Mexicans enjoy their hotel rooms and a week's vacation."

However, there was a favorable sequel for Bottomley. Palafox, who years later became McEnroe's coach, improved, and repaid Longwood by joining Rafe Osuna in thrilling finals the next three years against Ralston and McKinley, winning in 1962.

10

◯

Calliopes,
Please

It was the day the tennis circus came to town, and I was up early. Nervous. Excited. Impatient to get going. Was Kipling as unsure of himself, thrown in with Mother India, and wondering if he could capture her atmosphere?

Longwood wasn't altogether new to me by then. I'd spent about a dozen afternoons there, covering women's and junior tournaments. But this was a different Longwood, magically transformed for the National Doubles in sultry August to the kind of roofless pleasure dome that no longer can be found except in aging, wistful memories. All that mattered much in tennis then (1955)—a chain of grass-court tournaments linking Philadelphia, Long Island, Boston-and-environs, and New York—matters no more. Gone forever: floated away in the smoke of a fraudulent, yet enticing, system of amateurism that was the spine of the American tournament game for eighty-seven years.

Longwood Cricket Club, properly Bostonian in its unchanged nameplate (though cricket ceased as a diversion early in this century), is the elder among significant American playgrounds for tennis. Not quite the oldest, since the New Orleans

61

Lawn Tennis Club sprang up a year before, 1876. That fact was thrust on me in a copy of the NOLTC charter, forwarded by jocularly irate members chastising me for referring to Longwood, on TV, as the first. But Longwood, having entered the tournament business in 1890, is one of the last private clubs to stick with it, and remains a pleasant scene during its U.S. Pro Championships in July.

The U.S. Pro is fought out on an isle of clay in a sea of grass, with gigantic old oak and beech trees on Dunster Road as backdrop. However attractive, the tournament can't approach the vanished National Doubles in style or feel. Or essence.

Walking onto the broad veranda, just beyond the front door of the unprepossessing stucco clubhouse, I was unprepared for the spectacular changes in the usually placid retreat. Primped and painted for the Nationals, the wide-open plain before me had become a theater of the athletic, a stage made over by new sets. The courts were fenced off into neat, precise battle-grounds, approached by walkways. Small grandstands were installed here and there, tents pitched for the first-aid unit, ball-boys, officials, and concessionaires. Canvas sealed off the outer courts from peeping freeloaders. The stadium, a nondescript pile of planks on a metal skeleton, slouching idle and unused fifty-one weeks of the year, suddenly gained importance. Garbed for the occasion, it flaunted awnings, bunting, national flags, vari-colored umbrellas shading courtside boxes, and people.

Such people. The girls and ladies of Longwood in their summer skimpies still lead any spectating—and ogling—league I've ever encountered. And, sweet things, they tell me they feel the same about ticket buyers of the other sex, not to mention the hunks populating the U.S. Pro lists.

Estee Lauder herself couldn't have imagined a more be-witching facial than the patriarchal groundsman, Charlie Chambers—capped and clothed as white as a surgeon—applied to his sweethearts. His beloved courts were shaved close, watered, rolled, and made up with fresh lime. They were so green and beautiful you wanted to get naked and romp and roll on them.

They smelled fresh, alive, sensuous. The odor, the ambi-ence are missing from tournaments today, other than Wimble-don and Newport, the last resort of grass tournaments in America.

In 1955 tennis on the green stretched in every Longwood direction. A twenty-rectangle circus, dominated by the men's and women's National Doubles Championships, incorporated such amusing sideshows as the national father-and-son, senior men's and women's tourneys. Only doubles. Doubles, the game of most of us, had its distinctly championship days in Boston, separated from the National Singles that would follow at Forest Hills. Heroes and hackers, kids and crocks gamboled on adjoining courts as the seniors and fathers-and-sons shared terrain with internationalists in a whirl embracing hundreds of players.

There was eleven-year-old Chum Steele, abetting his papa, Chauncey, marking time, eleven years, before they would become champs. Nearby, seventy-seven-year-old Samuel Rockwell, who would never win with his heir, Bill, nevertheless enjoyed. Not far away were Rex Hartwig and Neale Fraser, stalwarts of Captain Harry Hopman's Australian Mafia, which had the world in its clutches, and beyond them Margaret duPont and Louise Brough, who would win a record tenth title. Wandering and sampling this smorgasbord, I gaped at all the good stories I wouldn't have room for in my reports.

Since 1968, men's and women's doubles and mixed doubles have been joined to the men's and women's singles championships beneath the flag of the U.S. Open in New York. Bad planning by the USTA. At Flushing Meadows the doubles tournaments are downplayed and devalued. The best players, consumed by singles, either skip doubles altogether or give them a halfhearted effort. Though more often the better game to watch, doubles is a mistreated poor relative of the singles, inconsiderately scheduled, seldom noticed.

The former, long-abandoned arrangement was superior. Standing on its own, the National Doubles gave the players a relatively relaxed week to tune up for the National Singles, and put deserving teams on center stage. Although John McEnroe and Peter Fleming may have been the strongest of all teams, their doubles at Flushing Meadows never got the recognition, nor generated the enjoyment, that would have come out of a U.S. championship devoted to doubles. Same goes for Martina Navratilova and Pam Shriver.

It isn't nostalgia that prods me to chant, "Bring back the National Doubles!" Unique, attractive tournaments should be preserved, particularly in this day of saturation tennis, the fifty-two-week season, and so much sameness.

Not that I would expect, or lobby for, a return of a doubles championship on grass. You might as well try to set up a tournament on the Sargasso Sea, which, as developed, would be a rerun of my writing debut at the National Doubles, ravaged on the third day by Hurricane Diane.

Those times past are rightfully consigned to scrapbooks, along with the parties and free-spirited fun that accompanied amateurism. As phony as it was, at least for the players at the top, the deceased system wasn't burdened by the pressures of big money and the ruthless computers, reviewing and ranking every move. Nor did it hold forth the temptingly perilous possibilities of overkill—overexertion and injury through overplay and overtravel—during an overextended season.

When summer ended, so did tennis. That was the logical way of things my rookie year on the *Herald*. I had been a very good and attentive boy throughout July and early August, hoping the Boss would send me back to Longwood for the Doubles, but well aware that a newcomer did not ask for specific assignments. Only very senior staff members could do that, and I was naïve enough to think that one of them would request the National Doubles.

Tennis, I accepted, wasn't baseball. Still, I thought the National Doubles, a big event with an international flavor, bringing the world's best players to town, would be claimed by one of our veterans. Request the Doubles? None of the others wanted to go near tennis. They were pleased by my interest so that one of them wouldn't get stuck.

Newspapering has changed drastically since those days when tennis was a beat in search of a beater, and there were no takers. It has changed even since 1968 when I began covering Wimbledon for the *Globe*, the lone American reporter sent over. Now there are nearly fifty. I heard from them in 1986 at the late end of a long, wet, discouraging day at the Big W. Nothing worth writing had happened. But people had to write anyway, and we were hopefully slapping the keys of our machines in the pressroom at about 11:00 P.M. Abruptly that fine reporter John Feinstein arose, pointed at me, and rasped, "If it wasn't for goddamn Collins and his TV, 'Breakfast at Wimbledon' and all the PBS crap, we wouldn't be stuck here tonight. I think we should boo him." And they did. And I was touched.

Lest anybody think I came to Boston as a complete novice

at covering tennis, I should recall the first stab. Three or four sober graphs in the *Enterprise* were granted a forgettable college match, Mount Union visiting Baldwin-Wallace, while I was working my way through high school English. I wrote that one of the players "displayed a stern backhand," because I'd read that somewhere.

Even sterner backhands were on display in those women's and junior tournaments the Boss had teethed me on two months before. I handled them okay in two hundred words or fewer. But now the sternest backhands of all would be displayed before spectators—paying, knowledgable spectators—in the Nationals. Was I ready to cope with it all in the five or six hundred words the Boss would permit me?

Could I compete with the acknowledged master, Allison Danzig, and the "omnivorous backhands" that delivered "ripostes" and "elicited errors" to be found in his expert, detailed accounts of a thousand words or more in *The New York Times*? Did I even know how to talk to Danzig? Would the archbishop of American tennis writing deign to nod to me?

My seersucker jacket was back from the cleaners, the lightweight flannels pressed. The loafers were shined, and the Madras bow tie in place so that my journalistic choking wouldn't be too noticeable.

It was impossible that I would measure up to the Brummelian standard of U.S. Davis Cup captain Billy Talbert, much less the literary mark of Danzig, but I went anyway. Stowing my supposedly portable (twenty-pound) Remington typewriter in the backseat, I pointed a fatigued Ford convertible toward the quiet, moneyed suburb of Chestnut Hill. There Longwood spreads bucolically across an enclave tucked in beside bustling Route 9.

In this instance, I obeyed the journalistic forefather, Greeley, by steering west. West of Boston. Twenty minutes was all it took. Yet it was the irresistible start, the first leg on a lifetime journey touching all the inhabited continents, wherever the *"Puh . . . puh . . . puh!"* of fuzzy ball on twanging strings could be heard. Quickly I was smitten by this circus, eager to run away with it.

I recalled later, in reading about the courtship of a president's daughter, how I'd felt in instantly falling for the National Doubles. A different sort of allure was involved, but the story about Margaret Truman was on the money. The successful suitor, Clifton Daniel, said on meeting Miss Truman, he chanced to look down the front of her dress—and never looked back.

11

○

Tokyo Typhoons

In the search for fragments, but not figments, of my reflection, I offer you Kamo and Miyagi.

Kamo and Miyagi? Miyagi and Kamo?

Give up?

Okay, then, perhaps a little multiple choice?

Kamo and Miyagi are:

(A) the latest Nipponese alternatives to Honda and Sony
(B) neighboring stops on the Kyoto-Okura line
(C) makers of Famous Amosuri Microchip Cookies
(D) Madame Butterfly's grandparents

Sorry, none of those. But if you can identify Kamo and Miyagi, separately or together, then you are unmasked as a certifiable tennis degenerate, lacking much hope of rehabilitation.

While Kamo and Miyagi are not threats to replace sushi and tempura they remain names dearer to me, a leftover taste of a bittersweet fortnight.

Kosei Kamo and Atsushi Miyagi, who constituted the entire Japanese Davis Cup team, were my first champions. They were grandly unknown survivors, really, of the deluge that very nearly swept Longwood and the National Doubles of 1955 out to sea and past Provincetown. Any other survivor who says memories of that catastrophic tournament keep flooding back applies a concise metaphor.

Hurricane Diane, christened by the U.S. Weather Service, was the name of that calamitous Jane. No lady was she, rather a wild-eyed, wet, and windy broadside that, with no warning, exploded on the New England coast in angry, destructive torrents.

When the Boss dispatched me to the Doubles, neither he nor I had any idea that the assignment would take so long: a record two weeks for a one-week tournament. Blame it on Diane. Blame Kamo and Miyagi on her, too, but that shrill wind did blow them some good.

Nobody was concerned with the smilingly quiet and polite Japanese, the No. 5 foreign seeds, as the tournament began in sunshine, high heat, and high hopes for a final between the Australian juveniles, Ken Rosewall and Lew Hoad, on one side and the American guardians of the Davis Cup, Tony Trabert and Vic Seixas, on the other. It was a keenly anticipated showdown, since the U.S. defense of the Cup against the Aussies was to take place the following weekend at Forest Hills, and the best-of-five match series might well swing on the middle match, the doubles. The Longwood committee wished to offer customers a preview.

My own high hopes of absorbing big-time tennis were rewarded, for three glorious days. I roved, enraptured. Especially enthralling was an engagement of cannonading servers, Clif Mayne and Eddie Moylan, defeating Robin Willner and Ed Kauder over five sets and two days, 3–6, 16–14, 9–7, 5–7, 14–12. Aces flew, and I was bug-eyed, squeezed into a low wooden barricade beside a remote field court.

Ninety-three games, one of the most wrung-out doubles ever played, and I thought it was wonderful. Jimmy Van Alen, forgive me—I didn't know any better. I was twenty-six. As life contracts, we appreciate the tie-breaker more. I could have watched that match for a week.

Even the great man from the *Times*, Allison Danzig, was there, pressed against the fence, taking notes on an envelope. Not only did this meticulous, seemingly withdrawn little guy in seersucker suit, striped tie, and thin mustache, nod to me, but he introduced me to his petite wife, Dorothy. We actually conversed. He was genial and helpful in a low, purring voice tinged with his native Texas as we exchanged observations of the day. Yes, amazingly, he wanted to know what I'd seen of interest, and was willing to share his sights. No one could see it all in that whirl of courts and matches, although I tried.

As we became friends, Danzig, an authority, too, on college football, rowing, and the Olympics, would talk about his past. He was known as considerate, but had overdone it in Columbus, after covering the famed Ohio State–Notre Dame game of 1935. He went out on the town with two friends, the syndicated columnists Grantland Rice (whose poetry included, "It's not whether you won or lost, but how you played the game") and Henry McLemore.

Rice and McLemore were being overserved. How they played the game of getting home looked like a loss. Conscientious Danzig intervened, and somehow managed to guide them onto the train for New York, and into Pullman berths.

"The next day, as we pulled into Grand Central Station," Al recalled, "they thanked me profusely for taking care of them. But then McLemore made a face. He looked at Rice, and said, 'Jeez, Granny, I remember now. . . . We drove to Columbus! Your car's still out there!' "

Danzig coined the phrase "Grand Slam" to hail the rarely turned trick of winning the four major championships within a calendar year. He used it originally in 1933 at Forest Hills to describe what might have been for Jack Crawford, the estimable Australian who had won the first three titles and led Fred Perry two-sets-to-one in the U.S. final. Crawford, who liked a taste of brandy occasionally during a match at a bucker-upper, may have overserved himself against Perry. After piling up that lead, he took only one more game.

Five years later, Danzig was able to use "Grand Slam" positively to illuminate the accomplishment of Don Budge, who made it by beating his engaging doubles partner, Gene Mako, in the Forest Hills final. He wrote about the climax of the second Slam fifteen years after that, by the concussive Maureen ("Little Mo") Connolly in 1953, and the third, by Rod Laver, in 1962. But when Laver recorded another in 1969, Danzig was newly retired after forty-five seasons with the *Times*.

Al was sitting near the court, though, and savoring Laver, wishing he could type a fanfare. Just as he was in 1970 as Margaret Court completed the fifth Slam. Also in 1984 to watch the fourth U.S. Open victory of John McEnroe, whose half-volleying Danzig heartily approved as "the best since Henri Cochet." High praise from a man who wouldn't budge—for Budge, Kramer, Laver, Borg, McEnroe, anyone—from his feeling that Big Bill Tilden had been the best of them all. Cochet had beaten Tilden thrice in the Davis Cup. First love is tough to beat, even after watching champions into a seventh decade.

Weeks before he died in 1987, at a lucid eighty-eight, Al told me a love story that amounted to his own serendipitous grand slam, begun grimly. He was pleased and relieved to have recently published his final book, *The Winning Gallery*. A treatment of an abstruse game out of the Middle Ages, court tennis, it was one of those devoted labors that would have few readers. Not many are even aware of court tennis, a favorite of the all-time mixed-doubles player, Henry VIII, and forerunner of the game we know as just plain tennis. It can be found in no more than seven private clubs in the United States and a scattering elsewhere. As virtually the sole American who could write knowingly about the marvelous game, Danzig was glad to get it into print, and was reminiscing about bygone bylines on the *Daily Sun*, the student newspaper at Cornell. Despite jockey-esque stature, he had been a 125-pound college football player as well as newspaperman.

"I was going to Cornell on a shoestring, watching every penny, and a writing contest came up with a prize of one hundred dollars. That was big money then, and I was determined to win it. The idea," he related, "was to have the most lineage published in the school paper over a certain period. My biggest competitor was a wonderful guy, E. B. White, who, of course, became a great writer.

"Well, a fraternity brother of his was the judge, and gave White the prize. I thought it was rigged. White was innocent, but I thought I got jobbed. I was so mad I quit school and joined the army. This was 1917; World War I was on. I came back and graduated in 1921.

"Anyway, they sent me to Camp Grant in Rockford, Illinois, and one night a guy came into the barracks and said, 'Come on, Danzig. Get cleaned up, we're going to a dance in town.' "

Al grinned and nodded toward his lovely wife. "That's where I met Dorothy. Well worth the loss of a hundred bucks."

A few days after Hurricane Diane bestowed her 1955 kiss of death on Longwood, and the rain looked as though it would never stop, the Danzigs were among those evacuating the forlorn outpost. Groundsman Charlie Chambers's sweethearts looked like 5 A.M. after the party was over. His courts were smudged, bedraggled, turning to mud, and the club was going under. Inundated.

Enough water, two feet in some places, stood on the courts to permit ballboys to fool around, paddling a soft-drinks cooler, and even swimming, for the benefit of news photographers.

When would Lake Longwood drain? Was the tournament drowned? Speculation on these questions was included in my first rainy-day story. And my second. And third, when I wrote that the National Doubles might be wetter and run longer than *South Pacific*. Quickly enough I was devoting more space to the absence of tennis than I had to the tournament itself. Daily defections included the Australian and U.S. Davis Cup teams, moving to anywhere they could practice for their battle at Forest Hills. Those persistent few who hadn't worn out their welcome with club members housing them stuck it out and were rewarded with victories even though they couldn't get on a court. Departing opponents forfeited matches to those who stayed.

The Boss was impatient. "Forget Longwood, I've got other things for you to do. Nobody cares anymore."

I did. Not out loud. "They're determined to finish, one way or the other, maybe indoors, Boss. Why not give it a couple more days?" I suggested softly while the copy editors chopped my rainy-day stories shorter and shorter.

At last the rain halted. The water receded, leaving Longwood a quagmire, and the men's tournament a national championship travesty. Survivors, not even a quorum of lost souls, could have been accommodated by a life raft. Even though the second round was only partially finished, merely nine teams from a starting field of forty-nine remained.

They were all strangers, including the patient Kamo and Miyagi. Defaults dotted the storm-torn drawsheet where results were posted. A Boston coffee salesman, Sonny Hunter, the only straggler with a genuine job, was also the only one disappointed by the sun's reappearance. Paired with college boy Ralph

Stuart, another local, Hunter laughed, "We're not going anywhere. If it rains long enough, and everybody else leaves, Ralph and I will become national champions by default."

It wasn't that much of a travesty. And not a travesty at all for the women. Maybe they were better houseguests. Not one deserted the women's tournament. It was won by the unmysterious and unyielding Margaret duPont, thirty-seven, and Louise Brough, thirty-two—their tenth of twelve titles. To connoisseurs of doubles, the portly duPont and willowy Brough, mixing craftiness with crash, were as zestful as finely aging wine.

The tournament, delayed exactly one week, resumed on the still-mucky high ground, the stadium and adjoining terrace courts. Startled and amused, California teenagers Greg Grant and Earl Baumgardner, who had played only one match, found themselves in the semis, the chief beneficiaries of defaults. Two more young Americans, Bill Quillian, twenty-one, and Jerry Moss, nineteen, got there on a default, too, and continued to an AA—Athletes Anonymous—final where Kamo and Miyagi were the white hats.

Quick and good-humored beneath creamy caps, the diminutive Japanese—called, naturally, the "Tokyo Typhoons" by the *Herald* correspondent—skittered across the damp turf like waterbugs. They captivated the diminished gatherings of the faithful, and were proud to attain Japan's first U.S. title. Why not? They beat everyone opposing them. What more can you ask?

In the records they're listed as 1955 champions, no asterisked apology for a watered-down tournament offered. The same for Jan Kodes, who won a substantially less than Wimbledonian Wimbledon in 1973, emerging from ranks severely diluted by the male players' strike. It's in the book for the champs to show their grandchildren; that's all that counts.

The Boss, who had been counting the days, disgustedly, said, "Thank God that's over. Forget tennis until next August."

I confessed thanks, too. Enough baptismal rainy-day accounts. There would be many more in years to come, mostly in England. But even if sticks and stones will break my bones, rain will never haunt me. Whenever a colleague bemoans Wimbledon showers and rain-outs, I'm bound to say, somewhat pompously, like a remnant of the *Titanic*, "As a survivor of the sinking of the National Doubles in 1955, I can state you ain't seen nothing."

In 1985, while playing with friends at the West Side Tennis Club, I noticed a slender, distinguished gentleman walking past my court. "Time out! Just for a couple minutes," I excused myself to run after the passerby. "I think this is our anniversary."

Overtaking him, I asked, "Are you, sir, by chance, Mr. Miyagi?"

Puzzled by the interruption, he said Yes.

"Happy anniversary—it's our thirtieth!"

At that, he looked ready to run himself. But as I explained, he began to smile. We shook hands, and he recalled Boston, to which he'd never returned, and the flood that was our bond.

Whenever I hear the song "Raindrops Keep Falling on My Head," I think of Kamo and Miyagi, and know they're playing our song. I hope they feel the same.

12

○

New Leaf
Lefty

Kamo and Miyagi's starburst was as fleeting as a cherry blossom. They had been one-shot tourists.

In 1956 the National Doubles was avoided by hurricanes, by the great black hope, Althea Gibson, and—sort of—by the controversy-to-be, Renee Richards. But not by the no-shows of 1955, Lew Hoad and Ken Rosewall, the Aussie twenty-one-year-olds, who won the tournament.

Twenty-one years later Kenneth Robert Rosewall, the Doomsday Stroking Machine, was still winning tournaments at the uppermost level, the Grand Prix. Thirty years later Rosewall, whom his first employer, Jack Kramer, dubbed the Little Master, was still winning tournaments as a masterpiece in miniature on a museum tour called the Grand Masters circuit. At the same five-foot-seven and 140 pounds, plus a few wrinkles and silver deposits in his black hair, he continues as a terror of that collection of golden oldies. The Grand Masters was originated in 1975 by a Cincinnati junk dealer named Alvin Bunis, who went from dealing in scrap iron to marketing priceless antiques. Like Rosewall.

74

There was no way of divining then that Kenny would become the greatest, longest-running success in shorts and sneakers. He holds the longevity mark: first major title, the French, in 1953; last, the Australian, 1972. Not to mention final-round bids for the Wimbledon and U.S. Open crowns in 1974, and a farewell Grand Prix triumph, Hong Kong, near the close of 1977.

Where, and if, it will all end, only Rosewall knows. He ain't telling. Certainly he wasn't telling anything when I first met him. None of the Aussies was talking through the gag fastened by their omnipotent Davis Cup captain, Harry Hopman.

"How's it going?" I stuck my hand out to Neale Fraser, then Rex Hartwig, as they came off the court following a first-round National Doubles victory in 1955. I was looking for a quote or two, and this is what I got from Fraser, apparently the spokesman:

"Can't say, mate. Better ask Hop."

Ask any of them about anything, even the weather, you received the same reply, if Hop were in town. Hopman could get away with such authoritarianism because of his brilliant record. After taking over the team in 1950, he had reversed Australia's Cup subservience to the United States. Following four straight postwar losses to the United States in the final round, the Aussies, under Hopman, won five of the next six. Eventually Hopman, before emigrating to the United States and giving way as captain to Fraser in 1970, won ten more.

It was clear to resentful Australian newspapermen why Hop kept his chaps from talking to any of them except under his close supervision. He had a newspaper column himself in Melbourne, and Captain Hopman saved the best news and quotes for writer Hopman.

Short, fair, and hard-nosed, he was sometimes referred to as Napoleonic. But Hop had a better backhand than Bonaparte, expressed with racket rather than stuffed inside jacket. He was in a lighter than usual mood in 1956, astride the world with Hoad and Rosewall. Another reason may be that he himself had won a National Doubles title, the seniors at Longwood, to celebrate his fiftieth birthday, in the company of the hand-kissing French Musketeer, Jean Borotra. They should have been called kiss and hell. Borotra never kissed me, but I caught hell from Hop often enough for trying to talk to his players.

Even ungagged, Rosewall had nothing to say. Young and

shy, he let an eloquent racket speak up for him. Loudly. He just knocked off everybody's jock with those beautiful ground strokes for which he was always in position. Kenny was fast all right, but he anticipated quicker than he ran. I anticipated Rosewall would become very good, but not that he would give me more pleasure for a greater length of time than any player I ever covered except Billie Jean King. They run a dead heat in my reveries.

How could anyone anticipate Dr. Renee Richards, the transsexual opthalmologist—isn't that an eyeful?—who would create a furor by crashing the women's tour two decades later? She was inconspicuously present in another life at the 1956 National Doubles, male-bodied and listed in the program as twenty-two-year-old Richard Raskind, a varsity letterman at Yale. As Dick Sorlien's partner he held up well for two rounds. In the third they lost to Sammy Giammalva and none other than Raskind's future blind date, Barry MacKay. Is that confusing? Not as confusing as the party that extra man MacKay arrived at in 1975. Barry discovered as his dinner partner the surgically recycled ex-opponent Raskind, introduced as Renee Richards. "I'd heard about the change, but it was a strange evening," MacKay said. "It felt a little funny when we said hello and I could see she expected a kiss on the cheek, which I delivered. It was a weird sensation. But that was momentary. I got used to the old Raskind being the new Richards pretty quickly. I think she's got a lot of guts."

Watching for a bit as Raskind and Sorlien fell to Giammalva and MacKay at Longwood, I noted Raskind's strong left-handed serve—and didn't look again for twenty-one years.

Though the serve had aged, it was still an asset. But its owner had grown chestier and was wearing a sunbonnet and short, barebacked dress as she entered Forest Hills Stadium again in 1977 where a curious U.S. Open crowd of ten thousand—the largest and most attentive of her life—awaited what several of them called "the freak show."

"I felt like a monkey in a glass cage, but people were much nicer than I expected," she said.

Wimbledon champion Virginia Wade, saying, "Renee played a little too well for a forty-three-year-old woman," nevertheless controlled the first-round show, 6–1, 6–4. The "social pioneer," as Renee called herself, was once more out of the Forest Hills singles at the outset. It had happened pretty much the same way in her last visit, seventeen years before, when Raskind was beaten by Neale Fraser, the Wimbledon champ of that year, 1960. However, no reporters had noticed or gathered around then. Was it because the same person, in an altered state, was now using the women's dressing room?

As history's singular player who stripped in both rooms, Renee made comparisons. "Men are louder, more boisterous, and tend to walk around naked. We girls are a little shyer, but we have a good-natured time."

One colleague on the female tour, JoAnne Russell, reported Renee's locker-room style to be a male hangover. "She struts around bare-ass a lot."

Renee described her social pioneering as "trying to help a minority, others like myself—transsexuals—to be understood."

Bright, sensitive—and brave—Renee, with her odd, seemingly forced female voice, has gone back to work as an eye surgeon. She made only a sensational incision in the women's tour, not good enough in her forties to support herself by playing. From time to time she reappears as a thoughtful, calming adviser to Martina Navratilova. "I think I understand Martina better than most," Renee says, drawing agreement from Martina, "because we both are outsiders. In slightly different, but comparable ways. We both left our homelands—I my sex, she her native country—for new lives."

Renee was a pioneer, all right. In making "a terrible psychological and emotional adjustment," she crossed a frontier, hitched to her heart, frightening and disturbing some, but giving comfort and hope to others. In a country where we're supposed to be free to change, she made the most daring change of all.

13

○

Follow That
Broad

Althea Gibson was another social pioneer, whose break through the color barrier caused a ripple that reached even my hard-boiled managing editor, George Minot, by 1956. Under his strict, penurious thumb, the *Herald* was the best of the conglomeration of Boston newspapers. Mr. Minot, as most of us called him, ran a taut ship from his bridge, a desk at the center rear of the noisy, electric city room.

Mr. Minot, as a real-life Walter Burns in *Front Page*, wouldn't have been a bad fit. Still, he has his own spot in American literature as editor of the rock-ribbed Republican paper in Ed O'Connor's Boston novel *The Last Hurrah*. Having been fired by Minot—the break of his life, as it turned out—O'Connor knew his Maine man, Yankee born and bred. A cost-shaver who moved around the office turning out lights, Minot was happy in his Yankee management's belief that closeness was next to godliness. He kept his bespectacled eyes on every department, and no reporter got beyond Harvard Square unless Minot okayed the expenditure.

Although a self-acknowledged sports expert who regularly strolled into our headquarters just off the city room, the managing editor had evinced no interest in tennis. And he certainly wasn't interested in that year's National Doubles champions, Lew Hoad and Ken Rosewall, Louise Brough and Margaret duPont.

Hoad and Rosewall had been the cry at Longwood. They went together like franks and beans, hot and sharp, as different, too, yet as well mated, in combination. By 1956 they'd been singles rivals for ten years, since Sydney childhood. You noticed Lew Hoad first, all crash and bash, with a broad smile above a broader chest. He was a gleaming life taker with golden hair, ivory teeth, and a hitman's devotion to his work of rubbing out tennis balls. He wanted them to hurt.

"When Lew was on his game, there was nobody better," said Pancho Gonzalez, the man-eater of those head-to-head pro tours of the olden days. Only because Hoad's back gave out did Pancho prevail on their 1957–58 odyssey.

But somber Kenny Rosewall, finer tuned for the longer haul, got your attention in subtler ways. His deft abetting of Hoad in their National Doubles triumph over Vic Seixas and Ham Richardson whetted my appetite to see what came next, namely Forest Hills. Stationed in the right court, Rosewall had returned serve so persistently and penetratingly, his first twenty-one without a miss—on capricious grass yet!—that the Americans were soon out of it.

Forest Hills, the National Singles, was supposed to be Hoad's extravaganza. As conqueror of the Australian, French, and Wimbledon championships, he was on the home stretch of a Grand Slam that would duplicate the respective 1938 and 1953 accomplishments of Don Budge and Maureen Connolly.

It was Hoad's quest for a Grand Slam that encouraged me to sound out the Boss about possibly covering Forest Hills—just the last two or three days, of course, sir. "Suppose I paid my own way?" I was trying to sound casual, aware that not even Red Sox, Harvard, and scoops were nearer management's heart than economy.

"Forget it. We'll get it off the wires," he said, echoing the policy of his fellow sports editors outside of the New York City area.

After that rebuff, I was startled when the managing editor

later stopped at my desk on one of his walk-throughs, and dropped a tennis question.

"How good is the colored girl?" He meant Althea Gibson. "Could she win at Forest Hills?"

I didn't answer right away. What was he thinking? I looked up from my typewriter to confirm that it was the managing editor. Definitely. Unchanging bow tie was clipped onto a 365-day model from the earliest drip-dry-iridescent-blue period of shirtmaking. Inquisitive countenance lay a few wrinkles below a bland bald head.

"The colored girl," he was saying, "would be the first of her kind to win, if she does, wouldn't she?"

I nodded deferentially, "That's right, sir. She's got a good chance." In truth, I didn't know much more than he did. Althea Gibson was but a name in the papers to both of us. Disappointingly, she hadn't entered the National Doubles, despite winning the Wimbledon title with Angela Buxton. I hadn't seen her play, but I wasn't going to say so because I was considered the resident sage on an uninteresting subject.

"She was unlucky to lose to Shirley Fry in the quarters at Wimbledon," I offered, "and Shirley won the title easily. She should have her Forest Hills jitters under control by this time." I was warming to Mr. Minot's attention, and vamping. Was he thinking of sending me to Forest Hills?

"Really? Well, it'd be a good story . . . if she wins. . . ," and he went away.

Althea was the Jackie Robinson of tennis, whose organizers were no more anxious to embrace blacks than baseball's had been. In fact, after her dramatic debut in the National Singles of 1950 at Forest Hills—four years after Robinson had signed with the Brooklyn Dodgers—Gibson still wasn't welcome everywhere on the tennis circuit. It took a Wimbledon championship and selection for the U.S. Wightman Cup team in 1957 to give her universal acceptance.

Althea's debut was "eerie." "There was a terrible thunderstorm during my first match at Forest Hills." She recalls the once-forbidden garden, guarded by stony eagles perched on the upper rim of the brooding stadium. "One of those eagles was struck by lightning. I couldn't believe it. The eagle fell to the ground, and luckily nobody was killed. It was sort of like a message that things were changing."

Even though Althea nearly beat Wimbledon champ Louise Brough in the second round, she wasn't able to bring about the changing of championship complexion until 1957. Tough, because she had to be to survive as an athlete in Harlem, and tall, she was thirty when she finally came through, denied the best competition in her developing stages by the color line.

Gibson was groomed and sponsored by Dr. Walter Johnson, a black physician from Lynchburg, Virginia, who would later do the same for Arthur Ashe. She was already twenty-two by the time careful lobbying of the USTA by Dr. Johnson, the American Tennis Association (the governing body for black tournaments) and other concerned individuals, such as ex-U.S. and Wimbledon champ Alice Marble, won her admission to USTA-sanctioned events.

Jackie Robinson, a Pied Piper, changed the face of baseball where thousands of blacks have benefited the sport and themselves. Gibson and Ashe didn't have that effect, unfortunately, because restricted private clubs were still the heart of tennis. Making it more difficult, few public courts and hardly any ca-pable instruction were available in poor neighborhoods, where the emphasis is on team sports. Even today, in only two or three locations, such as Boston's Sportsmen's Tennis Club, which offers a free youth program, is a black kid given the opportunity to utilize tennis talent to the fullest.

Talent in baseball, football, basketball can lead to subsidies in the form of prep school and college scholarships and professional contracts. But many years of heavy investment in coaching, court time, travel, room and board are necessary to develop a tennis player. Not many parents, black or white, can afford it. The challenge for the USTA, a wealthy organization, is to provide such help for needy cases among developing kids.

Althea, the hybrid, was lugging a double handicap as a female and a black, but she had the gumption to overcome. She had taken the French title in 1956, a negligible credit in the United States at that time, and was ready to win at Forest Hills on her seventh try. But she didn't; her basic, attacking game wasn't quite solidified enough to overpower the steadiness of Shirley Fry in the hungriest of finals. Fry, a very patient woman, would win on her sixteenth attempt, capping a Forest Hills crusade begun at fourteen.

But the thought of "the colored girl going all the way" intrigued the managing editor all the more when the Boss mentioned to him that I had volunteered to go for free. All right, I could go, the Boss said, letting me know it was against his sounder judgment. Just the last four days, and only if Gibson remained in the tournament.

"But there's Hoad's Grand Slam, too, Boss—"

"Never mind that, it's the colored broad we're interested in."

14

○

Keyboard Shushing

The Boss and the managing editor offered an extremely generous deal. Indulging my tennis degeneracy on a trip to Forest Hills as the *Herald*'s Althea Gibson correspondent, they permitted me to work on my days off, Thursday and Friday, as well as the weekend, as usual. In return for stories chronicling the tribulations of "the colored broad," they would approve moderate expenses for meals on two of those days and give me the pleasure of springing for all other costs, save telegraph charges for my stories.

What the hell? I was planning to go for a couple of days anyway, and now I could put my byline over that compelling dateline: FOREST HILLS, N.Y. Looking at it this way, and not as exploitation of the semi-working class, I was just paying my initiation fee, wasn't I?

Hitching a ride to New York and splitting a cheap Manhattan hotel room with Harold ("Big Z") Zimman, the Bostonian who publishes the tournament's souvenir program, I was at least with a guy who knew his way.

Dirty looks and shushing sounds were what I got along with

three FOREST HILLS, N.Y. datelines and bylines during a brief tenancy of the press . . . uh . . . stakeout zone. You couldn't call it a press box in the accepted form. Rather, we occupied three rows of writing shelves to the rear of the courtside boxes. Low railings were all that separated us from the swells, whose ears were easily violated by the gross sounds of typewriters.

What I didn't get in 1956 were historic stories of a giant (sneakered) step by Althea Gibson on behalf of herself, fellow blacks, and the game as a whole—or a Grand Slam by Lew Hoad. Shirley Fry and Kenny Rosewall made sure of that, intruding on bigger names and news by seizing the finals for themselves.

But I watched every point while the best possible stories didn't materialize, and felt a litle self-conscious as the new boy—an outlander. Maybe there were a couple of others. But the press corps appeared to be a thoroughly seasoned New York delegation that could have been accommodated in a pup tent.

Instead, we had a corner of a broader canvas-topped hut known as the marquee, sharing the worst seating area in the house with the socially prominent, the VIPs, and the Badgers and their guests. The marquee, a court-level lean-to of plywood and piping, roofed in blue-and-yellow-striped canvas, filled in the east end of the twelve-thousand-seat horseshoe stadium. If the marquee's location was the highest priced, at least it featured the most abysmal sightlines, along the court's sidelines.

But this was the sanctum, the place to be. Nevertheless, it was nearly impossible to see the court's boundary lines, particularly for reporters blocked by the incessant comings and goings of marquee squatters. Still, the lowdown upper-class shroud did shield denizens from the sun, and from the general public, who, sitting on backless benches in the stadium, could tell what was going on.

The principle of Wimbledon's Royal Box, close behind Centre Court's south baseline and reasonably high, indisputably the choice site for blue bloods, Badgers, and clubbies, was somehow lost on His Badgerliness, Julian Myrick, the USTA presidential force behind the 1923 erection of the Forest Hills stadium. Fifty-five years thereafter, it didn't elude the grits-and-greens chief Badger who never acted like one, W. E. ("Slew") Hester, out of Jackson, Mississippi. Hester, an oddity—that means "astute"—as USTA presidents go, had the vision to lift the Open from Forest Hills and transplant it at Flushing Meadows. In remodeling Louis Armstrong Stadium as the world's largest tennis pit, and America's center court, he included a less imposing but just as well-situated loge for the self-identified select.

Hester's blue-bordered Badgerville is also more rudimentary than Wimbledon's regal shelter. Inmates are democratically whacked by the same sun frying twenty thousand paying proletarians. When he sits in, though, Hester prefers his own box nearby, for which he pays. Bad form for a Badger.

Flushing's Badgerville exudes no more than the usual, everyday antipathy for the press, from which it is distantly and happily removed. Nothing today exists like the uncertain marquee truce at Forest Hills, shattered whenever a typist began knocking out a story. Malevolent glares and hisses—admittedly well groomed and relatively cultivated—suddenly were directed at the offending typist.

"Quiet, please! You're bothering the players!"

Possibly. But frequently the shushers, more devoted to their own conversations than to spectating, were on the receiving end of the athletes' scowls and pleas for silence. The marquee squatters merely passed those along to us in the press rows.

Maurice ("Red") McLoughlin, hailed as the California Comet when he broke the thirty-one-year eastern stranglehold on the men's title in 1912, cited similar difficulties before the Nationals shifted to Forest Hills in 1915 from Newport. "One of my most vivid impressions of Newport," he wrote, "was the lack of interest and attention to the actual play, displayed by so many, especially the fashionable occupants of the first-row boxes. There was always a continuous buzzing and gossiping during the rallies."

But that was downright tomblike, apparently, compared with the Philadelphia Cricket Club, where the women's Nationals came into being in 1887. In a memoir a half-century later, original champ Ellen Hansell recalled: "Is it possible for you to envision the gallery? A loving but openly prejudiced crowd standing within two feet of the court lines, calling out hurrahs of applause, plus groans of disappointment; and some suggestive criticisms, such as: 'Run to the net!' 'Place it to her left!' 'Don't dare lose this game!' The horrors of perfect silence, such as are evident today, had no place in our tournament thrills."

Horrors, it's just as well that John McEnroe wasn't there

to escort Miss Hansell in the mixed doubles. Mac, whose sonar ears can pick up two lovers cooing intimately in Flushing's upper deck, and disapproves of such on his time, would have gladly torched the Philadelphia Cricket Club.

The tones of Mr. Remington's typing machines have not been music on tennis players' eardrums, even though the rabbit-eared hearer might be undergoing canonization on typewritten paper at the moment of his bedevilment. Fortunately for us monkeys of press row, we were caged behind glass before the advent of McEnroe. He could accuse the press of everything but aural persecution.

McEnroe had a USTA president named Alastair Martin to thank for that. The 1970 spectacle of the ranking Badger, Martin, pacing before press rows and scolding its occupants in the interest of silence, led to a glass wall rising between shushers and shushed.

My own initiation-by-shushing was somewhat intimidating, but deadlines are fearsome, too. The thought of blowing one of them on my first tennis assignment on the road, and the Boss's reaction, steeled me to type on and on through whatever hostile barrage. Hopelessly I tried to emulate the discreet form of the good gray laborer of the *Times*, Allison Danzig.

No one ever directed a shushing rebuke toward Danzig of course. His was the Word they would read the next morning. But as a rookie I felt like the designated shushee, the rube whose clacking machine would be banned at any moment. I admired Danzig's concentration, superior to that of the players he watched, as he conducted a stop-and-go operation. At the instant the server was ready to launch a point, Al ceased fire at the keys. As the point ended, he quickly scrawled a detailed notation—his means of keeping score—recoupled his train of thought, and resumed typing fiercely during the fleeting interval between points. That way, in short bursts, feeding a telegrapher two or three paragraphs at a time, Al put together a graceful, informative story and made the earliest *Times* deadlines.

It's called writing under the gun, a required skill for the toiler on a morning newspaper. A fantastic energy grips you while you're at it, keeping you just out of range but ever fearful of the gunshot as your two fingers move across the keyboard like Van Cliburn's ten.

Imagine, then, the frustration, and fury, of Mark Asher, *Washington Post* reporter, whose missed deadline at the National Indoor in 1973, was caused by a shusher who, so to speak, gunned him down. Wounded in the line of duty, was Asher merely asserting freedom of the press as he continued to type during the doubles final? Asher's tap-tap-tapping in the open press row at the Wicomico Center in Salisbury, Maryland, disturbed two of the players, Clark Graebner and that all-time disturber, Ilie Nastase. Their complaints incited a few of the customers in the gathering of three thousand, one of whom began screaming at the reporter.

Not content to roar, the customer further imitated a lion, charging Asher, clawing the typist's offending hands and drawing blood. "Then the guy grabs my typewriter," Asher tells it, "and begins to run."

Sprinting faster than the *Post* man's twin typing fingers, the thief of Salisbury headed for an exit. "One minute I'm writing, the next I'm chasing this idiot, trying to get him arrested," says Asher, "but who do the cops grab? Me! And they throw me out!"

Eventually he got his typewriter back, but the ribbon was missing in action. Mark Asher regretted that he had only one ribbon to give for his readers. The bloodletting meant that he also had to get a tetanus shot. Asher should have been awarded a Purple Heart to match his prose.

You think covering this game is a garden party? Henry McKenna didn't, certainly not at Boston Garden. Henry, a staffmate at the *Herald*, wrote one tennis story, in 1957, and said that was enough. Because the Boss had sent me to interview a newly hired Harvard football coach, he was shorthanded, and he asked McKenna, the resident baseball and hockey writer, to drop in at the Garden to do a few graphs on the annual pass through town of the pros, Pancho Gonzalez & Co.

That was all right until deadline time neared, and Pancho and rookie Ken Rosewall were still locked in a long match. McKenna, who had gone through this all his adult life at football, baseball, and hockey games, unlimbered his portable in the balcony press section and began to bang away, oblivious to the howls of the Old Wolf below. Henry felt safe at that distance, and hardly imagined that his keys sounded like a firing squad to Pancho.

"I was just working, not paying attention to his yelling until a ball parted my hair and crashed behind me," Henry's eyes widened in recounting his brush with decapitation.

Enraged as the typing, not only McKenna's, continued, Gonzalez had started slugging balls at his literary tormentors.

"It was like a rocket attack, and we were, literally, sitting ducks in the front row upstairs," McKenna said. "Pancho scared the hell out of us. I've ducked foul balls in the press box at Fenway Park, but they come one at a time, and the batter isn't aiming at you. Pancho was out to get us, hitting balls as fast and hard as he could. They were smashing all around us."

McKenna prudently decided, "No deadline was worth risking much of that, especially for a tennis story." He stopped typing, and wished he'd had a white flag to wave. "You can have that game—and Pancho," Henry told me.

I have been threatened by shushers, and ducked a couple of balls slapped into a Washington TV booth by—who else?—Ilie Nastase. During a match in Melbourne, Nastase, after chasing a ball well wide of the court, even jumped onto the nearby TV platform. He grabbed a microphone, and told listeners what a terrible job he thought my partner, Donald Dell, and I were doing. He was being playful, then, not menacing.

But I never lost a corpuscle or a typewriter. Life is safer now that reporters use soundless writing machines, miniature video display terminals.

Life in Forest Hills stadium wasn't as safe as adherents of the power-playing Althea Gibson and Lew Hoad had thought it would be for their candidates. Neither could make a championship dent in consistently steady foes.

Rosewall, the Grand Slam–jammer whose deft backhand passing shots and clever lobs carried the gusty day, and the vanquished Hoad would not return in 1957. Kenny turned pro in January, Lew after winning a second Wimbledon in July. Lew thus preceded Bjorn Borg as the first of the two greatest players never to win the U.S. title. He came up empty five times, Borg ten, bowing out in the 1981 final to McEnroe. Martina Navratilova must have wondered if she'd join that illustrious company of American failures when she lost the 1981 final to Tracy Austin. But she succeeded the next year, her tenth try.

Althea, who couldn't get a set from Shirley Fry, had to wait until her eighth Nationals, winning in 1957 over Louise Brough.

It was the most mature U.S. final: Althea, thirty, and Broughie, thirty-four.

By then it was a foregone conclusion. Althea had taken Wimbledon, led the U.S. Wightman Cup team to victory over Britain, and the carpets and smiles had been unrolled for her at Longwood and other clubs that, previously, hadn't been so crazy about her complexion. There was no way to keep her out. She was No. 1. Her game and nerves had firmed, but she also had a thick chip on her shoulder.

Who could blame her? Nobody had wanted her to darken the door to upper-flight tennis. Now everybody acted as though black were the favorite color. It happened to Arthur Ashe, too: a token black for whom the Badgers and others of the tennis crowd could demonstrate their alleged liberal outlook.

"The hardest thing was finding out who was genuine," said Ashe. When he won the National Amateur title at Longwood in 1968, Ashe said he was amused. "Here I am, the toast of a club I'd never be admitted into as a member." He felt the same two weeks later at Forest Hills after completing an unprecedented double by winning the first U.S. Open, a feat unlikely to be duplicated. Thank heavens Arthur's "never be admitted" didn't hold up. Longwood and West Side, to name the two most prominent tennis clubs, have progressed beyond a whites-only policy.

Althea wasn't as good-natured as Arthur. As the unwanted pioneer, she was sometimes curt with interviewers and Badgers—suspicious, wary, even arrogant. She was entitled. Much of it was understandably self-protective, but in later years she let an inherent amiability flow. There was nothing more to prove.

Not to the Boss either. Confidently I supposed he would send me to Forest Hills again in 1957 because, as I hinted, "Looks like Althea's year."

"So what? She ain't news anymore."

"I'll pay my own way again."

"Not worth it. It's football season, junior. Get your mind back on real sports."

15

○

Doubles and JFK

Forest Hills was off my schedule indefinitely, simply because, as the Boss periodically pointed out, most readers weren't very interested. "It's all Australians and old broads anyway," he would say, stating in his way an accurate perception that there weren't many fresh young American faces capable of rousing even small headlines.

A summer visit to the Massachussetts state house atop Beacon Hill confirmed the secret state of the game in 1957 when the name Seixas became my barometer of tennis popularity, and I framed Seixas's Law. Seixas's Law (subtitled "Furcolo's Folly") was this: Anybody who could identify Seixas, and pronounce his name, was a member of an unidentifiable fringe group called tennis degenerates.

Other than the degenerates, who knew the identity of E. Victor Seixas (SAY-shuss)? The Boss knew, but certainly didn't care. I soon comprehended that Seixas, despite winning Wimbledon in 1953, the U.S. title in 1954, and a lengthy U.S. Davis Cup tenure, might as well have been the unknown soldier of Montenegro as far as the usual fan suspects were concerned.

One of those was the first citizen of the Commonwealth, Foster Furcolo, who was, and remains, a good, intelligent fellow. The U.S. team, with Seixas as mainstay, had arrived in Boston to face Brazil in an early-round Davis Cup match, and, trying to scare up some publicity, the organizers at Longwood arranged for Governor Furcolo to make the draw in his office.

As the teams entered for the brief ceremony, the Massachusetts governor looked at a list of names, and frowned at an aide, "Which guys are ours? Which team is Sex-ass on?"

The aide answered with a bewildered look.

It would have been a better story if the governor had grasped Brazilian Pepe Aguero, who looked like an American college kid (and, indeed, had won the National Intercollegiate title for Tulane two years before), and wished him well against Brazil. It's probably my fault that he didn't. "That's Vic SAY-shuss." I whispered to the Guv, indicating the No. 1 native, bearing a Portuguese name, "and the guys with him are the American team."

Furcolo nodded gratefully, and made the appropriate remarks.

Seixas became a code word for me. The secret society of tennis nuts would break the code, not many others.

Boxing, my regular beat, took up most of my time. It was a sports-page staple since Boston in the fifties remained a good fight town, supporting two and three shows a week and three or four promoters, notably the picaresque Sam Silverman. Sam operated six nights throughout New England, sustaining the manly art in such citadels as Fall River, Bedford, Holyoke, Providence, and Portland.

The Boss permitted me to moonlight in press agentry occasionally to supplement a meager income, as long as the projects weren't in sports. That's how I encountered another Massachusetts pol—John F. Kennedy—who was not as grateful as Furcolo for my assistance in getting his picture in the papers alongside a better-known face than Vic Seixas. Zero gratitude radiated from the photos of JFK, momentarily reunited with a former doubles partner, actress Arlene Dahl.

This was 1958, well before the revelations of his prowess as a roving eye, and Kennedy had his other eye on the White House as he campaigned vigorously for reelection to the Senate. Although he was a sure winner, and did not need to campaign at all, he sought to draw more attention by polling a huge vote.

I was doing publicity for another autumn campaign, the fund-raising drive of a charity, the Muscular Dystrophy Association, of which Kennedy happened to be honorary state chairman. As such, he had promised a half-hour photo session so that we could pose him with the poster child and a variety of volunteer workers, many of them firemen. In the press box at Fenway Park one evening, I mentioned this to a cunning public relations guy, Charlie Caruso, wondering what I could do to get the greatest mileage out of JFK.

"Perfect," Caruso was enthused. "I've got Arlene Dahl and Fernando Lamas in *The King and I* out in Framingham," he mentioned a summer theater account. "That'll make a good shot, them and the senator. Help us both out. Just don't make it early. Theater people aren't up before noon."

The time was 9:30 A.M. Caruso groaned, but the next day he phoned, "No problem. Arlene's all for it, although Fernando is pretty cranky. She'll get him there."

At the appointed time, a glowing Arlene Dahl arrived at our headquarters with a grouchy Fernando Lamas, her husband of that year. She was charming. He acted as though he'd walk out immediately, which he threatened to do as minutes, then quarter-hours, passed with no sign of Kennedy. Sweating and fidgeting, I tried to banter lightly with them while the poster child, not at all well, hung on with his mother.

Where was Kennedy? One of his people arrived to say it wouldn't be long. But it was, and still no senator. I wished I smoked. About an hour late, he streamed in with retinue, saying brusquely, "Only five minutes here. Let's go."

I shook his hand. "We've got a lot of volunteers here, a lot of firemen, senator. They've taken time from work, and they've been patient, and—"

"Five minutes! We're way behind schedule."

". . . and, sir," I prayed that he'd smile, "we've got a great picture here . . . Arlene Dahl . . . you know, the movie actress, and—"

"Absolutely not!" His voice and eyes were steely.

What? My voice and eyes were blank.

"Not with her. No, no."

"But, sir . . . why?" I was gasping. This was awful. "Wh-wh-why?"

"I will not have my picture taken with a divorced woman."

As I quivered, feeling dystrophic myself, and trying to figure what you say to a line like that, the fair Arlene sensed difficulty.

She strode toward us behind a magnificent smile while Fernando burned like Chicago behind her. Maybe he knew the history. "How are you, Jack?" her voice was warm and lilting. "It's so good to see you again."

She extended her hand. JFK was trapped, and knew it. He took her hand with, "Uh . . . nice to see you, too, Arlene."

Action. I motioned her to get closer, and she didn't mind. As gently as I could I shoved the poster kid into the act.

Camera. The photographer swiftly took the one chance he got before JFK broke away, looking to the assembled firemen to rescue him as tamer pictorial company.

Dahl, Kennedy, and Muscular Dystrophy kid hit some front pages in the Commonwealth. I can't remember if any of the papers bannered it MASS. KING AND I!

16

○

Easy Column,
Easy Go

Well before falling into the suspect trade of television commentary, I was a perfectly happy newspaperman—insecure and maladjusted—perched where I wanted to be: top left of the *Herald*'s front sports page as lead columnist. Five days a week.

That had been my aim since 1959 when the colossus who'd held the position for two decades, Bill Cunningham, was hospitalized with cancer. While he was out, the managing editor tapped me to substitute.

The absence of Cunningham's byline, one of the most commanding to stand forth in Boston, would be enough of a shock to readers grown accustomed to seeing it every single day since 1940, and now, to send Collins into the breach?

I wasn't too nervous about the first column: Oh, no, not much. Arriving at the office to dig in at noon, I wrote and tore up . . . wrote and crumpled . . . wrote and, unfortunately, did not possess a shredder. At 9:00 P.M., a half-hour before the deadline, I heard the kindly voice of Big Ed Cunningham (no relation to Bill), a rumpled, elderly copy editor. "Got something for me, my boy?"

I made a face. Like the mask of a Bhutanese ghost dancer.

"You're not writing this for the school yearbook, by any chance, are you? We come out tomorrow morning, like every day." His voice was still soft. But I nodded, finished up, and set four pieces of copy paper before him. They looked like a hockey player's face, scars wherever I'd penciled cross-outs and changes, trying to stitch it up.

"Good luck, Ed. You'll need it," and I was off to a night of little sleep and much self-recrimination. I couldn't look at the paper the next day. My only hope was that Ed had copped a plea for me while declining to put such crap in the paper.

But the managing editor smiled—that was an upset!—as I slunk past his desk. "Enjoyed the column," he said. "Keep it up. I see you more as a columnist than a reporter on a beat."

Elation. Followed within five minutes by depression. Jeezus, I had to do another one in a couple of hours. Then another one tomorrow. And the next day. Plus some other assignments, boxing, the Red Sox, the Celtics.

This was altogether different from looking at the assignment sheet and then going where the Boss directed. The column's subject, and its eight hundred words, were up to me. I'd wake up in the morning wondering, "What the hell am I going to write today?"

There was always something. Boston is one of the livelier domiciles for a sports columnist. But there was plenty of head scratching when those goddamn keys went on strike. Uncooperative, the little bastards just sat there, a keyboard looking like a team picture of lettermen from different schools, daring me to punch them. Bible method—seek and ye shall find.

"I'm the letter *R*—hit me if you can! And you better hit the others, too, and make it make sense!"

The clock would move, and my fingers wouldn't. The deadline cometh, and I fretted, there goeth my column—out the window.

Big Ed, ready to edit the piece as we edged on top of post time, could see me suffering at my desk with nothing regurgitating from the typewriter. He'd say something nice about wanting to see what I had in mind for the "goodly readers of this periodical," and never mentioned the lateness of the hour. That snapped me into it.

Couldn't leave the space blank, although I fantasized about

that. I wondered if I might start out like this: "My mother taught me that if you can't say something nice, say nothing. This column is about the Red Sox." Below my picture and that intro would be a hard-hitting eight-inch stretch of white beach within a black ocean of type. Nothing. It would convey my thoughts on the ball club tersely, offering the minimum in eyestrain.

That done, tomorrow's column would surely come easier. Also not at all, because even if I could have pulled off that blank beauty it would have been an amateurish admission that I wasn't up to columnizing.

The reverie passed, and I'd begin tormenting the keys. Big Ed would smile encouragingly, light another cigarette, waiting for me to slip him the first page. The race to the deadlines was always won, not always well.

The worst was on the road, dictating over the phone to a recording machine, an experience described by journalist Jack Mann as "swallowing your own vomit." He wasn't far off. It usually sounded grim in the interminable reading, and nearly every word had to be spelled. Otherwise "Swedish champion" might appear in print as "sweetest champion," as happened in regard to Ingemar Johansson, boxer, and Jan-Erik Lundquist, tennis player.

It was a good daily discipline. If you could write in a newspaper office amid the din of phone bells, conversations, and other typers, or in a press box, keeping an eye on the game and buffeted by crowd noise, you could write anywhere. Maybe not literately, or aesthetically. But you got it down on paper. If you were lucky you had an understanding repairman on the copy desk, like Big Ed, who would pinch and slash, append and correct, maybe rearrange, top it with a head, and get it into the paper.

Not all deskmen empathize. The war between writer and editor is unceasing. I have endangered lives at breakfast tables, as well as eardrums and sensibilities, by pitching a newspaper wildly, cursing some cretinish deskman for his abuse of my baby, my column. These maniacal acts frightened my young daughter and embarrassed me, and I had to convince myself that the day's paper was perishable, a suitable shroud for dead fish.

It still hurts. Nobody can hurt a writer worse than an editor—or help more. Good editors should get ticker-tape parades and be put in a writer's will. Won't Jerry Morris, Brent Banulis, Bob Duffy, and a few others at my current shelter, the *Globe*— not to mention book editors Peter Schwed and Laurie Colwin— be delighted to receive bequests of leftover alliterations stuffed in surviving cashmere socks for their kindness in not socking it to my copy too often? Still, I never could slip "Borgasm" (gushing enthusiasm for the performances of Bjorn Borg) past any of them.

Big Ed is gone to his reward, which precludes reading any more of my stuff. He was instructed by the Boss to "take junior in hand and teach him something about writing for English-language newspapers" after one of my rookie-year football reports. I had described Holy Cross as "encroaching on the end-zone proximity of the enemy."

"You mean," Big Ed said, "they were close to Dayton's goal line?"

"Uh . . . yeah."

"It's okay to write that."

He also taught me some useful things, such as: "People set records, not 'new' records. A record just set is new. Do not write, as everyone speaks, 'three A.M. in the morning.' Games are games, not tilts or brawls; and innings are innings, not chapters or stanzas. We do not pilfer hassocks; we steal bases at the *Herald*. I will pencil out 'internecine' and 'inchoate' or any other words like that you try to slide in from time to time to let people know you went to college and read a few books. They're hard on the reader's breakfast digestion."

He felt, too, that "beat" and "defeat" were appropriate to the processes of beating and defeating, particularly when one of Boston's myriad parochial schools was involved. Big Ed didn't think it seemly that St. Whoever stomped or slugged Our Lady of Whatever.

Thanks be to Big Ed for small favors.

He had me fairly well housebroken by the time I was dropped into the column slot. I was enjoying it. After several months, as Bill Cunningham worsened, and then died, I began to think of myself as a columnist. Hadn't the managing editor said that was his feeling? Well, if I had crossed over into that category, shouldn't I be given a raise? Nothing like Cunningham's opulent five-figure paycheck, of course—but a few bucks? I wasn't making more than $100 weekly.

It was time to visit the managing editor in his private office.

"Oh, hello, Collins." He was wary; he could smell such visits.

I made my case for a raise. Case closed fast. He nodded impatiently, peering at papers on his desk as his cheeks turned a grayer shade of gray. Parsimonious Yankee gray. Wordlessly he beckoned me to be gone. Within a day, his answer: a lowering rather than a raise was transmitted through the Boss: "We're going to have Sammy do the column for a while," he mentioned an older writer. "It wasn't anything permanent."

Ouch! What happened? Any raise would have been fine. Five bucks. I worked up some more nerve and asked the managing editor why I'd become an ex-columnist.

"Oh, you're doing fine work. Fine. I just see you more as a reporter than a columnist," he reversed his field completely. "Anybody can write a column," he disparaged. "You're more valuable on assignments."

Not valuable enough for a raise. The pain receded quickly. I was having fun covering fights and games, writing features, chronicling the allotted two or three tennis tournaments a year: the National Doubles, the National Women's Indoor, and sometimes the Women's Invitational at an old-money stronghold, the Essex County Club on the North Shore above Boston. But I'd had the taste, and a couple of years later, with a fair raise, the column was mine again.

However, a phone call from a TV producer named Greg Harney in the spring of 1963 would lead to another, only months later, from the *Globe*'s managing editor, Tom Winship, rearranging everything. Together they provided a life raft, allowing me to abandon the tight ship *Herald*.

In transferring to the *Globe*, and with a heavy travel schedule, I had to forsake a springtime job that I liked very much, coaching the Brandeis University tennis team. Two hundred bucks a season and an unlimited supply of nondesigner jocks and T-shirts. If Charlie Hollis was the coach who launched Rod Laver toward his Grand Slams, was I the coach who propelled Abbie Hoffman toward his grand tour of varied slammers?

At the *Herald*, when covering tennis was strictly a sideline, I wrote much about college sport and coaches who professed "building character." Then I became one of them. Did I build character? How many coaches have had a character like Abbie Hoffman, who made headlines and TV spots anywhere but the sports news, drove cops and judges whacko, and wound up as a humanitarian doing time in a federal pen? There was no need to red-shirt Abbie. He was already too red for many tastes—although now I realize that he was merely the kind of all-American boy who would have thrown out the first barrel at the Boston Tea Party or played engineer on the Underground Railroad.

When I told him in 1959, his senior season, to work on his serve, could I envision he'd spend nine months serving in two New York jails? But how many characters in the mold of irrepressible radical Abbie Hoffman have earned a varsity letter? While not presuming to claim full accolades for Abbie, I like to say, unprepossessingly, that I had a hand in building one of the great characters to ever grace intercollegiate sport.

As you may recall, Abbie Hoffman, bushy-haired revolutionary-with-sense-of-humor, helped liven the tumultuous 1960s by starting the Yippie party, whose squealing porcine candidate for the presidency in 1968, Pigasus, might have looked better in the White House, bellying up to the pork barrel, than what we got. As a protester against deranged governmental policies, among them the Vietnam War, Abbie spent more time in law courts than tennis courts.

Though Abbie, when he was on the lam, was able to create excitement from underground with furtive appearances and magazine stories, the distressing truth is that aboveground, on a tennis court, he was a boringly conservative—possibly right wing—performer. He camped on the baseline, content with reaction as a retriever, never venturing to the barricade to shake things up. This will hurt him, but the truth is he played like a cop—Inspector Javert?—doggedly pursuing everything. But he won most of his matches.

I had a terrific group of kids, and they gave me a winning record for five years among small New England colleges, although they couldn't have beaten Stanford's kitchen help. But we took trips south, once as far as Rutgers where we looked in vain for palm trees and grits. One of the kids, Mike London, became a judge. I'm not sure I should invite him and Abbie to the same team reunion.

17

○

Good Calls

A plaque at the corner of Harrison Avenue and Lafayette Place in downtown Boston informs: "Here Alexander Graham Bell transmitted to Thomas Watson the first completely intelligible sentence by telephone. March 10, 1876."

Is there life without telephones? How many lives have been changed by a phone call? Two of those life-reshuffling calls came to me in 1963, the first from a television producer, the other from a newspaper editor. Because of them, Greg Harney and Tom Winship, I have since transmitted countless unintelligible sentences to listeners and readers. But whose fault is it that they listened and read?

Romanian Ilie Nastase asked the same sort of question in 1974 at the U.S. Pro in Boston. During a doubles, he had insulted Yugoslav opponent Nicki Spear—and, collaterally, Spear's closest female relatives. Ilie's jibes were so obscene that Nicki tried to punch him, and then quit the match. "Sure I said those things to him," Nastase shrugged off the vileness. "But," he shifted the blame for the altercation to Spear, "I did it in Italian. Is it my fault Spear understands Italian?"

100

Is it my fault I understood Harney to say he wanted to buy me a drink and talk about tennis? Winship, who had a bigger expense account, offered drinks and lunch, and wanted to talk about newspapering at his place, the *Globe*. But that was five months afterward, when his call was the indirect result of Harney's.

"Mr. Watson, come here, I want you," were Mr. Bell's first words over the horn, embodying the most essential of telephonic messages ever since.

Mr. Harney wasn't as dramatic, although it worked out that way. We didn't know each other. He said he was a producer with Boston's Channel 2—"Uh . . . you know? The educational station?" I knew, vaguely.

Although WGBH-TV has evolved into a justly celebrated bulwark of PBS, it was then a learn-as-we-go, slightly advanced crystal set operating from a Cambridge garage, having been burned out of its room-above-a-drugstore. PBS, a sanctuary from commercial TV, also became a haven for tennis such as the sport would never enjoy again.

Harney's boss, David Ives, who shepherded WGBH into the big league, decided they'd try some tennis. Even if his station had fewer viewers than a Miss Death Valley contest, Ives reckoned those who existed were Ivy-tinged, likely to be tennis hackers themselves, or knew enough about the game not to confuse Forest Hills with the local subway stop or cemetery of the same name. Ives understood his audience.

I couldn't know as Harney and I chatted over martinis at the MIT faculty club that we would become firmest friends. We would do hundreds of shows together—he producing and directing, I babbling—amounting to the first significant televising of tennis in America.

"Since we're educational TV," Harney, a refugee from CBS, used the original description, "we've had indications that viewers would like an instructional program on tennis. I've got Jack Barnaby, the Harvard coach, to do the instruction. I wonder if you'd like to go on with Jack to introduce it, and comment on a couple of exhibitions involving local players?"

Sure. Why not? While I hadn't lusted for a chance to thrust another pretty face topped by gleaming scalp into American homes, who hasn't looked at a sports show and said to himself, "Hell, I could keep that going"? Harvey wasn't offering a career. Nobody ever has. It happened and, given the nature of the business, could unhappen as quickly as you change channels. One of my early NBC producers appraised my performances: "I wouldn't sell that typewriter, kid." I haven't, although now it's a teeny computer.

I had done the Pender-Downes middleweight title fight on radio in 1961. But that was a one-shot flyer I sold to the station in return for a plane ticket to London because I wanted to see the fight. A couple of reviews were good, noting I was able to fill nearly an hour of dead air when the start of the bout was delayed.

But Harney was unaware of that. "I saw your byline over some tennis stories. You seem to be the only one writing about the game here, so I thought I'd call."

He had no intention of endangering my amateur status by paying me—and, at that, I was overpaid. At the mellowing distance of a quarter-century, "ghastly" is the kindest adjective I would apply to my TV debut.

Was Mr. Watson, his ear wearied by taking those electrifying calls from Mr. Bell, the first to say, "Don't call me—I'll call you"?

That old line was what I expected from Harney.

18

○

Sputter . . .
Crackle . . .
Pop!

Have you known of anyone, outside of Howard Hughes or Greta Garbo, who could resist a TV camera? Point one at a presidential candidate, or any other pol, and whatever it takes to make the six o'clock news will be done. Including walking off a cliff.

None of us are impervious. Notice how folks ham it up when the camera looks their way?

As a guest on a televised exercise show led by a slender, supple hostess, I was in a group put through a series of stretches, bends, and kindred exertions that zing muscles you didn't know were yours. A physiotherapist friend who'd watched asked if we'd been given a physical beforehand. No. She shook her head. "Some of that stuff she had you do was dangerous for people whose physical capabilities weren't known. But once the camera is on, you—or anybody—will submit to anything, regardless of how it looks or feels."

My guide into the strange land of TV performing, Greg Harney, wasn't setting me up as a contortionist, although words did, too often, gush forth mortifyingly twisted. For our first show together, I was enlisted merely as master of tennis ceremonies

103

that were meant to be instructive. Jack Barnaby, the exceptional Harvard coach, also a first-timer, was to preside over a clinical demonstration, using area players as demonstrators on the town courts of suburban Lincoln, Massachusetts. It should be simple, Harney said.

It was. Simply awful.

The only thing worse than Barnaby and me was the station's equipment, which may have been Transylvanian war surplus. You've probably seen those huge TV vans parked outside of a stadium or arena, mobile units crammed with millions of dollars' worth of electronic gear that could cover a war in progress. But this was 1963, kindergarten time for a young and poor educational TV station. There was a mobile unit, all right, a reeducated school bus, aged and shimmying, with interior fittings left over from Baron Frankenstein's lab. It looked like a veteran of the Burma Road that had left its heart in Rangoon. That bus had more failures than a Norwegian orange grove, and four years later it collapsed, terminally, between Boston and Newport where we were covering one of Jimmy Van Alen's early pro tournaments. A trouper to the end, though, it was towed to Newport, kept legally alive through some sort of supportive wiring, and did one last show with smoke seeping ominously from various wounds.

By then I was used to equipment failures. But, as trembling tyros, Barnaby and I stood before the camera on a cool spring afternoon, looking like pregnant wombats in overly bulky sweaters, and forcing smiles that evoked Captain Smith on the *Titanic*'s bridge. The continual breakdowns were a little disconcerting. Either stammering incoherently or speaking pedantically, we were soon interrupted.

Sputter . . . crackle . . . pop . . . "Cut!" Another breakdown. "Hold it, Jack and Bud. Take a break. We've got to get this thing functioning again. Tape broke."

The fax (facilities, as the production people say) were definitely lax, inspiring as much faith in Barnaby and me as we did in Harney and his technicians. The tennis players weren't doing much better. Intimidated by the lenses, they tried too hard, missed too many shots. Jack is an articulate man, an authority on racket sports. I felt I could hold my own. But as nervous, uncomfortable, distracted rookies, we were chipmunks with toothaches.

Fortunately we were taping. A live show would have been

as decimated as we thought we were. Harney kept soothing, "We'll patch it together. Watch it and see."

I watched, for as long as I could take it, cringing. It was penance. I embraced my typewriter, promising, "Never shall I forsake you for the electronic temptress that makes me look and sound like Porky Pig."

Amazingly, th-th-that wasn't all, folks. I was resigned to the end of an unnoticed TV career, but sorry about the flop because I felt that tennis had something to offer to TV. Harney had been a nice guy. I hoped he'd do well. He did, winning an Emmy for producing a nationally saluted PBS show, "The Advocates." In doing so he selected an obscure young Boston pol named Mike Dukakis as the show's moderator, and that gave Dukakis his first splash of recognition on his way to the Massachusetts governor's office, and to within shouting distance of the Oval Office.

About a month later, Harney surprised me with another call. Were they doing a documentary on Porky Pig and looking for a stand-in?

"You see the show?" he asked.

"Mmmmmmm."

"Went over pretty well."

"With all six viewers? Don't crap me, Harney. I'm not looking for compliments on something like that abortion."

"No, no. I won't say you were good . . . but once you and Jack got over your nervousness . . . Well, there was some fairly good stuff—"

"When the truck wasn't exploding, and—"

"Very rough, sure. But really, the response was impressive." He must have been lying, but convincingly. "We think there are some people who want to see tennis, and the commercial nets aren't providing it. We've got some funding and permission to do the National Doubles at Longwood. How'd you like to be the commentator? I think you could get the hang of it."

"If you've got that kind of nerve, Greg, so do I. At least the tomatoes they throw will hit the screen, not us."

He said they could even pay me, $150 for seven days. That was a week's wage at the *Herald*. But I'd have done it for free, just for the fun of it. I still would, but don't tell my agent, or anybody at NBC.

19

○

The Late
Show

Was it prime time or primitive time?

Both, when WGBH-TV became the first—and, lamentably, the last—to televise a U.S. championship tournament from beginning to end. Or any weeklong tournament, for that matter.

Poverty bred success. Luckily the station couldn't afford to air the 1963 National Doubles live. A weekday afternoon audience would have been sparse. The day's principal matches, in the stadium, were taped and shown the same evening, and sometimes ran well past midnight, immediately developing a following wherever the signal reached in greater Boston.

Hour after hour of tennis. No commercials, no edited matches, no long-winded speeches by sponsors. And no idea what we were doing, at first. Harney said there weren't instruction books for pioneers. But it was BBC-style coverage—except for the babbler, me—and caught on in Boston as Wimbledon had in Britain.

Who were these talented athletes who began to appear on the screen, two by two, as though Noah's ark were unloading fantastic fauna? Margaret Smith (who would become Mrs. Court, most prolific of all champions) and Robyn Ebbern, a couple of longbodies from Australia, attracted attention, strong-arming to a title they won from a Brazilian-American coalition, Maria Bueno and Darlene Hard. Chuck McKinley and Dennis Ralston, who would end a five-year U.S. Davis Cup dry spell in Australia four months thereafter, became personalities as they climbed to the final against two Mexicans potent as tequila, Rafe Osuna and Tonio Palafox. Justina Bricka and Vicky Palmer made points with their aggressiveness, and Vicky jolted our sound man with grunting that would make Jimmy Connors's emanations seem infantile gurgles. Pat Stewart and Mary Ann Eisel were the pinups.

Nobody, including next of kin, had heard of Californians Billy Bond and Tom Edlefsen on one side of the net and Jim McManus and Allen Fox on the other as they stepped forth onto the Longwood green to be scrutinized by our cameras. Theirs was the first match to be shown by a public station, and very likely the first doubles to play start to finish on American TV.

Edlefsen, a rangy all-American at Southern Cal, was the subject of a story told me by Tom Gorman that I couldn't repeat on the air. Unacquainted with each other, they had been thrown together to play doubles in the Tri-State tourney at the Cincinnati Tennis Club, one of those long-deceased fixtures of the amateur heyday. "Edlefsen was kind of moody, uncommunicative," related Gorman, who became the U.S. Davis Cup captain in 1986. "We were getting beat, not very unified, and he had an easy shot at the net. He missed it, and screamed, 'Fuck me!'

"I wanted to hide. This was a very proper club, and the people watching were aghast. So we went on, uneasily, and then I had a similar easy shot. I missed it," Gorman said, "and Edlefsen screamed, 'Fuck us!' He looked at me and smiled. Suddenly we were a team, and rallied to win the match, although I thought we'd be asked to leave town when it was over."

Edlefsen didn't win before our cameras because his partner, Bond, a lanky towhead, persisted in double-faulting. Breaking in as commentator, I remarked, "If I double-faulted that much I'd quit and go home."

That night, watching himself on the taped show, Bond said to Dennis Ralston, his Southern Cal teammate, "You know, that guy's right. I'm going home." He packed up, and flew back to La Jolla the next day, skipping the upcoming National Singles at Forest Hills.

My advice isn't usually so helpful, or heeded.

McKinley and Ralston, whose championship triumph over the Mexicans, Osuna and Palafox, was a bang-up five-setter, were complimentary. They observed themselves almost nightly on the show, and said that watching—not my advice—helped them to make improvements and scout the opposition. They'd never looked themselves over before, and had played for the cameras only at Wimbledon, which was presented live.

Quickly we became known as the "Tennis Late Show." Taping from 1:00 P.M. to dusk, six years before Longwood was tarted up with floodlights, we had shows that started at eight and lasted as long as 6½ hours. Several shows provoked angry phone calls from viewers when a match was halted, uncompleted, by darkness. It might then have been around 1:00 A.M. as we signed off, urging them to tune in tomorrow night for the finish. Our clientele, to whom tennis was new, were unfamiliar with a tournament format, and thought they'd been cheated. Not realizing it was taped, they felt we'd inconsiderately pulled the plug on them.

"We watched for three hours, then you jerk it off the air. That's dirty pool! Why didn't you tell us at the start?"

We didn't know. Tiebreakers were seven years in the future, and the best-of-five set men's matches were uncontrollable in length.

During the 1966 National Doubles, a match that consumed practically the entire show, four hours and eighteen minutes, was a service to insomniacs. Manolo Santana, the Spaniard, and his Mexican partner, Luis Garcia, were overcome at nightfall by two other Mexicans, Joaquin Loyo-Mayo and Marcelo Lara, 10–12, 24–22, 11–9, 3–6, 6–2.

At 105 games it was then the third longest ever perpetrated, and prompted the tiebreaker's sire, Jimmy Van Alen, to step up his lobbying against "interminable deuce sets." He fired off a telegram to the USTA and the tournament chairman, protesting the "urological torture of officials, players, and spectators [what about the TV commentator?] inflicted by such unnecessary marathons."

Mercifully Jimmy persevered longer than those scores seemed, to liberate all forms of tennis from deuce sets.

Poor Santana. He couldn't know that his longest, most trying day was barely under way as he finally limped off the court with a sore ankle. For the gracious and gifted Manolo, the doubles loss was the least of it. A difficult night lay ahead. But, in the twilight, he said, "I wanted to play on grass to get ready for Forest Hills," where he would be defending the singles title. "But five hours is more than I wanted."

More than anybody wanted? Not always. Sometimes the customers, the few remaining souls, who may be homeless, become mesmerized at an elastic, superstretching contest, and hope it never stops. Fans, who count endurance as an attribute, want to be able to say they stuck it out for a twenty-inning ball game or a tennis match headed for eternity.

One of those accosted me as I left the TV booth, after interviewing Santana and getting off the air. "Hey," he said, "I hope you broadcast that Santana wasn't trying!"

It was true that he was dragging on that bum ankle in the fifth, but . . . *not trying?* I sounded like a teargassed bullfrog after nearly seven hours on the microphone, "Why would the guy stick it out for more than four hours? There are easier ways to go into the tank. And—"

To hell with it. Everybody's entitled, and I was in a rush to strip my TV guise and begin Act II as a newspaperman. There was a *Globe* column to be written, and fifty or sixty results around the grounds to peruse, some quotes to chase in order to write the news lead, too. Santana's continuing defeats weren't to come out until the next day.

After showering and having his ankle taped by Jock Semple, the tourney therapist, Santana walked across the street to his rental car, left in a no-parking zone. On the windshield was a ticket. Manolo shrugged. He did what a man who had been decorated by Generalissimo Franco does with a ticket at home in Spain. He tore up the decoration from the Newton Police Department.

It was a rip heard 'round the precinct. A cop on the clubhouse stoop witnessed Santana's violent abuse of document. He rushed over to offer the geographical and political advice that this was Massachusetts, not Spain. Obviously. Santana jabbered his objections in Spanish; the cop arrested him in English and escorted Manolo to jail.

It was a misunderstanding, Manolo kept trying to say. He

would be happy to pay the ticket. But he had been startled. His own quite serviceable English wouldn't work in his defense. After a while they let him make the permitted phone call, and he got through to Ronnie Barnes, a Brazilian who spoke Spanish. Barnes and some American friends reached the jailhouse, and bailed Manolo from his cell. The day after, in court, the judge, who had stayed up well past midnight to watch the Spaniard's televised trials on court, dismissed the charges, which included resisting an officer. Then he asked Manolo for an autograph.

The "Tennis Late Show" was reaching beyond the tennis lunatic fringe. Astoundingly I heard from the boxing promoter, Sam Silverman, in a somewhat sheepish confession that he had even monitored the educational channel. Why?

"There was nothing else on at that hour, Arthur," said he, the only person who addressed me by my given name (in Bostonese it came out AH-thuh). "I was desperate."

"What'd you think?"

"Not too bad. Better than I figured." Practically a benediction from Sam. "Some of the broads was okay, especially that Stewart kid. You give her money to be on TV? I'd give her money."

No doubt. One night, not long before, Sam had called me from Las Vegas where he'd attended the Emile Griffith–Jorge Fernandez welterweight title fight. He was pleased to report he'd made $200.

"How's that, Sam? You don't gamble."

"Naw, but I got a four-hundred-dollar broad for two hundred."

He wasn't the only one intrigued by Pat Stewart, tall and splendidly conformed. Pat was good enough to rank in the U.S. top twenty, which would be worth at least fifty grand in prize money today, plus endorsements, but not high enough then to avoid working. She was an underwear model, a breezy lady, uncorseted in her remarks, who laughed off losses with, "That's the way the strap snaps."

"A moving sight," my friend Death House Wogan called her. When Pat changed courts, moving from one end to the other, every other game, so did he. In order to stay beside her, although outside the court's fencing, Death House switched seats.

At Wimbledon in 1961 she was targeted by more than the

usual quota of photographers—from top to bottom—playing in a lavish wig and a pair of panties on which her phone number was embroidered. There was enough room for area and zip codes. This annoyed her fiancé of the season, an Englishman, who thought he was the only one who had her number.

Some of the numerous viewers introduced to Pat by us didn't approve of the way they assumed WGBH was conducting the National Doubles. Doesn't television influence all sports? We screened a Stewart match, a second-rounder, and she and Eisel lost. Thus those two were eliminated. The station received a number of irritated calls to the effect, "Why don't you put Pat Stewart on again? She was great yesterday. You oughta have her on every day."

Theoretically they were right, but a tournament doesn't work that way. As Pat might say, that's the way the draw's flawed.

Response to our program that exploratory year was encouraging. We knew somebody liked us, crude as the presentation was, because of the mail—containing checks—that came in. Throughout the tournament we had been begging in the unfortunate PBS manner. This programming is expensive. If you like it, let us know with your contributions. Mark "tennis" on your check.

The most impressive contributor didn't hold up. He was a viewer who wired to offer $1,000—"if you remove that abominable Collins."

A grand was a fortune to WGBH at the time. I'm sure the chief, David Ives, was tempted.

Such sentiment isn't isolated. That knocker and his ilk would have loved to learn of my situation in a swaying pressbox at tornado-struck Flushing Meadows in 1985. As 75 m.p.h. gales felled trees and carried off fences, the press coop, attached to the top of the stadium by steel beams, shimmied in midair like Sister Kate on the dance floor. For a few golden moments, unknown to them, the nation's journalism students stood to profit immensely if the press box went down with more than one hundred hands aboard. The pen didn't seem mightier than the Lord that afternoon. But as a remedy to Collins, I always suggest that the viewer needn't switch channels. Continue watching the match, but turn off the sound, and replace it with Mozart. Voila—the best of two worlds.

We got lucky with the finals, which left a good taste, but a commentator in pain. They were two of the better National Doubles windups. Ebbern and Smith beat Bueno and Hard, 4–6, 10–8, 6–3. Then McKinley and Ralston took the rest of the afternoon in nipping the lightning-fast Osuna and Palafox, 9–7, 4–6, 5–7, 6–3, 11–9.

An unseasonably cool August day became more uncomfortable as the hours went by and the wind rose, riddling me on my lonely aerie, an excessively high, and open, platform. My teeth hinted a chatter was imminent. I needed help, and they sent up hot tea. Well-meaning but very wrong. Where does steaming tea go on a cold day? Somewhere I couldn't go because I couldn't desert the mike.

I could have been exhibit A when Jimmy Van Alen cited urological torture. Cross your legs, and keep babbling, was my self-instruction. I looked down enviously when Osuna sprinted to the john at the base of my tower during one of the changeovers.

I stayed on duty, but if McKinley and Ralston hadn't somehow won in the twentieth game of the fifth set I might have been immersed like a captain going down with his ship. Closing the show in what may have sounded like a whimper, I vowed no more Boston Tea Parties on the TV bridge.

20

○

Pause for Nature

Sixteen years later, another town, another network, another call of nature. This one Roscoe Tanner said he couldn't put on hold.

It was London, the first Saturday in July 1979, well before we ever heard of Coach Reagan's trickle-down theory. But it was the alleged threat of same from Roscoe Tanner's message center—the bladder—that started the flooding of unsuspecting Americans' consciousness by this tennis tournament called Wimbledon. Later on that afternoon, putting Bjorn Borg unbelievably on hold for five sets, it was Roscoe himself who saved a day that would mean so much to the televising of tennis, to Wimbledon, and the game as a whole.

"Breakfast at Wimbledon!" was the invitation NBC sent across the United States, without a whole lot of assurance that anyone would respond by switching on a set to watch a game of tennis at 9:00 A.M. (7:00 A.M. on the West Coast). The breakfast motif was coined by Bob Basche, as aide to the imaginative, hard-driving NBC executive producer of sports, Don Ohlmeyer. A big, self-confident, sometimes abrasive, character out of a Dan Jenkins novel, Ohlmeyer had been brought in from ABC to enliven NBC's sports coverage. That he accomplished, establishing new standards of quality during a cyclonic four-year term.

Quickly he realized that although NBC had broadcast Wimbledon for a decade, those shows made not even semiquavers. The reason was clear to him—and anybody who cared for tennis: the finals show was a chop-and-paste, tape-delay production that aired late Saturday afternoon following a live baseball game. If the ball game ran long, possibly extra innings, the women's and men's singles finals were slashed accordingly. Excised tape one year contained Princess Margaret in the Royal Box. At the moment our camera picked her out she was picking her nose. "Great forehand," I noted. Her dexterity, along with a lot of other things, didn't get on the air. Naturally the results were known by the time we went on the air. The women's final had been played the day before, the men's at least eight hours before. But with an unalterable 2:00 P.M. start in London, there was no way a live telecast could reach the eastern time zone of the United States later than dreadful 9:00 A.M. Tape-delay was the pre-Ohlmeyer way of dealing with that inconvenience.

However, Ohlmeyer sized up Wimbledon accurately as the world's premier international sporting event, other than the quadrennial Olympic Games. NBC had been treating an extremely valuable property like an odd cousin in the attic. It wasn't even benign neglect.

Why not show it live? Wasn't it self-defeating not to televise the finals in their entirety? Wouldn't people arise a little early to witness the spectacle as it happened? All of it? That was Ohlmeyer's logical plaint.

He was answered, from higher up, that no seriously consuming American adult would face up to a TV set at nine, or earlier, on a Saturday morning for tennis. The only household viewers at that hour would be the "Sesame" set, tenaciously guarding the cartoon channels. The argument was reasonable, too.

But Ohlmeyer persisted, and got his way. It was a way that worried even the bluff, chain-smoking Ohlmeyer when the day of the first "Breakfast at Wimbledon!" arrived, and he didn't have the cast he wanted. Needed. Bjorn Borg, the resolute, angelic Swede, was in the final, all right, trying for a fourth successive title—but the Brash Basher, Jimmy Connors, was not.

Connors had played the previous two finals against Borg. He lost a five-set epic in 1977, and then was flattened in three sets beneath a steamrolling, Bjorn-again Swede. The difference was that Borg had added a Connors-befuddling chipped backhand approach shot to his arsenal in 1978. But Connors, who steadfastly refused to acknowledge the existence of that weapon, came to Wimbledon in 1979 looking for revenge on the breakfast menu. It wasn't to be. When the luck of the draw took over, NBC had lost its home-country heroes. John McEnroe, who had moved ahead of Connors in the seeding, to No. 2, was sideswiped by Tim Gullikson in the fourth round, opening the way for Tanner. Connors got his appointment with Borg all right, but this time it was a pre-"Breakfast" licking in the semis.

The considered wisdom was that "Breakfast at Wimbledon!" required an American challenging Borg in order to succeed in the only place commercial TV matters: the ratings. But Roscoe Tanner was not that American. Even though I called lightning-serving Roscoe "Bulletman," and the "Stanford Hillbilly"—he came from Lookout Mountain, Tennessee—these were fanciful appellations. Aside from his southpaw serve, there was nothing menacing about Roscoe, and he was the furthest thing from a hick. An ex-campus smoothie in a Buster Brown haircut, he looked like an insurance executive.

Almost as bad as the news of Tanner's ascension to the final was the late-hour refusal of the Wimbledon committee even to consider a five-minute alteration in their hallowed timetable that was requested by Ohlmeyer. Schooled in America where TV networks, backed by huge rights fees, call the tune for all sports promoters, Ohlmeyer had neglected to clear, well in advance, his production plans.

All he wanted—a paltry wish, Don thought—was for the two finalists to stride onto Centre Court at 2:05 P.M., rather than the traditional "precisely at two." Preparing to send the first live Wimbledon telecast to the States, NBC had charged up the prelude with the sort of ballyhoo and buildup it warranted: an elaborate "tease"—the lead-in pictures, music, and pronouncements designed to hook the viewer. Electronic foreplay. Of course, a commercial or two would be in there as well, and an appearance of the announcers to provide a "scene set."

"Just a lousy five-minute delay, for chrissakes!" Ohlmeyer

was steaming. Or was it that he seemed to be smoking three cigarettes simultaneously? "With all the millions we pay them?"

The Badgers of Wimbledon wouldn't budge. Not for all the T in TV.

"Not on, old chap. Never been done," was the usual answer whenever NBC, or anybody else, desired to innovate at the Big W.

It wasn't that they were unsympathetic, or even insensitive to money and the commerical realities of American television. No tournament is more commercial than Wimbledon. However, the huckstering is done so tastefully you hardly notice. Never will sponsors and underwriters be brought into the act, trumpeting their wares over loudspeakers as is customary at the high-crass presentation of trophies—and, of course, checks—during the U.S. Open.

(An uncomfortable blush covered Chris Evert, amid guffaws from the Forest Hills crowd in 1974, as she was announced winner of the Vaseline Intensive Care Award. That $35,000 honorarium was earned by Evert's performances in the Grand Slam tournaments. Her palm greased, Ms. Vaseline nevertheless accepted a tribute that would have made Wimbledonians cringe.)

The All England Clubbies are so zealous in protecting their traditions that inevitable change is as subtle as the sacraments of silence on Centre Court the last two days while the queen and king of tennis are anointed. A sporting coronation without commercials may be unimaginable to Americans, but it works at Wimbledon.

Wimbledon's overseers are as dollar-conscious as any other promoters, but they will not act without long consideration. When Don Ohlmeyer pleaded for a five-minute delay in starting the 1979 men's final, they could see his point, and suggested it might be acted on in 1980 if sufficient notice were given.

Twenty-four hours was not deemed sufficient pondering time, old boy, and Ohlmeyer was left high and desperate. He sensed artistic disaster for his highly publicized concept. By the time tease and commercials had rolled onto the screen, the match would be five minutes old. The first set might have been determined by an early service break. The critics, up at grisly dawn at Ohlmeyer's behest, would be stirring their coffee with harpoons, awaiting his "Breakfast" gaffes.

"Can you do anything for us?" Ohlmeyer turned hopefully to my commentary partner, Donald Dell, the agent and well-known power broker. Donald had been my first PBS booth-mate, starting in 1970, after I'd been soloing for seven years, but this was the first Wimbledon we'd done together. As U.S. Davis Cup captain, he'd appeared with me in Boston on a couple of National Doubles guest spots and impressed producer Greg Harney. Greg thought our contrasting deliveries and personalities—the sometimes imperious Yalie lawyer who detested the press and the Ohio rube newspaperman—would blend together well. I think he was right. Donald and I—dubbed "The Lip and the Scalp" by Jack Kramer—became good friends who agreed on little other than a love for the game, and are still at it, for one or two shows a year.

Nobody knew the game better—the playing and politicking—than Dell, who'd coasted perspicaciously from one to the other. If anybody could help out, it was him, even around noon, two hours before post time for the men's final. NBC was not quite bold enough yet to give the women their "Breakfast" due.

Dell, who was Tanner's agent, replied to Ohlmeyer, "I can't do anything with the committee, but . . . let me see . . ."

He returned a half-hour later, saying, "Maybe . . ."

Then there was the artistic problem of Tanner himself. Breakfast with Roscoe was a prospect as appealing as that grapefruit James Cagney shoved into Mae Clarke's face. On paper it looked like a ninety-minute debacle—but we had five hours of air time to account for. As Ohlmeyer, Dell, and I walked from the NBC compound, located behind the club grounds, and into the Centre Court complex, toward our broadcast stall, the boss said, anxiously, to Dell: "Can your guy win a set? Can he make any kind of match out of it?"

"You want it straight?" Dell looked warily at the distraught Ohlmeyer.

Acknowledging the boss's nod, Dell shook his head. "I wouldn't bet anything I valued on Roscoe winning a set, much less the match."

Wonderful, Was the sky falling on Ohlmeyer's ambitious undertaking?

But the gloom began to lift as 2:00 arrived, and Borg and Tanner didn't. Producer Ted Nathanson and director Geoff Mason commanded the proper buttons to be pushed, and NBC's peacock came onto the screen considerably more cocky than

Chicken Little. Host Dick Enberg's spirited voice was heard over the pretaped tease as a panoply of Wimbledon and London unfolded, offering more pomp and prestige than come together in any other playpen.

On flowed the images, gilded by Enberg—Beefeaters, double-decker buses, Queen Elizabeth presenting the 1977 trophy to Virginia Wade, Bjorn Borg kneeling in triumphant thanks, Martina Navratilova defeating Chris Evert in the 1978 final, Big Ben, the changing of the Guard . . .

Still no Borg or Tanner.

Minutes went by. Dell gave me a conspiratorial smirk. We were into commercial. Donald and I were getting ourselves organized in a chamber about the size of an outhouse, wedged into the southeast corner of Centre, a few rows from the court. Tanner, as we learned later, was sojourning in an inhouse outhouse.

After two weeks of scuffing, this most illustrious of tennis courts was suitably "bruised," as they say in English grass-court circles. "She's bruised but proud and ready, firm fast and true," said the head groundsman, Jack Yardley, who always accorded his honey the female gender.

I call her CeeCee (or C.C., for Centre Court), and never tire of her wiles and thrills. A changeable lady, she doesn't behave the same two days in a row. Her fickleness is one of the aspects that makes Wimbledon so uniquely challenging.

She was tattered and gouged, but as true of bounce as anybody could expect. Borg had feared her at first, in his 1973 debut, but grown to love her—"for sure," to use his stock expression.

That love, which he made happen with determined, unrelenting labor, was nowhere evident in 1974. Seeded fifth, recent winner of his first major, the French, a puzzled and dispirited Bjorn was run out of Court 1 by the pudgy Egyptian lefty, Izzy El Shafei, 6–1, 6–3, 6–1. Looking at each other knowingly during the third round fiasco, Mike Lupica, columnist for the *New York Daily News*, and I concluded, "The Swede will never master this place." Some experts.

More important than CeeCee's texture and genteel seediness—she looked something like a worn pool table—was her emptiness. The on-camera opening, with Enberg, Dell, and me discussing the final, had been taped ahead of time. Our faces appeared. We clucked away on the monitor, thus, presumably, across America, seen at breakfast, or blinked at from under the covers. Ohlmeyer had been ready to dump these three talking heads but there was no need. Borg and Tanner remained missing.

At 2:06, with everyone in the production truck feeling a lot better, Bjorn and Roscoe were sighted at last emerging from the doorway below the Royal Box, and were only yards from the court. Seconds before, "They're on their way," said a voice in my ear. "Plenty of time to set the scene."

Borg and Tanner were accompanied by referee Fred Hoyles, Centre Court usher Peter Morgan, and the dressing room attendant, tiny white-coated Leo Turner, who looked like a Christmas shopper with the finalists' rackets bundled in his arms. The posse was following the route trod since this version of Wimbledon (the second) opened in 1922.

In the tennis equivalent of the last mile, the finalists had stepped from the men's dressing room into the All England Club's main lobby—territory guarded by uniformed and beribboned military volunteers, and forbidden to all but players and club members. Taking a left, they descended a short flight of stairs, a brief passage through history that flashed at them on either side and overhead.

On the left, encased in glass, are the dazzling treasures— the crown jewels of tennis—championship baubles, cups, and salvers, that never leave the club. On the right, the dark green wall of honor is embellished with names of all the champions from 1877, lettered in gold. Above is the signboard bearing Kipling's admonition from his poem "If": ". . . if you can meet with Triumph and Disaster and treat those two impostors just the same. . . ."

In a game whose code and traditions are hangovers from Kiplingesque officers and gentlemen charged with maintaining the Empire, this short walk is as majestic an approach to a niche in sporting history as can be found.

At the bottom of the stairway, double doors open onto a small foyer. There, behind another door on the left, is the waiting room, the place of dual confinement for the combatants prior to their trial on Centre. The foes have only each other for comfort until summoned by the usher to move out to the holy of holies.

A spartan room furnished in wicker, it is decorated with photos of such champions as Maureen Connolly and Rod Laver, and a sketch of John McEnroe and Bjorn Borg sitting there awaiting the call to their 1981 clash.

Outside the waiting room, another double door bars the way to a narrow rectangular courtyard directly below the Royal Box, and behind the south wall of the enclosure.

Once outdoors and into that corridor, Borg and Tanner turned left and walked about ten yards to the end of the green brick wall, then right, through the opening to the court where they were first seen by the surrounding multitude of fourteen thousand.

Cheers and applause cascaded down on them as they stepped into the somber green cathedral and onto the turf.

"Here and now," says John Newcombe, the champ of 1967, '70, '71, "is the exam you've prepared for all your tennis life. All the questions will be asked of you, and the world will learn if you have the answers."

Tramping to the service line, Bjorn and Roscoe about-faced and bowed, like gladiators, to the Royal Box. Beneath a fluttering canopy that favors the club colors, purple and green, the duke and duchess of Kent, assorted other royals, and the Badgers of the All England Club accepted this anachronistic homage. It remains part of a dated ritual balked at not even by citizens of democracies and Communist states. The women curtsy. Form is varied. Prior to the 1972 semifinal, their wondrous first meeting, kids Chris Evert and Evonne Goolagong looked like a couple of Methodists trying to genuflect at the Vatican. They got better with experience.

Why had Borg and Tanner been late? Their tardiness, apparently unnoticed by the audience, was unremarked upon, except gratefully by our leaders, Ohlmeyer, Nathanson, and Mason. Whatever the reason, none of us knew at the moment. I would find out about Tanner's bladder-blaming stall from Dell only later, after he'd talked with Tanner. In the dressing room, Dell had told Tanner of NBC's problem, and asked him to dawdle somehow.

As Roscoe and Bjorn were notified that it was time to leave the dressing room, the American excused himself, saying he had to go to the bathroom. There, in one of dear Thomas Crapper's water closets, he sequestered himself for five minutes. Who would question the urgency, or break down the door and pull him out?

Saint Roscoe of the Lavatory.

As Bjorn and Roscoe engaged in the "knock-up," the English expression, always amusing Americans, for the prematch warmup, I slapped Dell on the back. That was my good-luck signal to my partner of nine years. We had first teamed by doing the 1970 Pennsylvania Grass Championships, a local telecast for WHYY, the public station in Philadelphia.

Working together sporadically the next three years, we were coupled on a regular basis in 1974 by Greg Harney at WGBH in Boston, my original producer. Harney was in charge of the PBS telecasts that for four summer seasons gave recognizable form to a game that had been pretty much ignored by the commercial networks. Those four seasons, 1974 to 1977, were, to my subjective mind, the shining years of tennis TV in the U.S.

Obviously Harney had neither the production resources of the commercial networks nor the most prominent events to focus on, Wimbledon or the U.S. Open to name two. But we had a lot of time before that became too valuable a commodity for even PBS, and an eagerness to let America in on the joys and skills of pro tennis during a time I recall as the Tennis Epidemic. We ranged coast to coast, and even abroad, thanks to Harney, who guided the production, and Dell, who largely raised the underwriting funds. Our usual tournament televising encompassed play on Saturday and Sunday afternoons and Monday night finals. The mail told us that people were watching, gratefully, and for a while most of the consequential men— Connors, Borg, Guillermo Vilas, Wojtek Fibak, Arthur Ashe, Stan Smith, Manolo Orantes, Harold Solomon, Eddie Dibbs, Bob Lutz, Vijay Amritraj among them—were first seen by Americans on PBS.

Leonard Roscoe Tanner III, a 1-to-8 shot in the eyes of London bookmakers, ought to get a medal from NBC for enabling the network not to lose its "Breakfast" in 1979. On a couple of counts. Once he came out of that latrine closet, after the prologue-saving interval, Roscoe gave us the match of his life. Not only did he win one set—"Thank you, Roscoe!" Ohlmeyer et al. in the production truck crooned when he took the first, 7–6—grabbing viewers and foiling the expected blowout, he went several steps and swings further, serving fifteen aces, terrifying

Borg, and damn near won the championship in five sets. It hung on a break point against the Swede's serve at 4–3 in the fifth. "If he breaks me, I lose, for sure," Borg said.

Roscoe lined up a forehand passing shot, and hummed it along the sideline. Borg reached vainly. The ball fell barely wide.

By that time, it didn't really matter to those of us involved in the telecast (except for Dell, understandably calculating what a Wimbledon title would be worth to his client and himself). We had a magnificent match. "Breakfast" had stretched to "Lunch at Wimbledon" and we were still going strong.

NBC got awfully lucky at breakfast time. The fact is that final-round matches are seldom the best or most exciting of a tournament. The players are usually drained after a tournament of straining to get to the final. Of the first ninety-nine Wimbledon men's finals, forty-eight went in straight sets, only sixteen the full distance traveled by Tanner and Borg. Yet the next year we got another five-set wowser, perhaps the greatest of all, with Borg overcoming young John McEnroe after losing the "War of 18–16," the excruciating fourth-set tiebreaker of thirty-four points. And the year after that, 1981, it was McEnroe smashing Borg's run at five straight titles and forty-one matches in four dramatic sets. Then came Jimmy Connors's resurrection in five thrilling sets against McEnroe.

How long could this go on? Ohlmeyer had been gone from NBC for a while, but his luck was holding. I warned his successor, Michael Weisman, that we were due for a dog, and we got one in 1983. Connors-McEnroe was the desired final, a rematch of 1982, but Kevin Curren served Connors out of the tournament with thirty-three aces, and then an acrobatic New Zealander named Chris Lewis spilled Curren in five bouncy sets in the semis. Lewis, unseeded and ranked ninety-first, was a wonderful story—for one day. When the reality of a Centre Court final with No. 1, Emperor McEnroe, dawned on him, he was a good story for about five more minutes.

Bjorn Borg was at Centre once again, but not where we really needed him, across the net from Mac. Instead, Bjorn was in the booth with me and Dick Enberg, as a commentator. None of this TV happy talk for the Swede. His answer to Enberg's question—"What does Lewis have to do to beat McEnroe?"—was as straightforward as his own game had been.

"He has no chance," Borg answered. Correctly. It was 6–2,

6–2, 6–2, in eighty-five minutes, and not as close as the score looks. Lewis was a tournament-wrecker, one of those wonderful can't-happens that sometimes do, spicing any sport, but he was abruptly out of his league in McEnroe's.

For his twenty-nine million compatriots (all but three million of them sheep), it was "Midnight-plus Snack at Wimbledon." The telecast came on at 1:00 A.M. in New Zealand, but by 1:10 the viewers could bleat compassionately and go to bed.

Chris, a nice kid, had a couple of big days, but he ruined ours. Contrary to what you might think, NBC didn't demand a saliva test for Lewis or suggest that his prize money be withheld for conduct detrimental to the ratings. There was just nothing Chris Lewis could do in his undoing, nor was he alone in his helplessness against McEnroe. A year later, scorching Mac beat Connors even worse. Executive producer Weisman took both debacles well—manfully, I believe it's called.

By then "Breakfast at Wimbledon" had been established, a double helping, the women on Saturday, men on Sunday. The concept was solid. And that's because Roscoe Tanner had raised his right hand and lied a little, saying that he had to go to the bathroom—before he raised his left hand and nearly brained Bjorn Borg.

21

○

Hello, Chrissie!

The intertwined coming and going of sixteen-year-old Bjorn Borg and thirty-five-year-old Roy Emerson at the U.S. Open of 1972, both of them en route to the Hall of Fame, was paralleled, somewhat, the year before at Forest Hills. Chrissie Evert was the freshly arrived Ice Maiden and Pancho Gonzalez was the used-up, departing Old Wolf. Naturally they didn't play against one another as Borg and Emerson were to do, but their accidental stadium encounter made an impression on her, and me.

Ponytailed and prim, although a delinquent cutting high school classes, the sixteen-year-old from Fort Lauderdale swooshed into the Forest Hills stadium like a Florida hurricane. During her seven-year run there, before the Open moved to Flushing Meadows, she played nowhere else but the thirteen-thousand-seat stadium because, as tourney director Bill Talbert explained, "People would have torn down the fences if I tried to put her on any other court. Everybody wants to see Chrissie."

Nothing has changed.

She was high-octane from the beginning. Starting by beating a seasoned German, Edda Buding (possessor of seductive blue eyes, to which Evert brought tears), she continued to stimulate the lachrymal glands of such older, internationally ranked, and bedazzled women as Mary Ann Eisel, Françoise Durr, and Lesley Hunt along the shining path of escape after escape to the semifinals. There, she couldn't find a way out against the champion, Billie Jean King.

Since she had helped the United States beat Britain in the Wightman Cup, and won twenty-five straight matches while approaching the Open, Chrissie was hardly an unheralded discovery. But millions did discover her in the second round, her TV debut, where our national romance with Chris America began. Talk about breaking in with a bang? That was a bang worthy of Los Alamos.

It was a grade-A reworking of a Hollywood B thriller, an escape from sure defeat at the hands of fourth-ranked American Mary Ann Eisel that has had no equal in Chrissie's long and brilliant career. At the TV microphone for CBS, I felt, along with everyone else, that the new kid had given a good enough account of herself in losing as Eisel served with a 6–4, 6–5, 40–0 lead. Three match points. And, after all, grass was Eisel's milieu, while it seemed something of an enigma to volley-disdaining, baseline-boomer Chrissie.

Nice try, kid.

Oh, yeah? However, . . . pow! The teeny kid began swinging from her heels, belting winners, and canceled the three match points. Before the game was over, in her favor, Evert had blotted three more. Eisel was reeling, and Chrissie was rolling, permitting her twenty-one-year-old foe just one more game, 4–6, 7–6, 6–1.

America was captivated.

After she had showered and dressed, Chrissie was brought back to the TV platform for an interview. The day's show was over, but the producer wanted to tape something for use the following day. The kid was hot.

Before the Open switched to Flushing, the TV broadcasting area was a small, rudimentary wooden platform, an outdoor perch at one corner of the stadium, dating to the radio days of my early guru, Lev Richards. Announcers, on their bridge just above the court, had to speak softly. The stage manager positioned Chrissie in a chair facing me. My back was to the court, where

Pancho Gonzalez struggled with Manolo Orantes in the third round. This was his last singles stand in the tournament he'd won twenty-three years before, in 1948 and again in 1949. Though Pancho was forty-two, and would not win another match at Forest Hills, he had taken the first set from future champ Orantes, and was a conceivable quarter, even semifinalist.

A large crowd was behind him, as always. To many of them the dark, appealing Gonzalez was tennis. With a dash of elegance and another of tough guy—an athletic Sinatra—he had done it his way, wooing fervent galleries and fawning gals in a way that frequently enraged colleagues of the compact gypsy troupe that constituted pro tennis prior to 1964. A pro stopover without Big Pancho was a big bust, most promoters felt.

"Pancho thinks we can't live without him," Rod Laver once remarked, acting as though he may have believed it. He and Rosewall, who had eclipsed Pancho on court, resented the general feeling that only Pancho kept the pro game breathing. They called him "Gorgo," for gorgonzola—the big cheese. Even in 1969, though open tennis was a reality, Pancho at forty continued as a Presence. Laver may have won Wimbledon for a second successive time, taking the third leg of his second Grand Slam, but the story from London that year was Gonzalez's improbable first-round triumph over twenty-five-year-old Charlie Pasarell, the No. 5 American.

It took two days, 112 games, and five hours and twelve minutes, the longest singles ever played at a major championship, and the score looked like a social security number: 22–24, 1–6, 16–14, 6–3, 11–9. But Grandpop Pancho, brushing aside seven match points, wasn't quite ready for social security. Pasarell looked, at the close, like somebody run over by a geriatric case in a wheelchair, and Laver, the champ, shook his head. "That's Pancho for you, always stealing the show."

I got lucky on that one, a titanic drama in two acts, five scenes. Covering the Joe Frazier–Jerry Quarry heavyweight fight in New York on the Monday, I figured to miss the first two days of Wimbledon. But Monday's rain in London pushed the opening back a day, and Pancho was still wheezing when I reported Wednesday. Barely. The Centre Court congregation had actually booed the Old Wolf to the showers Tuesday evening, for a couple of reasons. Storming about in the gloaming, Pancho was incensed that referee Mike Gibson had insisted on commencing the second set. "It's too damn dark to play," fumed fatigued Pancho, who believes that the eyes go first, not the legs, for a tennis player. "We can't see."

Dismayed by his impertinence to authority, the crowd was even more disapproving of Gonzalez's subsequent match conduct. Sulking, he was obviously not trying in the second set. Apparently dead, and behind two sets, he was sent home with a scolding—boo's—which was most unusual of the faithful. "He was so furious about the referee," reported Pancho's wife, Madelyn, "that he couldn't go to bed. I had to play backgammon with him until two A.M. before he settled down."

Twelve hours later he was back on Centre, possibly sleepy, but manifestly rejuvenated to take the crucial second act of three sets. Happily I was there, too, marveling—as foe and friend Pasarell did, along with everyone else—while Gonzalez twice served out of 0–40 match-point traps in the fifth, and closed on the crescendo of an eleven-point run. Yesterday's bad boy became today's St. Richard the Lion-handed. Everybody up. They stood and cheered and applauded him for thirty-five seconds, which in that territory is a marathon of adulation.

As he aged, Pancho became a master staller, raging to gain time, sneering and insulting court officials as a cover for the fact that he was resting. "We didn't like it, but we understood what he was doing and tried not to let our concentration be broken," says Laver. He may have bent the rules that way, but nobody ever accused him of vile language or pantomimes.

And he was ever a disciple of the creed: "The pro must go on." Gonzalez recalled the head-to-head, king-of-the-hill days. "Once, my first tour against Jack Kramer, I had a badly sprained ankle. 'I can't play tonight,' I told Jack, and I meant it.

"Jack was the promoter, too, and he wasn't in the habit of giving refunds. 'What do you mean—can't play?' he says. 'We always play.' He arranged for me to get a couple of shots of novocaine, and I played. The show always went on."

Times change. The pro game doesn't depend on one or two players anymore, and an athlete with an injury is probably wise to pull out of a match, possibly averting serious damage. Another factor is that the players take themselves much more seriously today. The good ones are solo conglomerates, worth tons as money-making vehicles. Are they going to let themselves be governed by the old, corny show-must-go-on credo, and risk income impairment? Not that we've noticed. Even Jimmy Connors, giving 100 percent-plus while he's actually playing, has a tendency to abandon matches when he doesn't feel just right. He has racked up more defaults, claiming disability before or during a match, than any other player: twenty-two times through 1988. The pros of the olden days may not have been hardier, but they had to act it. There was no other way to stay in business, whether it was playing in bad health or under outrageous conditions.

Gonzalez and Laver demonstrated the latter in perhaps the most remarkable match I've ever seen, the final of the 1964 U.S. Pro in Boston. Rain had pushed the final back a day until Monday when, despite the continuance of one of those wet gales New Englanders call a Nor'easter, Pancho and Rod vowed to play. "No choice," Laver explained. "We catch a plane tonight for London because we're scheduled to play tomorrow night in Edinburgh." It was a sporting reenactment of the Great Swamp Fight of 1675 as he and Pancho stormed through the storm— on grass, mind you—waging an astounding battle. No one should have even walked across that bog without doctor, lawyer, and clergyman in attendance, but Gonzalez and Laver ran, falling time and again, yet producing divine shot-making.

Laver won in four sets, halting the thirty-six-year-old king's bid for a ninth U.S. Pro title much as King Philip's Narragansett allies had been undone by colonists in the original Swamp Fight not far to the south. "Wouldn't have done it if I was still an amateur," said Laver. "It was bloody ridiculous." His paycheck was $2,200. Nobody, pro or amateur, would do it today for ten times that amount.

Gonzalez's rages, helpful as they may have been in his declining days, weren't necessarily contrived. He did have a thin skin, but, like John McEnroe, he seemed to concentrate his thickly grown competitiveness by getting into a jam.

One of the guys who put him into a jackpot was a surgical heckler named Dr. Edward Browne. He was lancing Pancho annoyingly from a courtside seat during a one-nighter at Boston Garden, getting the better of their verbal exchanges while Pancho tried to ward off another annoyance named Ken Rosewall. Unable to stand it longer, Pancho stalked over to Browne, and appeared ready to give the physician artificial expiration by applying hands to windpipe. But Browne, a team doctor for the resident Celtics and Bruins, had the good fortune to be seated next to a man who stood up for him.

Rising to his full and rugged six feet, five inches, Jim Loscutoff, known throughout the National Basketball Association as the Celtics' "enforcer," stepped between the enraged Gonzalez and the endangered Browne. "Now, Pancho, why don't you go back to playing tennis?" Loscutoff inquired pleasantly.

Gonzalez, a big man himself, isn't stupid. I have seen him brutalize locker rooms as a graphic commentary on defeat. But, gazing upward, as though at a lob, he saw the wisdom in Loscutoff's words, and eyes, and resumed a difficult subduing of Rosewall.

But on the September afternoon in 1971, he was having difficulty, also, with Manolo Orantes in the Forest Hills stadium. Not any more than I was having, at the same time, trying to pry answers from Chris Evert. I've interviewed her often since. She has become a delight, the consummate pro, true to herself, her game, her public, available to the press in defeat as in victory. She has also nailed me a few times, verbally when the interviews have piqued her. Touché. But in her first nationwide TV interview she was tight-lipped, nervous.

As I calmly, then a little desperately, sought some sort of interrogational hook for more than a yes or no answer, or merely a nod, I could sense that the stadium had become silent. Something was askew. Strange, since Gonzalez always inspired fervor in a New York crowd. But I was more concerned with Chrissie, especially as a look of puzzlement, even terror, began to spread across her face. Her mouth was agape, her eyes widened like a cartoon character's as she stared past me, at the court.

What had I said to unnerve her? Instinctively, I looked over my shoulder to find the answer: Gonzalez, directly below us, hands on hips, and glowering.

"Goddamn it, Bud!" he bellowed. "Don't you know we're trying to play a tennis match down here! Shut up!"

His words rippled across the arena as Chrissie and I jerked as if shot. Quickly the audience seconded with, "Yeah, shut up!" and thousands of personal versions of "Booo!" What a reception the heroine of Forest Hills was getting, courtesy of me and CBS.

I knew the interview was over. "Thank you, Chrissie, and

good luck," I whispered into the microphone, and then we slunk off the platform as though bailing out of a hotel without paying the bill.

It wasn't my first run-in with Gonzalez, but watching him play and talking tennis with him, a very thoughtful man on the subject, was always worth whatever trouble. Pancho was something like another attractive titan of his time, Ted Williams. On the job they were supremely confident, expert, self-centered, and vitriolic. Away from work, they could be charming, warm, intelligent conversationalists. Each was a loner.

During an uncharming conversation, in which he knocked the excitement and enthusiasm right out of me, I had encountered the historic Gonzalez stubbornness. WGBH-TV had gotten together enough money to present local area telecasts of the U.S. Pro of 1965 at Longwood. This wasn't easy for a striving public station, but Boston viewers were responding well to our tennis programs, which had begun in 1963. I was assigned to secure signed waivers from the twelve entrants, explaining that since this was a nonprofit venture, neither they nor their players' organization could expect a rights fee.

Eleven of them signed with pleasure. Since television never looked their way, they were pleased that our cameras—any cameras—would focus on them. Not Pancho. He wouldn't sign, snorting, "See, that's what's wrong with these other guys. They're so eager to be on TV they'll give it away."

For an hour we argued. He wouldn't budge. I tried to explain the concept of a public station, then known as educational TV. No commercials. No income. The station would probably lose money, but this one station in the United States believed in tennis. Didn't that mean something?

Nothing. Pancho had been around longer than anyone else, and had been conned by a variety of promoters who promised that his appearance would be good for the future of the game. For a guy seventeen years into his pro career, the future was now, and he wouldn't make a move for free. I said I understood, but, "If you don't sign there's no show. It has to be unanimous."

"Tough luck," he said.

"You'd let one guy spoil it for everybody, for kids who might be watching, Richard?" I was pleading, I was using his straight name, which I knew he preferred to Pancho.

"Maybe only one guy knows how to act in this situation. I gotta get paid."

My mind was whirling and searching. Would the station slip him something up front? I was aware that some promoters did that to guarantee his entry. It had happened at the U.S. Pro of 1963 that went bankrupt at Forest Hills. Pancho was the only one to get paid (and beforehand), and the other players were furious. I couldn't justify anything like that.

"Look, Richard, nobody's getting paid, and—"

"Don't give me that crap." For the first time he smiled, but his brown eyes were still hard. I'd been wasting his time. "Maybe the other players are stupid, but somebody gets paid. The cameramen don't work for nothing just to advance tennis. The producer gets paid. You . . . you get paid."

"Yeah." I couldn't rebut that.

"Then why should I be a sucker?"

"Richard, you're absolutely right. I do get paid. Twenty-five bucks a show, and I'm gonna write you a check right now for the entire amount—one hundred twenty-five dollars—if you'll sign this waiver. It'll be a pleasure to do the tournament for nothing."

Gonzalez is not a small-timer.

"Gimme the goddamn thing to sign," he shook his head. "I wouldn't take your money.

"Twenty-five bucks. . . ." He stomped out of the room.

We were on the air, the first time the U.S. Pro had been televised.

22

○

Masked
Ballyhoo

Frantic footsteps echoing along Cleveland's deserted Euclid Avenue one April night in 1958 may have belonged to a man fleeing his identity, but they were symbolic, too, of a sport suffering that fashionable malady called "identity crisis."

Pro tennis had slid so far into the well-known slough of despair by the late 1950s that the promoter of one of the few existing tournaments resorted to an ageless gimmick that has served professional wrestling (alias "wrassling") well: the "masked marvel." It was the masked marvel of tennis (alias "Mr. Nemesis") whose flight from the Cleveland Arena to further oblivion was noted by a slim gathering of witnesses at the World Pro Championships.

If there is a world championship in tennis, it is, debatably, Wimbledon, the first and foremost of tournaments. But this has never tempered the enthusiasm of any number of promoters, a breed seldom infected by taste, who modestly proclaim their own potboilers as World This-or-that. In Dallas, the promotional firm, WCT (World Championship Tennis), annually presents the World Championship of Tennis at its home base. The victor may thus consider himself world champeen, certainly within the city limits of Dallas.

"Classic" is another favored word, applied often, and instantly, to the nameplate of any newly organized tournament or make-believe exhibition. Like their rough-and-tumble cousins, boxing impresarios, tennis promoters—particularly in the highly commercialized present—are too liberal-minded to fall victims to truth in advertising.

It isn't unheard of for two different tournaments to go under the same name. Not too long ago an event sprang up in Houston billed as the U.S. Pro Doubles while a same-name exercise had been operating in Boston for several years.

Then there was a pretentious Florida exhibition event, designed for television, and to sell real estate at the site, a high-dollar housing project. Called the Grand Slam of Tennis, it has happily run its course (for now), but it especially enraged purists between 1977 and 1982.

Any moderately well-informed tennis follower knows that the Grand Slam is a Herculean task, requiring a total of two month's labor to turn the trick of winning the four majors within a calendar year. Two days were involved in the Floridian grand scam, which stole the name, Grand Slam, and cheapened it. Even though the Grand Slam lives not as a copyrighted entity but only in sporting lore, pulled from the ozone by Don Budge and *New York Times* sportswriter Allison Danzig, it has become, over the half-century since Budge's deed, the most exalted of tennis achievements.

Budge says he set out to do the undone, the unconsidered, and unnamed Grand Slam in 1938, without telling anyone beforehand. He also wanted to maintain his interest in the "amateur" game, which he dominated, before moving on to more money and less visibility as a pro. In writing about Budge's Slam-concluding win of the U.S. Nationals, Danzig indicated it was "something like a grand slam in bridge."

The name caught on, never discouraged by Budge, a pleasant guy who has dined out on it for decades. Nor did the hustlers of the abbreviated Florida version discourage the thought that their man had won a Grand Slam.

Such nonsense and obfuscation probably works less damage on the public mind than did the old White House quarterback Reagan's grasp of facts. What we're talking about is only a game. What really bothers me is that no promoter has been wordslicker enough to put all the revered words on one trophy and bill his brand-new flutter as the Traditional World Champion Classic. It will come, crafted especially for TV.

Tennis promoters, who are frequently player agents, have the instincts of boxing promoters in Ivy League suits. These Vultures would do almost anything at the expense of order and understanding so long as ever-increasing profits aren't disturbed. I use the adverb "almost" because I am fairly certain none of them would—in the spirit of London Bridge—try to purchase Wimbledon and move it to Dubuque. But, then, I'm an optimist.

Jack March, an engaging fellow who had played some pro tennis and supported himself mainly as a country-club instructor, could hardly be blamed for the liberties he took with his tournament between 1954 and 1962. Setting up shop at the Cleveland Arena, a ten-thousand-seat building constructed primarily as residence for the bygone hockey-playing Barons, March wasn't exactly in one of America's tennis hot spots.

Who could find fault with Jack for calling his clambake the World Pro Championships, even if a similarly named semi-attraction was also operating in London? Who noticed? The fact that he kept going in Cleveland for nine years, offering a purse of about ten thousand dollars, was a tribute to March's love for the game and a charm that enabled him to keep his sponsor, a local brewery, interested and sell a few tickets in a highly uninterested locale. His was a week-long payday in a world where such were scarcer than the players themselves.

As such, in that time and place, promoter March could be pardoned a little flimflammery with a game somewhat more respectable than hooking, but surely not as profitable. To juice interest, he tried Ping-Pong variations on the conventional scoring, pro-celebrity matches, and even the mystery strokesman, Mr. Nemesis.

The phantom of the Arena was shown off, suitably hooded at cocktail parties, and entered in the tournament. March was following a time-honored pro wrassling script: A masked mystery man, ballyhooed as unbeatable, comes to town to challenge all-comers. Anybody who can defeat him will be privileged to raise the hood and expose the marvel to public view. You have the promoter's word that this will be difficult because the marvel is invincible.

In a simpler time in Boston a masked grappler did exceedingly well, winning week after week, struggling heroically to prevent identification, building suspense and ticket sales. When, at last, the master plan decreed the moment of truth, the reporter for the *Post* wrote: "Everybody immediately recognized the Marvel as a total stranger!"

However, Mr. Nemesis was never recognized as anything but an ill-conditioned mystery guest who stroked the ball pretty well. Intent on fostering intrigue, March kept Nemesis in seclusion most of the time. The promoter intimated that Nemesis was a top amateur risking suspension by mingling in a pro tournament. March hinted that the World Pro was a furtive breakthrough for open tennis.

Actually Mr. Nemesis, Eddie Alloo, a teaching pro from California, had been a decent amateur who had ranked as high as thirteenth nationally. But this was seventeen years after, and it was no picnic to chase Bobby Riggs's drop shots and lobs in a first-round match. Especially for a guy with his head in a bag with only a small mouth-hole to breathe through.

Riggs was forty-one, midway through limbo between acclaim as the 1939 Wimbledon champion and the sugar daddy of 1973 who beat up on Margaret Court but succumbed to Billie Jean King in those flamboyant mixed-singles duels. But he was tough. Fortunately for Nemesis/Alloo, first-round matches were of one-set duration. Spectators near the court heard Nemesis gasping and panting, "I'm dying . . . I can't breathe. . . ."

Riggs mercifully beat him, 6–3, and, of course, Bobby felt it was his right and duty to unveil Mr. Nemesis and solve the mystery. As Riggs advanced, Nemesis fled. "March told Alloo he'd get paid only if he kept the secret," says a pal of the promoter. "So there's Riggs chasing Alloo up an aisle and out of the building.

"Alloo is bushed, but he keeps on going, out to the street, Euclid Avenue, still in his hood, and disappears. People on the street that saw him must have thought he was a bank robber making a getaway. I don't think he got paid anyway."

Poor, bedraggled Eddie Alloo was not alone in that predicament. Others more celebrated than he would be stiffed before America's professional championship found sweet stability in Boston six years later.

23

○

Road to Cloncurry

Professional tennis was four guys and a canvas court.

They jaunted wherever the schedule, made up by the boss, Jack Kramer, carried them. And they carried along their office rug, the green canvas playing surface that was plopped in arenas, gymnasiums, dance halls, ice rinks—any building large enough to accommodate a gathering willing to buy enough tickets to meet the local promoter's guarantee. Sometimes customers didn't materialize, and the promoter paid off in IOUs.

Numerous combinations formed the quartets. Over the Kramer years the limited casts were selected from among such as himself: Pancho Gonzalez, Frank Sedgman, Tony Trabert, Ken Rosewall, Lew Hoad, Ashley Cooper, Mal Anderson, Alex Olmedo, Butch Buchholz, Barry MacKay, Mike Davies, Luis Ayala, Rod Laver.

The pros' war cry was "Have court, will travel!" Kramer, who would conceive the Grand Prix, the framework for today's broadly recognized male pro game, employing at least a thousand players, must have scheduled with a copy of the *National*

Geographic in one hand and adventurer Richard Halliburton's book, *New Worlds to Conquer*, in the other.

His band of nomads went places where there were hardly places, locales so far off the presently regulated track that their whereabouts and doings were secrets from all but those in attendance. Here and there, hither and thither, they were as identifiable as Foreign Legionnaires.

Here were the best players in the world, nosebleeding their way through La Paz, Bolivia, no place to play tennis, at twelve thousand Andean feet above sea level. And there they were, finally beaten by the "bug curfew" in Khartoum. Hither they went to Warsaw, paid in złotys, worthless when they left the country. Thither they ventured through the Australian bush, hiding out among kangaroos and emus.

Wimbledon and Forest Hills were only memories of better days socially, if not financially, when they were somebodies in the sporting firmament. Now they were outlaws on the lam, banned from the legit territories of the so-called amateur realm, scuffling along on one-night stands. Very few tournaments were available to them. For one thing, not enough of their kind, professional bodies, were available to fill a conventional tournament. For another, considering the pros' drawing power, a promoter was better off hiring four of them for one performance than eight or twelve for a week. Not as much overhead was involved for a one-nighter, and the entire local hard core of tennis degenerates could usually be accommodated at one sitting. Interest in London was sufficient to support an annual tournament on the canvas. New York, Paris, Johannesburg, Los Angeles, Cleveland were sometimes scenes.

For the most part, however, it was a furtive activity, clandestine engagements conducted at outposts the customary amateur game didn't reach. There were, after all, tennis junkies under the rocks everywhere.

Rod Laver remembers the sanguinary recital in La Paz, probably the site of the world's most altitudinous courts, where exertion wasn't recommended for newcomers. "I was playing Andres Gimeno, and, besides our guarantee, there was a bonus prize of a watch for the winner of our match. We both had nosebleeds, but we were playing as if it was a Wimbledon final. Except blood was streaming down our faces, and we were laughing at the sight of each other."

The Sudan he remembers for the "bug curfew" in Khartoum. "We started late in the afternoon to avoid the worst heat, but it was still hot. When it got dark they turned on lights that attracted swarms of bugs. After a while the bugs got so thick on the lights that they were useless. We weren't through our program—but that was the end." Called by nature. "The crowd understood. They lived there, and they left very orderly."

Imagine television coverage of that event. The producer says, "We don't have to go to black—the insects just did it for us."

"On the Road to Cloncurry" is a plaintive lyric playing in the back of the brains of a few of them, rolling around like a loose pebble on an uncharted bush track. Of course there is no such tune, since nobody would be fool enough to compose a tribute to that arid, desolate settlement in the wilds of Australia.

"The Road to Mandalay" and "Flying Down to Rio" and "April in Paris" have flowed from the minds of romantics. There is nothing to romanticize about Cloncurry, a ramshackle cattle crossing. Yet those pros who traveled that road find something lyrical in looking back. It is their badge of honor that they made a trek no right-minded tennis player of this day would consider, or be offered. Oh, there are still some out-of-the-way spots—but within the framework of the organized satellite tour—in Nigeria, say, or India, where novitiates are battling to get to the big leagues. But nothing as raw as a Cloncurry where the cast consisted nonetheless of some of the very best players of all time—including Hall of Famer Lew Hoad—not fledglings.

But if you were a pro, there was only one road—the Kramer road—and once in 1961 it passed through Cloncurry. If you liked the Bataan Death March, you'd love the Cloncurry Caravan, according to one of the survivors, the Ohio Bear, Barry MacKay.

I suppose the veterans are as nostalgic as were those Englishmen who fought with a tennis player named King Henry V at Agincourt in 1415. William Shakespeare's account says Henry was stung by a gift of tennis balls from the dauphin of France, replying, "When we have matched our rackets to these balls,/We will in France, by God's grace, play a set/Shall strike his father's crown into the hazard."

And to his troops these words that could apply to Kramer's old pros: "From this day to the ending of the world, but we in it shall be remembered; We few, we happy few, we band of brothers. . . ."

The hardly remembered skirmishes among the brothers on the antbed tennis court of Cloncurry may not have been as rough as combat at Agincourt, but the transportation and amenities for the English army in France possibly were preferable.

This much is certain: If one of the king's men, the practical Sir John Falstaff, had come along later as a tennis player, between 1955 and 1967, there would have been no doubt in his mind about choosing between professionalism and the other side, pseudo-amateurism. The pros had set up camp as honorable men, supporting themselves on cash received above the proverbial table. You know what Falstaff said about honor: "Can [it] set to a leg? No. . . . What is that word, honor? Air. . . . Who hath it? he that died o' Wednesday." So you can imagine what Sir John would have said as a tennis player: "Can honor keep you in sneakers, clean sheets, comely wenches, and abundant grog?"

While the amateurs were leading the good life and taking their handouts in country clubs that Falstaff would have approved of, the pros were out there in never-never land like never-never-were men.

"Western Queensland," Barry MacKay sounds almost dreamy. "That's where you'll find Cloncurry. Boiling hot, dusty, practically inaccessible." After ranking No. 1 in the United States in 1960, Barry and Butch Buchholz, who was No. 3, made their decision to take the curious semantical fling—to go straight by joining the outlaws and travel the tennis underground with Kramer's troupe.

They were kids, Barry twenty-five and Butch twenty. As grown-ups they've become promoters themselves, operating Grand Prix tourneys whose budgets most likely exceed all the money involved in the yearly flea circuits they followed. Barry runs the Grand Prix stopover in San Francisco, and Butch the Players International at Key Biscayne, Florida.

Out in the cold when they abandoned their protector, the USTA, Barry and Butch have been along for the ride as pro tennis advanced from the ice age to the age of Tiffany's kind of ice. Considering what they endured at the start, you can understand them rolling their eyes whenever one of the entrants in their tournaments grumbles about working conditions.

"But I don't begrudge them," says Butch. "What we've got today is the dream the boys had in the old days. When Barry and I turned pro, we just wanted to make money playing tennis without all the phony expenses routine, and being controlled by the USTA. When I needed money, Bill Talbert, the Davis Cup captain, would slip me five hundred dollars. But I wasn't comfortable with the system. The money wasn't that good or that regular, and although we lived very well Barry and I wanted to get out and earn it on our own.

"We knew we'd be shut out of Wimbledon and Forest Hills, and the other amateur places, but we figured it was time to play against the big boys—Rosewall and Hoad, Gonzalez, Gimeno.

"We didn't realize how hard it was going to be. Those players were tougher than we thought, and it was discouraging to be getting beat, and getting no recognition."

MacKay recounts the night in 1960 they signed away their certified purity. "We were in the kitchen of Butch's house in St. Louis with Jack [Kramer]. It's really a laugh when you think of what the guys are making now.

"Butch decided that because I was the college graduate I'd do the negotiating. We had agreed we'd ask for a sixty-thousand-dollar guarantee, but settle for as low as fifty thousand dollars apiece for three years. But before I can get into my negotiating act"—MacKay grins —"Jack says, 'The offer is forty grand for three years, fellows. Take it or leave it—and here's a check for each of you for twenty-five hundred dollars to bind it.' "

"Twenty-five hundred! Neither of us had ever seen a check that big. Where did we sign? Fast. So much for negotiation."

Whereupon MacKay and Buchholz were off on the road to Cloncurry, and other places most people had never heard of.

"We played a lot of bush towns on that Australian tour," says MacKay, "but I remember Cloncurry because it was the toughest to get to. Hottest, most God-forsaken country I've ever been in. No roads. You just drove cross country. But there'd been some recent rain, and there was a gully we had to get over that was full of water. No bridges. So we found a railroad trestle, got the car onto the ties, straddling the tracks, and crossed."

Buchholz says it was "so boiling hot you had to play at night, and the lighting was awful," in telling of another bug curfew and a novel seating arrangement. "What they did was line up flatbed trailers beside two courts. Some were between the courts, the others on the sides. They put folding chairs on them, and that was the grandstand. We'd play on one court until the bugs got so thick on the lights you couldn't see. Then they'd turn on the other lights, and we'd move to that court.

"Some of the people moved to other flatbeds, and the ones in the middle turned their chairs around. We'd cut up a few hundred bucks a night, and these good country people were happy to see some fine tennis. Then we'd wind up in the ratty pub where we stayed, and sit around drinking with just about everybody who came to the matches until about four A.M."

Blond muscleman Lew Hoad, in his day maybe the best of all, but in 1961 four years past his last Wimbledon triumph, and lame of back, recalls this precinct of his self-exile and the pub. "Ah, yeah, Cloncurry. The whole town turned out to watch us—three hundred people," says the onetime toast of London. "We were so thirsty we could have drunk water, and we went to the hotel, the only barroom in town. It was dusty and dirty. The rooms were hardly ever used. Ah, the food in those country hotels. You couldn't possibly eat it—but you ate it."

His tale evokes one told by another Aussie, grizzled Vic Edward, the original mentor of the aborigine who twice won Wimbledon, Evonne Goolagong. "We were at some hotel in the bush, and you couldn't get near the dunny [outhouse], the flies were so thick. And the publican says, 'No worries, mate, you can use it at lunchtime. All the flies will be in the dining room then.' "

Hoad continues, "The manager met us at the door, and he was just as dirty as his place, wearing an awful-looking undershirt. And he says to us—this is unreal—'You blokes can't go into the dining room without a coat and tie. Rules of the house.'

"I doubt anybody in Cloncurry owns a coat and tie, but he made us dress, and it was about a hundred and fifteen degrees. But the beer was cold. The beer was always cold; only way you could live out there.

"That drive was strange," Hoad acknowledges, "but maybe not so much for us Aussies. The worst drive I had was in the States. It was common to drive all night after playing a match to make the next destination on time. Pancho Segura and I were going from Tampa to Houston, and we had to drive straight through. Segoo tried to duck the driving. He jumped in the backseat, stretched out, and fell asleep. After five or six hours behind the bloody wheel I couldn't see the bloody road. We got to Tallahassee and I made him drive. I passed out in back. After two hours I wake up and ask Segoo where are we. 'Tallahassee,' he says. We're still in bloody Tallahassee because Segoo's lost and can't find his way out. So I have to drive again.''

They were driving in reverse in terms of other sports whose professionals were treated as top of the line. They were fringe characters, gypsies flitting through, putting on an act like palm reading, a fleeting entertainment, then packing their canvas and stealing away. They were more proficient than the amateurs and got less notice for it. It was as though Isaac Stern had to fiddle his one-nighters in a subway station, like a busker, or Dustin Hoffman on tour with *Death of a Salesman* playing a round of storefront theaters.

Like Willy Loman, the memorable salesman who was out there in an inhospitable territory "on a shoeshine and a smile," the pros were selling themselves and a product not many were interested in.

But Willy's story was a tragedy. Theirs wasn't. Despite falling from grace and whatever limelight touched on tennis, don't get the idea these guys were hardship cases. True, sometimes they didn't get paid. There were momentary crises of lost identity, and the inconvenience of locker rooms that, as Mike Davis recalls, "could be a nail in the wall to hang clothes on. We brought hammer and nails ourselves. Showers were somewhere and sometime else."

But the money was quite good when cut up among a small gang, and a great esprit developed. They were earning a living doing something they loved, proud to be crusaders who believed that pro tennis did count, and would be accepted someday if they continued keeping it alive. They felt spiritually and athletically superior to their amateur colleagues, and financially better off than all but a very few of the handout-takers. Maybe they were a touch self-righteous, like all crusaders, in proclaiming that they preferred life underground to payment under the table.

Pancho Gonzalez was the granddaddy, the patriarch, when I came into contact with the pros, having forfeited his chastity late in 1949 by enlisting as an outlaw. He recounts, "Oh, I was out there somewhere in the world, making my thirty or forty grand a year when people were saying, 'Wonder whatever became of poor Pancho?' The spotlight was off. I wasn't getting the publicity of the years I won Forest Hills [1948–49] or my first head-to-head pro tour against Jack Kramer. But I wasn't starving, not by any means."

After retaining his U.S. Nationals championship at Forest Hills and helping keep the Davis Cup out of Australian hands, he signed a pro contract not only to follow the promoter's tortuous routes, but to try to beat the promoter: Kramer.

24

○

Ohio Bear
Tracks

If the Ohio Bear, Barry MacKay, hasn't done it all, he's done most of it, including what he modestly describes as "the world record racket toss in anger."

A lumbering, eager, good-natured teenager with a smile as big as his megatonic serve when I first encountered him at the National Doubles of 1955, he went on to become the No. 1 American five years later, a Davis Cupper, and an anomaly—a Yank winning the Italian title on the inhospitable clay of Foro Italico. One year he took time off from school at Michigan (for whom he won the National Intercollegiate title in 1957) to work as a roustabout for the touring pros. He drove the truck that carried their court from one one-nighter to the next, and helped lay the canvas rug wherever they played. That earned him the privilege of practicing with such virtuosi as Pancho Gonzalez, Lew Hoad, and Pancho Segura, whose select lodge he eventually joined.

The Bear kept smiling through the thin and thin of recognition during his career. He was the best of a not-very-scintillating lot during one of the periodic American depressions, a time of subservience to the Aussies in his amateur days. Then he was one of the spear carriers as a pro. But he had his moments, such as mauling Rod Laver in Boston Garden, spoiling the Rocket's U.S. debut as a pro in January of 1963. MacKay didn't spread the court that night, although Laver, fresh from his first Grand Slam season, may have suspected Bear's rough paw work. But it was the bull gang, the Garden's stagehands, who elected to cover the hockey rink with an uneven array of planking over which they stretched the canvas, rather than using the ice itself as a base, a common enough practice.

Maybe the laborers wanted to make sure that the illustrious rookie, Laver, as yet unfamiliar with life indoors, wouldn't get cold feet. But, squinting in the gloom of the decrepit building, and groping to cope with six-foot, four-inch MacKay's huge serve on a bumpy court, Laver felt chilled throughout, from bunions to brain. He might as well have tried to swat a jackrabbit with a whisk broom. Reviewing his ineffectual performance, attended by many unfilled seats, the well-thrashed Laver began to wonder why he'd traded the perpetual summer of amateurism for the dreariness and disinterest of North American winter on the pro track. Not only had Rod been creamed by Ken Rosewall and Lew Hoad when the 1963 tour commenced in Australia, but now MacKay, whom he'd mastered when both were amateurs, was giving him the business. This was ever the fate of Australian novitiates on the tour, though Laver was too good not to have a grip on the situation by spring.

That drug of perennial sunshine was a tough habit to break for anyone who considered turning pro. MacKay's pursuit of heavenly heat took him to Australia frequently, and even to India, not often visited by tennis players, where he had a sweetheart deal. "It was the sort of arrangement where you could put away some money as an amateur," recalls the Bear. "In 1959 Ramanathan Krishnan invited me and Mike Franks to come to India to play a tour against him and Premjit Lall."

Deceptively harmless-looking, Krishnan was possibly the greatest of all Indian players, a Wimbledon semifinalist in 1960. He slithered about like a lazy cobra, seeming half asleep, but his touch, sure and deadly, kept him among the game's elite for years. Krish carried the Indian Davis Cup team on his back. His son, Ramesh Krishnan, currently India's No. 1, though without Dad's somnolent appearance, carries on the family tradition.

"Krish," says MacKay, "paid me two thousand dollars for

a couple of weeks, plus all expenses, and I thought I was rich. Mike Franks got fifty dollars a match, and felt the same. But later a USTA official got wind of it and thought he could get us suspended. He confronts us at Wimbledon, and I'm scared. I figure the jig's up, and don't know what to say.

"So this official says to Krish, 'Mr. Krishnan, your tour was highly irregular, and I'm going to report it all to the Indian Tennis Federation, and request they send a complete report to the USTA.'

"I'm looking worried. But Krish flashes that great grin of his, and responds very courteously:

" 'Sir, I am the Indian Federation.'

"Case closed. Krish is so dignified, and the way he handled it let this official know there was no chance of anybody being suspended."

Good thing, because a suspension from overseas tournaments, as sometimes befell those the Badgers felt were profiting unduly abroad, would have caused the Bear to miss the Italian Championships of 1960. As the Orso Americano—American Bear—he achieved one of the more unlikely victories by a U.S. citizen on alien terrain. Once the tourney was revived after World War II, only one American guy, Budge Patty, had won, in 1954. Strictly an attacker, MacKay was as much at sea in the red dirt as most of his countrymen, yet he beat the two best Italians in succession: Hall of Famer Nicky Pietrangeli and Beppe Merlo. To do that in Rome to two such darlings of an extremely patriotic crowd might have made the Bear worry about his well-being, and certainly should qualify him for at least a citation in the Hall of Fame.

But, after cheering wildly against him for two days, the Romans took this big, smiling guy to their bosoms. His final obstacle was another born to clay, defending champ Luis Ayala, a Chilean, in a battle that resulted in this curious score: 7–5, 7–5, 0–6, 0–6, 6–1. No one before or since in an important championship has been double-bageled in the final, yet managed to win.

"I couldn't quite believe I'd beaten both Pietrangeli, who'd won the Italian twice, and Merlo," says MacKay. "I had no business beating Ayala in the final either because he was a better clay-court player, too. I couldn't trade ground strokes with those guys, so I just played like I was on grass or concrete, a fast court, even if it was slow clay."

Ah, the powers of self-delusion.

"I'm serving-and-volleying, coming in to the net on every-thing, and daring them to pass me. In the final against Luis, somehow I luck out the first two sets, but I'm dead, exhausted. I figure I'll rest the next two sets—6–0, 6–0,—and give it every-thing I've got left in the fifth, which isn't much. But by that time Luis's worn out, too, and when I start trying again he can't recover. After all these years I still don't believe I won in Rome."

His name is in the record books, nevertheless. The Bear stands as an ironic victor in one of the two most consequential clay-court tournaments (the other being the French), even though he could come no closer than the 1959 semis of Wimbledon and the Australian, and the 1958 quarters of the U.S.—grass-court conclaves that he was best suited to win, in style and temperament. Maybe he should have pretended he was on Ital-ian terra firma.

It was a grass-court defeat in Australia that fueled his least proud moment, a record he claims but is not listed with Guin-ness, the hurling of a gut-strung caber. "Losing in the South Australian to Bob Mark really peeved me," remembers the Bear. "This is at the Memorial Drive Courts in Adelaide, and I'm so mad I try to pitch that fourteen-and-a-half-ounce piece of wood, a Jack Kramer Model, over Lake Torrens, which is just outside the stadium. The racket sails over the fence, out of the grounds, and splashes in the water. I wish I'd had a tape measure. I'll bet it went over sixty yards."

Sixty yards, Bear?

"Well," he smiles, "I was really fired up, and there was a hell of a wind behind me."

25

○

Pros'
Face-Saver

Am I being overly romantic in describing Julie Hickey as the Helen of Troy of tennis?

According to old gossip, the Grecian princess, Helen, had a face so beautiful that it launched a thousand ships. That is, her comeliness inspired a Trojan stud named Paris to whisk her home for his private delectation. His mischief filled fifty-score sailboats with Greeks intent on retrieving her.

The frowning teenage countenance of Julie of Longwood in 1963 provoked nothing so warlike. But her words—"Where's Rod Laver?"—did, indirectly, launch innumerable professional tennis careers. While her utterance ranks neither with "Damn the torpedoes—full speed ahead!" or "Nice guys finish last," thirteen-year-old Julie Hickey wasn't an Admiral Farragut, a Leo Durocher, or a leader of any kind when she was smitten by the man with the gargantuan left arm, Rod Laver.

Julie, who has metamorphosed as a Boston attorney, was, in 1962, a schoolgirl out of neighboring Newton whose father had taken her to the National Doubles at Longwood. As the premier amateur of the year, Laver was brushing up his grass-court game by playing doubles alongside Australian compatriot

Fred Stolle before journeying to Forest Hills to win the National Singles and complete his first Grand Slam.

Julie loved watching Laver play. Who didn't? Freckled, crooked-beaked, and red of hair and face, he whipped the ball with carefree abandon, darted here and swooped there—a reincarnation of Stravinsky's balletic *Firebird*. When he and Stolle lost in the quarter-finals, Julie looked forward to the following summer and seeing him play again. But Laver wasn't at Longwood in 1963 when she returned to the National Doubles.

"Where's Rod Laver?" she asked her dad.

"Oh, he can't play here anymore. He's a pro," was the explanation.

"Huh!" Julie grimaced. "Can't play here? That's dumb. Doesn't everybody want to see him? He's probably better this year."

It was very dumb. Any kid could grasp a fact that eluded the officially certified Badgerly brains of tennis for decades. Her dad, Ed Hickey, public relations chief for the New England Merchants National Bank of Boston, thought it idiotic, too: Laver removed from the mainstream as he was approaching his prime.

Hickey's game was golf. But he was a sports nut, vaguely aware of the pro tour and its one-night stands. One of them, the troupe's annual appearance at a North End dump called Boston Garden, overflowed with unused seats and a hazy atmosphere more conducive to brawls between hockey players and prizefighters. Outlining this to Julie, her father said maybe they could go to the Garden if the tour came to town during the winter.

"But why can't I see him here at Longwood in a tournament?" flaxen-haired Julie persisted.

As he kept trying to explain the absurdities of a bankrupt system, the segregation of so-called amateurs and outright pros, Ed Hickey began to wonder, Why not here?

Uninterested in the possibilities, complexities—and improbability—of an open tennis system comparable to the golf tour, he asked himself, Wouldn't a straight pro tournament succeed in Boston? Wasn't there an audience? Weren't there people like me and Julie who would pay to watch Laver again on Longwood grass, plus Ken Rosewall, Pancho Gonzalez, Lew Hoad, and others they'd admired as amateurs?

Ed Hickey began thinking about it.

———————

A couple of months into cogitation, piqued by his daughter's loss of Rod Laver, Hickey phoned me and asked permission to buy my lunch. Sportswriters seldom deny permission. We sat down in the Parker House grille, and probably got scrod. Happens all the time in Boston. I knew Hickey only by his locally televised appearances, committing commercials for his bank: Soft-sells by a gray-haired, tweedy man with pipe. He was direct: What were the chances of holding a pro tournament at Longwood?

So was I: None, I said. It had been tried eighteen years before, 1946, and flopped. Longwood had enough problems running its old standby, the National Doubles, making a slight profit only because members handled so much of the work as volunteers.

As a Longwood member, I knew the board of governors would be overwhelmingly uninterested in taking on the responsibilities of yet another tournament, one of questionable appeal.

Case closed? Not quite. Suppose, Hickey mused, he had a sponsor? Like his bank?

Oh, really? Now I was interested for the first time. This was dessert, talk of a responsible sponsor who might underwrite and test my belief—and hope—that a pro tourney in a tennis setting, featuring the best players, could succeed. I was a realist, reinforced in my caution by the Boss. Never for a moment did I imagine pro tennis would grab the public as the Red Sox, Patriots, Celtics, and Bruins had.

But, as a certifiable/committable tennis degenerate, I did fervently believe the upper-level game, amateur or pro, was much better entertainment than the sporting public and press recognized. Tennis languished in the United States largely because of its prevailing reputation as a wimp sport, the stuffiness and reactionary nature of the establishment—the Badgers—and a split personality, the self-defeating separation of amateurs and pros.

I was convinced that most people who were exposed to the best players would be stimulated. Many would become converts, and a few even degenerates. The game had a magic, a beauty, a vigor and excitement that was too often hidden behind Victorian façades and proprietary customs so often found in the small, rich, and exclusive clubs that were the backbone of the game in America.

"I don't feel comfortable playing in private clubs," the best player in her world, Billie Jean King, would frequently say.

Imagine Ted Williams saying he never felt he belonged at Fenway Park?

Now here was this fellow, Hickey, a stranger, talking about staging a pro tournament in my town. Frankly, I wanted to help, but without becoming a cheerleader. The sponsorship, I told Hickey, would not only have to include prize money but indemnify Longwood against any possible loss. The club wasn't about to climb out on the point in the trembling cause of pro tennis. Also, it would have to be a genuine tournament, not a weekend exhibition with four or six players.

That was my own condition for writing about it in the *Globe*, and Hickey agreed. He was interested only in the real thing, too.

Hickey thought the proper financing could be arranged. But even though we parted like a couple of kids who'd shared forbidden fruit, I had my doubts about the project going any further. Were there even enough available bodies—eight, at minimum—to flesh out a tourney. Or was pro tennis too far gone to be resurrected? How would Longwood officials react? Was Hickey dreaming on the sly, or could he actually convince his superiors to come up with the cash?

If the bank was serious, my mission was to contact John Bottomley, the Longwood president, and Jack Kramer, the last-known promoter of pro tennis, a grave robber capable of supplying a cast, if anyone was. Bottomley, a hardheaded Boston insurance executive, figured to be the tougher sell, but he had vision. He liked the sound of New England Merchants Bank, and their product.

Jack Kramer had become very wealthy, parlaying the money he'd earned as king of the tour and then as its promoter. But he remained a purist—perhaps a naïf?—like some of us whose principal interest was the game itself, our own personal siren. We believed that pro tennis just needed a few breaks, and that if only the elusive dream of open tennis could be realized it would mean a bonanza in public interest, a broadening in following and participation.

As I talked to him in 1964, he was gloomy about tennis as a whole, feeling it was at a standstill. The amateur game, too, seemed to be receding. Tennis in the United States was televised but once a year, a few (unsponsored) hours during the Nationals at Forest Hills. There was no push among amateur officials for the obvious need—open tennis—and Kramer was weary of arguing an old, old case.

But it didn't take much to rekindle his interest. Kramer was pleased to learn of a Boston bank's tentative interest in sponsoring a tournament, happy to talk to Ed Hickey about it, and get in touch with the far-flung outlaws, whom he called "the boys."

The upshot was that the boys—principally Hoad, Rosewall, and Laver—said they'd like to come to Boston, but it was a long, expensive trip from Australia for just one tournament. Was there any other work?

Kramer awoke from hibernation, and began to look around. Armed with the word that a reputable Boston financial house was getting involved, he began to scare up prospects all the way from Washington to his hometown, Los Angeles. Meanwhile, Butch Buchholz, a young pro without a tour, and trying to keep himself in such essentials as diapers and mortgage payments, convinced a Volkswagen dealer in his hometown of St. Louis to sponsor a tournament.

Two tournaments would have been enough reason to invest in plane tickets from down under. Kramer found six to go with Boston and St. Louis—and, eureka!—an American circuit such as never had existed sprang forth. Not one-nighters, but a string of actual tournaments. True, total prize money was $84,000, which wouldn't pay John McEnroe's room and board for a season on the road.

It was small stuff, but maybe the farm was saved.

Banks are now among the mainstays of the game, backing tournaments across the world. Boston's New England Merchants was the first, a partner in an unlikely alliance of a sobersided institution and the oldest of the old-line tennis clubs. As copromoters, they seemed as giddy as itchy spinsters, climbing into bed with a sport lacking credit, credibility, or crowds of loyalists. Longwood, devoted to the National Doubles since 1917, was putting out the welcome mat for desperados.

Some of his colleagues in the Boston financial community thought Dick Chapman, president of the Merchants, was ready for the men with the nets—not tennis nets—when he reached under the mattress for $10,000 in prize money plus required promotional expenses and indemnification against the inevitable loss, an outlay of about $40,000. But others knew that despite a benign, bow-tied look, Chapman was a shrewd operator. Perhaps because Chapman came from Nebraska, he had pioneering spirit. But he may have been prescient when he declared that pro tennis had a future.

Where he got that, other than from his PR man, Hickey, I'll never know.

"To us," says Laver, who won the tournament, and $2,200, "ten thousand dollars seemed like a million. It encouraged us to see that a respectable bank had faith in us." But any top-flight pro asked to play a $10,000 tourney today would wail that his or her human rights were being threatened.

Nevertheless, it was the grandest ten grand in the history of tennis. That sum was the start of making the pro game a strong enough entity to enforce a growing demand for open tennis. If pro tennis, death-rattling in 1963, had expired, what impetus or incentive would there have been to permit the merger of pros and amateurs into open tennis? The fraudulent amateur system might well have continued, as in most Olympic sports, maintaining position as the preeminent phase of the game.

Rebirth was in the air—at least the air I breathed—as the summer of '64 approached. But what would the tournament be called? Something definitely commercialized like the Merchants Pro Classic?

But, I suggested, if the bank, a sponsor with less vanity and schlock-instinct than most, was looking for status, wouldn't the U.S. Pro Grass Court Championships sound nifty? You could free-form because there was no other national championship in the professional firmament. The same title had been used by a promoter the year before, 1963, at Forest Hills, but the tournament had been such a financial bust that it was done for.

The title was free for the taking; I urged Hickey, and he took. Presently the "grass court" part vanished, along with the grass footing itself. So did the National Doubles, and Longwood's surviving showpiece became what it is today, the just-plain U.S. Pro Championships, on clay. It is a continuation of the longest running professional championship, begun on a vacant lot in Manhattan in 1927.

In a way, the dawn of open tennis diminished the tourney's

significance. Once the gem of the pro circuit, the premier championship to which all the leading pros felt allegiance because Longwood had taken á stand for them, it became just another stopover on the unending Grand Prix calendar.

locked at 40–40 (three points each). Win the next point and you have advantage. And the next, you have the game, belonging to whoever wins two points in succession from deuce. The winner is required to be at least two points ahead. But if your foe wins your ad point, or you his, back you go to deuce.

Deuce, ad, deuce, ad . . . this seesawing symphony has limitless movements, and, according to Van Alen, limitless boredom as well. Same as a deuce set, a situation reached at five games each. After that, you can win only by being two games ahead. A set, minimally six games, thus has—or had, until Van Alen's tiebreaker—no maximum. Five games all . . . six games all . . . up and up . . . twenty games all. Thirty-four games all? These things could bloat into monstrosities resembling that produced by two guys named Brown during an amateur tourney in Kansas City in 1968: seventy games! After too many hours, it was finally determined that Australian John Brown had beaten Nebraskan Bill Brown, 36–34, 6–1. By that time nobody cared. Both Browns were black and blue, like the umpire's vocal cords. In fact, the umpire walked out on deuce-happy Brown and Brown somewhere in the tedious piece, and a replacement had to be found.

Strangely, nobody but Van Alen seemed disturbed by scores that looked like the budget deficit, for instance 36–34, 2–6, 4–6, 6–4, 19–17. That's what it took for Ted Schroeder and Bob Falkenburg to subdue Pancho Gonzalez and Hugh Stewart in the Southern California Championships final of 1949. Such long day's journey's into nightmare were merely possible results of the deuce-based and hallowed scoring system that had ever been with us. We accepted. Until Jimmy.

"Down with deuce!" became Van Alen's cry, a war whoop that would find fulfillment in the initially weird-looking 7–6 sets, settled by tiebreaker. An outsider, less affluent, couldn't have trod where Jimmy did, on the sanctified scoring principles, nor preached revolt against them. But the Badgers had to listen politely, if halfheartedly and scornfully, because he was one of them, superintendent of the amateur event in the cradle of American tournament tennis, the Casino at Newport.

That tournament, called the Men's Invitational, was a direct descendant of the seminal Nationals, staged at the one-year-old Casino in 1881. When the Championships (for men only) outgrew the exclusive playpen that rose from the drawing board of Stanford White, and transferred to New York in 1915, the Invitational Tournament was established, keeping Newport a respected dateline on the summertime grass-court circuit. Van Alen, who spent his boyhood summers on those well-groomed courts, and played in the tournament as a young man, presently became the house poobah, somewhat curt and high-handed with those not of his ilk—a majority of the players. They were treated like the help, somewhere between folks who bought general admission tickets and servants.

He seemed an archetypical Badger when I first encountered him in 1955, a remnant from *Brideshead Revisited,* and a bit rude to a new face from the *Boston Herald*—me. Still, I became very fond of him, and enjoyed his tilting against the freeze-dried brains in charge of the game, keepers of status quo. They regarded the crusading Jimmy as somewhat deranged but not certifiably dangerous—although a man who would change the scoring might be capable of profaning the Sabbath by not charging admission that day. They thought he would run out of breath and ideas, and go away. But Jimmy had remarkable staying power.

Inflation has always made his type nervous, and it was an inflationary score of the pre–tiebreaker era, 1954—Hamilton Richardson's 6–3, 9–7, 12–14, 6–8, 10–8, siege over Straight Clark—that drove Jimmy round the bend from Badgerism to bolshevism. He dates his bomb-throwing activities from that match, perpetrated before his very eyes at his shrine, the Casino, in the final round of the Invitational tourney. Immediately infamous in Van Alen's book were the perpetrators, Richardson and Clark, even though decent, well-bred college men of a sort who had dominated in the Nationals' earliest days of Newport residency.

After he cooled off from the eighty-three-game verdict, Jimmy realized that those two were inspirations rather than culprits, and the scoring rules were at fault. "Nice fellows, Richardson and Clark," Van Alen says, "but they spoiled our tournament that year. The match everybody wanted to see was the doubles final with the Australians [Ken Rosewall and Lew Hoad against Neale Fraser and Rex Hartwig]. But Richardson and Clark tied up our grandstand court for four hours, almost till dark, and we had to get the doubles final started on an outside court. People who wanted to watch it had to stand.

"It struck me then that there had to be a better, more exciting way to control the length of matches without those damnable deuce sets. Matches like that are Chinese water torture for players, court officials, and fans alike."

Tortured Jimmy, who hates deuce worse than income tax or welfare, went to work with his pal Winslow ("Mike") Blanchard, longtime referee and umpire. Their stated humanitarian objective was to eliminate the deuce principle altogether, so that you no longer had to be at least two points ahead to win a game, or two games ahead to win a set. "With deuce in there, matches are theoretically interminable," Van Alen said correctly, asserting that "you ought to be able to schedule tennis matches at specific times like any other sport."

After much experimentation, elation, and disappointment, he and Blanchard delivered VASSS: Van Alen Simplified Scoring System. Somewhere during a decade of puttering, amending, altering, and propagandizing, "Simplified" was changed to "Streamlined." I think. Jimmy's formula encompassed so much variety, and underwent such frequent updates—all the while he was bombarding the tennis community with rave notices on its glories—that you could say it was VASSSly amusing and refreshing, and not be wrong.

Of all the far-left provisions of VASSS, most of them intriguing and several worthwhile—but still too radical for the established order—two have made their mark, most stunningly the tiebreaker. Also no-ad scoring. No-ad, used in American collegiate tennis, is a schedule-maker's salvation. Deuce has been extirpated altogether. Each game is a maximum of seven points: first to four points wins. Each set is won by the now accepted maximum of seven games, with a tiebreaker played at 6–6.

Were that dastardly 1954 Newport final to be reframed in a no-ad, tiebreaker format, Richardson and Clark's eighty-three games would be trimmed to sixty-one (6–3, 7–6, 6–7, 6–7, 7–6), their playing time to not much over two hours. But those two birds of a filibustering feather served their purpose, just as the robins did for the Wright brothers.

They sent Jimmy Van Alen to the mountaintop, and when he descended, a WASPish Moses in Ben Franklin glasses, he declared, "Thou shalt not worship the false god of deuce, but honor the tiebreaker." It was the genesis of the most far-reaching change in the game since the emergence of the mother tournament, Wimbledon, in 1877.

27

○

Sudden
Death

They were squealing soon after they arrived for "The Guinea Pig Derby," as one of them, Mike Davies, called it.

"How did I ever let myself get talked into this?" wailed Pancho Gonzalez, an on-court soliloquy that brought sympathetic snickers from the customers, most of whom were bewildered, too. Unlike Pancho, however, they were enjoying their introduction to a suddenly surreal corner of the tennis world created by the dallying of Jimmy Van Alen, a veritable Dali in putting a new coat of paint on an old pastime.

This was the Casino at Newport in July 1965, an open-air laboratory for the game's mad scientist, his VASSS-inating experiment bought and paid for by himself. The legend of the signboard at the Casino's entrance told the scandalous story in one line:

$10,000 PROFESSIONAL TOURNAMENT

How low could Jimmy slip in trying to foment interest in his scurrilous VASSS? To the nether region of the game, that's where, to enlist the pros as his partners in the crime of blasphemy in the termite-ridden temple.

As the oldest tennis corral in the world, the Casino had been a pedigreed bastion of the amateur game since the very beginnings. It was filled with ghosts of Ivy-stained types from distinguished family trees who had won the National Championship within these wooden-shingled ramparts. Their line started with Saint Richard—Harvardian Dick Sears—in 1881. Professionals had never gamboled on the lawns where virtually every great male champion—some before their descent to professionalism—has appeared.

"A lot of the people," said Butch Buchholz, "thought the grass would turn brown when we pros set foot on it. I sure never thought I'd play here again."

Smudged courts would have been the least of the Casino's problems. With holes in her head, shivering timbers and creaking foundation, the venerable Sporting Lady of Bellevue Avenue was a broken-down beauty. Saggy of balcony, makeup peeling, suffering from acute pains in the sides, she was just about a fallen lady, fifteen years short of her one hundredth birthday.

Her condition resembled that of her latest lover, pro tennis. But, as it happened, both were on the way back, even though it would be a while before it was apparent. A concerted financial effort on behalf of the International Tennis Hall of Fame, located since its 1954 inception at the Casino, has rehabilitated the joint. The Sporting Lady, very proud and elegant even in her seediness, is today a shored-up born-again monument to the Way It Was, a regular, prosperous stopover on both the men's and women's pro tours as the last of the puritans. These are the only surviving grass-court tourneys in America.

Driving to Boston for the first time, from Ohio in 1954, I detoured specifically to see the Casino, although I could stay only minutes. It was dusk. As I peered, uninvited, from the entryway—the public wasn't welcome then, except during tournaments—I felt I'd stumbled into an F. Scott Fitzgeraldian idyll. Cavorting through the gloaming, men and women in white on the darkening green seemed participants in the midsummer evening's dream. I went away well satisfied with that tableau, hoping to return.

It was into this beatified mausoleum, overriding some con-

stituent objections, that Jimmy Van Alen brought the pros in
1965, his experimental swine before whom he would cast the
pearls of his tennis research—plus ten thousand bucks. He had
been encouraged by the resurrection of the U.S. Pro at Longwood, ninety miles away, the previous summer. Perhaps it was
a historic occasion in a historic place, but to the pragmatic pros,
readmission to an old haunt and a chance to try a VASSSly new
game were secondary to a purse whose amount was, at that
time, head-turning. It was only change from Jimmy's cookie
jar, but enough so that they'd barbecue any sacred cow to
get it.

That was the attitude Van Alen was looking for, and after
years of fruitless importuning he found he had to buy his own
tournament to get the guys to play it his way. The squealing
intimated that the piggies weren't happy to do Jimmy's kinky
bidding. But they had no choice.

But for Van Alen, the Casino would have become high-class
kindling, transformed long before into an American architec-
tural specialty called a parking lot. To him it is a plaything as
treasured as any teddy bear. "I grew up here during a wonderful
era before World War I," he recalls, a James Mason timbre in a
voice belonging to a Cambridge man.

It was a time for the summer people such as the Van Alens
and Vanderbilts and their "cottages," dwellings that make Loire
Valley châteaux seem dowdy. The question wasn't whether you
had servants, but did you employ enough of them to form a
bucket brigade to the vintner's if the champagne ran dry? "You
can't imagine the delightful times I've had in this place," sighs
Jimmy, "the games, the friends, playing and watching wonderful matches, the dances in the horseshoe piazza. . . ."

As interest in the doddering Sporting Lady ebbed, Jimmy
remained faithful. With the help of rich friends, he kept her
body and soul barely together. A scarlet reminder of her mortality was all too close, the supermarket next door on a Casino
parcel that had been sold off to forestall financial ruin. He also
oversaw the amateur tournament, and, at the suggestion of his
wife, Candy, convinced the USTA that it was time for a Hall
of Fame. Set up as the National Tennis Hall of Fame, in 1954,
and limited to American immortals, it occupied a few upstairs
rooms of the Casino, a not very striking project that received
little attention. Twenty years later, with interest and the base

broadened, it became the International Hall of Fame, unlimited in candidates for sporting sainthood.

Though nobody was sure at the time, Jimmy Van Alen's personalized and phantasmagorical tournament at Newport in 1965 turned out to be a giant step for tenniskind.

His ten guinea pigs—Rod Laver, Ken Rosewall, Pancho Gonzalez, Andres Gimeno, Barry MacKay, Pancho Segura, Mike Davies, Luis Ayala, Mel Anderson, Butch Buchholz—felt as though they were marching to the rear, to their pasts, when they crossed the Casino's timeless threshold once again. Banishment was rescinded. But quickly enough they realized they were being projected into a future, a region of Van Alen's whimsical mindscape, and not altogether to their liking or understanding.

But they were hired hands, with no voice in the matter. "Sounds half-VASSS to me," giggled the irreverent elder, forty-six-year-old Pancho Segura. "But Señor VASSS-oline is in charge of the dollars, so we play it his way."

Jimmy needed meaningful ingredients for his test tube, so the pros were it. His way was as different from any previous tennis tournament as dollars from blue ribbons, and never was a more entertaining tournament played.

It started with a usual focal point, the scoreboard. Remarkably enough, it wasn't until Jimmy that any tournament in the United States was monitored by an electric scoreboard. Manual labor was the time-honored method of informing customers, even at Forest Hills, where electricity would be introduced three years later, 1968. Jimmy's original remote-controlled board registered not only the score, but numbers even more meaningful: up-to-the-second prize money.

They were now pieceworkers, he informed the boys, their earnings determined according to how many points they won— at five bucks a point. That's how the $10,000 purse would be doled out, thus "every point has definite worth, and each is equally important."

Old line Newporters were taken aback by the financial information suddenly on view, the sort of thing they expected from the *Wall Street Journal*, not their tennis tournament. Were they at the racetrack? Did Jimmy's tote board actually blink this message:

DAVIES 30   ROSEWALL 30
$150 $150

Indeed it did, amusingly more crass than even today's scoreboard messages. Freed of the constraints of the USTA and convention, Van Alen was improvising dazzlingly in a jam session of his own invention and comprehension.

Not everything was new. But the used ideas were refurbished with a VASSSly fresh touch, having been Jimmied with. Round-robins had been played before, but Jimmy borrowed medal play from golf for the two five-man groups. Single-point scoring, pirated from Ping-Pong, was incorporated. First to 31 points won the match, but each point won was rewarded not only financially but counted in a man's chances of "making the cut," as in golf, after four rounds. Thereby the top scorers in each group became the final four, reaching a round-robin among themselves. A man taking all four of his group matches would clearly survive to the last day with a perfect medal score, 124 points.

But no one did. The shorter matches gave "us donkeys a better chance," Segura declared on behalf of the usual first-round losers. "And we get to play four rounds, four different guys, instead of usually one," he added complimentarily. Rosewall lost to Davies, Laver to MacKay, and Gonzalez was edged out of the final four by Anderson. It was exciting.

Meanwhile the board was clicking off those five-spots with every point, and Abraham Lincoln's head became a bouncing ball. It was like playing with five-dollar bills wadded up into spheres. After beating Rosewall, 31–30, Mike Davies exulted in his $155 windfall, an extremely decent afternoon's work in 1965. He and Kenny, unaware of their historic moment, had also taken part in the first tiebreaker.

At 30-points-all, they were instructed and guided by the umpire through the unknown, the playing of an "added game," as the historic overtime passage was known. Known, at that, only to a few of the inner circle, Van Alen, his lab assistant, Mike Blanchard, and one or two others. Davies, who would one day, as executive director of World Championship Tennis, devise another form of tiebreaker, won the granddaddy of them all, 5 points to 3, and thus the match.

Was nothing safe from Van Alen? Robbing the venerable

grass blades of their nightly rest, he installed portable floodlights, extending tournament hours beyond dusk. Lighted outdoor courts had been around for years, mostly at public parks.
No one had lit up a grass-court tourney until promoter-player
Bobby Riggs turned the switch at Forest Hills for the U.S.
Pro in 1951, which was a business failure nevertheless. Jimmy
went blithely along with electrification, the first to do so prof-
itably.

Then there was the new and controversial line that stuck
in the pros' craws. Three feet behind the baseline was the Van
Alen belt to constrain the serve-and-volley belters—a limed
stripe. "You must serve behind that line as though it were the
baseline," he told the astounded guinea pigs.

Simple marks on the grass at either end of the court, but
they enhanced those VASSS tournaments tremendously, and
would have the electrifying effect of the Berlin Wall if adopted
by Wimbledon or any other fast-court tournament. Forcing the
net rushers to travel a yard farther, those stripes proved just
enough of an impediment to the serve-and-volleyers, provoking
more ground stroking, longer rallies, better points.

"You serve one bloody way all your life, and Jimmy says
you have to serve another way," Rod Laver shook his head. But
he got used to it. Despite all the razzle dazzle of VASSScapades,
the perilous nocturnal skidding on dewy and mist-draped grass,
Laver demonstrated his primacy by winning the tournament
and, at five bucks a point, $1,774.

Pancho Gonzalez was not, like some of the ecstatic among
us, saying that he had seen the future and it worked. While the
old Harvard Bolshevik John Reed may have been whirling happily like an eggbeater in his Kremlin sarcophagus, applauding
Van Alen, the sullen Pancho was spinning in fury.

Boiling over, he rebelled against the resident Bolshevik. As
a man who had profited from one of the more glorious and destructive serves, Gonzalez did not care for its artificial dimi-
nution by the decree insisting that he propel it from the Van
Alen line. Nor was he thrilled by night games in darkest Newport, where the sod was treacherous and the floodlights approx-
imated the wattage of birthday candles.

Colleagues were reminded of the night their tour paused at
Salisbury in a country now called Zimbabwe. Pancho and his
opponent had completed their warmup and were introduced to

the assemblage by the umpire. "Mr. Gonzalez will serve. Ready? Play."

Gonzalez didn't move. "We're ready. Please play, Mr. Gonzalez."

"Not until somebody turns on the damn lights."

"They are on. Please play."

"Now," snarled the Old Wolf, "I know what they mean by darkest Africa."

Early in the Newport going, Gonzalez blew up during a match. His language, though rough, never approached the vileness level of Nastase, Connors, or McEnroe. But it scalded Van Alen in his temple. Trotting onto the greensward, Jimmy confronted and scolded Pancho. Looking up at the volcano, elderly, round Jimmy shook his finger, "You'll have to behave yourself here."

Startled at this effrontery, Pancho growled, "If you don't like it I'll leave."

"Then leave, if you can't behave like a gentleman!" Jimmy stood his ground as few umpires have done against Gonzalez, or McEnroe for that matter.

Momentarily subdued, Gonzalez continued playing. But he said he would leave when the match was over, annoyed as he was by the rules and the Van Alens.

As Jimmy was rebuking Pancho, his wife, Candy Van Alen, in the family box, remarked to friends, "What a terrible man that Gonzalez is! Can you imagine how horrible it would be living with him?"

That year's Mrs. Gonzalez, seated nearby, overheard, and reported to Pancho. "That's it for this dump," the Old Wolf fumed in the dressing room. "Do you know what that Van Alen bitch said about me?" he turned to his old comrade, Segura. "She said I must be horrible to live with."

Segura, the one person who could approach Gonzalez during an eruption, grinned. "She doesn't know the half of it, does she, buddy?"

Gonzalez did not quit the tournament. He was a professional as he had been since the beginning, his rookie tour against the champ, Jack Kramer, during the winter of 1949–50. Pancho might blow up, but he wouldn't give up. His behavior could be atrocious, but he fulfilled his commitments professionally. All those pros did.

As proud as Mussolini making Italy's trains run on time, Jimmy crowed about the first tennis tournament ever to stick to a timetable. The matches never lasted much longer than a half-hour, and the flow of high-grade players into the main enclosure was constant, adhering to the schedule.

To let the uninitiated know that a match had ended, Van Alen himself stood beside the court like a town crier and rang a handbell. "Jimmy ought to bring in the Liberty Bell for that job," said Mike Davies. "They go together—they're both cracked."

Lights flashed, bells rang, the purse jingled at five bucks a point. But Jimmy did not yet wave the red flag of tennis bolshevism. Such joyous flapping of scarlet banners—announcing the commencement of a tiebreaker—would come later, most noticeably at Forest Hills during the five-year U.S. Open sway (1970–74) of his purest strain of breaker: Sudden Death.

Particularly dramatic was the gigantic flag unfurled in the stadium whenever a set reached the six-games-all deadlock. Small red pennants signaled similar crises on the outer courts. "It's eerie what the tiebreakers do," said Arthur Ashe. "Those flags are out and the crowd is absolutely silent." Like most of the players introduced in 1970 to the new, abrupt shortcut, Ashe was no fan. It may have been "a definite cutoff, or finish line," as applauded by tourney director Bill Talbert, largely responsible for the breaker's adoption, but Pancho Gonzalez said, "I feel like I'm getting a heart attack playing the tiebreaker." Sadly, the flag-waving did not continue at Flushing Meadows.

"Extraordinarily nerve-racking," said Cliff Drysdale, who was caught up in the first Sudden Death situation to be televised, at the U.S. Pro in 1970. In a second-rounder, he and Ken Rosewall reached six-games-all in the second set, then 4-points-all in the breaker. Since Drysdale had won the first set, this was simultaneous match point for him and set point for Rosewall. "Never been in anything like that before," said Rosewall, who lost the point and the match.

But Rosewall had felt like that before, and would again. As one of Van Alen's lab volunteers, he not only had lost the first recorded breaker, to Mike Davies at Newport '65, but was involved in the hilarious and perplexing tiebreaker windup of the tourney the following year.

Tied for the lead in total points at the completion of the tournament, Rosewall and Mal Anderson wondered, "What do we do now?"

Van Alen answered by leaving his canopied courtside preserve and taking the microphone: "Mr. Rosewall and Mr. Anderson will now play a tiebreaker for the championship." The overtime, called "extra game" the year before, was now called a "tiebreaker."

Jimmy superintended as they played the flawed "best-of-8-points" version. Of course Kenny and Mal got to 4-points-all.

"What do we do now, Mr. Van Alen?" the crowd guffawed, as confused as the two Aussies.

"Simple, gentlemen. You play another tiebreaker."

Play it again, same. However, as they tried once more, and Rosewall won, 5–3, Jimmy recognized the weakness. He and Mike Blanchard cogitated some more and conceived "Sudden Death," the best-of-9 points ulcer-maker.

Of course, the nerve-racking aspect was a collateral attraction to Talbert and other promoters. Drysdale was among the majority at Boston who signed a petition urging Talbert to drop his plan to install the breaker the following week at Forest Hills.

Talbert sagely answered the petition: "Players don't buy tickets."

But one of them, the best of the time, Rod Laver, did have some influence earlier in the year at the Philadelphia Indoor (since 1972, the U.S. Pro Indoor). The tournament's efficient founding father and mother, the demon husband-wife promotional team of Ed and Marilyn Fernberger, were eager to be the first to present the tiebreaker beyond Van Alen's Newport preserve. Buckling under Van Alen's assault—as unending as a deuce set—and logic that was becoming obvious, even to the Badgers, the USTA had given approval for optional use of the breaker in sanctioned tournaments.

But this Sudden Death of Jimmy's seemed suddener than a thunderbolt to the groaningly cautious pros, who'd grown up believing you couldn't lose if you stayed within one point. A game just couldn't be lost by a margin of fewer than two points, nor a set by fewer than two games. That was gospel.

Laver, who was to win the tournament, could see that the Fernbergers were unyielding in their determination to take in the bastardly tiebreaker that had given him jitters at Newport.

The Rocket, a quiet man, was no troublemaker. Only months before he had completed his second Grand Slam, and was a man whose few complaints were listened to. "We ought to be able to have a tiebreaker where you have to be two points ahead and win," Laver raised his objections to Sudden Death. "And five points to win is too sudden."

At the Spectrum was hatched Laver's variation on a theme by Van Alen, the impetus for the tiebreaker that has been practically universal since 1975.

A committee, including Laver, tacked together a Philadelphia Version. To win you had to get to seven points, but with two to spare, and serve alternated on every point. Van Alen howled, long-distance. He had campaigned so relentlessly to get his baby accepted, and put on display in just such a setting, a major arena, and now the infant was in the hands of plastic surgeons. In the women's final, Margaret Court closed out Billie Jean King in one of those jerrybuilt tiebreakers, 12–10.

That wasn't a sudden enough expiration, complained Van Alen. "Lingering Death, that's what it is," he groused, relishing what the pros dreaded: the possibility of a simultaneous set or match point at 4–4 in the breaker: Sudden Death!

If Jimmy was disappointed in the Philadelphia Indoor, he relished happenings in the same town later that year in July, at the Pennsylvania Grass tourney. Tom Gorman beat Haroon Rahim in the ultimate sudden death encounter, 6–7 (3–5), 7–6 (5–1), 7–6 (5–4). Surviving the last point, the both-ways match point, in the closest of all matches, Gorman was shaken. "This destroyed the precept of tennis that has governed my life—if you don't lose your serve, you can't lose. Not anymore."

Three months later, Cliff Richey made a diving save of the ninth point of a fifth-set tiebreaker at the Pacific Coast championships to beat Stan Smith for that title by one point. Never had a single point meant so much, not only a championship but the No. 1 U.S. ranking for the year. It went to Richey over Smith on the strength of that last point in the last tournament of the 1970 ranking period.

But Lingering Death is the kind of mortality and mentality we have today, the so-called 12-point breaker, a misnomer because, obviously, it can stretch well beyond a dozen points. As far as 50, the last time I looked. Four lingerers (malingerers, in the Van Alen view), were entwined in a 26–24 breaker at Wimbledon, won by Jan Gunnarson and Michiel Schapers over John Frawley and Victor Pecci in 1985.

Laver's improvisation was presently spruced up in 1971 to become the official ITF version, but for five years Van Alen had his Sudden Deathly way in the United States. Finally, in 1975, the USTA caved in to the ITF.

Ironically, Laver was the victim of his variation in the biggest money match of his career, and the tightest finish yet of a significant tourney, a two-point loss to perennial thorn, Rosewall.

That was the 1972 WCT final in Dallas, which may have been the best match ever played over five sets, and it entranced the American public as no tennis encounter had up to that time. Jim Simpson and I voiced it for NBC at Moody Coliseum, and as the match stretched on and on, and the two diminutive giants of stroke-making got better and better, we worried that the network wouldn't carry it to completion. The sacred six o'clock news was approaching, and Rod and Kenny crossed the three-hour mark gloriously, with no end in sight.

Fortunately, the unprecedented commercial decision was made, higher up, to forget the world and go with Laver and Rosewall to the conclusion. Laver rebounded from 1–3 in the fourth set, forced a tiebreaker, and won it to square the match. They were in the fifth-set tiebreaker at 3½ hours, having packed more brilliance into that space than the longer-dragging matches of the present, and Laver had edged into winning position: 5–3. He would not win another point, which seems unbelievable when you consider that two of them were on his own serve.

But Rosewall, the creator of elegant backhands, was about to unleash three of magnum opus quality. The first got him to 4–5, and then it was Laver's serve. Rod delivered two hooks that could have been knockout punches—but Kenny sent them back as crackling, disarming winners while the building shivered and Laver gaped in disbelief. Simpson and I were shocked into unaccustomed silence.

Now it was the exhausted Rosewall's serve at 6–5. It was clear he had nothing left as he pooped the ball over. However, Laver was so startled by the flutterball that he banged it into the net. It was over: 4–6, 6–0, 6–3, 6–7 (3–7), 7–6 (7–5). Had it been sudden death, Laver would have plucked the $50,000 first prize. Instead the unlikely four-point spurt gave it to Rosewall.

But some outposts didn't fall, among them a precinct called the People's Republic of China. As a member of an American tennis delegation to China in 1977, the first contact on court between the countries since Chairman Mao's 1949 takeover, I was pleased and surprised to learn in Shanghai that our hosts, within their closed society, had not only heard of and smuggled in the tiebreaker but maintained revolutionary fervor and retained the Sudden Death model. Chairman Jimmy, a rebel, maybe, but no Maoist by any stretch of any political imagination, grudgingly felt there might be hope for the People's Republic when I related the news.

Mao Tse-tung himself had been a tennis player, according to a biographer, Edgar Snow, who was with him during the self-imposed exile in the north following the Long March. The daily games came to an end in a sudden-death manner when, one night, a goat ate the net.

28

○

Eight Handsome Piggies

The last I heard of Dave Dixon he was selling antiques in New Orleans. Would I buy a used carpet from this man? Better Dixon than Nixon, although I usually associate Dixon with attempts to peddle something new and contrary to the established order. The U.S. Football League, briefly breathing as a competitor to the National Football League, 1983–85, was his scheme.

I also associate David Dixon with Richard Nixon, not only the rhyming surnames, but because both are hustlers, sports nuts, innovators in foreign policy. Both got to the top of chosen heaps in 1968. It took us six years to get rid of Nixon. However, Dixon was gone in weeks.

Considering what he accomplished for pro tennis, and misaccomplished during only days in the game—a flash flood—Dave Dixon, a handsome guy whose toupee didn't restrict his brain waves, should not be forgotten. Probably it isn't kind to Dave to lump him with Nixon. But it should be said for Coach Nixon that during his first term, 1972, two important changes for the United States took place: the rapprochement with China, and the massive switch to yellow balls. In getting it together with the Chinese, mightn't Nixon have masterminded a CIA plot to infiltrate sporting equipment manufacturers, influencing them to deluge America with yellow tennis balls as a sly tribute to Mao Tse-tung?

I wouldn't doubt it, but perhaps I give Nixon too much credit. Yellow balls, easier to see than traditional white, were an idea whose time had come. Some, especially the English, who believe their country to be the wellspring of all tennis blessings, may say I give Dixon too much credit as well. But for him, though, I believe that open tennis would have arrived later, and the prosperity of pro tennis delayed considerably.

Dave didn't look to China for his big score. His foreign coup, as founder and boss of a tennis promotional outfit he called WCT (World Championship Tennis), was the simultaneous corruption/reform—depends on the definer—of two Australians (John Newcombe, Tony Roche), an Englishman (Roger Taylor), a South African (Cliff Drysdale), and a Yugoslav (Nikki Pilic).

His act of pulling that quintet from beneath the amateur table and signing them to professional contracts commencing in 1968 was regarded as corruption by many of the Badgers. Not since the promotional forefather, Cash-and-Carry Pyle in 1926, had an entrepreneurial-minded reformer enabled so many amateurs to go straight at one time by introducing them to honest cash. On the whole, Dixon outdid original promoter, Pyle, by also enlisting the already tarnished Butch Buchholz, Dennis Ralston, and Pierre Barthes. That made eight in the WCT road show, sufficient to conduct an authentic tournament wherever they went.

"Pro tennis doesn't have enough color," pronounced Dixon in 1967 when he was preparing his descent on an unsuspecting game, and an ascent that never came about. He meant ballyhoo and provocative change as much as actual tones and hues, although a tint-up was part of it. First off he baptized his octet the Handsome Eight, announcing instant recognition and stardom for all of them. If not many people were listening, Dave went on undeterred.

Color was very much on his mind that chill January evening in 1968 as Dave feverishly prowled his messy Kansas City hotel room. His wife, Mary, was on her knees, straight pins in her mouth, fiddling with the waistband on Roger Taylor's fire-engine-red tennis shorts. They didn't fit. Mary was making alterations.

Dixon was more upset than Taylor, who seemed resigned

to the madness swirling about him. If Boston '64 had been the rebirth of pro tennis, with the U.S. Pro's arrival at Longwood, Kansas City '68 was the unexpected revitalizing of the patient through a transfusion of all this new blood. Dixon's octuplets. Each of the Handsome Eight was to be clothed in a different shade of a rainbow envisioned by Dixon as they danced to a pot of gold. Dixon just knew a gold strike was waiting for him and these pros he was choreographing.

These were guys who had grown up following the lead that any color was permissible for tennis as long as it was white. They couldn't have been more apprehensive if Dave had asked them to play in fig leaves. But Dave was betting his bankroll on radical change, as well as some loose change his partner, Texas petrocrat Lamar Hunt, may have collected from the Tooth Fairy.

The critical initials here weren't WCT but LH: Lamar Hunt. Hunt would become the muscle, spiritual as well as financial, preventing pro tennis from floundering in the first chaotic days of open tennis, days that Dave Dixon never entered, although he was instrumental in bringing them about.

Why would Dixon choose Kansas City, a place with a minimal tennis background, for the American debut—disastrous debut—of the Handsome Eight and his concept? Dave thought there was a tie-in between Hunt and Kansas City and professionalism because Lamar had transferred his pro football team there from Dallas a few years before, renaming them the Chiefs. But Kansas City was widely uninterested, especially when the ballroom hired for Dixon's coming-out party was a sporting flophouse called the American Royal Arena in the stockyards.

Now, only hours before they were to appear, the main concern was getting the eight dressed in their spangles. "This is going to be sensational . . . Roger, you look wonderful," Dixon burbled as his harried wife continued making adjustments. None of the uniforms created by Sears, Roebuck for the Handsome Eight fit the trim athletes very well, but Mary Dixon was bravely seamstressing right up to post time.

Roger Taylor wasn't convinced it was sensational or that he looked wonderful. The Yorkshireman's dark, brooding face was tinged with embarrassment as a woman he hardly knew fussed with his shorts, trying to adapt to his body an outfit that seemed to him and his colleagues as garish as a New York pimp's. Taylor was a rough-and-ready type, a steel mill worker's son from Sheffield, an unlikely spawning ground for a first-rate tennis player. But he was also the product of one of the most strait-laced societies in sport: British tennis. Take away the security blanket of alabaster playclothes, and Roger felt "tarted up," naked to his enemies.

Sure, a guy might have some red and blue trim along a sweater neckline and, discreetly displayed elsewhere, a tiny green reptile or laurel wreath, emblems of the designer. Other than that, tennis garb was supposed to be riotously pale. It took longer to crack white supremacy in tennis raiment than race relations.

But here was a revolutionary of the palette, ready to let his Technicolor guinea pigs run wild: John Newcombe in rust and green, Dennis Ralston in lime that seemed seasick green, Pierre Barthes in lemon, Cliff Drysdale in a blue plaid. . . .

These piggies were rooting out numerous sacred traditions. Dixon's court was Astroturf, a plastic rug that had gotten much attention as the carpeting of the huge playroom in Houston, the Astrodome. The promoter had found a soul brother in Van Alen, and adopted his VASSS single-point method, with tie-breakers, for WCT events. Dixon stomped on protocol further by taking a microphone and urging the customers to cheer and boo, yell at the players as they would in any other sport. "Tennis is exciting," he told the thousand souls who showed up at the nominally heated Royal Arena. "We want you to show your excitement. Enjoy yourselves."

In a space of days, Dixon was trying to turn a ninety-five-year-old sport of rigid custom upside down. The balls, rackets, and court looked familiar, but what was happening surely wasn't tennis. Not to seasoned tennis spectators, for whom stillness, punctuated at appropriate intervals by applause, was accepted etiquette. But nothing much came of his ballpark motif because for people to make a lot of noise it was necessary for there to be people.

His guinea pigs made it to fame and fortune in varying degrees. Dixon did not, not in tennis anyway. Nevertheless, Dave deserves remembering, perhaps a mention of some sort one day in the Hall of Fame for the positive push he gave the game toward opens. Albeit unwittingly.

His brainchild, WCT, remains with us, a tournament-producing firm in Dallas where Dave's name is seldom mentioned, except with discouraging words and a giggle.

Dave was merely a couple or three ideas ahead of himself.

That night in the Kansas City stockyards, his piggies were slaughtered by nonattention, and their own mortification was a harbinger of more promotional doom. In their new clothes of many colors they felt as self-conscious as nuns in bikinis. Their base, the court, was all wrong. Astroturf, which worked for baseball and football, was too fast for tennis. The balls leaped disconcertingly like gazelles on uppers. Not only that, but at Kansas City the rug, spread on ice in a building used primarily for hockey, was too small, barely extending beyond the painted lines. That meant the players had to do some running on ice, a substance more conducive to highballs than high-stepping.

Dennis Ralston took some of the hardest pratfalls in the opening match. He stormed to the dressing room, screeching about lousy conditions. Once inside, he began to shiver. The heat was off. The room was as cold as a witch's mitt. Denny decided to try to warm up with a shower. Cold water. "Jeezus!" he yelled, and retreated to a toilet stall, hoping possibly to hide from the nightmare. He entered and slammed the door. The door fell off.

The older pros of the Gonzalez-Rosewall school would have shrugged off the breaking-in pains of the Handsome Eight as "the breaks of our game." Why should Kansas City be different from anyplace else?

Butch Buchholz, the senior pro at twenty-seven, beginning his eighth season in limbo beyond the amateurs, tried to counsel and encourage Dixon's traumatized rookies. Open tennis, approved by the United States only hours after Kansas City, hadn't yet been tested or taken hold, and they were out on an unfamiliar limb. It had always been that way for the new boys defecting from amateurism. Abruptly an amateur big shot was dumped into an inhospitable environment, joining the "donkeys"—the consistent losers—until he became accustomed to the faster company. If he did become accustomed. At least the WCT gang, five of them anyway, were new at it together, and they were cushioned by guarantees richer than any novitiates before them, ranging from John Newcombe's fifty thousand dollars on down a slightly graded scale.

Dave Dixon primped them and promised them they were the bright, handsome new wave of a better day who would earn more than their guarantees, more even than professional golfers. It came true, after their psyches hit some rough spots.

View from the Bridge—Rubbing elbows with NBC boothmates JoAnne Russell and Dick Enberg. *Suzanna Collins © Carol L. Newsom Associates*

The Magnet—Jack Kramer, man for all seasons and reasons, drew me to Forest Hills.

ABOVE LEFT: *Boy Boris*—Only eighteen in 1986, Boris Becker wins his second Wimbledon. © *John Russell.* ABOVE RIGHT: *Same Time Every Year?* Martina Navratilova wins her eighth Wimbledon in 1987. © *John Russell;* BELOW: *You Don't Say*—The Chrissie Show has been running on TV since 1971. © *Carol L. Newsom*

ABOVE: *Volley-Packin' Mama*—Evonne Goolagong scores a rare Wimbledon title victory on behalf of motherhood in 1980.
© *John Russell.* RIGHT: *Hacker and Hustler*—Always yell "Yours!" when you've got a partner like Bobby Riggs.
© *Carol L. Newsom*

Madras Monsoon—Never an ill wind blows from Vijay Armitraj, the peerless sportsman.

ABOVE: *Who Won?* Hard to tell, but in 1977 at Wimbledon, it's ex-Teen Angel Bjorn Borg over Jimmy Connors. © *John Russell.* BELOW LEFT: *Goldilocks Unseats Swedish Bear*—John McEnroe stops Bjorn Borg's five-year Wimbledon streak in 1981. © *John Russell.* BELOW RIGHT: *Champion of Breakfasts*—Roscoe Tanner didn't win in 1979, but he did save NBC's "Breakfast at Wimbledon."

ABOVE LEFT: *Heavy Lifting*—Arthur Ashe wins Wimbledon, 1975. © *Russ Adams Productions.* ABOVE RIGHT: *Public Launching*—Tennis, Arthur Ashe, and I received unprecedented exposure in the first nationwide PBS sporting telecast of Arthur's 1968 win of the National Amateur. *Courtesy WGBH.* BELOW: *Trailblazers to be Trailed*—Althea Gibson was the object of my first reportorial assignment to Forest Hills; Arthur Ashe became a global assignment. *Courtesy* World Tennis

ABOVE: *Lovebird Double*—Rookies of Wimbledon '72, Chris Evert and Jimmy Connors (in the stands) met there, became enamored, engaged, and won the titles two years later. Hardly less enchanted were Steve Flink, her foremost chronicler, and I. © *Associated Press.* BELOW LEFT: *The Other Dracula*—Transylvanian Ion Tiriac. © *Albert Evans.* BELOW RIGHT: *Unblinking in Bucharest*—Stan Smith (left) and Erik van Dillen withstood enormous pressure in the U.S. Davis Cup win over Romania in 1972. *Le-Roye Productions Ltd/Courtesy* World Tennis

The Firebird—Redhead
Rod Laver's Grand Slam year,
1969, was the finest of all
seasons. © *Russ Adams Productions*

Euphoria in Prague—Jan
Kukal (left) and Jan Kodes (right)
win doubles to spearhead
Czechoslovakia's Davis Cup
triumph over Russia in 1971.
© *Paris-Match / Courtesy*
World Tennis

Prone to Volleying — Gail Hansen senses her hackerly partner will go flat-out in National Doubles of 1969.

ABOVE: *WCT's Handsome Eight*—Standing (left to right): Dennis Ralston, Roger Taylor, Tony Roche, Pierre Barthes. Seated (left to right): John Newcombe, Nikki Pilic, Butch Buchholz, Cliff Drysdale. *Courtesy World Championship Tennis*

OPPOSITE ABOVE: *Good Gray Gentleman—New York Times* correspondent Allison Danzig (left) and his wife, Dorothy, at Forest Hills. © *Hans Knopf*

LEFT: *Gang's All Here* at U.S. Pro Championships. This was the entire cast of pro tennis in 1967. Front (left to right): Andres Gimeno, Sammy Giammalva, Luis Ayala, Ken Rosewall, Dennis Ralston. Rear (left to right): Alex Olmedo, Butch Buchholz, Barry MacKay, Fred Stolle, Mike Davies, Mal Anderson, Pancho Segura, Rod Laver, Pierre Barthes. *Courtesy Longwood Cricket Club*

LEFT: *Little Miss Moffitt*—Billie Jean at Essex Country Club in 1967, seven years after I first spied her there, creating the initial stir for metal rackets. © *Paul J. Connell.* BELOW: *The Rosebud*—Rosie Casals at seventeen, with a legs-bisecting volley at National Indoor of 1966. © *Paul J. Connell*

BELOW: *Emmo and Fiery*—Roy Emerson (right) and Fred Stolle winning National Doubles in 1965, a season when they never met a foe or beer they couldn't subdue.
© *Jack Sheahan*/Boston Globe

ABOVE LEFT: *Angel at the Bank*—Ed Hickey led a revival of the U.S. Pro in 1964. © *Hal Sweeney*/Boston Globe. ABOVE RIGHT: *Up Your VASSS*—Pancho Gonzalez didn't care for Jimmy Van Alen's revolutionary scoring system at Newport in 1965, so Jimmy felt obliged to deliver an on-court rebuke. *Courtesy International Tennis Hall of Fame.* BELOW: *Mexican Thumping Beans*—National Doubles favorites Rafe Osuna (right) and Tonio Palafox, 1963. *Courtesy* Boston Globe

Apples of the Camera's Eye—My first TV champs, at National Doubles of 1963. Robyn Ebbern (left) and Margaret Smith Court. © *Paul J. Connell.* Chuck McKinley (left) and Dennis Ralston. *Courtesy* Boston Globe

ABOVE: *New Boy on Pancho's Block*— Novitiate pro, Ken Rosewall (left), at twenty-two in 1957. *Photo from European.*
ABOVE RIGHT: *Tokyo Typhoons* Kosei Kamo (left) and Atsushi Miyagi survived Hurricane Diane to become my first champs at the National Doubles of 1955. © *Samuel Cooper/Courtesy* World Tennis
RIGHT: *Homeland Heroines* of my first Wimbledon final, Karen Hantze and Billie Jean Moffitt won 1961 title. Here they receive 1962 National Doubles runners-up loot from Lady Tennis, Hazel Wightman.

Friends and Foes—Ken Rosewall (left) abets Lew Hoad in National Doubles title of 1956, but jammed Lew's run to a Grand Slam at Forest Hills. © *Russ Adams Productions*

ABOVE: *Record Start*—Louise Brough (left) and Margaret Osborne duPont (right) win the first of twelve National Doubles titles in 1942, as Hazel Wightman passes out silver. I covered their tenth, eleventh, and twelfth, starting in 1955. © *Gil Friedberg/Boston Globe*. BELOW: *The Voice* singing the siren song of Forest Hills belonged to avocational radio announcer Lev Richards (right), a fourth for clubhouse bridge with Sammy Giammalva (left), Vic Seixas (center left), and Kurt Nielsen (center right). © *Samuel Cooper/Courtesy* World Tennis

Today opportunity is broader. Though talent is deeper, job opportunities have expanded a hundredfold. It's no longer an either/or proposition. Instead of leaping blind and unpadded into the pit, nonprofessionals on the way up—exceptional juniors, collegians—can test themselves against pros in opens without having to declare themselves careerists. A man or woman deciding to play for money can get a taste of how difficult it will be, and may want to defer the decision longer, as John McEnroe wisely did by attending Stanford for a year even though he'd been a Wimbledon semifinalist as an amateur in 1977.

The new pro in the old days was a pitiful case, a whipping boy in every way, like Fred Stolle one winter night in 1967 at Boston Garden. The Old Hacker, as he called himself—never looked more like same. As the U.S. champion at Forest Hills four months before he was a prince among amateurs. Huddled in an overcoat—the first he'd ever owned—over a sweatsuit, he seemed as miserable as a pauper.

"Never been in bloody, snowy winter before, mate," he shivered, the usual moan of a rookie Australian pro, whose movements as an amateur had been dictated by those of the sun. "Look at me—wearing this bloody coat indoors. Can't get warm. Wish I could play in this bloody coat. Can't get used to the conditions. Never played much indoors before. And I can't win a bloody match against any of these guys [Laver, Rosewall, Gimeno, Buchholz, Ralston]. Gotta stick it out, but I wonder why I ever turned pro."

Fred was too good not to start winning, and his lugubriousness presently melted. Numerous others couldn't adjust, and departed, among them the 1958 Wimbledon champ, Ashley Cooper. Another of the Aussies who received his baptism by snow in Boston, Coop seemed to be having more fun when he passed through in 1959 than Stolle. It may have helped that he was honeymooning with the recent Miss Australia, née Helen Wood, she playing rookie bride to his rookie pro. Delighted by snow in the streets of Boston, they performed, Mrs. Cooper reported, "a scientific experiment of our very own, the making of ice without a fridge. I put a glass of water on our hotel windowsill last night, and this morning it was real ice." Cheaper than room service.

Helen Cooper's enchanting glass of water wasn't any more frosted than Dennis Ralston and the rest of Dave Dixon's Kansas City rainbow boys, who skated and stroked their way as

WCT first-nighters. But Dave wasn't discouraged. Yet. One bad night wasn't going to floor him, or cloud his vision of pro tennis as a splendid enterprise, a diversion the world couldn't do without. The schedule he had drawn up—two and three tournaments weekly—was too full and frantic to permit the mourning of a momentary disaster.

His players thought Dave was loony, but they were getting paid well, and they followed him along a path of empty auditoriums through night after disheartening night. Not to mention matinees. For Dave, the tennis trail that had begun six months back in the unlikely town of Binghamton, New York, would dead-end a few weeks out of Kansas City.

Dave Dixon may have been on his way out of business, but I'll remember him as the imaginative pebble who, in September of 1967, unwittingly started the avalanche toward open tennis.

Three largely unnoticed stories were being played out during the summer of '67 that, in converging, buried the amateur system. Dixon's. Wimbledon's. And George MacCall's.

Here's the way the tangled tale went, a scenario that gathered a momentum of its own.

In June, despite British advocacy, open tennis was voted down again in the ITF. The British, led by Herman David, the influential boss of Wimbledon, were distressed. They countered by deciding to find out if their regular Wimbledon customers were interested in the pros, and scheduled an eight-man, pros-only tournament for Centre Court in August.

In July, David was discouraged. Although Wimbledon had drawn the usual full houses and a record attendance of over four hundred thousand, the tournament was a bore, won by raw Aussie John Newcombe over indifferent German Will Bungert. If that wasn't bad enough, the All England Clubbies were being sniped at by the only substantial tennis press—their own in London—for being part of an increasingly hypocritical system of phony amateurism. Why were they paying top dollars for less than the best players? That made Herman David and fellow Wimbledon Badgers all the more eager to see the best, the great old pro names on Centre Court once more in August.

Also in July, Dixon experienced an epiphany in an improbable location. Scouting prospective attractions for the New Orelans Superdome (also his idea), which was in the planning

stages, Dave was curious about pro tennis. Did it exist anymore? Research had uncovered a small tourney in Binghamton,
New York. Seeing Laver and Rosewall, he became an immediate convert. "Here were two of the greatest athletes I'd ever
seen and they were unknown. All they needed was a promoter—me."

He was excited, but needed a partner flusher than himself.
It took him about 3.5 seconds to think of Lamar Hunt, whom
he knew through pro football. Lamar didn't know a tennis ball
from a matzo ball when he got a call in 1967 from good old
Dave Dixon, tipping him off about the next sports bonanza.
Get in on the ground court—there's gold in them thar halls,
Dixon urged. Hunt was smart enough to turn to his nephew,
Al Hill, Jr., who did know something. "Little Al," as he's known
around Dallas, had made his letters at Trinity University, a
tennis power in San Antonio from whence Chuck McKinley
had sprung to the 1963 Wimbledon title. Little Al agreed with
Dixon that the time was ripe. Hill and Hunt each went in for
25 percent, leaving half for Dixon, and WCT was in business.

Dixon wasn't alone in his admiration of Laver and Rosewall. While he was having this revelation, a Los Angeleno named
George MacCall, a first-rate hacker who had won U.S. senior
titles, and a shell-shocked refugee from three troubled campaigns as U.S. Davis Cup captain, shared Dave's goal. He, too,
wanted to promote pro tennis, under the colors of the National
Tennis League, backed by a syndicate at home.

In August, both Dixon and MacCall followed the pros to
the tournament at Wimbledon, intent on signing them.

"We couldn't wait to get there," says Laver, one of the eight
prodigals invited back. Most of them had been honorary members of the All England Club, a reward supposedly in perpetuity
for winning a Wimbledon singles championship. They had been
rudely stripped of that membership, which was revoked whenever a man accepted straightforward dollars by turning pro. "I
got a letter from the Club in 1963 asking me not to wear the
club tie anymore," says Laver. The missive didn't quite suggest
that Laver fall on his sword, but he didn't have one anyway.

The temple didn't crumble, or even jiggle, when the heath-
ens entered. It only shuddered romantically, especially for the
Laver–Rosewall final, a grateful response to the pros' rapturous
brand of tennis so long absent. Though heresy to some of the

faithful—tantamount to installing Muhammad Ali at Poets' Corner in Westminster Abbey, or Mick Jagger as choirmaster at St. Martin's-in-the Field—it was a grand homecoming and a box office success.

Though the pros were well received in London, Dixon wasn't well received by the pros. Laver says, "Dave was a persuasive bloke, and he was talking big money. But he didn't know a bloody thing about tennis. We'd been romanced before by dreamers, so we were wary. But George MacCall, who was offering good money, too, talked our language."

MacCall signed the cream for NTL: Laver, Rosewall, Andres, Gimeno, Pancho Gonzalez and Fred Stolle. He already had a commitment from the No. 1 amateur, Roy Emerson, at last going straight at thirty-one after spurning several earlier offers from Jack Kramer. No sexist he, MacCall deserves a salute for bringing women into pro tennis in a bigger way than ever before. He also signed Billie Jean King, Rosie Casals, Ann Jones, and Françoise Durr.

Disappointed, but not surrendering, Dixon had little trouble enlisting the three guys MacCall didn't want for WCT: Butch Buchholz, Dennis Ralston, and the attractive Frenchman, Pierre Barthes. Three players weren't enough.

Dixon turned in another direction: toward the amateurs at the Nationals in September, hitting Forest Hills like a tornado. Getting Hunt and Hill's permission to go at it like all the promoters before him, Dave, however, did it in Texas style. He didn't cut the prime steer out of the herd—he bought the herd. "Tell you what I'll do as a friendly gesture," Dixon was sweet-talking Newcombe and Roche. "You fellows just go across the street to Abercrombie's and pick out any suit you'd like. It's on WCT."

"We were easy all right, " Newk remembers. "The pro game was looking stronger, and we were young and didn't know much. When Dave told us to pick out suits, we were really impressed. We hadn't met anybody like this. But the money Dave talked about was really there, too."

"I went after the best amateurs money could buy, and I got them—Newcombe, Roche, Pilic, Taylor, Drysdale. I was surprised how simple it was to make the deals, and I was glad I missed the older guys. I had the young, vibrant future stars."

Abruptly, Dixon had peeled the grade-A flesh from the amateur game, crippling it, and the ITF was forced to the brink of sanity. They hadn't regarded MacCall, one of their chums, as a threat. George's only amateur catch was Emerson, past-prime. But Dixon was alarming. He hadn't skimmed—he had decimated.

Presto! Gone as attractions were Newcombe, Roche, Taylor, Pilic, Drysdale, along with Emerson. (The nonchauvinist minority noted that MacCall had nabbed King, Casals, Durr, and Jones, too.)

Change-o! The top ten was a disaster area: Newcombe, Pilic, and Taylor had been three-quarters of the 1967 Wimbledon semifinals. Dixon's kidnapping of the choice quintet was the last nudge the British needed to launch the Tennis Court Revolution in December of 1967. Really, self-interest in presenting the best tipped the Wimbledon impresarios in the better direction, away from sham amateurism.

As David Gray, the bright reporter for the *Guardian*, was to write about the pros in Centre Court: "Having grown used to margarine, it was good to be reminded of the taste of butter."

29

○

Getting Their
Goats

Margarine suited the majority of the ITF Badgers just fine. They were comfortable in a nineteenth-century mind-set, and feared a grave new world of dealing with professional promoters and players. And they did not relish the thought of rustling up prize money and losing control of the players painted "amateur" and beholden to their respective national federations and associations. The ITF fired paper salvos at London, where the sires and keepers of the tennis flame had turned into fiery rebels.

Arm in arm with Wimbledon, its financial keeper, the LTA (Lawn Tennis Association of Britain) trumpeted in December 1967 that henceforth Britain would recognize no distinction between amateurs and pros, and all tournaments within the British Isles would be open to all.

Hopefully, but without much conviction, the ITF countered that Britain would be a pariah, evicted from organized tennis. But that couldn't stand up if the USTA joined the LTA in flinging the game into the twentieth century. Eternally stodgy leadership in the United States had lost out to a progressive president, Bob Kelleher, who stepped into office at the propitious time. A Los Angeles lawyer who later became a federal judge, Kelleher was forceful enough as an upper-grade hacker to win several U.S. senior titles, and as an administrator to maneuver the sleepy USTA into siding with the British. It was inconceivable that the ITF would throw out its two most important members.

Still, Kelleher couldn't give open tennis an American okay all by himself. He had to shepherd the sort of resolution that had failed several times before through the narrow lanes of the USTA annual meeting—only hours after Dixon's calamitous WCT bow in Kansas City—at an unlikely location for a revolt. The Del Coronado Hotel beside the sea in San Diego was a patrician hangout, an eighty-year-old retreat of alabaster planking that appeared more suitable for status quo.

David Gray, the English reporter, and I had flown in from Kansas City to find Kelleher uncharacteristically jittery. He had worked hard and cleverly to wire the proceedings, lining up the votes to put across open tennis that had been historically opposed by leading Badgers. Imposingly tall, sometimes combative with a sharp judicial tongue, Kelleher was all softness and caution early that morning as he waited for the hotel newsstand to open. He was determined to enter first to buy up every copy of *Sports Illustrated*, a healthy stack, before anyone else got there. The magazine carried a speculative story on the fateful meeting, quoting Kelleher as mixing his zoology, referring to the anti-open Badgers as "backward old goats."

Kelleher confessed, "Sure, I said it," defending his scorched-magazine policy with, "but I don't want the old goats reading this and exploding." The jurist-to-be even committed larceny, pinching a copy from the hotel reading room. "I'm a man of the law, but, under the circumstances, I think this theft is defensible."

As Gray and I recounted the Kansas City fiasco of Dixon and the Handsome Eight, only hours before, Kelleher winced. "For God's sake, will you keep that to yourselves until after the meeting? Otherwise the old goats will say, 'See, we don't need the pros. They're a flop. Why should we give them our game?'"

The two reporters, leading with their hearts, were momentarily co-opted.

While British emissaries to the meeting Derek Penman and

Derek Hardwick of the LTA, dark-suited and proper preachers of rebellion, fidgeted outside the convention room, America stumbled into the open era. Although Penman and Hardwick had appeared as moral support, Kelleher greeted them as though they were undertakers, and urged them out of sight.

"At that point the Brits were rebels," Kelleher recalls, "and I couldn't risk having the old goats think I was following their lead, and disregarding the ITF. I wanted open tennis to be accepted legally, as it was in an emergency ITF meeting, specially called for by the United States and Sweden, in April. Naturally, if the USTA voted in a normal, legal way for opens, but not breaking away from the ruling body, that would be a powerful persuader for a reconsidered ITF vote. And that's what happened."

Support for Kelleher from within his own organization, however, was far from wholehearted. Parliamentary roadblocks were constructed—and vaulted. The resolution had to be passed by a two-thirds count of seventeen sections of the USTA, each containing hundreds of votes. A section's voting strength depended on the number of member clubs therein. Kelleher and his allies were sure they had the numbers to carry the motion for opens. But imagine their annoyance and apprehension when good-natured old Henry Benisch, delegate of the Eastern Association, the guy who was supposed to second the motion, didn't respond. He was asleep, not an unusual or unwise posture at a USTA gathering.

Somebody kicked him, he wiggled his head to promote consciousness, and blurted, "Uh . . . second the motion!" And it carried. Kelleher was relieved. For a long instant he thought it might be 1962 all over again when the question of relief stymied what might have been the triumph of an unexpectedly broad-minded conclave of the ITF. That year a resolution favoring open tennis was voted on favorably. However, the proposal went down the drain, failing to obtain the necessary two-thirds majority even though sufficient votes were assured. At the time of the roll call, the delegate representing the votes that would have approved the rational scheme was in the men's room. Nature had beaten reason, and we had to wait six more years.

Approval of open tennis didn't light up Dave Dixon as it had those of us who had campaigned for it over the years, envisioning the change as beneficial beyond imagination. Dave said, sure, the Handsome Eight could play Wimbledon and Forest Hills if his guys felt like it, but the main business of WCT was its own American circuit. That was the breadth of his picture: eight variegated characters playing two tournaments a week at $10,000 per, their individual winnings marked off against guarantees. WCT would put up the prize money, hire the hall, and reap magnificent profits from sellouts ensured by the presence of the Handsomes.

Trouble was, Dave didn't give America enough time to share his excitement or catch up with his scheme, only three days in one town before they moved on to the next. By the time one town had an inkling that the Handsome Eight were in the vicinity, they were leaving. Gate receipts didn't begin to cover the ten grand in prize money and accompanying overhead. WCT was going broke, and the players were going crazy, even though paid. They sensed the WCT tour was a trip to oblivion.

"We know open tennis is approved," said Tony Roche, who rated his own pulchritude as "No. 14 in the Handsome Eight." "But nobody knows what open tennis means yet. WCT can't last, and when it folds, where does that leave us?"

In a movable sanitarium. I looked in on the Handsomes just before the end in the cavernous, and empty, St. Louis Arena. Dave was on the microphone, an unfazed and indefatigable sideshow barker, haranguing the scattering of customers on the beauties of Astroturf. "I'm surprised he doesn't replace his own toupee with a slice of it," said an aide, Ron Bookman.

"Come down here and walk on it, folks. . . . See Astroturf for yourself after the match. Now, our scoring system is modern and different." Dixon kept trying to explain his other conversion, to the radical gospel of Jimmy Van Alen's 31-point matches. "I want you to cheer for your favorite player, or your favorite color," his voice echoed throughout the auditorium as he pointed out these guinea pigs dressed like jockeys. "And boo if something—a player, anything—displeases you."

Pierre Barthes was close to tears as Dixon counseled onlookers, "If you don't like De Gaulle or his policies, cheer against our Frenchman." Looking as though he'd been dropped on a strange planet, Pierre groaned, "Thees ees a circus . . . but we are not aneemals!" Then, sounding like Peter Sellers's Inspector Clouseau, "I am not a cloon!"

Pierre wanted to walk out and catch the first plane for Paris, but Butch Buchholz talked him out of it. Butch was a settling influence. No matter how bad it got, he'd been through worse: the exploration of the Australian bush as well as a Kramer tour they called the "Texas Death March"—thirty matches in thirty days in small towns throughout that state.

It was Buchholz who suggested to Dixon and his aide, Bob Briner, that they bring in a former Kramer tourist, Mike Davies, as play doctor.

A shrewd young man with a Welsh lilt in his voice, Mike Davies had escaped the Swansea coal mines to become Britain's No. 1, then enrolled with Kramer's desperadoes. Facially he could have qualified for the Handsome Eight, but, no longer up to them competitively, he would eventually settle for Dave Dixon's job and straighten out WCT financially so that it became the first viable promotional force of the open era.

Davies put his finger on the problem. "Dave, we're paying for everything—players and rent particularly. What we've got to do is find sponsors to cover our expenses. Then we can make a profit if we promote properly, which we haven't done. There's been no groundwork. It's too new for people to turn out just because we announce we're coming to town."

Ron Bookman, the press agent then, could see that Americans were yet largely unfamiliar with the game. "One of the first tournaments was in the gym of a Catholic high school in Houston. That tells you where pro tennis was in early 'sixty-eight. After the final was over, the priest in charge of the school came up to Dave and said, 'That was very interesting. Who won?' "

Who lost was clear. In a matter of weeks, Dixon was broke, losing fifty thousand dollars of his own money. In March, Lamar Hunt and Al Hill, Jr., assumed total ownership and began a reorganization under Bob Briner. Hunt could have written it off, and forgotten tennis. Too proud and stubborn for that, he began to take an interest. Nobody knows how much his pride and stubbornness cost him. At one time, with more astute management and bolder commitment of his staggering resources, Hunt might have become the dominant figure in the game. Nevertheless, WCT was an extremely positive entity in the early professionalization of an amateurishly operated sport, the first to bring American network television into the game on a regular basis in 1972, and the first to brandish serious prize money, offering a stratospheric $50,000 first prize for the initial WCT Championship in 1971.

Those who tried to push Hunt out of the game—there've been a couple of attempts—have found this mild-looking fellow, who cultivates a "jest folks" reputation, to be a relentless antagonist guarding his position and few lasting tournaments with rock-hard, dollar-plated resolve.

Pro tennis has been good for Lamar, too. He took up the game and became a fair hacker, playing on a court on his Dallas estate that makes Versailles seem a housing project. Like his shoes, the court sometimes had holes, but he laughed that away as "the home-court advantage."

As the boss of WCT he has shared royal boxes, here and there, with Prince Rainier and Princess Grace at Monte Carlo, the duke and duchess of Kent at Wimbledon, and the shah of Iran at Teheran. The last, in 1971, was a meeting of good old boy oil barons. In that better time for both, the shah owned Iran, and the Hunts a goodly chunk of a livelier land called Texas. It was the sort of gusher for WCT that Dixon had imagined: the shah paid $100,000 for a tournament as part of the festivities celebrating an anniversary of his rule. That was sitting pretty for Lamar, a onetime Southern Methodist substitute football player, in a royal box alongside the shah.

Dave Dixon never made it to any of those places. We mustn't leave him labeled a total commercial bomb, though. In fairness, I should point to his one WCT tourney that did make money. Dave got lucky at a surprising outpost—Shreveport, Louisiana—because his court didn't arrive on time. "It was being trucked in from the previous tourney," remembered Ron Bookman. "We marked off lines on the basketball floor at the gym we were using, and Dave opened the doors and let in free anybody who was interested. A few came in.

"How we made money was WCT sued the trucking firm for five thousand dollars for nondelivery. They paid off, and Dave had his only profit."

30

○

Open at
Last

The year that Abbie Hoffman, that old tennis protégé of mine, started making his name as a nuisance, novelty, nut, or nugget—your pick—the world was generally convulsed. Tennis, no less than many other endeavors, seemed affected by the rebellious mores of 1968. The staid old game, whose radicalism was carefully contained within Jimmy Van Alen's mind and manor at the Newport Casino, erupted in a cataclysm long feared and fought off by the Badgers: open tournaments.

The integration of the underclass minority—the pros—with the privileged keepers of castles such as Wimbledon and Forest Hills—the amateurs—came in not with a bang but with the whine of a cold, wet dog.

That uncomfortable, unknown hound was one of a hundred or so shivering spectators as open tennis commenced on the raw, drizzly morning of April 22, 1968, at Bournemouth, England. Tournament tennis may have lurched into being July 10, 1877, at Wimbledon, a two-hour train ride distant from Bournemouth, but this April Monday ninety-one years later was nonetheless a birthday of consequence. This consequence is a thoroughly professionalized game, barely two decades old, only toddling through its infancy. Renaissance may be a better characterization.

Despite the infighting, the periodic tennis wars, the glaring acts of irresponsibility, I sometimes comfort myself by remembering that the game of today dates merely to 1968. How far along, after all, were baseball, football, basketball, or any other of the professional sports only years beyond inception?

It was all glistening—with raindrops—as the British Hard Court (that means clay in America) Championships convened at the cozy West Hants Lawn Tennis Club in Bournemouth, a seaside resort on the English Channel. Opponents of the innovation said the marrow-piercing downpour meant that the gods of amateurism were displeased. Realists huffed that amateurism in sport was considered to exist only by those who worshipped Jove.

Besides, it always rains at English tennis tournaments.

Also quaking, but not so much in reaction to customarily invigorating and bronchitic English springtime, were a band of untouchable outlaws abruptly and unexpectedly covered with a blanket amnesty: the pros. And scared stiffer than the upper lips of the scattering of Limeys (plus that lonely dog) who wouldn't have missed the historic opening day for all the tea at London's Ritz.

The pros felt like the count of Monte Cristo, out of jail and restored to polite society, invited in from exile for a proper cup of tea, with cream and sugar and cakes. Permitted to mingle with amateurs as equals, returned to a former life, they found it unnerving after operating outside the law for so long.

To be sure, they'd crept into Longwood, Newport, and Forest Hills when hardly anyone was looking, rummaging through those upper-class haunts while the acceptable tenants, the amateurs, were elsewhere. As long as they didn't try to mix with the amateurs competitively—"Beware miscegenation!" was the Badgers' segregationist bark—the pros were tolerated.

Now that integration was decreed, the pros, considering themselves a meritocracy, were nonetheless jittery. Would they know how to act, and hold their teacups without spillage?

Some of them had trouble holding their rackets at all, and proud professional blood was spilled, making the daring Bournemouth caper all the more exciting. "Ah, yeah, I'm bloody nervous," said Fred Stolle after a bloody nervous performance, a tremble past nondescript English amateur Peter Curtis, in four sets. "The pressure is all on us pros. We've been saying all along that we're the best in the game, and now we'd better prove it." They did, overall. "But the amateurs have nothing to lose, and it seems like our prestige is tied up in this first open this week. If I lose, I'm letting down my mates and pro tennis."

Lines were drawn on the landscape of Euphemism as defenders of whatever faith—amateurism or professionalism—had their say, and their day. Thus the Bournemouth mood that fourth week in April was starkly dramatic as a blustery wind of change blew in from the Channel.

Was it appropriate that victory came from the left in the very first of the radical confrontations, amateur versus pro? Left-handed Australian pro O. K. Davidson was momentarily ashen in losing the starting point to Scottish amateur John Clifton, but he won the breezy decision, and they were off. Constant gusts made the assignment all the more difficult for the men with reputations, whose game was conducted largely indoors.

The fact was that the assembled men and women, regardless of A or P labels, made their livings playing tennis. A's dough came from "expense" payments and subsidies from national federations, P's from prize money or a percentage of the gate. The absurd and self-defeating situation should have been remedied long before.

The fiction of amateurism and the practice of barring pros from recognized events, so long fostered by the Badgers, began to die in Bournemouth.

The pros were shaky because they'd become ingrown, playing only one another, and no longer played the best-of-five-set matches this British championship called for. Each new amateur face was a problem. "There are so many we've never seen or heard of," Rod Laver was to say as the season wore on. Promoter Dave Dixon's pros, the Handsome Eight of WCT, ducked Bournemouth, leaving it to George MacCall's NTL troupe of Laver, Stolle, Ken Rosewall, Pancho Gonzalez, Andres Gimeno, and Roy Emerson.

Absent as well were the most prominent amateurs, who also had reputations to protect. Arthur Ashe, Clark Graebner, Manolo Santana, Cliff Richey, Ilie Nastase, and Jan-Erik Lundquist; Margaret Court, Maria Bueno, Nancy Richey, Kerry Melville, and Helga Niessen were waiting and seeing what open tennis was all about. Wimbledon, two months distant, would be soon enough for most of them, even though the French was scheduled as the next open. Besides, the money wasn't that enticing: $8,856, total purse.

Rosewall got $2,400 of that for beating Laver in the final. But the newly confessed female pros—Billie Jean King, Rosie Casals, Ann Jones, Françoise Durr—declined to accompany their NTL brethren, sneering that the $720 first prize was insultingly low.

The British Badgers were astonishingly straightforward: everybody welcome, take the money or not. No distinctions between columns A and P.

The amateurs were justifiably unsure of their reception at home and abroad. "Suppose . . . ," hesitated Mark Cox. An English amateur who was about to engrave a historical plaque for himself with racket, Cox had decided beforehand to decline cash. "Suppose I accept money here? That's fine with my own association. But will that prevent me from playing leading events in other countries because I've been tainted," he smiled, "by prize money?"

Wise man. How open was open? At that juncture it was uncertain where open tennis would go beyond the no-hands-barred attitude of Bournemouth. Instead of the thousand dollars that he startlingly earned, Cox had, like his still-cautious colleagues masquerading as amateurs, elected to accept a pittance as "expenses." His absent betters of the amateur gang—Cox was about the twentieth-best—could understand. They didn't care to jeopardize their usual exorbitant expenses to come to Bournemouth and be humiliated by a pro for lunch money.

But their absence increased the stress load for the pros, who risked their names against nobodies. Stolle might have been able to rationalize a loss to Santana. But to Peter Curtis?

The West Hants Lawn Tennis Club seemed an unlikely place for the tempest in a test tube—the long-awaited maiden open.

With a stadium holding no more than five thousand (one thousand of them standing), West Hants was small, tidy, and out-of-the-way, a New Haven for the tryout of a brilliant drama that might make it on the tennis Broadways. Although determined to lead the world into the open epoch, the British weren't so brave or brazen as to drop the bomb at the sacred Big W. Better to start slowly, well down the railway tracks, with an off-Wimbledon trial. If it didn't work, they could close open tennis quietly after a one-week engagement, and Wimbledon would be unaffected.

But it did work. Before Rosewall and Laver dueled in another of their wondrous finals, before the week was half over, the apprehensive Mark Cox had put his face on every front page in the British Isles, assuring the success and thrills that propagandists for integration promised. By Wednesday the stands were full and there was no longer room for that freeloading matinee-idling dog of opening day.

Looking like an athletic Harpo Marx in his blond curls, Cox, a twenty-four-year-old left-hander, played strings as sweetly for two heady days in beating Pancho Gonzalez, then Roy Emerson, to crash the semifinals. The plaque in the cranny he may have in the Hall of Fame one day will read: "First amateur to defeat a professional," and go on to recount Cox's heroics of Bournemouth.

First to crumble was the aging emperor of professional tennis. Sure, Gonzalez was a grandfather, a forty-year-old beginning to creak, but the Old Wolf was nonetheless regal and malevolent.

"It's one hundred—to—one against Mark," said Cox's less-than-confident wife, Alison, with whom I was sitting in the grandstand as the two men warmed up. "And I wouldn't bet a pound against a hundred."

After losing the first set, 6–0, Cox was in tune with his roommate, and a withering thought "flashed through my mind: I may get beat, 6–0, 6–0, 6–0. God, I hope that doesn't happen."

It didn't. Gonzalez hadn't worked a best-of-five gig on clay for nine years, and as Cox steadied, and began to pump balls back, the Old Wolf began to feel his oldness.

Cox won the second set. Now it was a match, and the attractiveness of open play was heightened: a good amateur was playing it close against one of the great pros. Gonzalez was laboring, and Cox allowed himself to hope he might win. It was possible. "I didn't think so beforehand. All I wanted to do was put up a good show," said Cox, who was observing Gonzalez on court for a second time. "The first, I think, was fourteen years ago on the telly, against Frank Sedgman. The pro tournament was in London. I was ten."

A crammed-in crowd was torn. Cox was their countryman, and an underdog, yet the magnetism of Gonzalez was undeniable. Scores of uniformed and straw-boatered schoolgirls seemed puzzled by their affections as they applauded for a fine shot here by Cox and there by Gonzalez. They would grow up to marry men like Cox, a nicely mannered graduate of Cambridge—but they could dream of running off with Pancho, a Rhett Butler in short trousers. Cox was their kind. They should want him to win, but . . . Pancho, oh, God . . . come on, Pancho!

Pancho won the third set, but he was disintegrating before our eyes like an old fighter, as Sugar Ray Robinson had done in 1960 at Boston Garden, losing his middleweight title to a lesser, but younger, man, Paul Pender.

Pender had picked apart Robinson with his left and Cox was doing the same to Gonzales. Pancho and Sugar Ray were soul brothers: sleek, quick, powerful, willful, rakishly attractive, they hung on into their forties, periodically dipping into a box of slickness in the attic and rubbing it into their bones to facilitate brief impressions of their former selves.

Noteworthy victories still lay ahead for Gonzalez. He would beat Tony Roche at the first U.S. Open, trim Stan Smith, Bob Lutz, and Arthur Ashe in succession to win Las Vegas in 1969, jolt Rod Laver in a 1970 Madison Square Garden challenge match shortly after the Aussie had completed a Grand Slam, and continue as a danger man on the circuit into 1972.

But on this surprisingly mild Bournemouth afternoon, in too much sunshine, Pancho was trying to cope with a killer-for-an-hour who "immortalized himself," according to some London reporters.

Pancho was groping and grunting as Cox became firmer and surer. At one change game Pancho had to change shoes, removing a pair waterlogged with sweat. His damp feet were blistering. His omnipotent smile of the first set was replaced by a hounded, harried look, no longer "superhuman," as Cox's wife had described Pancho to a friend. He let Cox escape by bungling a volley at 3–4, 40–0 in the fourth set. After that, Gonzalez got only three more games.

In 3½ hours Cox won, 0–6, 6–2, 4–6, 6–3, 6–3, and the

story circled the world that an amateur had derailed the most eminent pro. A semantic sensation, really. Pancho had the name if no longer the standing. Cox was a pseudo-amateur.

Never mind. Don't spoil a good story with the facts, as Sam Silverman used to intone his gospel. The facts are too involved, and the reporter is cramped by limited space.

It was a hell of a story. Amateur beats pro. Barely known amateur beats best-known pro. Man bites Wolf. Big, black, up-front headlines saluted Cox's career triumph. He wasn't through, though. Next day it was Emerson's turn, to be the second pro to lose to an amateur. Cox was back on page one. Would he be knighted? Maybe canonized, someday, as Saint Mark, slayer of sneakered dragons?

Emmo had conquered Cox with ease a few months before when both roamed the amateur sphere, but as rookie pro he was transformed to wobbly loser, feeling pressure to uphold his new label. When Emmo emerged from his coma in the third set, one of his worst thrashings, 6–0, 6–1, 7–5, was almost complete.

"It's up to me." Laver was grim, thoroughly un-Laverian. This wasn't another tennis match; it was the brotherhood on trial, and somebody'd better hit the saboteur, Cox, before he dominoed the pros right out of Bournemouth. Laver was a meat grinder in those days, as confirmed by Cox after Rod had restored order, 6–4, 6–1, 6–0: "He made mincemeat out of me."

Then Rosewall, ever trouble for his old pal and adversary, did a little grinding of his own, 3–6, 6–2, 6–0, 6–3, to conclude the opening of unchartered territory in the name of his majesty, Kenneth I of Bournemouth.

Was Gonzalez still seething like the nearby English Channel, tossed by a hearty storm that delayed completion of the tempest in a test tube by one day? Pancho seemed pacific in losing the doubles final beside Andres Gimeno to Emerson and Laver. But he dumbfounded us reporters who, after the defeat by Cox, hesitantly followed him down that long pathway to the clubhouse. Thrushes sang in the trees, but it seemed an ominous passage. Expecting a turbulent, even hazardous dressing room scene, something Caligulan, we wondered if we would emerge to hear thrushes again.

I have been thrown and cursed out of better dressing chambers than Bournemouth's. Comes with the turf. Others have more dangerous jobs. War correspondents get shot at and killed, reporters have been assaulted, jailed, maimed, murdered trying to get stories. But sportswriters may be the only ones who routinely trail a beaten man to his lair, circle him, a pack of hyenas, as he disrobes, and delay his passage to a comforting shower by trying to probe his innermost, probably troubled, thoughts. It is in such times that athletes may break furniture or even take a shot at breaking a reporter's head.

Gonzalez was a celebrated throttler of prying photographers. I'd watched him punch out a steel locker after a loss, abuse chairs and shoes, and snarl menacingly at questioners.

I didn't think this was going to be a lot of fun as we tracked the Old Wolf, at respectful distance, into the spartan changing room. Guardedly we waited for him to raise his eyes and pull the wooden clubhouse down around us . . . scream an eviction notice . . . snatch for the nearest jugular. None of that. Expect the unexpected from Pancho.

He felt weary, not humiliated. "Somebody had to be the first to lose to an amateur. It might as well be me." He smiled. "I was glad to be part of this. Didn't think I'd ever see it happen. Now let me take a shower. I've been working pretty hard."

We smiled, too, relieved, and escaped, unbattered, to our typewriters.

Derek Hardwick, chairman of the LTA, toasted the tournament, "We've set financial and attendance records for the week. Tell them in America," he directed, "tell them what a success open tennis is.

"There's no going back after this."

There's no going back after anything, as novelist John P. Marquand pointed out some time ago, but I knew what Derek meant, and shared his enthusiasm. As well as his sherry.

31

○

Welcome to Chaos

Bournemouth '68 made the future look as rosy as the cheeks of the entrants contesting each other and gales off the English Channel—and as green as the pound notes shoved into the box offices of the West Hants Lawn Tennis Club. And it was, despite almost unrelieved chaos below the surface. The game was being remodeled drastically by the forces of professionalism and commercialization, and by the transition of power and leadership from national federations staffed by amateur volunteers to player unions and player agents.

The tempest bubbled out of the Bournemouth beaker and beyond in 1968, a fuzzy year for those who tried to figure who's who—and why—among the cast stocking the eleven other tournaments certified as "opens."

A seeker of order should avoid tennis. Example: Use of the tiebreaker varies from country to country. At the U.S. Open a tiebreaker is played to conclude any set that reaches 6–6 in games. At Wimbledon, no tiebreaker is played when the ultimate set (fifth for men, third for women) reaches 6–6. Instead, the old-fashioned deuce set is restored, and the set carries on until one player, or team, is two games ahead. Such contradictions and paradoxes abound, making tennis infuriating to the precise and orderly, and charming to the rest of us.

Still, it took five years of fuzziness, the Badgers' steadfast resistance to the broom of honesty and straightforwardness, before the spirit of Bournemouth was fully realized to the satisfaction of progressives. Only when participation in the international men's team tournament, Davis Cup, became completely unrestricted in 1973, was full competitive homogenization a reality. That year Rod Laver, Ken Rosewall, John Newcombe, and Mal Anderson reappeared on the Australian side after long hiatuses, seventeen years in Kenny's case. As the strongest team in the history of the Cup, they hatched a goose egg in the big silver birdbath, taking it away from the United States, 5–0.

Go back to 1969. Arthur Ashe and Laver were both pros, but Laver wasn't eligible to play for his country in Davis Cup while Ashe was. How did you explain that to the customers? Well, in the eyes of the Badgers, some professionals, like Laver, were more professional than others. Laver, under contract to WCT, agreeing to play some WCT tournaments, got a guarantee plus prize money, and was labeled "contract pro." Davis Cup was a no-no for such naughty fellows. Ashe, making similar wages on prize money but not under contract, and playing non-WCT tourneys along with Laver, was labeled "independent pro." Davis Cup was an option for him.

Then, in the early days, there existed a rare amateur bird labeled "registered player," a hybrid concocted by Badgers who still found the word "professional" obscene. Along the lines of "only slightly pregnant," a "registered player" could accept prize money but was not a pro and could play Davis Cup. One of these was Tiny Tom Okker, the slight but facile Dutchman who underlined the absurdity as losing finalist of the introductory U.S. Open in 1968.

Since the champ, Ashe, had to preserve his amateur standing for a very plausible reason, the runner-up, nonprofessional professional Okker, stepped right up and accepted the first prize, $14,000.

Ashe labored for $28 daily expense payments because only amateurs were acceptable Davis Cup timber that year, even though the game was supposedly open. Also, as a U.S. Army lieutenant, he was granted government permission to play as much tennis as he wished under one condition: He had to belong to a national team in international competition—Davis Cup. Once out of the army, Arthur became an "independent pro."

It got so laughable that in 1969, preparing the souvenir program for the first important indoor open, at Madison Square Garden, publisher Harold Zimman pondered trying to get his readers through the semantical maze. "Practically everyone is in it for the money, but we've got all these categories, so I guess it's time to fall back on my asterisks.

"I'm putting one asterisk beside the names of the out-and-out pros, whether they're with WCT or NTL.

"Two asterisks go beside the 'players'—that's 'independent pros' in the U.S., and 'registered players' elsewhere.

"Three asterisks go with the ones getting $28 a day plus a variety of perks—the 'amateurs.' The program will look like 'Stars Fell on Alabama,' but I'm just trying to be helpful, separating the moneymakers from the moneymakers."

Only the Badgers, men capable of splitting hairs on Kojak's head, could have elevated the euphemism to such delirious heights, creating this situation, and others similar: Margaret Court entered in good standing (and won) the National Amateur Championship of 1968 even though she'd been collecting prize money. She was a "player," a nonprofessional vying with pros for cash, so it was perfectly logical.

The Badgers of tennis were hung up on the cloud of amateurism. Some, notably Olympic Badgers, still are. Nevertheless, it was amusing that tennis, of all sports, might be credited in the 1988 Games with leading a parade eventually to an open and honest Olympics. Through the political maneuvering of the Big Badger himself, ITF president Philippe Chatrier, all players nominated by national federations, whether deemed amateur or pro, were certified as contestants for Seoul.

Most Badgers didn't detest pros. But, in their Victorian time-lock, they dreaded the mongrelization of the amateur mainstays of their tournaments through competitive intercourse with pros. They weren't bad guys, those pros, but would you want one to play mixed doubles with your sister?

It was bound to happen, the first such misalliance at revolutionary Bournemouth in 1968, where the Chilean pro, Luis Ayala, was linked with California amateur Valerie Ziegenfuss. They were the first genuinely mixed pair in mixed doubles.

Valerie didn't seem corrupted by contact with Luis on court, and he looked quite pleased to have her in tow. For one thing, since she signed in as an amateur, Ayala didn't have to share prize money with her. That meant their staggering $28 score as losing semifinalists was all his. I hope he gallantly took her to dinner, or at least bought Val a meat pie and a beer.

Squat and jovial Ayala, who had paid his way from Puerto Rico just to be in on the historic gala, and thus lost money, grinned at the reward. "I did better on legitimate expenses at Wimbledon my last year as an amateur. I enter the mix doubles with my wife, Maria, so she gets expenses, too. Some people thought we shouldn't do that because she's six months pregnant, but we need the money.

"Then I ask the committee for expenses for two more people. They say, 'Two more players? What do you mean?'

"I say, 'Maria gonna have twins, and there be four of us playing the match.'

"They don't buy that," Luis smiled. "Pretty soon I have to turn pro because I'm not like some guys. I can't support a family as an amateur. Maria didn't have twins. Just my boy, Luis Jr., but he tells his friends he play Wimbledon even if he don't know what the place look like."

Open Tennis, an exalted term at the end of the 1960s, has lost meaning and significance as professionalism settled in, and only a scattering of amateurs—American collegians or juniors for the most part—popped into tournaments from time to time hardly noticed. Eighteen-year-old Sammy Giammalva's victory at Napa, California, in 1981 was the only tournament triumph of the decade for a male amateur. Rodney Harmon, quarter-finalist at Flushing Meadows in 1982, was merely the fourth amateur to do so well at the U.S. Open. The first was Arthur Ashe, the startling victor in the first, 1968. Following him were Chris Evert, semifinalist in 1971–72, and Pam Shriver, finalist to champ Evert in 1978.

Legitimization of wide-open play wasn't necessarily embraced on the spot. Some didn't want to recognize the fact, and acted as obstructionists, but they were eventually bypassed.

From there to here, that era to this . . . tennis went from a penny-ante operation and thank-you notes, in return for room and board, to a sport awash in millions of dollars in prize money, marketing profits, and television revenue. Practically overnight.

Historically, Bournemouth now seems like Saint Francis's tiny rustic chapel dwarfed by the gaudy Cathedral of Santa Maria degli Angeli that surrounds it in Assisi. The game has gone so far beyond Bournemouth that the West Hants Lawn Tennis Club, where the heresy began, couldn't keep up. Bereft of a tournament since 1983, it is today a shrine for hackers, as Francis's eight-centuries-old place in Assisi is for hagiographers. I recommend pilgrimages to West Hants for Lendl, McEnroe, Navratilova, Evert, and all the others whose overflowing bank accounts can be traced to Bournemouth '68.

Bob Kelleher, who helped condemn the Lost Civilization as USTA president in 1968, said, "We don't know what we're getting into. Nobody's prepared for open tennis, or even knows what it means. But I believe the time is now, even if I get tarred and feathered for it."

Twelve tournaments approved as opens were on the 1968 calendar. Three women and three men purporting to be amateurs were among the winners.

The old order was changing subtly. But everything looked deceptively the same. The eastern grass-court circuit clung to its American primacy for a while. However, it was as ill-fated as the British Empire, and its organizers were as oblivious to their numbered days as His Majesty's garrison at Singapore in 1941, whose officers danced and partied while the Japanese closed in.

The parties were nearly over at the Lost Civilization's clubby retreats where John O'Hara characters paid the dues and called the tennis players' tunes. Making money and waltzing to the computer's rhythms would become utmost as tennis grew in prominence and joined professional sport as another business game. Players would compete as fiercely and profess their love of the game, without which, originally, they couldn't have become so proficient. They would be affluent and better known, but they wouldn't have as much fun. Unless their idea of fun was hanging out with agents and tax accountants.

32

○

Long Way
from Rome

Rome, the place where Guido Tommasi stood up Chris Evert, and Billie Jean King got pinched, is my favorite tennis town. If I am ever rationed to one tournament a year, make it the Italian Open, please.

The English may have invented tennis, but the Italians humanized it. Possibly too much, and in ways that would scandalize the English creation called Wimbledon. Such as the time Ilie Nastase picked up a bottle that was thrown at him while he was struggling to beat a local hero, the "Pasta Kid," chunky Paolo Bertolucci. Nastase looked at the empty mineral water bottle and sneered, insulted, "They should throw champagne. A full bottle."

"If Romans had any real style, somebody would," scoffed my journalist friend Gianni Clerici of *La Repubblica*, who, you must understand, is a Lombard, from Como.

Il Foro Italico, an amusement park for strings, was built in fiddler Nero's town in 1932 by one of his successors, a bombastic hacker with suspect backhand, the dictator Mussolini. It is a gem of lush landscaping, marble tiers, sunken clay courts in a shade of smoked salmon, gigantic statuary, and excitable patrons. Situated at the base of a verdant hill called Monte Mario, a short distance from the Tiber, it might have inspired the native composer Ottorino Respighi to write another tone poem, about tennis.

His pines of Rome form a tiara above the outer rectangle of courts where a chorus of thousands keeps time to racket strings and percussion of winning shots.

Would the world have been a better place to live if the Foro's architect, Benito Mussolini, had possessed a decent backhand? Have historians searched Mussolini's character to determine whether his invasion of Ethiopia in 1935 was the result of backhand blues?

I learned of the one-sided nature of Il Duce, as his followers called him, from his personal tennis coach, Mario Belardinelli. Belardinelli, nearing eighty, stooped but robust, can still be seen in attendance at the Italian Open. Recalling the private lessons he gave Mussolini at Villa Torlonia, Belardinelli says that the boss had a pretty good forehand, and preferred to be fed balls on that side. "One day," says Belardinelli, "I decided we should work on the backhand, and began to hit there." This was a time when a favored Fascist slogan was *Noi tirreremo dritto!* (We must always go forward.) *Dritto* also happens to be the Italian word for forehand. When Belardinelli pumped a few shots to the dictator's left, he reacted by scowling and projecting the famous jaw, ordering: "No, no, no, Belardinelli! Remember— *noi tirreremo dritto!*"

The noblest Roman of them all, of recent times, was handsome, slick-stroking Adriano Panatta, who stirred adoring throngs to frenzies. They would have boiled in oil any opponent, even the admirable Bjorn Borg, to further the cause of their man, whose name was sandwiched around hand claps in an intense singsong chant of *"Ad-riano! Ad-riano!"*

Indeed, his townsmen roasted the ears of such dangerous challengers as Harold Solomon, Jose Higueras, and the great Borg, driving them right out of town. Since the customers were allied in a communal conspiracy, spontaneous and unplanned, with some extremely patriotic umpires and line judges—hanging judges, really—anybody facing Panatta in the Italian Open was outnumbered considerably.

Between the noise and the thievery on Adriano's behalf, it

took a strong, determined man to bear up, much less win. The catcalls from the stands and the Panatta-catering calls from selectively blind linespeople caused Solomon, a doughty American, to walk out in despair from a 1976 semifinal, even though he was ahead. Solly's surrender was a victory for the Unfriendly Society of Adriano's Friends, rewarded by his championship that year, first for an Italian in fifteen years.

It happened again in 1978 when the harried and intimidated walker was the Spaniard, José Higueras, also leading. The crowd was so naughty that the umpire, an English neutral named Bertie Bowron, abdicated, too.

The outrageous home-court advantage that had beaten Higueras in the semis almost felled Borg in the final. Pelted by coins—"low denominations . . . bloody cheap Romans!" appraised Clerici—and jeered incessantly, Borg needed all his skill and resolve to carry the final in five sets. But he was faithful to a vow never to return and play a martyr's role in another of Panatta's passion plays that went on for several more years.

It can still be trying to play against an Italian in Rome. Nastase, who speaks Italian, stopped playing one afternoon to inquire of an abusive spectator why the fellow kept urging Ezio di Matteo to "Kill Nastase!"

"Because I bet ten thousand lire [then about seventeen dollars] on di Matteo at six to one," the heckler answered.

"Very bad bet at any price," advised Nastase with a smile, but he couldn't shut the guy up until he won the last point.

However, the emotions and pandemonium of the past have been curbed by the Italian Federation's stricter observance of crowd control, and recently implemented universal code of officiating, drastically reducing instances of local theft.

Law-and-order doesn't necessarily please those of us who experienced Roman barbarism. Those turbulent scenes, sometimes requiring police intervention, were unfair and traumatic for visiting victims—but marvelous theater. Still, Romans remain naturally exuberant and boisterous, and they seem to have more fun than any other tennis crowd, making their tournament the liveliest.

Although the Italian Open isn't one of the four majors, it strives mightily to be regarded as No. 5, and remains No. 1 in my heart, a position it seized when we were introduced in 1973. The English, longtime seekers of sun in Italy, and global propagators of the faith, planted the tennis seed in this climate superior to their own in 1878, a year after Wimbledon was launched.

Ah, but how different from Wimbledon. As a refugee from New England and a claustrophobic winter of indoor tournaments, I stretched out in the Foro, taking heart from the sunshine of May, before Rome grows hot. The mood is languorous, relaxed. The ice cream called *gelato* and the women called *signorinas* are fetching. It is a good way to break into the European swing, prior to the bustle and mobs of Paris, where more often than not the weather is chilly, and London, historically soggy. Smaller in area than the major sites, the Foro offers manageable spectating, since there are only seven courts. Campo Centrale, the marble enclosure guarded by towering and militant figures of soldiers and athletes in various states of nudity, is the main arena. At some distance across a landscaped piazza, are the remaining half-dozen courts. There are places you can stand, in the shade of those elegant pines, offering a vista of four matches at once. Or you can wander off to the rear of the grounds and take a nap alfresco.

Not a bad walk across the Tiber are small restaurants in a residential neighborhood, for quiet, pleasant lunches and dinners. Unfortunately, the organizers of the Italian Open, which accommodates a friendly eight or nine thousand at a sitting, have felt compelled to keep up with the financial race by recently installing floodlights. Night-and-day tennis, of course, doubles the profits.

"It is an abomination," agrees Clerici, "but necessary in this day to keep the tournament in the top six. Only with big money do the players take it seriously. When I was a player, everybody wanted to come to Rome because—it is Rome. But we wanted to enjoy the life as much as the tennis. Life doesn't seem very important to players today, but they have to please the bloody computer and their bloody agents."

Clerici, who held an Italian ranking, is happy to point out the back court where he opposed the 1952 champion in the first round, the Australian since elevated to the Hall of Fame, Frank Sedgman. "Clay was not Sedg's best surface, and I was having a good time. He doesn't know who I am, but of course I know Mr. Sedgman, and know he isn't playing well. I am serving for the first set, and thinking, Why not? By then, though, the news gets around that Sedgman is losing to an Italian, and the place isn't peaceful anymore. I am sheeting my pants with all these people watching. And Sedg is getting serious and beats me in straight sets. But it is a nice memory."

It was the kind of "good loss" that tennis players have cherished across the years, a hard fight, a decent score, against a personage. Not so much anymore, though, because the ruthless pro computer decrees that a defeat is a defeat, regardless of the defeater. There was a time when such a defeat was an attractive credential, negotiable for tournament entry or to be dined out on. No more.

Even the goodest win: The championship itself wasn't that satisfying a memory for Christ Evert in 1975 or Billie Jean King in 1970. It was the disrespect involved. Not only did they have to get up too early, like real working folks, to play ungodly 10:30 A.M. finals, but the hour guaranteed that they would be watched only by an expanse of empty pews, those dead-eyed statues, next of kin, and a few loiterers. The truth was painfully evident to Billie Jean and Chris, two of the biggest attractions in the game's history: They were as popular in Rome as Pizza Hut. Women's tennis in Italy had the status of breakfast: something to be gotten out of the way fairly early and fast, before the day's consequential business began.

A chauvinistic feeling pervaded and reached even a nine-year-old ballboy named Guido Tommasi, who had the gall to stand up Evert. Scheduled to work her doubles final in which Chrissie and Martina Navratilova won the title, Guido boycotted Signorina Macchinetta ("Little Machine")—as she was called at the Foro—and stayed home.

"Women's doubles is not for me," he told his mother, disdaining the supposed honor of ballboying a championship match.

"That's not the proper attitude," said his mother, trying to shame him into fulfilling his assignment.

"It is the Italian attitude," said his father, who told the kid he could stay home and watch TV.

Later, the father, Rino Tommasi, a journalist, related the story to Chrissie with a smile. "I think, Signorina Evert, Guido is the only man in Rome you haven't charmed. But he will learn."

Billie Jean King felt she and her sisters were losing too much to their brothers on the circuit that day she got pinched at the Foro. Such rudeness, considered conventional and jolly male sport in Rome, and commonly practiced on tourists, didn't actually happen to BJ. It was the symbolic tweaking in the wallet area that caused her to scream. She didn't stop screaming about financial inequality for years. By that time the indecencies of Rome 1970 were well past, but Rome was the fiscal turning-away point for the ladies. All roads upward led from Rome.

During that third year of openly paid tennis, the prize money ratio, set by male administrators, generally favored the men, two to one. But the painful fact for Billie Jean in Rome was that she collected $600 for her championship while Ilie Nastase got $3,500 for his. A six to one payoff made her "realize we'd get nowhere at the mercy of the men who ran the federations."

Although the ratio was about three to one at the U.S. Open, at least the female first prize, $7,500, was richer than the men's first prize at Wimbledon. Nevertheless, separatist talk was heard in public at Forest Hills where a group of women called a press conference to protest the disparity in prize money, and, as one of them, Patti Hogan, put it, accurately, "male greed. The men want all the money in the game." They also brought up a prospective boycott of the forthcoming Pacific Southwest Open in Los Angeles where the ratio was to be a feudalistic ten to one.

The women found no friends in their brothers. Even Mr. Minority, Arthur Ashe, who undoubtedly regrets his words, said that women's tennis would fade away because no one would pay to watch them.

If Rome fired up Billie Jean, Los Angeles kept her ablaze. But in boycotting L.A., the foremost women decided to go it on their own in what *World Tennis* magazine publisher Gladys Heldman called a "little broads only" event, put together by her in Houston. Through her friendship with the boss at Philip Morris, tennis junkie Joe Cullman, his Virginia Slims came in as sponsor of the $9,500 tournament.

Rosie Casals, who'd picked up a trophy and nothing more aor winning the Italian doubles in concert with Billie Jean, banked $1,700 for beating Judy Dalton in the Houston final. The intrepid nine women who defied the Badgerly USTA demand to desist were, naturally, suspended. It didn't matter to the historic Houston Nine—Peaches Bartkowicz, Casals, Dalton, Julie Heldman, King, Kerry Melville, Kristy Pigeon, Nancy Richey, Valerie Ziegenfuss—or the sponsor. Virginia Slims put on another separate-but-more-than-equal tourney at Richmond,

Virginia, at which winner Billie Jean pinched $2,400. So well received were those two tourneys that Cullman okayed a full circuit for 1971.

The ball-busting Babies had started on their Long Way. They were as confident and productive behind Chairman Ms., Billie Jean, as Chinese were in Long Marching behind Chairman Mao. By 1973 prize money at the U.S. Open was one to one. Equal. John Newcombe and Margaret Court got $25,000 each for winning. As 1988 closed, the top prize money grubber in the game, male or female, was Martina Navratilova. She, who had won $2,500 as runner-up to Evert in Rome in 1974, sat astride a career pile of $14,058,200.

As for Rome and the women, it was a distressing decline and fall until 1987. Italian Badgers, appearing to be misogynists in their policies of short money-shabby working hours, confirmed my worst views of them by evicting the women from the Foro altogether in 1980. This was but one symptom of the mismanagement and neglect of my favorite by inept caretakers. While the women's end of the Open was shunted off to a small, out-of-the-way club in Perugia, the men's operation withered in Rome, no longer a port of call for the best guys. Faithfully I continued to attend my love at the Foro, where attendance became so slight that you could hear the birds singing.

I hung on, though disheartened by the collapse in prestige, indifference of the Romans, and the absence of the women, pushed further into the wilderness, Taranto, in 1985, then abandoned altogether. In 1986, for the first time in thirty-six years, since the tournament was revived on an international basis after World War II, there was no Italian championship for women. This was worse than a pinch or a kick in the posterior.

But the Eternal City has seen all the boom-and-bust stories, from a phasing out of lions as matinee idols to the restoration of various ruins, including the Italian Open, which stands proud again. As one of those who regrets the saturation of the game by agents, I must also credit and thank IMG and its Roman stalwart, Cino Marchese, for the marketing and counseling that has resuscitated the tournament.

Like the majors, Rome is now a two-week fiesta, embracing both sexes, although the Italians have imposed their own form of segregation at the Foro. The women have the first week to themselves and are replaced on the second Monday by the men. Record crowds greeted the return of the women, who have a constituency after all. Even Guido Tommasi, ex-ballboy, and his father, Rino Tommasi, could be seen paying attention.

Though the women have been better received and better compensated since their return to Rome, pay equity is not exactly around the corner. While the 1988 women's champion, Gabriella Sabatini, received $40,000 (a respectable piece of change), the men's champion, Ivan Lendl, received $145,200.

33

○

Robber
Barons

If Bob Kelleher, a prime instigator, couldn't imagine in 1968 where opened-up tennis would go, a couple of his American friends had definite directional ideas: Jack Kramer and his disciple, Donald Dell.

Kramer had made a fortune promoting the old, lightly manned pro tour, the outlaws. Dell, seventeen years his junior, and fresh from law school, had played well enough to rank No. 5 in the United States in 1961, and was on his way to a fortune as trailblazer among the Vultures—player agents. Together these establishment shakers put together a new establishment. Theirs is a decent legacy for men's tennis: the Grand Prix circuit and the union, the ATP.

Few today would consider the tentacled Dell motivated by anything but power and profit. But somewhere within my sometime broadcasting partner is still the guy of vision and capacity who saw and utilized ways and means of elevating the shuffling, stumbling game he adored. He was a preeminent mover, a positive one, and could be again if he decided he's rich enough to become an elder statesman like his preceptor, Kramer.

Dell was in good position to carry the ball for open tennis, and he made the most of it as Kelleher's 1968 appointment to the U.S. Davis Cup captaincy. Besides his patriotic mission to win the Cup, which Australia had held since 1964, Donald intended to force open tennis, in actual practice, down the Badgers' gullets.

Even though the Aussies—Rod Laver, Ken Rosewall, John Newcombe, Roy Emerson, et al.—remained world-beaters, they were among those semirehabilitated ex-outlaws categorized as too pro for Davis Cup. With them ruled off, Dell's guys reclaimed the Cup in an easy final against Australian leftovers, certified as amateurs. Dell's guys—Arthur Ashe, Stan Smith, Clark Graebner, Bob Lutz, Charley Pasarell—weren't merely exceptionally talented young tennis players. They were also as exceptionally committed as their captain to remaking the system.

With Ashe and Smith as the nucleus, the United States won the Davis Cup five straight years—until the Aussie strong-arm guys were fully pardoned and permitted to partake again. By that time, although Dell had traded his captain's chair for the office furniture of an agent, the leading American men remained his. They were clients rather than team, and he a strong influence on them. He used that influence to help players as a group, thus the game, by making it plain that Dell's guys would enter no tournaments that didn't post appropriate prize money.

In the eyes of many American Badgers, open tennis meant business as usual, that is, the amateur monkey business at most of the old stands. Sure, there'd be a U.S. Open and a couple of other prize-money events such as the Pacific Southwest in Los Angeles. Those were the only American opens in 1968. But, by and large, the Lost Civilization would be maintained.

Not if you want my guys, said Dell. Get the dough up. Announce it out front as prize money, so everybody can play for it—or we won't be there. He knew he could haggle for just as much, or more, for his gang in "expenses," no matter how they played. But that wasn't the premise of open tennis. He also knew that the thought of prize money offended some Badgers. They and their small clubs didn't want to get into the business of pro tennis, and would fold up their piece of the tradition.

That was all right with Dell, who believed the game belonged in bigger, more accessible arenas, promoted by go-getters like himself who could land sponsorship money. No pay, no play was the rule for Dell's guys, waving good-bye to the Lost Civilization before signing its death warrant.

Ironically, as professionalized as tennis became, and as remodeled the surroundings, the sin of the fathers remained. Although supposedly worn out, that convenient old table, the cover-up for illicit handouts, wasn't put out with the trash. The male pros use it still. The idealistic spirit of the reformers, such as Kramer and Kelleher, was twisted by greed.

The theory driving open tennis was an equal start for all in tournament play: earnings in prize money based on wins. Soon enough, as tournaments proliferated, it was clear that the best players had to be selective when their agents raffled them off. That is, except for the four major tournaments, and a few others, the big guys went only where their agents could make undercover deals for substantial guaranteed amounts—appearance money—up front.

Although it's against the rules, and the spirit of the profession, these bonuses, only for the richest, of course, have become accepted practice. Kramer, who thought that putting up decent prize money would be enough to erase the sins of professional amateurism, was correct, but only for a while. Who could predict the encroachment of the Vultures, who believed that abundance wasn't enough for their new class of clients, the overly predatory professionals? Or for themselves. Or maybe they were just following their instincts, as usual, with little regard for the game, and applying the time-honored American business credo: Get all you can while you can.

"Everybody does it." John McEnroe, one of the robber barons, spoke out on behalf of Guillermo Vilas, the only pro to get caught breaking what has become an unenforceable rule by collecting a secret $60,000 payment at Rotterdam in 1983. So much time and money and anguish were spent on prosecuting and defending the popular Vilas in 1984 that it seems certain the Wise Old Owls, the MTC, won't have the heart to go through it again.

It appears that Vilas got nailed, as an object lesson, because he was easy—managed by the loner Ion Tiriac. Vilas was unattached to one of the three powerful agencies: Mark McCormack's International Management Group, Dell's ProServe, or a breakaway from Dell, Advantage International. Taking on one of them in such a case seems unlikely for the Wise Old Owls, and it would require the FBI to ferret out all the rule-bending.

Bjorn Borg may have been the first beneficiary of his agent's (IMG's) zeal in extracting extras from tournament promoters. No one profited more. But the history of that kind of "chiancery"—to use one of boxing conniver Sam Silverman's favorite malapropisms—is secret. Is such bribery exacted in the women's game? Probably, but not so prevalently. Their opportunities may not be as great. But the dolls have always been more responsible to their game and profession than the men have been.

However, nobody ever said the New Civilization would be paradise.

34

○

A Ticket
to Ride

Follow that carcass, was the directive of the *Globe's* managing editor, Tom Winship. Happy to oblige. The carcass in question was unimpressively skinny, yet usefully whippy, like a bamboo pole, and capable of landing trophy-size fish. It was sandy-hued, and belonged to Arthur Robert Ashe, Jr., who had to get out of town to become a decent tennis player.

Jim Crow ran him out of Richmond, Virginia, where the tournaments were off-limits to black kids while Arthur was growing up. Even after he was grown up and the name Ashe had international meaning, there were tournaments in the South (Dallas Country Club's, to name one) that ceased operating rather than accept him. How satisfying it was for him to enter Dallas not long after, in 1965, to represent the United States in his first significant Davis Cup assignment, brilliant triumphs over Mexicans Rafe Osuna and Tonio Palafox at Samuell Grand Park.

He left home young to tune his obvious talent for the game. Attending high school in St. Louis, and college at the University of California at Los Angeles, Arthur has been a moving man since. For that I'm forever grateful. The man was my ticket

213

to ride, a wonderful horse who carried me and my typewriter to every continent.

He even drew me to Richmond, where Arthur's homecoming was a bust in a recycled bus garage called the Arena. It was 1966. Since Jim Crow was at last out of style, Arthur was welcomed back by Morrill Crowe, the mayor, at a city hall reception. Then he was put on display in a local tournament for the first time, an eight-man tournament arranged specially to showcase the native son who had been thrown out of Byrd Park five years before for the crime of trying to play tennis with white kids. Imagine, then, his quiet pride in heading the U.S. lineup in a 1968 Davis Cup victory over the West Indies at the very same Byrd Park. That was a more comfortable homecoming. But, in 1966, he was embarrassed by losing in the first round to Frank Froehling.

But my thoroughbred didn't pull up lame very often, although his greatest triumphs were unexpected—Wimbledon '75, and the U.S. Open '68—which made them all the better.

When the earlier black champion, Althea Gibson, motivated my managing editor at the *Herald*, George Minot, to send me to Forest Hills for the first time, it was only a two-day story. Minot lost interest in spending money on Gibson afterward. But that was 1956, and the *Herald*. Tom Winship's *Globe* a decade later was a different proposition. The civil rights struggle was in full force, and the *Globe*'s publisher, Dave Taylor (who marched in Selma) and the editor in chief, Larry Winship (Tom's father), were keen exponents of the black cause. Larry was also a tennis buff who had hired a Harvard classmate, a marvelous writer named John Tunis, to file the *Globe*'s first tennis stories from France and England during the 1920s and 1930s. He was extremely interested in Ashe's progress, as was his son, Tom, and the *Globe*'s president, John I. Taylor. John I. spearheaded the newspaper's longtime financial and spiritual commitment to the Sportsmen's Tennis Club, an inner-city organization carrying on an ambitious and free instructional program for Boston kids.

With this kind of support I had no trouble clutching Arthur's shirttails regardless of his destination. Writing five or more sports columns a week, I was attending to the affairs of the professional sports—following Muhammad Ali's boxing career, looking in on the local Bruins, Celtics, Patriots, and Red Sox, as well as keeping an eye on tennis. Having fun with some bedraggled Red Sox clubs, I labeled them Our Olde Towne Team, and it stuck, through good years and bad. But I didn't have to be urged further when Tom Winship said, "Ashe is a good story. Hang on for all it's worth."

I hung on as Arthur swung, through Africa, Australia, Asia, Europe, and Latin America, right down to the sea-breezy afternoon in 1985 when he checked in with the saints at Newport's Casino, anointed for the Hall of Fame. He had done practically everything, missing out on only the French title, but grasping the other three majors as well as taking a powerful hand in four victorious Davis Cup campaigns, and captaining two more winning U.S. teams. Throughout he remained balanced and thoughtful, eloquent and dignified. His demeanor and appeal set him apart, much as Jack Nicklaus in golf, the stylish sort of guy nowhere evident on the men's side of tennis today.

It would take too much time to thank Arthur for all the mileage he put on my body, as a story of both social and athletic interest, but I should acknowledge his help in getting me a TV job.

The sixth year of WGBH's coverage of the Longwood tournament took on a brighter meaning for Greg Harney, the producer, and me, the babbler, along with a greatly increased audience. In that expectant and curious first summer of open tennis, 1968, the dual cities National Championships were remodeled. What had been the National Doubles in Boston became a hybrid called the National Amateur, comprising both singles and doubles. Forest Hills's production, usually the National Singles, was to be the first U.S. Open, also embracing singles and doubles, and with prize money at stake.

Did this mean what everyone suspected: that the well-flouted concept of amateurism at the uppermost level was embalmed? Not to those Badgers fearful of losing their treasured and alleged amateur national championship tradition while pros sought Open treasure at Forest Hills. They felt it should be continued at one of the venerable way stations.

Thus Longwood conducted a contrived carnival for that transitional year, the National Amateur, played in by several suspicious characters who posed as amateurs but weren't averse to accepting prize money wherever it had been offered, as at

Wimbledon. Identities of contestants and championships would get sorted out eventually. The USTA still holds a National Amateur, justifiably so, even though the appellation may seem dated. Lately it has taken place in rural Kiamesha Lake, New York, attracting little notice, and entered by reasonably amateur types, college kids, and others who don't pursue prize money. Presumably they have more fun than most of the tribe at the Open.

But in 1968, laid out on the Longwood green as a prologue to the introductory Open in America, the event had some standing. We were especially revved up at WGBH. Not only would we show championships in singles for the first time, but we had joined the big league on our own side of the game as part of a genuine nationwide network. Our telecasts, beamed only to the Boston area at first, and then to a few other eastern cities, were going national. Little old PBS finally had a transcontinental hookup, and—fanfare, please—color pictures. We would give Longwood the proper true-green treatment.

Although black-and-white telecasts were now past for us, we thrilled to the black among whites as Ashe made a tremendous debut for an American TV audience, winning his most meaningful title at that stage. It was an enthralling ace-splattered five-set skirmish in which he trailed another popular young American, Bob Lutz, 2 sets to 1. In that pre-tiebreaker day, a ten-minute refreshment pause was permitted after the third set. The players walked about seventy-five yards from the stadium to the Longwood clubhouse for a shower and change of clothing.

But Arthur started a fashion now common. Having asked permission of the referee, he did a minor striptease, changing his shirt beside the court to spectators' gasps and giggles. Then he sat contemplatively, awaiting Lutz's return, and promptly ran up eight games to take charge of the 4–6, 6–3, 8–10, 6–0, 6–4, victory. Ashe explained his radical public changing act, "It's terribly distracting to walk through a crowd, well-wishers and otherwise, to the clubhouse. So I thought I'd change on the court and stay there, and just concentrate on winning."

It was the second successive day of shirt shock. Beating Jim McManus in the semis, Arthur had added even more tone to the picture by performing in a revolutionary garment, a blouse of "trophy yellow," one of the two shades authorized by the USTA that year in a crossing of the clothing color line. The other was "match blue." Never before had a nonwhite shirt (or man) intruded on a national semifinal.

In the light of today's overly drawn-out matches (even with tiebreakers), the Ashe-Lutz five-setter was a shorty—two hours, forty minutes—though plenty long enough. But there were no ninety-second intervals at change games nor thirty seconds allowed between points. The game didn't drag as it tends, unfortunately, to do now.

Ashe by then was weary of being referred to as the first black male to win whatever—"Do the sportswriters still refer to Willie Mays as the 'black' outfielder?" Yet he was an original, and accepted the obligations and opportunities that went with it. After mounting the TV scaffolding to my booth, he sat through an interview of about forty minutes, a lifetime compared with the time allotted such postmatch chats now. But on PBS we had the riches of enough time to dig into a subject. We talked about Arthur's role in the black spectrum, his views on the "Black Power" leaders, such as Stokely Carmichael and Rap Brown, and where he fit in with them. While he supported the "Black Power" movement and understood some of its radical leaders, Arthur was a moderate. "Not a stone-thrower, although I sense the hopelessness of those who throw stones, the rioters."

His father as well as his tennis benefactor, Dr. Walter Johnson, had counseled turning the other cheek, with unfailing dignity. "It was the old Jackie Robinson stuff of his early years in the big league that Dr. Johnson preached whenever he was allowed to enter me in junior tournaments that had previously been whites-only. Don't give anybody the slightest reason to throw you out. He told me I'd be cheated on line calls—and I was—but to never complain. Just play the points, and keep everything inside."

That made Arthur a cool cat, seemingly unconcerned, although he was concerned. During this period as an army lieutenant teaching at West Point, he had made a couple of civil rights speeches at public gatherings. And he had been chastised by the commander of the military academy and warned that this was out-of-line for a serviceman and could result in his losing his tennis-touring privileges. Unlike Jackie Robinson, who was sometimes belligerently outspoken once he'd established himself, Ashe maintained his detached manner, though working hard for black advancement "through the system." I asked his thoughts on South Africa (he was considering resigning from the Davis Cup team as a personal protest to that country's inclusion in the Cup tourney), and his feelings about playing at clubs where he would not be admitted as a member—that meant every club he played at (and made money for) in the United States, where private, narrow clubs were the backbone of the circuit. "I don't like it at all, but I'm resigned to the fact that if I'm to play tennis I have to play at these clubs because that's where tennis is. But not forever, I hope. I hope I see changes."

Certainly he has. I felt good about his victory and the interview. Greg Harney and his crew felt good about presenting a telecast that had been historic in its breadth, and the color of its winner and images. We toasted ourselves and Arthur with beer before I had to write the story for the *Globe.*

A message awaited me at the clubhouse, a phone number in New York. Answering my call was a sports executive at CBS, Jack Dolph. "Liked the job you did," he said, "especially the interview with Ashe. Would you be interested in doing the Open for us next week at Forest Hills?"

Thank you, Arthur.

CBS had acquired the Open because ABC, after three years, wasn't interested in carrying it any longer. None of the commercial nets were interested in the old Nationals, a time salesman's dread. But the Open was blessed in having Joe Cullman as its chairman that baptismal year. Cullman, the boss at Philip Morris who was to boost the women toward heaven two years later by pouring Virginia Slims cash into their tour, was well connected in New York communications and advertising circles. He persuaded CBS to take over the Open for a minor rights fee—it has soared into the millions in recent years—and the tournament has become one of CBS's jewels.

Jack Kramer and I were the commentators through 1972, the year that NBC hired me. I did both the Open and Wimbledon that year, and I thought neither network cared that I worked for the other. But both were starting to regard tennis respectfully, and each suggested I had to make a choice. I picked NBC because of Wimbledon.

In 1968 Ashe came into New York seeded fifth, but a longer shot than that. It was logical to believe he'd had his limit of fun at Longwood, safe from pros such as Rod Laver, winner of Wimbledon where, as always, he'd beaten Arthur. But Cliff Drysdale cleared a path at Forest Hills for First Lieutenant Ashe by stunning a strangely ineffective Laver, and the new American hero charged through the breach to beat Tiny Tim Okker in a blizzard of twenty-six aces during the course of another five-set final. Ashe, by the American definition, was an amateur restricted to $28 daily expenses plus a hotel room. Therefore Okker got first prize, $14,000, Ashe the tributes and, for the first time, at twenty-five, utmost respect throughout the game.

As I went onto the court to interview him, Arthur was elated but couldn't quite comprehend all that he'd done in fifteen days. I was as exhilarated as he at having broadcast his unique winning of the U.S. Amateur and Open titles in the same year. Ashe was a drought-buster of epic proportions. Those bemoaning the state of American tennis in the late 1980s don't know what suffering is. Thirteen years had passed since the last American, Tony Trabert, had held the men's trophy. Now *that's* a dry spell.

Standing there, I imagined a reprise of our Longwood interview, but for a far larger audience. Friends who were watching told me I looked as though I'd been stabbed for a moment. Why? The voice in my ear, belonging to producer Howard Reifsnyder, said, "Don't get into all that black stuff—just tennis."

I was furious as I asked routine questions, wondering what was up. Was CBS afraid of controversy? Were they worried I'd offend the host club by asking how Arthur felt about winning at a place that wouldn't countenance him as a member?

Numerous members of the West Side Club had been affronted by Arthur. Not so much by his own tint, but that of the recently USTA-approved "match blue" and "trophy yellow" shirts that he had worn until tourney director Bill Talbert asked him to put them aside in the interest of harmony. West Side has dropped its more deplorable color ban—on humans—but retains to this day its white-only clothing regulation.

After we went off the air, I went after the producer, livid. "I had so many good, important questions to ask. . . ."

"I know, I know," Reifsnyder said. "But we aren't PBS with all that time to spare like you had in Boston. You had sixty seconds for that interview. That's all, no matter what. If we'd cut you off in the middle of the first serious answer, how would that have looked?"

I nodded in agreement, understanding his position. Welcome to commercial television, Bud.

Having been given the facts of commercial television life, and realizing that Greg Harney (a refugee from CBS himself) had told me so—"All you'll have to do is collapse a thirty-minute PBS interview into thirty seconds"—I went searching for Ashe. I still had a story to write, about his high-powered Open triumph over Okker.

Beneath the stadium I came across an Arthur Ashe, all right, but this was a fifty-two-year-old model, A. R. Ashe, Sr., who was weeping and didn't want anybody to see his tears. But we knew each other, and I felt it wouldn't be intruding to offer him a congratulatory handshake. He was mopping with a handkerchief, but smiling, too.

"Waited a long time for that boy," he was saying, sounding like an American tennis devotee who had given up hope that there would ever be another native champion. But I knew that wasn't what he meant, and I listened.

"I waited five years for that boy, and I never thought he was going to arrive. You see, the doctor told my wife, Mattie, after we'd been married five years, that she couldn't have children. I guess he wasn't up on everything medically. Anyway, some white folks I knew sent us to a specialist, and he said an operation would fix her.

"It didn't take long, a three-minute operation, but it made her all right. We had the two boys, first Arthur, then Johnny. Mattie was frail, never weighed over ninety pounds, and died of a stroke when Arthur was seven.

"It's hard for me to understand really how this day happened," said Papa Ashe, stocky and broad-shouldered. "Arthur was a frail child, weighed five and three-quarter pounds when he was born, and never would eat much. But he was good to see when we got him finally. My, we were happy. I don't think I've ever been so happy again until this day, watching him win this."

I'd met Arthur's father, a serious-minded yet jovial man, three years before at Forest Hills, after Arthur lost in the semis to Manolo Santana. Driving from Richmond to New York, he learned from the radio that his son had beaten the defending champion, Roy Emerson, in the quarter-finals. "That was a shock. I almost drove off the road." Watching made him nervous, and he had high blood pressure. But it was safer than following Arthur's results while at the wheel.

The United States had waited five years, too, not only for Arthur to fulfill his promise but to win the Davis Cup again, an accomplishment his presence in Adelaide three months later guaranteed. It wasn't the same Adelaide of my first visit of 1963, buzzing over the Davis Cup and the chances to prolong another reign of Captain Harry Hopman's defense force by withstanding American invaders. Adelaide was resigned to a dreary no-contest, so atypical of the greatest of rivalries. John Newcombe, Tony Roche, Fred Stolle, and Roy Emerson, the nucleus of a five-Cup run, had run away with the pros, and there was no chance for the ragtag home guard of Bill Bowrey, Ray Ruffels, Allan Stone, and the last of the seemingly unending Hopman Line, eighteen-year-old John Alexander.

Open tennis may have been approved in 1968, but an open Davis Cup was not. Australia's destitution was reflected in the striking cordiality of Captain Hopman. At sixty-three, Hop, who saw the futility, jumped ship to the United States in 1969 to begin a late and successful career as a professional coach. Usually sharp-edged and secretive, he even welcomed American journalists to his team dressing room in a glasnost-like gesture.

As the Aussies would say, Ashe and Clark Graebner in singles, and Bob Lutz and Stan Smith in doubles, went through the home side like salts.

That was the culmination of Captain Donald Dell's proclaimed "crusade" to regain the Cup, and the beginning of his career as the game's foremost power broker. Although captain of the team only one more year, he remained an éminence grise since Ashe, Lutz, and Smith were clients. So was Dennis Ralston, captain from 1972 through 1975. The 1968 victory earned the team a White House audience with President Nixon. They returned for more Nixonian commendation following the 1969 championship victory over Romania, although the chief didn't make as good an impression on the athletes because his choice of door prizes was small and hard. He handed them golf balls imprinted with his name.

35

○

Enemy
Camping

Arthur Ashe was imbibing oxygen from his private stock, courtside at Ellis Park, Johannesburg, six thousand feet above sea level.

"I know he doesn't trust us," murmured a South African spectator, "but did he have to bring his own air?"

There was something in the local air, all right, that you didn't want to breathe: hate, oppression, cruelty. Evil. Even if you were a white visitor, unhassled, you couldn't be comfortable in this police state. Especially if you were white, and paying attention, you realized that South Africa wasn't as bad as you'd imagined, and read about. It was worse. But you couldn't imagine how much worse unless you were a black South African.

A billboard in the rusting stadium seemed sarcastic. Or was it prophetic?

TIME TO SERVE BLACK AND WHITE

But it pertained to whiskey. However, as Arthur played Texan Sherwood Stewart in the opening round of the 1973 South

222

African Open—the first black man to beat a white there at tennis—a scintilla of hope appeared. It was an illusion of sorts, but Arthur's brief incursion had some meaning. "Apartheid pauses for you, Arthur," a black man said to him.

"You're opening a door, brother," the black poet Don Mattera told him.

It was the best of weeks and the worst of weeks in tracking Arthur Ashe, a stimulating time of "walking a tightrope," as he put it. "Arthur's playing well, and I don't know how he plays at all," said Jimmy Connors, who beat him in the final. "There's so much emotion for him."

Ashe was determined "to win this title for my brothers," and to see as much as he could in a brief time. At least he came away with the South African doubles championship in the company of Tom Okker, and, as one local black pointed out, "He beat two white South Africans in the singles. That is a small thing, but something to be pleased about." He had put the lone black face on a championship roll of a tournament dating to 1891.

As houseguest of a wealthy white, Ashe received the first of many culture shocks when the servants addressed him, quite properly in their line of duty, as "master."

"How embarrassing that was for me, the descendant of slaves," he said. "I finally got them to drop it, but it wasn't easy to bring about a temporary suspension of habit."

Refused visas on two previous occasions, Ashe was walking and speaking softly, observing, listening, disturbed not only by the conditions in which blacks were straitened, but by those blacks who told him bluntly that he shouldn't be there at all, that he was "a tool of the government."

"You make the government seem to be bending a little by letting you in, and letting South African blacks play in the tournament for the first time. They are using you," said a disapproving journalist. "This is window dressing, helping us not at all."

Actually, Ashe did not break the color bar. An American of little playing consequence, Bonnie Logan, had done that, followed by the Australian aborigine Evonne Goolagong and the New Caledonian Frenchman Wanaro N'Godrella. But Ashe, who had publicly denounced South Africa's government, was considered a hot potato even though hardly a firebrand. It took some skillful negotiating by the liberal-minded tournament promoter, Owen Williams, to get him a visa, and permit nonwhite South Africans to play, too, as well as integrate tournament seating. Those were Ashe's conditions, for which he agreed not to speak disparagingly while in the country.

Ten local black players, none, understandably, of international caliber, were allowed into the qualifying tournament, where they lost swiftly. But as South African–born champion Cliff Drysdale (the TV commentator, now a U.S. citizen) pointed out, "It was incredible to see blacks alongside whites in the changing room. That was a revelation to some of the Afrikaners, that they could change clothes in the same room with blacks and the place didn't collapse. And I don't think it was intimidating for the blacks either. A small dent in the system, perhaps."

Nothing you've read or seen can prepare you for the ghastliness of Soweto. It gives new and more disheartening meaning to the word "ghetto." But Arthur brought a spot of cheer by playing an exhibition there, on a dusty, cracked public court where two thousand gawkers crammed themselves around the wire fence or clung to nearby billboards and a railway platform. Never have cheers, including those that would salute his Wimbledon triumph twenty months later, touched Arthur more deeply. He was called "Sipho"—gift, in Zulu. "You are a gift to us, an inspiration," said Reginald Ngcobo, president of the Black Tennis Association. "You show our young how good a black man can be in his profession. It is important for them to see."

We departed those meanest of streets, aching for the people trapped in them, yet buoyed by the flickers of happiness Arthur brought to faces decreed to be the wrong color, and by the kindness shown his companions of the legally favored shade.

At a tense, poignant reception for Ashe by the Black Journalists Union, he—we—were startled by pointed, thoughtful objections to his presence mingled with congratulatory expressions. The meeting of about fifty newspaper people was split down the middle on pro and con, and extremely tense because what seemed free speech might be very costly. Informers, dotting the assemblage, were indicated to us, ready to report antigovernment oratory, which was heard.

"What good does Arthur do the poor black who has never heard of tennis? No good," said one. "But, being here, he makes the government look a little better."

But another drew laughter with, "You're kicking the system in the backside, Arthur, if only for a few days. That makes us laugh at the system, and it's important for us to laugh."

Even the man who wasn't there, an embodiment of the terror routinely practiced on blacks, could laugh. Don Mattera, journalist and poet, who had arranged the reception, had been "banned" for five years only that morning for his allegedly seditious views and writing. He stood outside the hall, closely watched by men from BOSS (Bureau of State Security), explaining that a banning, a form of nonpersonhood, meant "I can no longer work at my profession, be published, or gather with more than two other people."

But he smiled broadly as he shook our hands, and said, "Go well, brothers. Don't heed those who say stay home, Arthur. All blacks and whites who can should come here, and see conditions for themselves."

That seemed reasonable, an antidote to the South Africans who insist that critics from abroad, who haven't visited, don't really understand. Anyone who gives me that line gets the response: "Have you been to Soweto?" The answer is, invariably, no.

We left that beautiful, awful country in anguish, and hope, remembering the kindnesses and warmth of blacks and whites who yearned for change, true freedom, the dismantling of apartheid, and who kept on going, cheerfully, somehow. After all these years it seems extraordinary—and outrageous—that the South African Open remains within the tennis community, an outpost on the men's Grand Prix schedule. When will the MTC, apparently oblivious to its callousness in sanctioning world-class entertainment for the ruling class, show a conscience and throw South Africa out of organized tennis? Soon, I hope.

I'm disappointed in the nondomestic players who enter Grand Prix and satellite tourneys in South Africa, particularly since there are so many other lucrative opportunities elsewhere. But as unfeeling or uninformed as such guys may be, I do believe it's their choice, their business, and also that South Africans—who certainly aren't reps of their government—should have free access to tournaments worldwide.

If the journey to South Africa rendered me depressed, anyway there was also the delayed reaction of being scooped. In the departure lounge, Chris Evert, who had won the women's title, sat beside me. "Did you see what Jimmy gave me?" She lifted her left hand, which glowed like a searchlight, decorated by a diamond the size of Kareem Jabbar's big toe.

"Very nice," said I, acknowledging that South Africa was a good place to purchase diamonds. As Mr. Obtuse, I didn't even say, "Best wishes," even though the considerate Chrissie was trying to tell me something.

When her engagement to Jimmy Connors was announced not long after, my boss at the *Globe* said, "Strange you didn't have that story first."

A light suddenly went on in my neural mush, evoking that diamond at the Johannesburg airport. "Oh, yeah," I said, "that's what that diamond ring must have been all about."

"There you were sitting next to the story and didn't write it?" Dave Smith roared. "If you'd been at Pearl Harbor, December 7, 1941, I imagine you'd have written the fireworks for Chinese new year went off a little early."

36

○

Good Old
Guzzlers

From five bucks to fifty thousand dollars. From a furtive basement transaction in Boston to a televised world championship in a Dallas arena. Fifteen years it took Kenny Rosewall to make that transition in peddling his wares, from nickel-and-dime to the big time, and even then he couldn't quite believe he'd done it. It wasn't what he set out to do when his father, a Sydney grocer, put a racket in his right hand. He was just a little kid, who didn't get much bigger, but instantly loved the game so much that he would embrace it unquestioningly and carry on a lifelong affair.

Champions have to play. They aren't concerned with financial terms at the start. They just have to play. Rosewall didn't go into tennis for the money, but, winding up a millionaire, he never turned down a chance to pick up some change either. That's what he and the other Aussies were doing at Longwood in 1956 where he won the National Doubles with Lew Hoad, and I first came across him. Forest Hills in New York was the next stop, where they'd be reoutfitted with rackets and clothing. So they were selling same, off their backs and out of their hands, to the ballboys, children of the club members. It was a way to supplement stipends doled out by the traveling team's captain, usually Harry Hopman. Also it was a nice way to do something for the ballboys in the generous Aussie manner.

The rackets, virtually new and strung with the best gut, worth about thirty-five dollars retail, were priceless to the ballboys because they were foreign models, seldom seen around there, and had been used in battle by their heroes. The Aussies would sell only to ballboys, regardless of how much an adult offered, and the price that year for a Rosewall Slazenger was $5.

"Imagine Rosewall's financial rise!" laughed Pierre Whalen in 1971. Pierre, a friend of mine who purchased one of those rackets, was noting that Rosewall, who might still have that five spot, had just won the heaviest payoff in tennis history—fifty thousand dollars—for beating Rod Laver in the WCT finale.

Rosewall, the onetime equipment merchant, was stunned himself to be the cutting edge as the truly serious money began to pour forth. Fifty grand to win an eight-man tournament considered the professional championship! The U.S. Open's fifteen-thousand-dollar first prize was the closest any of the majors came to that figure in 1971.

Rosewall, who at one stage of his career felt blessed to receive a cup of tea and free lunch for playing, got started back when Australia seemed so remote that most people took it on faith that the island down under existed at all. Still, the fairly well informed did know of Australia as the exotic hatchery of a number of strange creatures. There were kangaroos and koalas, wombats and world-beating tennis players who sometimes hung from a racket with both hands while bashing the ball, and appeared to be having a better time than anybody else.

Little Miss Two Hands, Chrissie Evert, was unborn, her father, Jimmy Evert, in grammar school when the first double-fisted backhand was seen—swung by an Aussie named Viv McGrath. McGrath came to attention by astonishing, and beating, U.S. champ Ellsworth Vines, who had taken one of those rare, infrequent, and interminable boat rides to reach the Antipodes. It was 1932, two years before the birth of Kenneth Robert Rosewall, my candidate for the position of most remarkable player of the game. Ever.

Although he hasn't won a major championship since 1972, or graced a major final since 1974, Rosewall must never be spoken of in the past tense because "The Little Master" or "Muscles" or "The Doomsday Stroking Machine"—whichever sobriquet you prefer—continues to work his strong and enduring artistry somewhere in the world sometime during yet another year.

Long married to his sweetheart of teen years, careful with a penny and his two beers, and hardly the life of any party, Rosewall—the dark-haired Dorian Gray of tennis—is nonetheless a landmark in a couple of ways. He may not sing, dance, hoist, or enliven spirits in the manner of the beloved ringleader Roy Emerson, but Kenny surely does typify the Aussie tennis player. Fit, competitive, and sporting—championship class all the way.

As tennis players go, they were the best of breed, those good-old-boy Aussies, the down under–taking mafia of godfatherly Captain Harry Hopman, stretching from Frank Sedgman and Ken McGregor in 1950 to John Alexander and Tony Roche in 1977, when the world-conquering line ran out. Of course, Rosewall still runs, never in danger of running out of anything except, possibly, opponents who can keep up.

During those twenty-eight years Australia won the Davis Cup 17 times to America's 8, and 62 of a possible 113 major men's singles championships, while Americans were next with 24.

This nation of fewer people than inhabit the Greater New York City area took great delight in beating up the rest of the world on tennis courts. No country's citizens have made a comparable record, before or since. One of the more mournful aspects of the game recently has been the disintegration of the Aussies. Not only because they were so good, but because they were so good-natured about it.

Any Aussie well knows that the saddest song ever written in his language is Slim Dusty's "The Pub with No Beer." Australians have been known to drink beer. Australians also have been known to have fun and play tennis—and to combine all three activities, although the ones who play tennis in public generally wait until the game is over before they start swilling. Gentleman Jack Crawford, one of the more popular Australian players, winner of the Wimbledon, French, and Australian titles in 1933, was known to sip a little brandy during the course of a match. But that, he assured friends, was medicinal, a help with his asthma.

Were the Aussie good old boys malt-powered? Not exactly. But they probably wouldn't have done as well without it. "It helped them unwind," said an American, Marty Riessen. "They'd get together at night and have a few, and they were in such superb condition that it didn't hurt them."

Margaret Court liked her beer, too. A rangy, long-armed six-footer, probably the strongest woman ever to play, Mighty Maggie sipped on her own, or with her husband, Barry. "Sheilas" weren't included in the communal swill. Men only.

If Margaret ever got "a skinfull," as the Aussies sometimes describe being overserved, she never gave any indication. Ever the lady. But the boys knew how to throw 'em down and whoop it up.

Considering some of the parties and partyers, it may seem appropriate that in Australia a colloquial synonym for intoxi-cation—"Adrian"—is the name of a splendid tennis player. Adrian Quist, a Hall of Famer who led Australia to the 1939 Davis Cup, is not noted as a tippler. His name alone caught the fancy of some anonymous dabbler in that curious lingo, Cockney rhyming slang. It follows the same reasoning for another word also meaning tipsy—"elephant's."

Drunk rhymes with trunk. Whose trunk? Elephant's. Pissed rhymes with Quist. Who's Quist? Adrian.

Now that's fame, wouldn't you say, to live on in the language long after anyone would recall your 1950 Wimbledon doubles championship?

Adrian or elephant's, the Aussies were never disorderly or objectionable that I knew of. The most jovial were Emmo and Fiery, Roy Emerson and Fred Stolle, who could turn any gathering up a few notches into high-proof high jinks.

Emmo and Fiery enjoyed themselves immensely while scorching American lawns the summers of 1965 and '66.

They were undeniable hits, unbeaten in doubles and dominant in the singles. Attractive and gregarious, they played and laughed their way into the hearts of anybody watching. Emmo gleamed from head to teeth—patent leather hair and a Fort Knox lineup of gold fillings—a superb athlete covering court like a greyhound. Stolle, a big-serving cornstalk with maize locks, walked as though every step was the last. Together they were murder, hanging tough whether or not hung over.

Quickly they instituted a sort of split-shift program to get them through the American summer. "We either go to bed at a reasonable hour or stay out all night," Stolle explained. The way they partied and won their way across the Northeast showed how far the Aussies were ahead of their American rivals at that time. Those who bemoan the recent European takeover of men's tennis may have forgotten the hegemony of Australia. Americans fretted about ever getting out from down under. But they did. It's cyclical.

Emmo and Fred's energy was prodigious. Stolle recalls a doubles match at the Meadow Club at Southampton, one of the venerable Long Island watering (and boozing) spots. "We were just getting home from the party. It was about nine-thirty in the morning, and Emmo says to me, 'Fred, we've got to go finish our doubles. Remember?' Right he was. We'd been playing a couple of lightning-serving college kids from California—Jim Osborne and Jerry Cromwell—in the semifinals, back in an area they called the paddock. Terrible grass courts. Nobody could return serve.

"They won the first set, 24–22. That was before tiebreakers—God bless Jimmy Van Alen for inventing them. We won the next, 9–7. It was going on forever, and finally it's bloody dark, so it's put off, to finish the next morning at ten.

"There's Emmo and me, a little fuzzy, and when we get to the club Cromwell and Osborne are out practicing. Bright-eyed and eager. They've got a big upset going, and they want to be right to start the last set.

" 'You want to hit some, Emmo?' I ask him. 'God, no,' he wrinkles his face and blinks. 'Be right with you fellows,' I say to Cromwell and Osborne. Then Emmo and I run and jump into the club pool, hoping that'll clear our heads. We put on our tennis gear, walk to the court, and say, 'Let's go!'

"Cromwell says, 'You want to hit a few, don't you?' And Emmo says, 'Naw—couldn't stand it, mate, Let's just start and get it over with so we can go to bed.'

"Well," Stolle beams, "that just bloody psyched those two right out, although it wasn't intended that way. Emmo and I couldn't stand to look at a bloody ball. We figured they'd go through us like salts, and we didn't care. But damned if they couldn't put a ball in the court, and we won easy."

For the National Doubles in Boston, however, they amended their approach to a split formation: one-in-bed and one-in-the-beer. "If either of us decides to stay at the party, the other goes back to the hotel early and gets enough sleep for both of us. We alternate," Emmo outlined the game plan for pursuing a national title. This was not only considerate of themselves but of the hosts and hostesses around town who were assured of entertaining one or the other of the celebrated pair.

The eve of the 1965 semifinals was Stolle's night out, and he arrived at my house on Beacon Hill early to get a good fielding position beside the kitchen icebox, from which he didn't budge all night. "Emmo's back at the hotel, sleeping the good sleep." He delivered his partner's regrets and snared his opening Foster's—mother's milk from home. My roommates and I called it the Fuzzy Ball, and everyone in the tournament was invited. Most of them came, it seemed, and so did the police— eventually irritated by the impenetrable shoulder-to-shoulder camaraderie that was embellished by a band in one of the bedrooms.

The fuzz were always at the Fuzzy Ball, a tradition starting with the inaugural—an impromptu bash in 1958. Lots of cheap beer in jelly jars and the obligatory bag of potato chips mixed with hordes of tennis players, stewardesses, and newspaper people at a Back Bay roof-garden apartment above Marlborough Street that I shared with two other guys.

"It's all right, Officer," I had said to the sergeant as he was alluding to the patrol wagon. Nodding reassuringly to the guests, I was going to handle it with aplomb. "Sergeant, you don't want to create an international incident, certainly," I began. "Possibly you aren't aware, but six of these gentlemen are the Australian Davis Cup team."

I looked firmly at the sergeant. He smirked at me, and I was at once dismayed, sensing that even a plea of diplomatic immunity would go unheeded as he replied:

"What the fuck is Australia? And what the fuck is the Australian Davis Cup team?"

I suppose he was being straightforward, but the Aussies looked a little wounded, as well as fearful.

Seven years later, the August evening (and morning) in 1965 that Fred Stolle guarded the kitchen icebox was atypical: The cops barely stepped in, glanced about, requested that we close the windows, and were gone.

"Poor performance," Stolle grimaced. "This dinger of yours

must be losing its touch, mate. Cops weren't toey [disturbed] at all."

The fellow next to him, with a villainous mustache and a felonious grin, offered, "It would have been amusing, Fred, if you'd been carted off, and spent the day in jail instead of playing." He was the engaging Longwood member and college instructor Joe Vay, a good player who called himself the Baron of Hungary, insisting he was such, in exile.

"Ah, Baron," Stolle replied, reaching for another Foster's, "Emmo could win it without me. No fears. Who we playing? Just bloody Riessen and Graebner in the semis, and probably Pasarell and Froehling in the final. No worries there that I can see."

"Really?" said the Baron, sniffing at a cognac. The Baron and cognac were practically inseparable. He also liked to make a bet, and, being Australian, so did Stolle. "No problems, you say, Fred?"

"Absolutely none, Baron. I make Emmo and me two-to-one over anybody you can name."

"What about later today? Marty Riessen and Clark Graebner. Not a bad team, Fred. . . ."

"Two-to-one for twenty bucks, Baron?"

"Fred, you're on. You're a sportsman," said the Baron, who spent the next few hours trying to be sporting himself, as a one-man bucket brigade keeping Stolle from burning up with thirst. "Let's drink to your match," the Baron kept saying, working hard to protect his wager. Stolle appeared to be working just as hard helping him.

As three o'clock in the morning approached, and they'd drunk the whole night through, Stolle murmured, "Baron, I think I ought to ring up Emmo and tell him about the bet. I want him to know so he realizes how important his sleep is."

"Capital idea, Fred," the Baron whispered from the kitchen floor.

Fred dialed. After innumerable rings from the hotel switchboard, Emerson was on the line.

"Did I wake you, Emmo?" Fred inquired.

"Ah, no, had to be up to answer the phone. Lovely to hear your voice and know you and the Foster's are well, you bloody idiot." Stolle related the proposition with the Baron, offered Emmo half the action, and then hung up. "No chance for you,

Baron. Emmo's very clear-headed and determined," he said, trying to help his adversary out the door.

Even muddle-headed, the Baron knew he had a sure thing. Never had he worked so strenuously to give himself an edge.

Stolle and Emerson together, however, were beyond the Baron's control. He sat in the stands groaning, perhaps more in recognition of his post-dawn squash than his losing bet.

"Baron," Fred smiled as he collected the money, "you should know that beer is like popsicles to us Aussies. But the cognac doesn't seem to have agreed with you."

Though he lost several tennis bets to Stolle, the Baron had his revenge four years later, after the demise of the National Doubles, with the U.S. Pro settled in at Longwood. Gaining the kind of edge that would make any gambler gleeful, he actually wormed himself into the contest he and Stolle were betting on—as an official!

Stolle had selected the favored Cliff Drysdale in a first-round match, offering the Baron an appealing price against Ron Holmberg. Looking around for the Baron when the match began, Stolle couldn't believe where he spied him. "Why . . . he's on a bloody line!" Stolle screeched. "What the bloody hell's he doing out there?" We would see.

Tennis was that casual not so long ago, before officiating was regulated by the MTC. Any kindly soul known to the chairman of officials could volunteer to take a line, and was gratefully seated. And . . . there was the Baron, on the court, tactfully having left the cognac bottle in his locker, seated in a folding chair as a sideline judge.

If Drysdale had been aware of the situation, he would have strangled the Baron. He very nearly did anyway, because—it was inevitable—after a diligent stretch of flawless decisions, the patient Baron had his chance. As the match came down to a third-set crunch, Holmberg hit a couple of balls a trifle wide of the Baron's line, and, predictably, the Baron officiously signaled them good, with his palms parallel to the ground. Drysdale spluttered, glared at the Baron, and complained, vainly. Stolle fumed, accepting that he'd been had, and the Baron turned his felonious grin on and quickly off.

He had stolen the match from Drysdale and won the bet as neatly as tossing back a cognac. Or an Aussie chugging a beer.

Rosewall and Laver, forever linked, like gin and vermouth, Lewis and Clark, Romulus and Remus, are the prime freaks: the guys who were kings of three realms. First, they rose to the top of flimflamateurism, bowing out of conventional society by winning the U.S. Nationals. Ken in 1956, Rod in 1962.

Then, electing to play for money that was outright and over-the-counter cash, they descended to the wilderness of professionalism, peripatetic outlaws folding their canvas court and sneaking from one one-nighter to the next, and ruling there, too.

Outlasting their status as outcasts, they were returned in 1968 to respectability and all the old familiar throne rooms that open tennis comprised. It wasn't too late, fortunately, and Kenny and Rod were monarchs again, of this new and lasting order.

Rosewall was forty-three when he won his last on the adult professional circuit, in 1977, a year he played twenty-four tournaments. Listen to the whining of one of the top guys or gals today whenever it's suggested that they engage in excess of fifteen.

At forty-four Kenny was still formidable, ranked thirty-first in a world he had begun traveling, immediately successful—a U.S. quarter-finalist, for instance—twenty-six years before. At the close of 1979 he announced his "retirement," though only from the big league, the Grand Prix circuit. That was just a convenient line of demarcation. Upward and onward he moved, to a gathering of hyperactive relics called the Grand Masters circuit, a repository for champions aged beyond forty-five. His 1987 championship in that precinct, at fifty-three, was his fourth in six years. No one who knows him doubts that Rosewall will be the terror of the eighty-and-over tournaments when he becomes eligible on January 1, 2014.

First sightings of Rosewall reported in the United States came in early 1947 from the lips of that astute champion Jack Kramer. Kramer found Kenny more beguiling than any other Australian flora and fauna he'd encountered during his first visit, a quest for the Davis Cup. Jack and Ted Schroeder, as teammates, had repossessed the old punchbowl from the Aussies in the December 1946 revival of the competition shut down by World War II. Kramer related that they were taken to the final of a twelve-year-olds tourney in Sydney where a couple of amazing kids named Hoad and Rosewall were flailing away at each other. The robust Hoad was hitting the ball harder than any kid in Jack's experience—but the slight Rosewall was winning most of the points.

Little has changed. Kenny grew up to five-foot-seven, 140 pounds, a killer of giants of several eras. A wondrous retriever at first, he developed an attacking game, too, unerring smash, deft volleys, and a wimpy-looking but well-placed serve. His knifing backhand remains an aesthetic joy, one of the great weapons. I would be willing to bet that if the financially shrewd Rosewall were to encounter unlikely reverses, and had no alternatives, he could yet make a comfortable living as a plus-fifty returnee to the Grand Prix. Picking his tournaments carefully, say about sixteen of them, I believe he could rank within the first one hundred, none of whom earns less than $60,000 annually. That may be wishfully hypothetical guff from an unreformed admirer. Anyway, his prize money on the Grand Masters tour would easily ward off starvation.

Kramer, who would be Rosewall's employer a decade later in 1957, says, "I gave Kenny his first look at bills bigger than those fives that Harry Hopman handed out to the Aussies as meal money. He didn't know there was such a thing as a hundred when I signed him, but he grew fond of them fast."

Aussies used to leave home in April, heading for clay-court tournaments in southern Italy and France that prepared them for the Continental bigs in Rome and Paris. Then it was grass in England, en route to Wimbledon. More grass in the United States led to Forest Hills, followed by a spot of concrete in California. Not until October were they home again, to bone up for their own grass-court summer circuit that would begin soon.

It was a hard proving ground, putting up with that much life on the road, homesickness, the iron rule of Hopman, and constant competition. But few who came away failed. Carefully picked by Hopman and other official selectors as lads who could be counted on, they were eager for the extraordinary chance to leave ordinary homes and see the world, knowing their country was banking on them. Davis Cup victories were the financial backbone of development of more good players. Why were they so well behaved? Bad actors didn't get to travel, at least not for very long.

They quit school at the legal age of fifteen to put aside everything for tennis. From then on they were professionals in fact, if not label. Those who did really well, one or two of them every once in a while, would defect to genuine professionalism, accepting Kramer's money. But amateurism, though modestly compensated, was a better life than most of them could have imagined. They were on the payrolls of sporting-goods firms, and had all their needs on the road taken care of. Nothing lavish. But no worries.

Hopman dealt with tournaments for his players' money, and handed it out as he saw fit. In exceptional cases, if Hopman and his fellow Badgers were trying to prolong the amateurism of an older, married player, keeping him out of Kramer's clutches, they permitted him to make a "private tour." He traveled on his own, made his own deals, and did whatever with the dough while official eyes were averted. Frank Sedgman, Lew Hoad, Fred Stolle, Rod Laver, Roy Emerson, and Margaret Court eventually won these most-favored deals.

The Hopman/Aussie system was a winner, perfect for the time when no prize money was available as a temptation to individualists, and for an isolated country whose traveling team concept built tremendous esprit de corps. Tennis was a major sport in Australia. Making Hop's team was as good as becoming a big-league ball player for an American kid.

Maybe the talent did run out along with Hopman, or maybe Australian kids became interested in other things. Possibly Patrick Cash, in 1987 the first male Aussie to win at Wimbledon in sixteen years, signals a resurgence. Neale Fraser, a Hopman protégé and successor as Davis Cup captain, has managed to win two Cups with post-Hopman players, notably Cash, in 1983 and 1986, by rejuvenating the family feeling of Aussie Cup teams for brief periods.

But the good-old-boys era is gone forever. Cash, who can't make up his mind whether to be surly or sunny, is certainly no throwback to the Hopman days. He would have shaped up fast, or been left in Melbourne by Hop. Fraser, who has had his jams with Cash, swallowed his memories of Hop and began praising Patrick as one of the greatest of all Aussies. Why bite the hand that swings the Cup-winning racket? Hop could afford to bite a few. But then the supply line looked endless.

Not until that One Great Scorer hands out a celestial stats sheet will we know how many times Laver and Rosewall dueled. Nobody counted between 1963 and 1968 when they were the stars of the limbo league, playing every continent in all conditions, good and bad, adequate and abysmal. Sometimes money was good, sometimes it wasn't. They played magnificently wherever, to large houses and empty seats, going at each other life and death every time. They think Laver won more, but can't be sure. "I know I lost some of the best matches I ever played against him," says Laver.

Occasionally they would appear where it mattered, Forest Hills or Longwood, Wembley in London or Roland Garros. Customarily their doings were but a rumor from the Andes, darkest Africa, the Australian bush, or a dance hall in Scotland.

By the time Rod and Kenny got to Dallas in November 1971, to launch an open-era tradition, the WCT finals, they had been through the mill of indifference, but still aiming to please and drill each other.

"One match for fifty thousand dollars . . . ah, my," Rosewall mused the day before they played the final. "More than I made for a year several years. Hard to imagine that I'd be doing this now." He was thirty-seven, just getting warmed up. "When I started as a pro fifteen years ago, I reckoned my traveling days would be over by now. I'd be settled down in Sydney, maybe selling insurance, giving a few lessons or coaching youngsters, and working on my golf game.

"But this?" He shook his head, bemused.

In the final, though struck in the eye by a ball that glanced off his racket, Kenny kept his blurry eye on the money and beat Laver. Accepting the unprecedented check, Kenny did have the decency not to peddle his rackets for walking-around money.

37

○

Big League

The Big W.

What else could you call the cathedral on Church Road? Like pilgrims to the Vatican, every year the last week in June and the first in July, the faithful stream toward the Doherty Gates on one side of the verdant lot, or the Perry Gates on the other.

Wimbledon-crazed lemmings. Hundreds of thousands of them appear during the fortnight whether they have a place to sit or not. Most of them don't. Only the eleven thousand or so who clutch daily Centre Court tickets, and a few thousand more with Court 1 admissions—scarce as hockey players' teeth—can be sure of good bottom land in a reserved pew with a clear view of the services. The rest line up like petitioners at the pearly gates, willing to undergo any indignity if only they are admitted.

Once inside, they're prepared to wait even longer for unreserved seats, or merely places in standing-room pens for an upright vigil of hours. There they are stacked like cordwood on end, lifted out as though steamer trunks by first-aid attendants whenever anyone faints—and quickly replaced. It is the sort of merry arrangement that, if attempted in America, would lead to a jolly old riot. Especially on rain-out days. Hard luck, old boy. After seven soggy hours and not a ball struck, you may leave and burn your ticket. There are no rain checks at Wimbledon.

This, however, is the masochism of the British Wimbledon patron. Following British tennis is a sort of death-wish pastime anyway. Limeys may have bred tennis, but they long ago forgot how to play. But, as one of their infrequent champs tells it, tennis isn't all that popular in the homeland. "You get the wrong impression from Wimbledon," says Ann Jones, the doughty left-hander who snuffed Billie Jean King's bid for a fourth successive title in the 1969 final. "We aren't mad keen on tennis, but we are mad keen on Wimbledon."

The occasion. Just being there, regardless of who plays, and crashing those gates seems enough. Open to the public for two weeks a year, Wimbledon is an enduring monument to a Victorian outing. The tournament, entitled formally "The Lawn Tennis Championships," seems incidental to the place.

They could set up TV screens on each court and show reruns of old matches, and it wouldn't make much difference. Just as today, some devotees might pay attention to the slapping of backhands and forehands, but greater numbers would wander, casing the joint and each other, patronizing the champagne and strawberries-and-cream emporia, and the souvenir shops, perhaps passing out, overheated, during one of those widely separated days when overbearing sunshine pays a welcome, though astounding, call.

During the last days of the tourney, when the important stuff is played entirely for the relatively few with visas for Centre or Court 1, many patrons are content to stand in front of Centre Court stadium, taking in the match via a large scoreboard on the outer wall that registers each point. Seeing the illuminated numbers, and judging the match from crowd noise seeping out, is, apparently, sufficient.

Possibly no other sporting event is as thoroughly covered as Wimbledon by press, radio, and TV, yet the scoreboard gapers and grounds roamers persist, stoking their own Wimbledon imaginations in their own way. They don't actually have to see Boris Becker or Martina Navratilova, Pat Cash or Steffi Graf, to be fulfilled. Merely being in the same precinct may be a kind of sensual experience.

"Well, we're British," said David Gray, who wrote for the *Guardian,* feeling that explained it all.

It is this phenomenon, an orderly mob's flooding of the All England Lawn Tennis and Croquet Club's estate in the southwestern London suburb named Wimbledon, transforming it into the Green Hole of SW 19, that is the centerpiece of tennis. Wimbledon—usually pronounced and spelled *Wimbleton* by Americans, I have no idea why—is the first tournament, in age and influence, from which the game has radiated throughout the world. Its 1877 birth predates the next eminent championship, the U.S., by four years, the French by fourteen, the Australian by twenty-eight. Long before its would-be emulators had captivated substantial followings, Wimbledon was socko-boffo, swollen with customers. Soon after World War I the original Worple Road Grounds, whose Centre Court held 4,500, was overrun.

The answer was the "new" (present) Wimbledon, christened in 1922, roomy enough for about fourteen thousand (three thousand of them standing) in Centre Court. Quickly the new ballpark was besieged. Precious Centre Court tickets sold out as soon as they went on sale four months prior to opening day. It is one of the world's toughest tickets, and if attendance were limited to those possessing ducats for specific seats, as at the U.S. Open, you could move about as comfortably as you can at Flushing Meadows. However, you may find as many as forty thousand pilgrims paying their shoulder-rubbing respects at the Big W, no place for a claustrophobe.

Isaac Stern, a connoisseur of strings fixed either to racket or violin, delivered the classic answer to "How do you get to Carnegie Hall?": "Practice, practice."

The same could be said of Wimbledon, although the most common, fastest means is by subway (to watch, not be watched). Spilling forth from Southfields Station of the underground onto Wimbledon Park Road, the Charge of the Sight Brigade is constant, aimed toward the All England Club. You can take a bus or taxi, but, as the crowd flies, it's only about a mile, and the direction is unmistakable. Join the parade.

A friend and colleague, Harold Kaese, and I, did in 1959,

curious to inspect this whale of a tournament that, so we'd heard, could swallow all the others put together. We'd heard right. Kaese was a precise, thoughtful *Globe* columnist with whom I sometimes played tennis. As a reporter with the rival *Herald*, I'd been thrown up against him in England. It was typewriter-to-typewriter competition on a stroking story, but one about as far from tennis as you could get: the Henley Royal Regatta.

A couple of hot Harvard crews were entered, and the *Globe* had trumpeted that its all-rounder, Kaese, would be beside the Thames to provide stroke-by-stroke accounts. Such an expense ran against the spiritual grain of the richer yet chintzier *Herald*. But, with a heavy Harvard readership, Mr. Minot, the managing editor, had no choice but to keep up with the Joneses: his *Globe* counterpart, an old Harvard, Vic Jones.

The Boss was on the phone on a June Thursday. Did I have a passport? Did I know anything about rowing? Could I leave two days later on a flight to London? The answers in order: No; oh, sure; absolutely.

The passport was easy. And didn't everybody living in Boston know something about rowing? I mean, who could avoid noticing the racing shells skimming along the Charles? One opinion of the sport stuck with me. Sam Silverman, the boxing promoter, was forever decrying the "wasting"—that is, allotment—of sports-page space for "college boy crap" that might conflict with his own business. Of the Harvard-Yale boat race he said, "I hope they both capsize and drown. How can anybody be interested in college boys paddling them canoes backwards—and without any broads on board?"

Sam had assessed the situation pretty well. He wanted romance with his boat rides, and liked to see where he was going. I had no clue where I was going with this one. For twelve hours, the length of the pre–jet age flight, I nervously pored over books and other literature on rowing, particularly Harvard rowing. It was like an all-night cram for a final exam. Would I pass, justifying the editors' faith?

Henley turned out to be the most delightful event I've covered. Set in the pastoral Henley Reach, a straightaway between two bends in the Thames, the Regatta is a retreat to an Edwardian panorama. Straw skimmers and garish blazers that only English gentry can get away with adorn the young and old boys.

Gorgeous women in flowery dresses and big hats are seen in the members' enclosure while a red-coated military band plays "Roses of Picardy," and the bankside crowd roars, "Come on, Jesus!" for a boat from the Oxford college of the same name.

Wimbledon, which Kaese and I had yearned to see, was running at the same time. We couldn't resist stealing a day before the Regatta began to slip off to London for a look. One-day press passes were arranged. About two and a half hours on train, subway, and foot was the distance to the Doherty Gates, past those interminable columns of Wimbledon degenerates waiting serenely on the outside for their chance to enter. Many of them had slept the night through on the sidewalk to get better line position.

The well-managed crush at the gate was staggering. We were unprepared for the bustle of ticket-holders, scalpers, and neatly landscaped, grassy parking lots where picnickers fueled themselves for a long day. Large, black Daimler limousines, ferrying players and officials, streamed in and out of the gate. Neither Forest Hills nor Longwood could approach the efficiency, the quiet good taste, and the cosmopolitan air of this presentation.

Crossing the threshold, I was in a green and floral land that I couldn't associate with tennis. Hydrangeas, roses, and people lined the way to the looming, overpowering presence of ivy-clad Centre Court, a Yankee Stadium of this game.

Two words hung in my mind: big league.

I could feel myself smiling broadly. Of course I knew that Wimbledon was the oldest, biggest, and best-attended tournament. But how big? How engulfed in worshippers? Not until this moment did I begin to grasp.

Big league. I didn't know until then that anything in tennis was truly big league in the sense of size and interest and impressiveness. It didn't matter because my love for the game was enough, and there was much joy in smallness and intimacy, too, of tournaments I had covered and would cover. But Wimbledon was an "additional category," as my Italian pal, Clerici, would say.

I had never seen so many reporters at a sporting event. There are ten times as many now. The press dining room—bar looked opulent, the writing rooms extraordinary although they would seem drab and minuscule today.

We were ushered into the press stand of Centre Court. No,

I didn't genuflect or bow, or wet my pants. But this was clearly the holy-of-holies. The Green Room.

Dusky green and high, the walls at either end of the amphitheater provide the best background in the business. Champion after champion will tell you he and she sees the ball better in Centre, that it is the heart of their universe.

Alex Olmedo, the Peruvian carpetbagger (and University of Southern California tennis scholar) who had worked the Good Neighbor Policy in reverse to win the Davis Cup for the United States over Australia the previous December, was impressing a decorous full house with his volleying. The day was overcast, but a divine light seemed to pierce the mauve clouds and settle on the slender Olmedo as he sparred with the chubby Chilean Luis Ayala. Was this ray anointing Incan-blooded Alex as the next chieftain of this somber green-on-green tennis jungle? Or was I getting divinely light-headed in my first Centre Court ecstasy?

Olmedo did win the tournament, but I didn't stay for the entire quarter-final against Ayala. I was anxious to see my fellow Buckeye, and friend, the Ohio Bear, trying to bring down the cofavorite, Aussie left-hander Neale Fraser, on Court 1. Barry MacKay came through all right, in five grueling, exciting sets and fifty-two games, and I ran down to courtside to shake his hand. I thought Barry could win the tourname t, and so did he. But another Antipodean lefty lay in wait in .he semis, whose time was approaching for the greatness that the Bear would never achieve: Rod Laver.

So aroused was I by the 1959 pilgrimage that I borrowed a typewriter in the pressroom. Knocking off a feature story of my impressions, I cabled it to the *Herald* where the Boss's impression of my enterprise was negative. When I asked later what had happened to the piece, he answered, "Space was tight that day, and we sent you over there to write about rowing, not to run up a cable bill on tennis."

Not much progress for this pilgrim.

Despite my immediate affection for Wimbledon, there was no point in requesting to be assigned there. The Boss would have scowled, then laughed, convinced I was attempting a bad joke.

My next visit, as purely off-duty pilgrim in 1961, was the fortuitous by-product of covering the middleweight title fight in London between Bostonian Paul Pender and hometownie Terry Downes. While aching to write a story for the *Herald* about that finals day, I was reconciled to the wastebasket fate of any such effort, and just settled in to enjoy three title bouts in the Green Room. One of them, a doubles, produced the first of her record twenty championships for a seventeen-year-old named Billie Jean Moffitt.

It was the last evening I could walk away from the Big W like an ordinary pilgrim, without thinking deadline, and assaulting keys. But I wouldn't return for seven years. Even though the *Globe*'s willingness to send me in 1964, my first summer on that staff, was apparent, my interest in the hopeful stirring in the professional game was stronger.

Under way was the salvaging of the U.S. Pro Championships at Longwood. The tournament that would save pro tennis was to begin two days after Wimbledon concluded. Why go to London when the finest players had arrived in my own backyard? Anyway, I'd be able to view the top amateurs in the National Doubles and Singles at Longwood and Forest Hills at the close of summer.

Then, as Jimmy Van Alen lined up his Newport pro tourney to precede the U.S. Pro in 1965, '66, '67, there was even more reason to stay home. Wimbledon may have had the ballpark and the trimmings, but New England had the ball players. Then in 1968 the bars were dropped, the pros were admitted, and the first full-service, homogenized Wimbledon burst forth, open to everybody entitled to play. For that one I would have paid my own way.

It was an especially blessed event to the defending champs, Billie Jean King and John Newcombe, who had since joined the outcast pros. Wearing invisible scarlet *P*'s, they were uncertain, on signing professional contracts, of ever treading the hallowed ground again. Billie Jean won for a third straight year, but Newk was beaten in the fourth round, by Arthur Ashe, and had to wait until 1970–71 to collect crown numbers two and three. He might have won again in 1972 and 1973 but for his exile by a couple of the wars that periodically upset the game. Open tennis, after four successful years, was partially closed at Wimbledon first by All England Club fiat in the form of a ban of WCT pros in 1972, then by an imperious Badger-headedness that caused the leading men to pull out the following year.

But the amnesty of 1968 was a true, unduplicable celebration of tennis made whole, if uneasily so—the first presentation of a very best face. Technically, you might say for the first time since 1926, before the incomparable Suzanne Lenglen and outstanding Americans Vinnie Richards and Howard Kinsey had been siphoned off as debutants on the introductory pro tour by promoter C. C. Pyle. However, in that time, before the development of air travel, none of the best players could be counted on to show up at all the major occasions, and only a few made most of them. Even playing both Wimbledon and the United States in the same year was unusual. In fact, no Americans played the four majors within a calendar year until Don Budge and Gene Mako stretched their sea legs in 1938.

Thus a united front, with all the prodigal pros returned to the mother church on Church Road, made 1968 a distinctive Wimbledon. Pancho Segura, forty-seven, had been missing for twenty-one years, Pancho Gonzalez, forty, absent for nineteen. It was too late for them to win titles, as it was for three other Hall of Famers, ex-champs Frank Sedgman, forty, away for sixteen years; Lew Hoad, thirty-three, for eleven; and Alex Olmedo, thirty-two, for nine.

Andres Gimeno, thirty; Butch Buchholz, twenty-nine; Fred Stolle, twenty-nine; and Dennis Ralston, twenty-five, had strayed for varying lengths of time. But Rod Laver, thirty, blackballed six years, and Kenny Rosewall, thirty-three, readmitted after twelve, were still factors. Laver was better in taking up where he'd left off in 1962, unassailable and registering a third successive championship.

Whatever they had left to offer, the exiles at this sentimental reunion reveled in their return and the welcome they received from loyalists too long deprived. The success of the seminal open at Bournemouth two months before was nothing in comparison. Unlike Bournemouth, cautiously avoided by the best of those characters living out the last days of the fiction— the amateurs—Wimbledon had a full-house cast. Arthur Ashe and Clark Graebner, twenty-eight-dollar-a-day U.S. Davis Cup players, were among those nominal amateurs who kept up the excitement of a "them and us" separation of the cast, and attained the semis. Never will that happen again.

First-round fun included one of those amateur-beats-pro reversals: Herbie FitzGibbon, not long out of Princeton and ranked only fifteenth in the United States, tormented sixteenth-seeded Nikki Pilic, the Yugoslav rookie pro, who had been a semifinalist twelve months earlier. Pilic, confined mostly to indoor arenas by the faltering WCT tour, anguished on a windy afternoon, wailing, in English, "Why we have to play in such weather this tennis? Why?" Two rounds later Ray Moore, the Wolfman, a young South African known thusly for his abundance of hair, terrified and beat a nervous No. 3 seed, Gimeno.

The added pressure of a pro trying to uphold his fraternity against an amateur would be evident for a season or so, until everybody was playing unapologetically for the cash. A rarity, it still happens now and then, as at the U.S. Open of 1987 where precocious fifteen-year-old Michael Chang, not yet ready to desert amateurism, startled Aussie Davis Cupper Paul McNamee.

The most resplendent Wimbledon up to that time was this junkie's fantasy fulfilled. And I had it all to myself, from an American standpoint. While the tennis sphere bubbled and crackled in the delightful pangs of re-creation, the world outside wasn't unduly stimulated. No American newspaper other than the *Globe* sent a correspondent, and no network cared to televise the transformation. NBC arrived the following year, but stuck with a barely noticeable tape-delay format until the first live "Breakfast at Wimbledon" was shoved in America's face a decade later.

It was impossible to see every match, meet every player, catalog every style in my mush, and to ferret out every story—but I tried. In trying, I arrived at noon when the gates opened, hunted down a feature to bat out for the *Globe*'s evening edition that day. Finished with that, I dashed, shoved, wormed among the courts from 2:00, when play began, until the last ball was poked at nightfall. That could be well past nine in the generous English summer. Then I would sit down to write for the next morning's paper. Practically everybody else was leaving the press rooms, having met their local or European deadlines. With that five-hour jump on Boston time I never, thankfully, blew a deadline. Even if I finished at 1:00 A.M., it was only 8:00 P.M. in the Bean, plenty of time for the first edition. But only the saintly forbearance of the telex chief, Alec Downing, who waited for my copy, kept me going.

I was taken by how Wimbledon-struck the town was. Because of saturation newspaper and TV coverage, everybody knew what was what and who was who. Autograph seekers were rife. Folks lined up outside the gates just to gawk at players arriving and leaving by auto. You could purchase a picture postcard of almost every player in the tournament.

Promptly I purchased one of the forgettable Nicky Kalogeropoulos, who played Davis Cup for—who else?—Greece. I wanted to send it to a pal of mine, Bill Kipouras, sports editor of the *Salem News*. As colleagues on the *Herald*, we had seen Kalogeropoulos's name in wire stories, evidence satisfying and pleasing Kipouras that there was at least one Greek tennis player, even if he seldom won.

Seeking out Kalogeropoulos, I introduced myself and thrust the card at him. "Would you sign this for a Greek friend? And, please, write a couple of words of greeting in Greek."

Kalogeropoulos wrinkled his face like most athletes being asked for an autograph by an alleged adult. "I can't write Greek."

"What?"

"Don't speak it either. I was raised in Costa Rica. My father's Greek, so the federation takes care of me to play for the team."

I sent the card anyway, with the message: "Sorry, Bill, but Greek happens to be Greek to your favorite tennis player—the imposter."

Burlesque is entertainment, and so is Wimbledon. But is Wimbledon ever burlesque?

Sometimes.

Come off it, old top. Don't be crude.

But it's true. There have been choice moments of naughtiness perceived when the "Take it off!" theme has taken over. Of course, it was all in the eyes and minds of the perceivers, the All England Club's committeemen, to whom a glimpse of stocking was once truly shocking.

Right up to the present day, the censorious committee, scrutinizing with an Elmer Gantry-ish gaze, presumably on behalf of public morals, has amusingly sought to uphold the manners of, say, 1889. The 1988 hounding of Barbara Potter, who, justifiably and discreetly, changed shirts on court, was the latest example of perfectly agreeable men gone ga-ga when collectivized. They seem to regard Wimbledon clientele as a continuing Victorian brood, exemplified by the two elderly women in a story London writer Lance Tingay tells.

Tingay, whose tennis reporting for *The Telegraph* earned him a journalistic niche in the Hall of Fame, relates, "This was about 1962, a genteel tournament at the Hurlingham Club, with a gallery composed mostly of retired pensioners. A couple of young women of temper, Virginia Wade and Carole Rosser, were playing, and they were both swearing like sailors.

"Seated near me were these two aged ladies, and they were responding to the players' language with puzzled looks.

" 'What's that she's saying?' said one.

"The other replied, 'I don't understand a word of it, my dear. I think they're Spanish.' "

It was the plain, yet voluptuous, Parisienne, Suzanne Lenglen, who, after World War I, first gave stirring indication that there might be a desirable young thing beneath all the yard goods that customarily encapsulated female entrants during Wimbledon's first four decades. Suzanne raised hems and temperatures thigh-high. But her hoydenish ways were excused ("she's French, you know"), then applauded, because she was the greatest champion to emerge up to that time—and because her presence lengthened ticket lines.

But once Suzanne had emancipated the female form, and sent previously de rigueur whalebone corsets to the boneyards and museums, there was still a good deal of official tut-tutting whenever someone like Billie Tapscott, a young South African, dressed (or undressed) to her own drummer.

In her own impromptu statement on behalf of freedom of the human limb, Billie Tapscott abandoned garter belt and habitual white stockings before appearing on Centre Court in 1929. Sensibly, she deemed such equipment foolishness, hurting her effort by impeding comfort and mobility.

Even though Lenglen rolled her stockings to below the knee, she had worn them. Brazenly baring her legs, Tapscott was regarded as a strumpet. But she persevered, an act deserving everyone's gratitude.

Not long after came Helen Jacobs in shorts, and, after World War II, Ted Tinling's assaults on decency. Now, nearing eighty, the lively elder statesman—the Towering Totem of Tennis—Tinling then was the Dastardly Dressmaker. It was Teddy who titillated and tempted by creating fluffy costumes that drove the committeemen to fits of Puritanism—and photographers and spectators to rapture.

He made frilly fillies of such as Maria Bueno and Lea Pericoli. "I put four hundred ostrich feathers on Pericoli's backside once," he recalls. But his lace panties for Gorgeous Gussy Moran were banned like Henry Miller novels were in old-time Boston. And the gold lamé drawers for Karol Fageros were looked at askance. Julie Heldman's see-through dress raised a few eyebrows until eyes discerned that it was only flesh-toned material behind the diamond-shaped opening at cleavage zone. "What's the difference? I haven't any cleavage anyway," Julie cracked.

Alas, Teddy's out of the designing business because nobody has worn a dress for years. Skirts and tops doomed his elegant touch, at least for the present, and the committeemen gave up as knicker inspectors. Though not as arbiters of wardrobe miscreance.

The last of Ted's dress-wearers, Rosie Casals, whom he spangled and glittered in a variety of amusingly showy minigowns, got in trouble with the committee in 1972. It wasn't sex, but a nonetheless purple passion that brought down authoritative wrath on Rosie. Splashed with purple squiggles, this frocked-up number from Tinling's sewing machine defied the "predominantly white" sartorial code that governs Wimbledon to this day.

Never darken our door with that sinful garment again, thundered the apoplectic committee—intimating that disqualification would be the penalty for the world's No. 7 player. For all I know, the little purple dress was removed to the Tower of London for drawing and quartering.

None other than the defending champion was hauled off Centre before he could open the tournament of 1984, caught defying the committee's predilection for alabaster attire. To them, John McEnroe seemed the pits of the fashion world as he stepped onto the sanctified sod to oppose Paul McNamee. Noted for blue lines, McEnroe accelerated his risqué routine by showing up in blue shorts. The committee saw red during the warmup. Get thee to the changing room forthwith, Mac was ordered. Returning in the prescribed pale, to get on with winning the championship, he said he'd made a forgetful mistake.

Unlike a puckish Hoosier, John Hennessey, back in 1925, the era of white trousers. Hennessey wanted to see how far he'd get on Centre in blue pinstripes. No further than McEnroe fifty-nine years later.

Shockingly enough, white was too much of a good thing in

1985 when the white-on-white lycra getup of the greatest player in the history of West Virginia smacked of wickedness on Court 2. Anne White, a willowy blonde in a gleaming ivory body stocking—sort of upscale longjohns—lit up the court at dusk like hellfire. While the committee had often fretted about skimpy togs, here was White, thoroughly covered from shoulders to feet to wrists.

But undeniably slinky. Anne spooked the committee, and even her highly favored opponent, Pam Shriver. They split sets before night fell for good on what Shriver's fashion review termed "bizarre and stupid."

Since it was a late-starting match, not particularly important, most press room occupants were writing their stories for the following day. My wife came in, excited and breathless, having run about a hundred yards and up four flights of stairs. "You better come and see Anne White," she advised me and John Feinstein, then of the *Washington Post*.

"We've seen her. Marrrvelous, but . . ."

"Not like this you haven't."

The next day the fun was over. Instructed that she had been "improperly attired," White turned up in the usual scanty work clothes and lost the decisive set. But she had her historic place in the Wimbledon Follies.

Barbara (Potsy) Potter has one, too. Unwanted. In London, a city where all the nudes fit to print can be found daily on page three of *The Sun*, Potter's rather tame topless tease of '88 was, incredibly, all the rage. Maybe not so incredibly when you consider that anything occurring at Wimbledon (or, possibly not occurring at all) is magnified to elephantine proportions on the sensational side of the London press.

Potter, a victim of numerous back problems, had been quick-stripping for some time, at the suggestion of her physician, to avoid dampness and possible chilling of her back.

She had the referee's approval to enter "Potsy's Bath-house," as I've called the improvised shelter on TV—a shielding of towels held by ball kids. Even photographers who managed to snap her through the draping showed Potter in a hammock bra more modest than a nun's swimsuit.

"It's a nonstory," was Potsy's sane response to reporters. Not, however, in London, where it was further inflated by the committee's terse bulletin to the effect that "the Practice is not encouraged," and that the referee would have a further word with the left-handed ecdysiast.

A sympathetic referee, Georgina Clark, scheduled Potsy's third rounder on Court 6, within yards of a public toilet where a shirt change could be made in private. No notification of such an arrangement was given us persistent reporters and photographers who gathered at courtside, and so we weren't prepared for what became the Great Potty Chase. By the end of the ninth game, a glowing Potter—ladies don't sweat at Wimbledon, old chap—suddenly grabbed a fresh shirt, bolted from the court, and sprinted around the corner. Immediately one of the line judges left her chair and dashed in pursuit. The green-blazered official was followed by reporters and camera-clickers, who came to an abrupt halt at the women's john into which Potsy and her tail disappeared.

Under the rules, she had ninety seconds to get herself together, which she did. Why was she accompanied by an official? Later, the answer came back that the shadow was to make sure that Potter didn't receive illicit instructions in the latrine from her coach. Her coach said that he neither frequented ladies' toilets nor gave seminars therein.

It made us wonder what the committee would have done if Potter had progressed to an inevitable Centre Court date. Is there a loo in the Royal Box?

Involuntary disrobing, too, has invested Wimbledon with touches of burlesque, from such stars as Martina Navratilova, Margaret Court, and Betty Nuthall, and bit players Shirley Bloomer, Linda Siegel, and Tim Wilkison.

"My most embarrassing moment in tennis," says eight-time champ Navratilova, was when her skirt began to fall during her 1983 championship triumph over Andrea Jaeger. Serving and rushing the net, she was saved by an ambidextrous reaction as the wraparound skirt descended. Making the winning volley with her left, Martina clutched the skirt top with her right until she could make repairs.

Betrayed by loose straps while playing Billie Jean King in 1979, young Californian Siegel found her escaped bosom on several front pages the next day. Worse than a service break was Wilkison's zipper break on Centre in 1987. Like Siegel, he was threatened by a mortifying falling, but he excused himself to don new shorts.

Worse still were the elastic breaks of Court, Bloomer, and Nuthall. Not long ago, just before his death at ninety-two, Colonel Jackie Smythe, tennis historian and member of the Wimbledon establishment, was queried as to the most memorable occasion of his innumerable Wimbledons.

Unhesitating, smiling fondly, he replied, "Why, it was the day in 1926 that Betty Nuthall's knickers fell down in Centre Court."

Same thing happened to the aptly named Bloomer on Court 1 in 1958, and three-time champ Court in 1975. Wasn't that a horrendous experience for Margaret, Ted Tinling was asked some time afterward.

"For her?" he shot back. "What about me? I designed her outfit. I'd just had a heart attack, and there I was in hospital, watching the telly, and her pants came down. I had a cat fit—it almost put me back in intensive care!"

38

○

Fireman's Daughter

As the sort of prodigies Southern California used to turn out regularly when old Perry Jones was minding the shop, teenagers Billie Jean Moffitt and Karen Hantze were beneficiaries of Los Angeles–London plane tickets, and very little expense money. Those goodies, rewards for achievement and promise, were doled out by Jones, a martinet who ran the Southern Cal. province of the USTA, and held the power of life and travel over the kids coming up in his system.

When young Pancho Gonzalez, who would win the National title in 1948 and 1949, was playing truant as well as juvenile tennis, Jones ruled him off local tournaments until he got his educational act together. Jones, a prim and rotund bachelor who wore bow ties and dark glasses, courted money for his tennis projects from society and movie people.

Headquartered at the well-heeled Los Angeles Tennis Club, he had a condescending manner that early wounded Billie Jean, offspring of the public courts of Long Beach. Mr. Jones, as the players always referred to him, in or out of his presence, once yanked her out of a lineup of bright juniors about to have their picture taken, and issued a scolding. Her shorts and T-shirt were not the acceptable costume. When she had a proper tennis dress, she might return.

Betty Moffitt made one for her daughter, who was to become Mr. Jones's finest female export. "But I always was uncomfortable in snooty private clubs," says Billie Jean. Except, somehow, for Wimbledon, which the fireman's daughter sensed was her place.

The fireman, Bill Moffitt, for whom she was named, was a meat-and-potatoes guy, a basketball and baseball player, and one of the most unusual of sporting sires: Billie Jean became a world champ, and her brother, Randy, pitched for years in the National League, mostly with the Giants.

Softball had been Billie Jean's first passion, but her father felt there ought to be something a little more "ladylike" that would satisfy her competitive urge, and "keep her running." That eliminated swimming and golf. Given a cheap racket, she soon was a pupil of Clyde Walker, a coach employed by the Long Beach recreation department.

Walker would move from park to park to teach, and Billie Jean showed up wherever he did. He was dying of cancer in 1961, but made himself stay alive in the hospital until his student's first Wimbledon was complete.

Nobody dreamed that she would stay the two-week course to claim a first prize on the very last day. "Clyde defied the doctors and hung in there with me, thousands of miles away." It is a comforting memory. "He died knowing I'd won at Wimbledon."

Another teenager on the verge of prominence, mighty Margaret Smith (presently Mrs. Court), teamed with Australian compatriot Jan Lehane against Billie Jean and Karen in the Saturday doubles final. By that time, late afternoon, the Wimbledon crowd, indeed all of Britain, taking it on TV, were burned out. They had exulted and suffered through the first home-cooking Wimbledon singles final in nearly a half-century.

Since British winners of the Big W are scarcer than hens' dentists, the most recent having been Dorothy Round in 1937, this was an unbelievable smorgasbord: Angela Mortimer against Christine Truman with a domestic queen assured. The last such yoking had been a hyphenated headache for sportswriters back in 1914 when the "old" Wimbledon was pretty much an intramural English tea party. Dorothea Douglass Lambert-Chambers beat Ethel Thomson-Larcombe.

The Brits, so practiced at losing, were giddy. They couldn't lose this one, a thriller right down to the wire with spindly Angela Mortimer nipping towering adolescent Christine Truman, 4–6, 6–4, 7–5.

Sixteen years later an identical no-lose situation loomed after Virginia Wade deposed the champion, Chris Evert, in a semifinal that was Chrissie's most heartfelt defeat. "I didn't come out of my hotel room for three days, I was so upset." Next on Centre was another native, charming blonde Sue Barker, against intruder Betty Stove. Millions held their breath through teatime as Barker struggled gallantly, and was deliciously within sight of victory.

However, Barker blew it, and the resultant letdown was wonderfully captured in the dispatch tapped out by my Italian friend, Gianni Clerici, for his paper: "Britain suffered a national case of coitus interruptus."

Nothing could interrupt Billie Jean and Karen, although they were strictly anticlimactic, an added filler after the Mortimer-Truman drama. There was no indication that "Little Miss Moffitt," as English writers called her, was commencing a historic run.

As Mrs. Rod Susman, Karen would win the singles the following year, aided considerably by sidekick Billie Jean's opening-round win over No. 1 seed Margaret Smith. An auburn-haired beauty with fluid strokes, Karen was the apple of any male spectator's eye. In any groundskeeper's eye, however, she was as associated with original sin as Eve. Her indiscretion was a right foot heavier than Richard Petty's, dragged as an accompaniment to her serving, and tearing divots at the baseline. But since she was also the only woman I ever saw who could copycat Jackie Kennedy's bouffant hairdo and look as stylish as the instigator—even maintaining an unmussed and royal air while playing tennis under the damned thing—all divots were forgiven.

Karen, whose husband was a very good American player, would have made her millions had she stuck with the game into the open era and the Virginia Slims paydays. But she did what was expected of pretty female tennis players then. She became a housewife, had a baby. Marriages between top-flight tennis players have seldom succeeded. The Susmans', still going, is one of the few to last. Maybe because they both quit tennis at that level to make their way elsewhere.

"Margaret and Jan [Aussies Smith and Lehane] were nervous," Billie Jean recalls about the 1961 final, "and we were loose. Karen and I were just having an unexpectedly good time, and laughed a lot."

Since they also had to wait for a five-set men's doubles final, it was well past teatime before the four kids were ushered onto Centre. After eight sets, at least one witness was yet eager for more, even though I spent a night without sleep on a flight across the Atlantic. This was my first finals day at Wimbledon.

I was immensely pleased by Billie Jean and Karen's victory, particularly since I'd met them the summer before at a women's tournament north of Boston, and been taken by their enthusiasm and obvious talent. Like a stage-door Johnny I stood at the club's main entrance, hoping to congratulate them before one of the imposing limousines chartered for the players rushed them off to what I imagined would be an adoring victory party.

When they emerged, we shook hands and I mentioned my name, hoping they remembered me.

"Sure . . . Boston. Last summer at Essex," said Billie Jean.

"Well, I just wanted to say nice going, but I don't want to keep you from the celebration—"

"What celebration?" they chorused.

I thought they were being modest. "Why, you're the Wimbledon champions. You'll be toasted at the Wimbledon ball, and—"

Billie Jean tossed her head, "We're going home and going to bed. We're broke. We don't have clothes for the ball." They laughed at what they seemed to regard as my naïveté. But they weren't bitter or feeling unappreciated. The facts were they were down to almost nothing but their return plane ticket. Wimbledon furnished lunch, but they were junking it on the cheap for the rest.

No ball for the Wimbledon Cinderellas.

"Well, could I take you to dinner?"

Never had pretty ladies—any ladies—whooped "Yes!" to me so quickly. I didn't know much about London and neither did they, but we found a basement Italian joint in Chelsea. They ate like Marco Polo discovering pasta in Cathay.

"I'm gonna order champagne," I said.

"We don't drink," they said.

But they didn't mind that I had a goblet of wine with which I pinged their water glasses in a salute to the champions. It was even better than Cinderella clicking her heels in glass slippers.

39

○

Stalking
Bunny

Bunny Ryan could hear the sneakered steps behind her, and she didn't like it. "That woman is trying to take my record," she glowered when the subject of Billie Jean King came up.

Elizabeth ("Bunny") Ryan, a Californian who preferred to live in London and was generally thought of as English, had an unobtrusive sparkle as one of the gems of Wimbledon, although few people other than fellow All England Club members were aware of her. She lived on Centre Court, first in deed—amassing nineteen titles between 1914 and 1934—then in spectating spirit. And she died a few steps away in 1979, as though willing her departure while still clutching the precious record, only hours before Billie Jean would snatch it.

"I always liked seeing Miss Ryan at Wimbledon, and I'd try to be friendly, but she didn't seem to want it," says Billie Jean, who ran and swatted through nineteen Wimbledons to supplant Ryan as the all-time champ with a total of twenty titles in singles, doubles, and mixed doubles. "For me, it wasn't personal," King says. "Sure, I wanted the record, but I wasn't trying to steal a possession of hers. Eventually, somebody will break mine, probably Martina."

No tennis player will ever have a career as rich in romantic trappings as Ryan's. Not much money involved, but the perks and the style kept her in the upper reaches of a world forever gone.

A visitor to her London apartment could get glimpses of it in sterling-framed photos of Bunny with this maharajah, that king, and other royal figures as she traveled the world on a racket. A tennis-court partner of Czar Nicholas II of Russia during a 1917 visit, she escaped the country barely ahead of the Revolution.

As Wimbledon celebrated its one hundredth birthday and she neared her eighty-seventh in 1977, she was the only one in the nostalgic cavalcade of returned champions whose championship accomplishments spanned the "old" and the "new" Wimbledons. All her nineteen titles had been in doubles and mixed doubles. The first, with Agnes Morton, was achieved at the original Worple Road grounds, on the eve of World War I; the last, alongside Simone Mathieu, on the present Centre Court.

Little was made of the record until Billie Jean King's chipping away at it got serious in 1974 with her eighteenth title, the mixed doubles. Most tennis nuts were surprised to see that Bunny Ryan was still alive when the centenary was celebrated. But there was no mistaking her presence among the returned champions.

Stout and broad-shouldered during her reign, a veteran of the "whale-boned corsets we all once wore," Bunny was now slight, white-haired, gimpy. But the will remained firm. As she labored onto Centre Court on two canes and managed to curtsy to the duke and duchess of Kent, presiding over the ceremony, the crowd cheered and clapped mightily.

Ryan remained the all-time champ, but Billie Jean had edged in as co-holder with No. 19 in 1975, her sixth singles triumph.

If the doddering spinster, a daily Wimbledon communicant in the members' box, was rooting against Billie Jean in the finals of the 1976 doubles and the 1978 mixed doubles, you could understand. "That record's all Bunny has left," said one of her old friends. "No children. Not many of us friends remaining."

King failed in both those finals, and she, too, was getting older. But Wimbledon was as much an enchanted cottage for her as it was for Bunny. She would keep on grasping for recognition as the champion of champions if she had to win No. 20 in a walker such as had become Ryan's vehicle. In 1979, at thirty-five, she appeared a lock in the doubles, having acquired the destructive left arm of Martina Navratilova at her side. Though I tried to put together Bunny and Billie Jean for an NBC interview to be used during the Wimbledon telecast, Miss Ryan would have none of it.

Bunny and Billie Jean both had waistline problems the years they arrived in England from California and fell in love with Wimbledon. "It was the Devonshire cream, and in those days it was really Devonshire cream," Miss Ryan smiled the day in 1978 I visited her at home. Reminiscing appeared to make her happy, and she forgot about "that woman" trailing her for a while. "My sister and I put on quite a few pounds, but tennis helped."

She regretted never winning the singles, losing the 1921 final to the glamorous Suzanne Lenglen (with whom she won six doubles), and 1930 to Helen Wills. "Elizabeth wasn't fast enough for singles. Too heavy," says historian Ted Tinling, who was there.

Corsets had gone out by 1961 when pudgy seventeen-year-old Billie Jean Moffitt arrived in the company of her svelte eighteen-year-old partner, Karen Hantze. Billie Jean's only restrictive device was "a safety pin to hold up my skirts. I couldn't button them anymore."

A friendly London journalist, Gerry Williams, had walked Billie Jean through an empty Centre Court before the tournament began, and it was like strolling the streets of Oz with Dorothy. "Right away," she says, "I had a wonderful feeling. I knew this was the place I wanted to play a lot. It's perfect. The high dark-green background is especially good. You can see the ball so well.

"Even though I lost in the first round of the singles to Yola Ramirez, I was lucky because the match was on Centre. It was a long match, suspended by darkness and continued to the next day, so I spent a lot of time there. Playing there right away, I never had any fear of Centre as some players do. It brought out my best."

It was a sanctuary where she was destined to live a substantial part of her competitive life—twenty-eight championship rounds among scores of appearances—and the shiniest times. "It's funny about the crowds. They're very good and well behaved, of course, but they change in their appreciation. At first, when you're a kid, they're crazy about you. They want to see you do well. But if you win a lot, they think, maybe, you're doing too well—give somebody else a chance, you know?—and they cool on you. But, if you're around long enough, as I was, they love you again, as you grow old."

She felt all the sensations. Such side shows as women's doubles and mixed doubles, considered blah by most spectators in other countries, are dear to British hearts. Billie Jean and Karen, total nonentities as the 1961 tournament began, picked up steam and followers while they giggled their way, unseeded, to the title round, the greenest pair of champs in the event's annals.

Perky, talking aloud to herself, wearing rhinestone-rimmed glasses—and volleying ferociously—King compounded her popularity by winning the singles in 1966, '67, '68. In '68 she did it hurt, on a bum knee.

But the next year, a finalist again, she was opposed by an Englishwoman, Ann Haydon-Jones. Not only were the home folks getting a little tired of the bouncy, too successful, American, but the presence of one of their own in a Wimbledon final occurred as frequently as a sighting of Halley's Comet. Their support of Jones was boisterously un-Wimbledonian, and the buxom left-hander came through in three sets to their unrestrained joy. "I could feel some animosity that day," says Billie Jean.

In later years, though, she had them back in her palm again, especially during her singles farewell, 1983. No longer a factor in the game, she nevertheless came on as Saint Billie Jean of the Grass Blades, resurrected once more, at thirty-nine, and committing miracle after miracle in wending her way to the semifinals. One last singles final became a distinct possibility, and with her guile and steely nerve, mightn't she call forth an ultimate miracle to bring down Martina Navratilova?

But the magic had run out with her quarter-final victory over Kathy Jordan (eliminator of Chris Evert), and Billie Jean was flatter than a leftover glass of beer in the semis against eighteen-year-old Andrea Jaeger. There would be no singles final reprise, no renewal of the first time, two decades before.

As she and Jaeger, twenty-one years her junior, walked together from the sanctum, Billie Jean turned and paused for a last lingering look from battleground level. Look homeward, angel?

"Yeah, it was a long look. I knew it would be the last time."

Bunny Ryan must have dreaded the thought that her last look would encompass Billie Jean winning the doubles with Navratilova, and breaking the record that had endured thirty-five years. On the eve of King's championship No. 20, at the close of play, Miss Ryan entered a restroom, collapsed, and died, taking her record with her. She went out at Wimbledon, still champion of champions. Bunny knew Billie Jean would finally move ahead—but let her do it on somebody else's time.

40

○

Hills and Meadow

Queens Boulevard, despite the fresh-squeezed breakfast orange juice at the T-Bone Diner on the corner of Continental, hasn't qualified as the road to romance for a long time. Still, before the USTA uncoupled from Forest Hills to set up U.S. Open housekeeping at Flushing Meadows, Queens Boulevard was, indeed, a compelling route for tens of thousands, on (or under) which they traveled the same time each year for a festival of graceful movement and determined competition, an annual concert of the world's virtuosos with rackets.

Fans found sporting romance for generations in the feats of champions such as Little Miss Poker Face, the sun-visored and beautiful Californian Helen Wills, who officiated at a dual inaugural in 1923. Her defeat of Kitty McKane launched both the newly built stadium and the Wightman Cup rivalry between the United States and Britain.

The delightful Kitty, who in 1988 was still making her shopping rounds by bicycle at age ninety-two, would gain revenge the following year, 1924, at Wimbledon, beating Wills in the final, despite Helen's big lead. That was Helen's lone Wimbledon defeat of fifty-six matches. The one time I met her, by then a reclusive person, I asked how such a remorseless competitor had let a 6–4, 4–1 lead slip away.

"Oh, I remember that," she recalled fifty-five years later. "I made a very bad mistake that day, and learned a very valuable lesson."

Oh? What was that? I felt some great secret was to be imparted.

"Why, I lost my concentration," Helen said, but as someone else might say, she broke a leg or was felled by a sniper. How many times had I heard a player lament a concentration lapse? But never what followed, so matter-of-factly: "I learned I must never do that again. And I didn't." Obviously. Strong-minded Helen Wills won the next eight Wimbledons she entered, ringing up fifty consecutive match victories, a record as distant as the moon. I thought Martina Navratilova would be a moonwalker when she arrived at her forty-seventh in a row by beating Chris Evert in the 1988 semifinals. But Steffi Graf brought about an eclipse of that bid in the final.

Three years before Wills and McKane opened the Forest Hills stadium, the customers had, momentarily, feared for their own safety. Ten thousand witnesses gasped, as a sputtering biplane circled the temporary wooden grandstand and crashed just beyond while Forest Hills's soon-to-be hero of heroes, Big Bill Tilden, was beating Little Bill Johnston for the title.

Stalwartly, the umpire of the torrid five-set struggle, Edward Conlin, asked, "Can you continue, gentlemen?" They nodded affirmatively, unwilling to be upstaged by a mere aircraft disaster, and Conlin cried, "Play!" The show went on, although scores of curious spectators deserted to inspect the wreckage.

Of course, distraction by airplane wasn't even a consideration when the Nationals shifted to Forest Hills from Newport in 1915. Trains bolting along the southern edge of the property were more of a hazard to deepthink when the tournament began squatting at West Side Tennis Club, just as they were at the original Wimbledon grounds on Worple Road.

It isn't true, as many assume, that Kenny Rosewall was one of Bill Tilden's antagonists. But Rosewall was at Forest Hills before smog. "My first year, 'fifty-two," recalls the champ of 1956 and 1970, the longevity record-holder, "you could actually see the Manhattan skyline from the clubhouse deck." His last year, 1974, Kenny outdid Tilden by playing a final at thirty-nine. But Jimmy Connors, twenty-one, like a snarling young Richard Widmark pushing a wheelchair rider down a flight of stairs in *Kiss of Death*, beat up Rosewall mercilessly (as he had in the Wimbledon final) for the first of his five U.S. titles.

Sometimes the wheel does come full cycle. By 1987 Connors, nearing his thirty-fifth birthday and now the revered elder, the people's choice to win, as Rosewall had been, was blasted in the Wimbledon semis by twenty-two-year-old Patrick Cash.

Not always does a geezer looking for one last call's jigger of glory get shut off. I think of Darlene Hard at Forest Hills in 1969.

Thirty-three and overweight, Darlene had been out of the picture for six years, and no longer fit into a championship tableau. She looked like an incongruous fourth wheel on a tricycle with her fit, well-tuned companions—partner Françoise Durr, and the strongly favored foes, Margaret Court and Virginia Wade.

Although she had twice commanded this arena, winning the singles in 1960 and 1961, held nineteen major titles, and was destined for the Hall of Fame, Hard drew impatient remarks of "Who's this?" and "What's she doing here?" from the small crowd. It was a chill, wet Monday afternoon. The Open had been saturated by record rains, and the only reason anybody showed up in the gloom of the added afternoon was to see if Rod Laver could complete his second Grand Slam by beating another "bushie," an Australian country boy named Tony Roche. That's what they'd paid to see and, with the weather threatening, weren't overjoyed to have to endure a women's doubles first. Especially the way Darlene was so obviously out of it. She was pitiful.

Waiting the women out in the clubhouse, Rod and Tony sat on a leather divan in the men's locker room, kibitzing with friends and reporters. These were Aussies at their best, good old boys before the money got so big that the elite began to think of themselves as just that, and even take themselves seriously. Nobody hid then, gave you the brush, mumbled "See my agent" if you wanted a few words, or looked for an alibi.

Laver was doubly pressured in '69. The Slam loomed, as did the birth of his only child. The baby was already overdue as Rocket and Rochie waited to play. Usually pleasant, Mary

Laver was no fun that month. She was past the usual child-bearing age, and angered that inclemency had extended the tournament by a day, delaying Rod's return to their California home. Mostly, she was concerned with a Grand Slim, and issuing the kid, and she wanted her husband at her side.

A Grand Slam, Roche was saying, should have been dead before it started, eight months back, and would have been if Laver hadn't benefited from a dubious line call during their monster semifinal (ninety games) in the Australian Open. "Should've been my point, a break point giving me 5–3 in the fifth set. Would've been my match," Rochie needled.

"Reckon you're right," nodded Laver.

"Glad you'll at least admit it, Rocket, because I'll never forget it. But I'll say this—I was cheering for you to make the Slam in 'sixty-two." The butcher's son from Tarcutta was seventeen then. "Couldn't wait to get the report on the telly from Wagga Wagga to see if you'd made it. Then I read about it when the Sydney papers got to us two days later."

The news in Tarcutta, via Wagga Wagga, would be sadder this time. Roche, although he had a winning record for the year over Laver, couldn't keep up in sneakers with the claw-footed Firebird in the stadium morass. Inexperienced in spiked shoes himself, and suspicious of those once-common antidotes to slippery grass, as dated today as high-button shoes, Tony opted not to try them. For him the court was the "Slough of Despair," according to the account by London's David Gray.

Once he'd lost the first set and been granted permission by the referee to don the claws, Laver scratched through like the cock of the barnyard. According to the Chinese, 1969 was the year of the rooster, and this bandy-legged, cockscombed, sharp-beaked Aussie did his part as the human embodiment.

Look at Laver's stats for his two biggest of nearly twenty years in the big league: His first Grand Slam year, 1962, he won 19 of 34 tournaments on a 134–15 match record. Seven years later, age thirty-one, and Slamming again, he had slowed to winning 17 of 32 tournaments on a 106–16 match record. And he was also playing a full doubles schedule.

Put those beside the most productive years of the giants who followed: Jimmy Connors, 1974, age twenty-two—won 15 of 21 tournaments on a 95–6 match record; Bjorn Borg, 1979, age twenty-three—12 of 19 on 93–6; John McEnroe, 1984, age twenty-five—13 of 15 on 82–3; Ivan Lendl, 1982, age twenty-two—15 of 23 on 107–9; Ilie Nastase, 1973, age twenty-seven—15 of 31 on 118–17; Guillermo Vilas, 1977, age twenty-five—17 of 31 on 134–14; John Newcombe, 1974, age thirty—8 of 22 on 72–13; Stan Smith, 1973, age twenty-six—8 of 19 on 81–22.

By 1983, when both men were thirty-one, Connors won 4 of 15 tournaments (one, the U.S. Open) on a 52–11 match record and Vilas 3 of 20 on 56–18. Arthur Ashe held up productively well with his in 1975, at age thirty-two, when he won Wimbledon and 8 other tourneys of 29 on a 108–23 match record. Only Connors came close to a Grand Slam, winning three of the four prizes in 1974, but was locked out of the French by the Gallic Badgers because of his participation in World Team Tennis.

Even at thirty-three Laver was still the leading match winner (82–18) and took 7 of 26 tournaments. I remain unconvinced that there was ever a better player.

But Rod had stopped playing mixed doubles some time before, in 1961, on the advice of his old coach, Charlie Hollis, who believed that he'd never win the singles at Wimbledon if he persisted entering all three events. His last partner, in the Wimbledon mixed victory of 1960, had been none other than Darlene Hard, the unexpected heroine of his murky Monday at Forest Hills.

Open tennis arrived too late for Darlene, a teaching pro in California who returned to Forest Hills to test the waters for a comeback. They were too deep and swift by then. She lost in the second round of the singles, and got into the doubles with the proficient Françoise Durr only as a stand-in for injured Ann Jones.

Like her close friend and sometimes doubles partner, Althea Gibson, Darlene didn't give a damn what anybody thought. Both came from working-class backgrounds and found the private clubs' atmosphere prickly. Darlene wore shorts that were too tight, drove a souped-up Chevy that was too loud, worked as a waitress when she needed money, and didn't conform at all to the pattern the Badgers had for a champion. But she'd been a champ, all right, hard-serving and attack-minded.

But now it was embarrassing to watch her, the pudgy tag-along with three exceptional doubles players—Durr, Court, and Wade. Darlene had been a better practitioner of doubles than any of them, yet those qualities had disintegrated.

Every match had been a war for the newly yoked Darlene and Françoise while Court and Wade flowed dynamically, beating top-seeded Rosie Casals and Billie Jean King in the semis. The first painful half-hour of the final flew past. Darlene flubbed, Françoise fretted, and Court and Wade flogged to win the first eight games. If it had been boxing, a merciful referee would have stopped it at 0–6, 0–2, to save the deteriorated champion from further battering. Get her out of here.

But then a beautiful transformation occurred. Darlene remembered who she'd been. She began to make herself prove it so that the diehards in the stands wouldn't go home feeling sorry for her. She wanted desperately to make a match of it, and so did Durr, who said, "I theenk we looze love and love." Despite her bizarre strokes that made her seem a woman warding off an attack of mosquitoes, Durr was clever and competitive, a champion doubles player as well as the most recent Frenchwoman to win her country's title in singles, 1967. As Hard rummaged her hope chest to find the barely remembered clout to blend with Durr's angled volleys and nimble retrieving, they became a juggernaut-for-an-afternoon. After building a seemingly unscalable wall, Wade and Court were washed away, securing only six more games as Durr and Hard triumphed, 0–6, 6–4, 6–4.

It was one of the lovelier times at Forest Hills, though blanketed by clammy, sooty clouds. Not only did Laver have his Grand Slam, but nobody in either the men's or women's doubles had ever recovered from a first-set bagel to win the championship. Darlene Hard, forgotten, down on her luck, still bitter from social slights and putdowns, cranked it up one last time, and trudged away from the stadium proudly, a champion.

The flushing of Forest Hills, after more than six decades as the scene of the Nationals and then the U.S. Open, was fittingly chaotic. That last Sunday, September 11, 1977, blended elements of the evacuation of Saigon, *Twilight of the Gods, Day of the Locust*, and a fiesta.

But should such a monumental divorce have occurred in a dignified, untraumatic, "so long, it's been nice knowing you" manner? Of course not. Since 1915 those two words, Forest Hills, had signified tennis in America. Only the degenerates knew that the game was played elsewhere, too.

"Forest Hills" stayed put as a mental landmark, although

the U.S. Open had skipped the old neighborhood. It would continue rolling mistakenly off tongues at least into the early 1980s, despite the Open's separation from the West Side Tennis Club, Forest Hills, hot to move in with a new suitor down the street, Flushing Meadows. "How do you think Borg will do at Forest Hi—uh, I mean, Flushing Meadows?" You heard that all the time, and, for some, the uprooting was so painful that they never went near Flushing Meadows, regarding the eclipse of Forest Hills as a death in the family.

The eclipse was accompanied by riotous noise, confusion, the fear of an actual riot, and the unseemly flight into the night of the defending champion—the one and only James Scott Connors—who seemed to feel the shrilly excited mob of 12,644 was on his heels. Beaten in the final by Guillermo Vilas, Connors neither shook hands nor paused for other niceties such as the presentation ceremony. Instead, shielded by minions who blocked for him, Jimmy raced down the walkway from the stadium to a getaway car on Burns Place, outside of the clubhouse, and sped off before reporters could sample his thoughts. But it wasn't lasting twilight for the god Connors. He would regain the title a year later in the U.S. National Tennis Center, Flushing Meadows.

If the Open's last gasp at the old homestead was uproarious and uncharacteristically uncouth, it figured. Jimmy Connors, the most uproarious of creatures to imprint himself indelibly on the game, was one of the principals. The other—Guillermo Vilas, the burly and intriguing Argentine—was everything Connors wasn't, except for tennis genius. The Young Bull of the Pampas, a sensitive, well-educated product of Latin gentry, who wrote poetry and songs, made the deceptively slight Connors look scrawny and particularly crude.

As the Brash Basher of Belleville (Illinois), Connors was a rude, tough kid born on the wrong side of the courts in East St. Louis. There, one day, as a boy with his grandfather, he happened to be sitting in a barroom as a murder took place. When he spoke of his rivalry with Bjorn Borg, Jimmy said, "We tried to murder each other. That's the only way we know how to play tennis. I was lucky to have a rivalry like that, and with [John] McEnroe, too." His rage to win made him truly one of the all-time greats.

It took some time, but eventually Connors (snails and puppy-dog tails) began to reap the sort of popularity in America rivaled only by his onetime girlfriend, Chris Evert (sugar and spice—and a blacksmith's backhand). Their images, flung farther and wider by TV than Big Bill Tilden and Helen Wills's in newsprint, were enhanced by incredible longevity. The two great and good friends were still playing, and winning, well into their fourth decades. His and hers were the records for most professional singles titles: 107 and 157, respectively, by the end of 1988.

But in 1977 Americans weren't quite sure how they felt about Connors, whose "me against the world" attitude stuck out spikily. A loner who listened to—and sometimes fought— his mother-coach, ex-player Gloria Thompson Connors, he declined to play Davis Cup for his country and refused to join the men's union, ATP. In fact, in his disputes with the ATP and its leaders—such tennis heroes as Arthur Ashe and Jack Kramer— he had been involved in multimillion-dollar lawsuits and countersuits.

The 1975 Wimbledon championship victory of the one-to-ten long shot Ashe over seemingly invincible Connors—Jimmy was suing Arthur in law court as well as firing at him in Centre Court—generated more warmth within the sporting public than any tennis victory I have known.

Connors had never been very well thought of at Wimbledon anyway. The first year he showed, 1972, his mother was cautioned about disturbing the peace. She was asked to lower to imperceptible volume her shouts of "Come on, Jimbo!" Gloria had nervously demolished her rosary during a prayerful— hail, Jimmy?—Centre Court vigil while the kid wrecked eighth-seeded Bob Hewitt, a memorable and prophetic debut.

His feelings about Wimbledon were mutual. "They're a little too proper, too stiff for me," Connors said of the All England Clubbies' attitude. Nor did he help himself with vile language at play, or collaborating with doubles partner Ilie Nastase in simulating a sexual coupling when both tumbled to the ground trying to field a shot down the middle.

Surprisingly, that wasn't cut from the taped version NBC beamed back to the United States, and in supplying voice-over, all I could say was, "Connors and Nastase have brought *Oh, Calcutta!* to Wimbledon."

Even worse in British eyes was Jimmy's standing-up the

All England Clubbies and fourteen thousand faithful at the Centenary party on Centre Court in 1977. While the Parade of Champions, marking the one hundredth anniversary of the Big W, filed in to enthusiastic, nostalgic, and respectful applause— the elder, eighty-seven-year-old Elizabeth (Bunny) Ryan, hobbled in on two canes—Connors, the 1974 champ, made his statement by ducking. But he was on view, practicing on an outside court, while such among the galaxy as Don Budge, Althea Gibson, Alice Marble, Bjorn Borg, Chris Evert, Billie Jean King, Rene Lacoste, Rod Laver, Ashe, and Kramer linked hands and sang "Auld Lang Syne" along with the audience.

To the hosts, Connors's response was like picketing one of the queen's tea parties at Buckingham Palace. It was the first leg on Jimmy's Grand Slap that year, the back of his hand to the three elders among the circuit's prominent way stations. The next questionable antic came at Longwood Cricket Club when he vanished from the U.S. Pro, failing to appear for a quarter-final after apparently feigning an injury. He left the clubhouse a few steps ahead of reporters, who sought a quote on his abrupt departure. First in line, I received a grand slam of his car door in my face. We jumped aside, unwilling to sacrifice our typing fingers and other limbs as the car bolted out of the club driveway. Shortly thereafter he completed the Slap by bugging out from Forest Hills.

That wasn't the last time Jimmy would close a car door practically on my nose, or shove me away as I tried to interview him. But it comes with the territory, and just adds to the Connors saga that, above all, means excitement.

It always has since I first glimpsed him in 1970, at Forest Hills, the eighteen-year-old left-handed tagalong in a remarkably unlikely doubles team guided by the Old Wolf, forty-two-year-old Pancho Gonzalez. Here was Raggedy Andy in tennis costume, a rag doll throwing himself into every shot with such exuberance that it couldn't possibly last beyond 1990 or so. Hair, arms, legs flew along with plenty of fur as Connors bashed away in a game he so obviously loved. He and Gonzalez laughed and scowled their way to the Open quarter-finals, beating fifth-seeded Tom Okker and Marty Riessen along the way.

The excitement of his singles style, the all-out hitting backboned by a double-barreled backhand, was apparent twelve months after that as Jimmy won the first of a record total of ninety-one matches at the Open, dumping ex-Wimbledon champ Alex Olmedo in the opening round. By 1977 he was contesting his fourth successive final, having won in 1974 by dynamiting Kenny Rosewall in the last grass-court title bout, and again in 1976, launching Bjorn Borg's New York miseries, a string of four fruitless finals. That was on clay, a championship pivoting on the most momentous of final-round tiebreakers, which put Connors ahead, 2–1 in sets. Although Borg held four set points in the overtime passage, Connors made Herculean saves to win the breaker, 11–9. A ballboy named Eric Koller may have prevented pandemonium with a nifty save himself during the hectic tiebreaker. The flustered umpire had somehow lost track of the score, but Koller, sensing the problem, discreetly set him back on the correct track.

It was largely a Vilas throng that settled in for the farewell fight in the stadium, illuminated in late afternoon sunshine that would give way to floodlights. Americans were particularly high on Guillermo then, and Connors had unnecessarily alienated many of the customers the day before in the semis against the Italian, Corrado Barazzutti. At a critical stage of the third set, as Barazzutti pointed to a mark in the clay indicating that a Connors shot was wide, Jimmy loped around the net to the spot and destroyed the evidence, scuffing away the mark with a shoe. Hardly fair play, but he got away with it.

Connors had his loyalists, to be sure—more in New York than anywhere, his town above all others. They would expand dramatically in number at Flushing Meadows, where he picked up three more Open titles as well as the habit of "pumping myself" by twirling his right arm like a propeller and baying at the moon, or the sun, in a competitive dementia.

The Connors of the 1980s was no less feisty and belligerent, but he papered over the rough spots with a seeming mellowing-out, the sort of maturity that told him the right times to say the right things. Astonishingly, he began to say a few nice things about his opponents' accomplishments, startling those of us who had never heard him credit someone for beating him. For years it had been Jimmy who had won or lost; it was always in his hands. Perhaps he wouldn't let himself believe that someone could outplay him, seldom as that happened.

He and Borg had waged an extraordinary five-set struggle

in the 1977 Wimbledon final. The following year, Borg, having juiced up his repertory with a chipped backhand approach shot, slaughtered Connors. "What backhand?" Connors looked annoyed when asked about the Swede's additional weapon. "There's nothing new about Borg. He's the same guy."

But Jimmy has won over even his most critical audience, the Wimbledon crowd, starting with his tremendous five-set jarring of John McEnroe in the 1982 final. He solidified his position as one of the chosen with the stirring five-set comeback in 1987 against Mikael Pernfors, rising from two sets, and 0–3 down in both the third and fourth. "He's so courageous," the duchess of Kent remarked to me two matches later, after his semifinal loss to Pat Cash.

Even though the tasteless pantomimes remained—his "masturbatory dumb show," Dudley Doust in the *Sunday Times* of London called it—Connors had become a revered figure, an elder strokesman in whom such peccadillos were overlooked.

"A con man," sizes up McEnroe—although, grudgingly, "the guy actually does still love to play . . . after all these years. Can you believe it? Nobody understands it. You'll never get him off the court."

Vilas was certainly Jimmy's opposite. For four years, in fact, Guillermo had rated No. 1 in appeal to Americans. We knew that at WGBH in Boston, the flagship of PBS coverage between 1974 and 1978, because he consistently led our mail polls, drawing a huge response. Those were the days when PBS focused on the men's tour throughout the summer, weekend after weekend, Saturday and Sunday afternoons topped by a Monday night final. We like to believe we built a large constituency for the commercial and cable networks to inherit.

There was a mystique to Vilas, though no mystery to his game. It was built on conditioning and strength, an outlasting of the other guy by a constant slugging of heavily topspun ground strokes. He played, and won, like a caveman—brown hair, arrested by a headband, streaming to his shoulders. Then he sat for interviews like a noncombatant. A sinewy matinee idol, he spoke in a low, gentle voice of sportsmanship—sportsmanship in 1977?—poetry, and his hopes for Americans missing in action in Vietnam whose names he wore on necklaces and bracelets.

He captivated our viewers, winning tournament upon tournament that Connors avoided. Jimmy was busy on the "Riordan Circuit," a tour operated cleverly apart from the Grand Prix by his agent, Bill Riordan, and showcasing Connors and Nastase.

So captivated by the Argentine lefty were tournament patrons that they nearly rioted on Labor Day when the referee attempted to switch Vilas's match against José Higueras from the matinee to evening session. "We won't go!" chanted more than twelve thousand customers who refused to leave their stadium seats. Referee Mike Blanchard felt the late afternoon hour was too late to start Vilas-Higueras. He wished to clear the stadium and get it tidied for those holding tickets for the evening session, due to start in little more than an hour. But, observing and listening to the ruckus that might grow ugly, Mike smiled, "They obviously won't let us change the schedule." He put on Vilas and Higueras, and let the evening crowd wait a while outside. "In fifty years around here I've never seen that kind of disobedience from a crowd."

The 1977 season was Vilas's zenith. He was in the midst of a record fifty-match, eight-tournament streak when he beat Connors for his second major title of the year, following up on his French triumph. If looks could have killed that day, neither man would have made it through the first set, struck down by the glares of their seconds: Ion Tiriac, in his Draculean mien, was Guillermo's mentor; Gloria Connors, impersonating Medusa, was Jimmy's. After losing the first set quickly, Vilas began to play one of his smarter matches, changing his patterns, offering variety, and finally even attacking Connors at the net as the Argentines in the stadium went wild.

His head of steam carried him through a third-set tie-breaker and the next five games. At 0–5 Connors was serving to stay alive, and the crowd was whooping as though they'd seen to it that he didn't. Jimmy asserted that it was frightening—but to this day he will not accept that he lost the match, or that it even concluded. His last shot, a forehand, landed near a sideline. As soon as the ball touched, the partisans were chorusing, "Out! Out!"

"My shot was good. There wasn't any out-call from the linesman," says Connors, "which means it was good—my point. The match isn't over."

In a sense, he's correct. No hand signal or squawk of "Out!"

came from the sideline judge. But as jubilant followers of Vilas exploded like a bursting dam and came pouring onto the court, the aged umpire, John Coman, made a rather wise announcement: "Game, set, and championship to Mr. Vilas!"—and hoped he and his high chair wouldn't be carried off in a human undertow.

The joyous multitude lifted Vilas on a tidal wave of arms and shoulders, similar to the one that swept him around a similar stadium at the Lawn Tennis Club of Buenos Aires six months before, as he powered a Davis Cup victory over the United States. "It was a little frightening for me, too," he said, "because they all were grabbing for my headband for a souvenir. I thought they might pull off my head."

But only the defrocked champion lost his head. As receding hosannas of "VEE-LAS! VEE-LAS!" rebounded from his eardrums, Connors was sprinting for the exit. After a while the spontaneous fiesta subsided so that the trophy presentation could be made.

Never had a Forest Hills crowd cast itself so wholeheartedly into a match. It was ominous only for a moment, until the good nature of the revelers became apparent. The brief Latinizing of Forest Hills recalled the delightful triumph of Manolo Santana in 1965. A troupe of folk-costumed dancers from the Spanish Pavilion at the World's Fair had carried him from stadium to clubhouse after his victory over Cliff Drysdale. Barred from entering the clubhouse, they serenaded Manolo when he appeared, like Juliet, at a second floor locker room window.

It was the same World's Fair grounds at Flushing Meadows Park that would catch the public eye once again, thirteen years later, as the 1978 U.S. Open settled in the following September.

Twenty-one years had passed since I typed my first of about two hundred stories from that canvas-roofed West Side press box, a cramped cubicle that would not be missed. And thirty years elapsed since the teenage pilgrimage to Forest Hills had revealed that what's in a name did not mean the courts were on wooded sloops with spectators perched in branches. The place itself, repository of so many splendid memories and ghosts, would be missed. How did you reach nirvana? Head east on Queens Boulevard and turn right at Continental. But nirvana seemed to have shrunk.

My first story with a FOREST HILLS, N.Y. dateline had been

a "wait till next year" for Althea Gibson, who didn't make it in the 1956 final against Shirley Fry. The last, written as a smoggy night deepened, said that there would be no next year for Forest Hills.

Before smog there was Forest Hills. Before short pants, and before the women shed their garter belts and stockings. Before Big Bill Tilden came along to put tennis in a prominent position on the sports pages.

We thought of that after completing our stories, five reporters who climbed a stairway and the tiers to the heights of the venerable, ivy-draped stadium. It was empty and silent. I had commandeered a bottle of champagne and plastic goblets for the valedictory, and poured for John Powers of the *Globe*, Neil Amdur and Jane Gross of *The New York Times*, and Barry Lorge, then of the *Washington Post*. There were toasts, reminiscences, good-bye pats on the tailfeathers of one of the stony eagles on the ramparts.

The eagle we chose as host to the party, had, like his brethren, little regard for tennis. All ten of them are turned away from the stadium courts, peering into the distance. Ours was looking toward Flushing, where the courts would be as hard as his beak. And so were we.

The day the U.S. Open almost burned down returned me to my roots as a rookie reporter chasing fires for the *Herald*. Even though I'd been hired as a sportswriter, the managing editor thought all his recruits should put in time on general assignment, which included police and courthouse beats, political and educational details, obits, and fluff pushed by press agents.

Fires were stinkers. Literally. You got back to the office reeking, in smoked-up clothes that required cleaning immediately. Or, if funds were short, you went around trying to tell yourself that eau de conflagration was a wonderful, manly scent that would set female hearts aflame. It did not, and I could never find a female reporter of similar experience and aroma so that we might mingle while canceling one another out. Interviewing people who had been burned out of homes and possessions, and who were frightened and dazed, wasn't much fun either.

But I thought those days were over until the afternoon in 1981 that fearless Fireman Second Class Craig Groth charged to the rescue of Flushing Meadows, swinging his hook in a two-fisted Chris Evert manner to quell the blaze. Does Groth deserve a niche in the Tennis Hall of Fame or the Firefighting Hall of Flame?

Smoke signals, not standard scoreboard equipment, indicated that Ivan Lendl might be in trouble on the grandstand court, which adjoins the U.S. Tennis Center's main arena, Louis Armstrong Stadium. Sure enough, when I got there Lendl was leaving, followed by his foe, a diminutive left-hander named Mark Vines. "The joint's on fire," an usher informed me, nodding toward a black and smelly mist rising behind the south wall of the grandstand. "I never seen a tennis match called on accounta fire."

Neither had I. In the past, matches at the Nationals had been delayed by rain, traffic jams, darkness (of both a nightfalling and power-failing variety), a hurricane, a gunshot wounding a spectator, player injuries, the assassination of a net by Roscoe ("Bulletman") Tanner, and fiery tantrums. But never by a fire. A tornado would intrude in 1985, prompting the sort of flooding downpour that probably would have been welcomed the day the alarm bells rang at Engine 289 in nearby Corona. Captain James Spillane of the New York City Fire Department said that he and his men had not been summoned before to save a tennis tournament, but they go wherever the alarm beckons, and would do the same for any event.

The captain, gas mask at the ready, was standing only feet from the offending blaze, which, though closeted, was nonetheless roaring within a huge steel garbage compactor parked next to the grandstand. To some, this is the essence of the Open: garbage. It is the world's ripest tournament, and by the second week, if either the wind or your position are wrong, the whiffs can be overpowering. Fortunately it is an outdoor tournament, but garbage disposal has never been a strong point of the Flushing operation.

It may just be the place's heritage. Flushing Meadows Park was a flaming ash heap long before it claimed the title aspirations of Bjorn Borg or drew Engine 289 to the Open. Prior to its redemption as a public park, the Meadows existed as a vast dump for the burning of Brooklyn's garbage. A politically well-connected hustler from Flatbush named Fishooks McCarthy, holding the contract to remove his borough's trash, spread mountains of it over the meadow in the 1920s. A staggering, repulsive sight then, the future tennis playground was described by F. Scott Fitzgerald in his novel, *The Great Gatsby*, as: "... a valley of ashes—a fantastic farm where ashes grow like wheat into ridges and hills and grotesque gardens, where ashes take the form of houses and chimneys and rising smoke. . . ."

It didn't stay that way because of the foresight of Robert Moses, New York's longtime commissioner of parks, who transformed the dismal plain into a verdant recreation ground. Much later, in 1978, Slew Hester's variation on a theme by Moses came to pass: the construction of the Tennis Center, luring the Open from neighboring Forest Hills.

But was the promised land of Moses—albeit an earsore from the traffic of two other neighbors, Kennedy and LaGuardia airports—about to go up in smoke? Not quite. Certainly Lendl was coughing, he said, from the noxious fumes that had halted his match with Vines. "The guy has always been a choker," remarked a customer—this three years before Ivan broke his jinx in major championships by beating John McEnroe in the 1984 French final. Umpire Adrian Clark felt the backdrop of smoke was no reason not to play on, and remained in his high chair as resolutely as Captain Smith on the *Titanic*'s bridge while Lendl walked. Vines, ranked 195th, also wanted to continue, figuring sagely that his only chance was the asphyxiation of Lendl.

Summoned by the interruption, referee Mike Blanchard sided with Lendl, and the match was formally halted. Blanchard, though unaware of the smoke's origins, assured me that it wasn't a fire for insurance purposes since the Open is an eminently successful commercial enterprise.

Shortly the match resumed. Twice more it was interrupted as the intrepid firemen cracked the compactor's door to shoot streams of water that brought forth more sooty belches. The last time was the worst, and even the doughty umpire, Clark, decided not to go down with his chair, and fled, along with a drove of spectators. It was then that Fireman Second Class Groth gave a first-class performance, wading into the compactor with hook to probe and prod and find the blaze's source and handle the last, snuffing hosing.

He was modest about his role in saving the Open. "I've

been here before, to watch," said the surprised participant, "and it was nice to be back, if only for an hour." Groth did not, he said, knowingly copy Chrissie's grip on his hook.

Bjorn Borg seemed ready for the hook himself when he exited Flushing Meadows, glazed of eye, and for the last time, eight days later, beaten by McEnroe in the championship match. He was zero-for-ten in U.S. Opens. Enough. But if one moment could epitomize the great champion's discomfort and anguish in the Borough of Queens, it was that raw September evening in 1979 when the Bulletman, Tanner, made the webbed wall—then Borg—come tumbling down.

Borg had narrowly escaped Tanner's trigger two months before in broad daylight, at the rousing five-set Wimbledon final. But now, dealing with that high-velocity left-handed serve after dark in the stadium was like trying to catch rabbits with a teaspoon. Tanner led, 2–1 in sets, and, serving at 5–3, deuce, he fired the shot that seemed to symbolize another liquidation of the favored Swede.

Whap! The yellow bullet aimed at Borg was on its way. Snap! The ball struck the net with such force that it collapsed, expiring with a broken cable. If Tanner could destroy the wall separating them, what hope was there for Bjorn?

Time was called while the stricken net was dragged away and a replacement raised. During the intermission of six minutes, Borg paced and shivered, blew on his hands. He looked cold and helpless, a rare state for him, and Tanner's resumed attentions only served to accentuate the negative.

Six days after Fireman Groth put out the fire behind the grandstand, a discourteous Englishman, Philip Greenwood, kindled another one of a vocal nature in the upper deck of the stadium that heated up more people, two of them named Evert and Navratilova, and disrupted their semifinal.

The hero of that slow burn experienced by Chris Evert, Martina Navratilova, and a large crowd, was an anonymous usher, later identified as Ron Calamari. His was a honey of a flying tackle, extinguishing the annoying Mr. Greenwood, and cheered by 18,588 witnesses.

From the remote reaches of the northeast balcony, the penetrating voice of Greenwood was heard in loud and obscene heckling of Navratilova, who was having a tough enough time coping with Evert. Martina was starting to feel like Borg. Although twice a Wimbledon champ, she had come up empty in eight previous U.S. Opens. She hadn't yet overtaken Evert in the Rivalry, trailing 28–13 in matches, and had never beaten Chrissie outdoors in America. But despite the raucous opposition of Greenwood, amid a raffish group in Row Q characterized by police as "known scalpers and gamblers," Martina was playing Chrissie even in the tense third set. The rowdies were drinking, screaming, generally antagonizing the rest of the audience and the players, acting as though they were auditioning for an "I Love New York" commercial.

"They were in the wrong stadium," said Martina. "They sounded like Yankee fans." In his geographic delirium, Greenwood kept yelling at her, "Go back to Russia!"

Once Martina retorted, "Have another beer, and shut up during the points!"

The first delay occurred when a fight erupted between the hecklers and security guards, who were trying to enforce rudimentary decorum. Play was halted for a few minutes. It was the second disturbance—with Martina serving at 3–4, and on her harried way to victory—that enshrined the rugged Ron Calamari. To the crowd, he was every bit as much a liberator from obnoxiousness as Fireman Groth had been from greasy noxious clouds. And just as nameless.

Free speech was one thing, but public nuisance was quite another the cops decided, and closed in on Greenwood. It turned into a chase scene as Evert and Navratilova paused in their labors below to watch. Usher Calamari, a college student at St. John's, led the pursuers, and in excellent linebacking form launched himself at Greenwood to make the soaring stop. It was football season, after all. The cops took over, making an arrest for disturbing the peace, and Navratilova continued disturbing the pace of defending champion Evert.

But Martina, newly certified as a U.S. citizen, wasn't any luckier the next day in the U.S. Open than she had been as a noncitizen. Tracy Austin beat her in a third-set tiebreaker. She had to wait two more years, too long to tell Borg (retired from major activity in 1982) the old Bohemian proverb—that the eleventh time never fails. In 1983, against Evert, with flying volleys as impressive as Ron Calamari's flying tackle, Martina burned down her U.S. Open hex.

41

○

Nasty Acts

Ilie Nastase was never given his due, but I haven't given up hope. If there is any fairness in the world of tennis, the MTC (Men's Tennis Council) will change the cold and lifeless name of their behavioral statutes from Code of Conduct to the Nastase Act, honoring a man who put more life in the game than some wished, but thereby provoked the Code into being.

There is ample precedent for fully crediting the all-Romanian boy—a childish but magnificent champion—who was clearly responsible for these tennis regulations. In suggesting this tribute, surely earned by all the mischievous trouble Nastase caused during a bumptious fifteen-year career in the spotlight, I ask that the MIPTC consider the conventional system of identifying laws and acts by their namesakes. For example, the Gramm-Rudman Act, seeking to balance the U.S. budget, named for Senators Phil Gramm and Warren Rudman. Or the Volstead Act, sponsored by Congressman Andrew Volstead, that ushered in the aridity of Prohibition.

Of course, not even Gramm-Rudman could balance Nastase, the Bucharest Buffoon, nor would Volstead have prohibited the high-proof high jinks that drove court officials to high-balls. But in making the Code of Conduct necessary, and unavoidable—and available for trying to deal with John Mc-Enroe—Nastase rendered a service to the game he loved so well, and played as such a gifted free-flowing spirit, perhaps the Nijinsky of tennis. In its way, the Code is as much Nastase's contribution to mankind, and curbing the headstrong, as Joseph Ignace Guillotin's advocacy of the machine that bears his name and serves a similar purpose.

There may have been times when guillotining him seemed too good for this darkly handsome gazelle, but who couldn't quickly forgive "Nasty" his antics and think only of his art? "I am a little crazy," he conceded, "but I try to be a good boy."

Some may say, correctly, that another wayward artist, McEnroe, broke all of Nastase's records for fines and suspensions. Aside from the obvious, that great athletes of the present always surpass the marks of great athletes of the past, how could McEnroe have achieved such outrages if Nastase hadn't defined them?

Records be damned, McEnroe could never approach Nastase's panache. Did Mac ever moon a referee well before the moon rose? Or remove a shoe and throw it at a baseline judge who ruled he was footfaulting? Or change both his shorts and shirt on court during a match? Nasty did.

Disagreeable as he was at Wimbledon, did John ever scandalize the joint by simulating an unnatural act in view of TV cameras and speechless commentators? Or hide from an admonitory umpire behind a fence of Court 2 while spectators tittered and opponent Andrew Pattison fumed? Would McEnroe have painted his face black, drawing a laugh from his mimicked partner, Arthur Ashe, to archly comply with an apparel rule of the time stipulating that doubles teams must present matching (sartorial) appearances? Was Junior ever guilty of spitting in an opponent's face? (Well, he did expectorate at a female spectator in Boston.) Nasty did those, too.

Has the American miscreant cursed foes and officials in at least a half dozen different languages? Might he have borrowed an umbrella from a spectator, and stood beneath it, ready to receive serve, to let a stubborn umpire know that it could be raining too hard to continue play? Nasty did that, and much more.

Though McEnroe may be a genius at work, he hasn't been very imaginative or amusing in his boilovers. Saving graces aren't his attributes. In penitent moments, John has said that he doesn't want to be remembered as another Nastase, but he shouldn't worry. He won't come close. True, churlishness and vulgarity did spill forth from Nastase, too, but not enough to overwhelm his endearing impishness, a basically naughty little boyishness.

These pages could be filled with Nastase's escapades alone. Vitas Gerulaitis tells of their arriving late at an airport, apparently missing the flight. But Nastase bolts through the gate, races after the taxiing airliner, and pitches a racket at the cockpit window. A startled pilot looks out, beholds a grinning Nastase begging for a ride. Who can refuse the delightful rogue? The plane returns to the gate, and they board.

Nastase shouldn't be left behind in this matter of crime and punishment either. There can be no doubt that the Code of Conduct, first put forth for professional play in 1976, was a direct response to Nastase's tweaking of court officials and twisting of decorum. Certainly there were suspensions (though no fining) of bad actors before Nastase appeared in 1966, still the amateur era. But a stern word or two from an umpire was generally enough to quell an argumentative, abrasive, or disruptive soul, and get a match going again.

But the eccentric Ilie, with his fragile psyche, and predilection for showmanship and gamesmanship, dropped on tennis as a brass band parading through a chamber music recital. He was a comedian whose humor could grow tediously coarse. His pranks, sometimes an antidote to boredom, might be aimed at smashing an opponent's concentration or mocking an official. At times he seemed gripped by the furies, unable to control the histrionics, coming apart as a player.

Umpires, unfortunately not trained as riot cops or wardens, were unable to cope with him. The rules seemed as inadequate. Additional regulations were needed, specifically setting forth actions that would not be tolerated, and a variety of penalties that could be levied during a match as an alternative to summary disqualification. That step seldom found favor with the customers, suddenly deprived of what they'd paid to see.

A frequent traveler along the steps of the code, McEnroe seemed to reach his zenith of boorishness during a win over

Bobo Zivojinovic in the U.S. Open of 1987. His repeated vile outbursts at umpire Richard Ings resulted in $17,500 in fines and a two-month suspension, well beyond the accomplishments of any of Nastase's greatest outrages (though short of Jimmy Connors's record assessment of $20,000 for the most heinous of Code batterings: leaving a match unfinished in 1986).

For his first punishable infraction, McEnroe received a "warning." The second reaped a point penalty, the third a game penalty. Another would have meant disqualification, but McEnroe was cynically mindful, "I've been there before. I'm too much the pro to take that last step."

Each step of the way umpire Ings carefully enunciated the punishment like this, for the second one: "Code violation, Mr. McEnroe. Point penalty."

Wouldn't it have sounded better, more respectful of tennis history and tradition, if he'd been empowered to put it this way: "Nastase Act violation, Mr. McEnroe . . ."

Since the Code inspired by Nastase has most often been applied to McEnroe, there might be some grounds for baptizing it the Nastase-McEnroe Act, but that seems an unwieldy dilution of the progenitor's bad works.

The Nastase Act, as I would have it known, seemed to be a last-straw response to a couple of his more glaring offenses in 1975, a season during which he was disqualified in three tournaments. The first occurrence was the Canadian Open final in Toronto against Manolo Orantes. Angered by a line call that went against him in the opening set, Nastase sulked the rest of the way. Shamefully he stopped trying. He won only one more game, spoiling the afternoon—my most disheartening on TV—for the on-scene and at-home audience, as well as his very sporting Spanish foe. He was so appallingly unprofessional that during the telecast I ruefully advised viewers to tune us off. Verbal suicide.

Four months later, at the Masters in Stockholm, Nastase was involved in the only match in tennis annals with two losers. That figured, but the identity of his harried accomplice in this anomaly did not: the exemplary Arthur Ashe. Bringing together the top eight players of the men's season in a playoff that began with a series of round-robin matches, the Masters had been Nastase's meat, won by him in 1971, '72, and '73. The round-robin feature, giving a player a chance to lose a match yet remain in the tournament, had been a boon to Nastase in 1973 (along with the leniency of the rules), and was again in 1975—his last diddling with those rules before adoption of the, uh, Nastase Act.

Throughout the extraordinary Double Knockout, a round-robin match, Nastase had been bickering, stalling, heckling both the umpire and Ashe, a thoroughly objectionable performance. Ilie presently got to the usually imperturbable Ashe, who communicated by word and gesture his disgust, and the message: How long is Nastase going to be permitted to get away with this?

Astoundingly, although he had built up a 4–1 lead in the decisive set, Ashe exploded. "Unbelievable!" he yipped while Nastase emoted—and picked up his rackets and left the court. Ashe, convinced that Nastase had fiddled him out of their 1972 U.S. Open final with the same sort of unchecked foolery, refused to take more.

But by walking out, Arthur, though sinned against, committed the cardinal sin. He was surrendering, and the umpire had no alternative but to disqualify him.

Taking a highly unethical tack, officials followed Ashe to the dressing room, and tried to talk him into returning. Nothing doing. The match was apparently defaulted to Nastase.

But was it? Wait a second! After an hour of wrangling with the two contestants, leaving a full-house crowd at the Kungliga Tennishallen restive and baffled, referee Horst Klosterkemper announced a bizarre decision: Nastase was disqualified because, "It was in my mind to do so just at the moment Ashe walked out."

The belated disqualification-of-Nastase solution in the mind of the German beholder, Klosterkemper, came out later because, he insisted, he hadn't been quick enough to voice it before Ashe disqualified himself. Here, then, was a historic match with two losers, a parody of that tiresome sentiment so frequently mouthed at trophy presentations: It's too bad one of you had to lose.

They stayed losers overnight—a pox on both your rackets, gentlemen—but, of course, that would never do. If Christine Jorgensen, the former George W. Jorgensen, could get a major change in Stockholm, why not Ashe? A bit of official, and inventive, surgery the next day transformed him into a victorious quitter. Arthur's sin of premature departure was altered to a hastily created faux pas called a "misdemeanor," a lower-grade transgression than whatever prompted the Nastase disqualification that had lurked in referee Klosterkemper's cerebellum. The dilemma of the double defeat was resolved in Ashe's favor, a gift for clean living—deserved, maybe, but unwarranted under the rules.

Sir Arthur, the knight in shining sneakers, was declared winner over the Romanian dragon, who wailed, "How can I lose a match when I stand on the court and the other guy quits?"

Odd, all right, but poetic within an odd career. Not as poetic as Ilie's complete turnabout at Stockholm. Feeling wronged, he got revenge by behaving and playing like an angel to win his fourth Masters. His one defeat didn't keep him out of the semis, and once there he turned the tourney upside down with such eloquence of racket and feet that he was irresistible.

This was the greatness—which surpassed even the imagination of his contemporaries when it was plugged in. No ball was out of his reach. Ilie's shots were tinged with such delicate spins and angles, and power, that his last two foils, all-timers Guillermo Vilas and Bjorn Borg, groped like charwomen in the dark, totaling twelve games between them for six sets.

It was marvelous to watch him in form that he wouldn't find again on an important stage. While giving Ilie credit for a recovery, Ashe, influential in tennis politics, said, justifiably, that the affair pointed up the need for a code of conduct spiked with point and game penalties. The putative Nastase Act was on the way, and yet it was unable to trip the hero himself, although it was enforced against him in 1979 at Flushing Meadows. Nastase, eventual victim in the match with two losers, became the man who lost the same U.S. Open match twice!

That was not unique compared to the Stockholm farce, or even to the ever-embroiled Nastase, who was also the loser and winner of the same match during the 1973 Masters at Boston. Then he had quit a round-robin match against Jan Kodes in a pique, griping that the crowd and officials were against him. Since he had lost his opener to Tom Gorman, Nastase was ostensibly out of the running. However, the avuncular referee, Mike Blanchard, talked Ilie into continuing the match, over the understandable objections of Kodes, who thought he'd won. Reconsidering, Ilie did go back on, won the match—and presently, the tournament.

But nothing weirder has splotched the U.S. Open than Nastase's twice-lost decision to his successor-in-crimes, McEnroe, in the second round of 1979. Dark had fallen on the Meadows before the rules fell in a shambles. What else would you expect in a late summer night's dream meeting that might have been presided over by Puck—McEnroe vs. Nastase. Getting them together on the same court was a remake of *Frankenstein Meets the Wolfman.* For that reason, an understanding, extremely competent umpire, Frank Hammond, was stationed in the stadium high chair, an item of domestic furniture better suited to the mentalities of McEnroe and Nastase.

But the overflowing Hammond crashed along with the rules, a needlessly disgraced judge thrown out of court instead of the offender. It was just one more instance of Nastase being followed by his little lamb—bedlam. Ilie, just about phased out as a meaningful player, was still out to provoke his ascendant nineteen-year-old rival. He succeeded, although not sufficiently to make McEnroe waver from the path to an initial Open title. As the two railed at each other like fishwives, Nastase clowned and stalled, argued, erupted, pulled all the tricks against the only guy whose deportment could turn a crowd of ten thousand solidly pro-Nastase.

The match, a scheduling disaster, begun after 9:00 P.M., went from disorder to chaos to anarchy as an overly bibulous audience threw paper cups, soda cans, and other trash—and umpire Hammond was tossed to these wolves in spectators' clothing. Egged on by the crowd, Nastase became impossible. Not even his old pal, Hammond, could coax him to behave, and, as the match progressively deteriorated, he regretfully nailed Ilie with provisions of the Nastase Act: a warning, a penalty point, then in the fourth set a penalty game. Nastase, behind 2–1, found himself ordered to become the server at 1–3 as the penalty game was levied.

Unruly spectators either didn't understand, or refused to accept, shouting, "2–1! 2–1!"—which was their version of the score. Nastase refused, too, pacing the baseline with the balls as a discomposed Hammond blurted, "Play, Ilie! Come on . . . you have to play right now!" The umpire was begging.

Nastase, sensing "the low point" of the umpire's thirty-two-year-career, as the pitiable Hammond would acknowledge, ignored his friend. "First time I ever lost control of a match," sighed Hammond.

Step four was disqualification. In the wings was referee Mike Blanchard, the same conciliator who had sidestepped bouncing Nastase in Boston, thereby saving the 1973 Masters for him. But this time, amid the ugly din, Blanchard nodded to Hammond, properly, to go to the clock. If Nastase didn't serve within thirty seconds, he merited the fourth violation—and the hook. After fifty-eight seconds of inactivity, Hammond reluctantly shrieked, "Game, set, and match to McEnroe!"

Garbage and boos cascaded down from the pews. The customers were not amused that their bear-baiting was shut down. But it was over—though only for the moment.

Tournament director Bill Talbert, fearing, he said, a riot, disqualified the disqualification. He directed that the match resume, and rather than removing Nastase, he yanked Hammond, substituting referee Blanchard in the chair. The unruly thus ruled in this travesty, the nadir of U.S. tennis jurisprudence. The Nastase Act had been mocked on behalf of Nastase. An Italian journalist, Rino Tommasi, veteran of numerous miscarriages of justice at Il Foro Italico in Rome, laughed, "Tonight, American officials make our Italians look like amateurs in falling apart."

It wasn't lost on the adolescent McEnroe, who needed only four more games to hand Nastase his second defeat of the raucous evening, well after midnight. Mac could see that law-and-order didn't necessarily apply to a willful bigshot, and would make use of that knowledge. Nor did it assure common courtesy or respect for an opponent.

At one juncture in the brouhaha Nastase had complained, vainly, to the umpire, "McEnroe keeps calling me a son of a bitch. Make him call me Mr. Son of a bitch!"

42

○

Together
Nests

You've heard about wife-swapping, but could a man legally banish his thirty-one-year-old mate to Pittsburgh in exchange for a twenty-one-year-old blonde?

It happened early in the foible-filled five-year life of a delightful sexual aberration called World Team Tennis. So did a form of communal living that came to sport during WTT's 1974–78 existence when player-coaches Billie Jean King in Philadelphia and Rosie Casals in Detroit became the first women to boss men on professional teams.

"Separate-but-adjoining are the men's and women's locker rooms," said coach Billie Jean. At least she knocked before entering the hired guys' domain of her Philadelphia Freedoms, a team whose bubbly coach inspired Elton John to compose and record the equally bubbly rock anthem "Philadelphia Freedom."

Mother Freedom and her husband, Larry King, were among the WTT founders, enthusiastically jazzing up an individual sport by throwing men and women together in a perky professional-team concept. Billie Jean still believes. As commissioner of

Domino's Team Tennis, she presides over a watered-down revival that has been operating since 1985 with lesser players and payrolls, convinced that the public fancy will yet be caught.

But DTT hasn't attracted anywhere near the attention, and none of the anxiety, that greeted WTT's arrival and shook the power plants of the game in 1974. It was during the original boy-girl lineups mixup that Clark Graebner, player-coach of the Cleveland Nets, got rid of his brunette spouse, Carole, exiling her to the Pittsburgh Triangles in exchange for the blond Laura DuPont. Laura, rather than Carole, now shared Clark's bench, but, she said, that's all.

When the newly formed league was stocked at a 1973 draft meeting, Cleveland was given a special "family selection" in the interest of domestic harmony so that owner Joe Zingale could pick Mr. and Mrs. Graebner in the same round. They were a rare couple in tennis annals, only the second husband and wife to have played in major singles finals. Carole lost the National title match of 1964, Clark the National of 1967. Before them, Sarah Palfrey Fabyan Cooke Danzig, National champ of 1941 and 1945, roomed with Elwood Cooke, Wimbledon finalist in 1939.

But domestic disharmony shortly embraced the Graebners, and Clark gave a new twist to the familiar sporting refrain, "Play me or trade me." Graebner advised owner Zingale, "If you want me to play, trade my wife!" The deal was made, to the pleasure of all involved.

Not so pleased by a first-year trade was Paul Gerken, who felt backhanded in his macho. "You mean they traded me for a woman?" he gasped when told he'd been shipped to Baltimore by Boston for Janet Newberry.

There were times when Frank Froehling, the player-coach of the downtrodden Miami Flamingos, thought he should trade Betty Anne Grubb for anybody who could lift a racket, and other times when he wouldn't have traded her for John Newcombe, Jimmy Connors, or any other man in the league. The coach had a lot of competitive men on the team: They were all competing for attention from the alluring Ms. Grubb—including Froehling, whose romance with her chilled when her regular boyfriend came to town. "Then we had a triangle in Miami that was the talk of the league—much more so than the Pittsburgh Triangles," chuckles teammate Donna Fales, a happily married mother of two young boys. "After a while Frank and Betty Anne weren't speaking. So if he, as coach, wanted to tell her something he used one of the other players as an intermediary. 'Would you please tell Betty Anne we leave tomorrow at nine'—that sort of thing.

"Betty Anne was a fantastic player for one set, which is all you played in WTT. So, maybe, to keep her happy, the team actually signed her boyfriend, Ken Stuart, who was a fair player. Imagine what it was like with the triangle on the same bench. Frank said one night, 'There may be bloodshed,' but there wasn't." Fales indicates that if the male side of the lineup hadn't been so distracted trying to win over Betty Anne, the Flamingos might have won a few matches.

Other sports leagues didn't have such hormonal flutterings to cope with, at least within the structure of a franchise. That was part of the beguiling nature of WTT, whose San Diego Friars fielded the self-proclaimed "all-time minority mixed doubles team"—John Lucas, black moonlighter from the National Basketball Association, and Renee Richards, transsexual.

Females may have been different as teammates for the men, but were as important on sixteen franchises across America. You couldn't win without winning women, a readily evident feature of the new coeducational undertaking.

Popping up like crocuses on many sports pages in the spring of 1974 were a new set of daily standings containing numerous cities also associated with the American and National Leagues of baseball. It was WTT with a forty-four-match May-September schedule and such teams as the Boston Lobsters, Detroit Loves, Los Angeles Strings, New York Sets, Houston EZ Riders, and Hawaii Leis. Some felt the last two should have merged as the EZ Leis, and the New York Sets renamed Zets—Yiddish for swats. Eventually the New York name was fixed nicely, altered to Apples.

The innovative league was a paradise for players and their agents, who peddled the athletes at fancy prices to green owners, otherwise sane businessmen eager to prove the theory that everybody in America wants a team as a plaything; and plenty of suckers could afford it. In the ripe climate of the mid-1970s, the height of the Tennis Epidemic, anything labeled "tennis" sold. Except tickets for WTT matches. Teams changed hands or folded fast. Millions were lost. A few stayed the five-year course, and at times the Golden Gaters in Oakland outdrew their baseball counterparts, the Athletics.

But the payrolls were too big, along with the expectations, and the teams didn't build fan support as quickly or thickly as had been hoped. Evonne Goolagong was supposedly guaranteed $1 million to play five seasons for Pittsburgh, considerably above Mrs. Graebner's divorce settlement, although the team didn't last very long. That first year, the rush of name players to WTT scared the Badgers and others involved in the conventional game. Was WTT going to knock out the summer tournament circuit?

Fiercest reaction came from the European tournaments, foremost among them the French Open. Players who signed WTT contracts were banned from events on the continent. Most deeply wounded by that unfair stand was Jimmy Connors, who had enrolled with the Baltimore Banners. Since he had won the Australian Open in January, Jimmy was the only guy that year with a shot at a Grand Slam, and the $100,000 bonus that went with it. The extra remuneration, a publicity gimmick, was put up by a cologne merchant. But it was fairly difficult for Connors to win the second leg, the French, because his entry was rejected.

Too bad. And it became worse as Jimmy went on to capture the other two, Wimbledon and the U.S., completing one of the three best seasons compiled by an American man. Budge's Grand Slam year and Tony Trabert's 1955 bag of French, Wimbledon, and U.S. were the others. Connors wasn't a lock to win the French, the one major that has eluded him. But he was robbed in being denied the opportunity, and he snubbed the tournament until 1979.

As it turned out, Howard Fine, owner of the Banners, wished Jimmy had repudiated his exorbitant contract and gone to Paris. Fine never knew when he was going to show up to play for the team. Ever individualists who take only their own games seriously, tennis players seemed to feel that WTT was a nifty little prank their agents were playing on the owners, a secondary enterprise at which they marked time between important tournaments—at very high wages.

Maybe the wages were the problem. Tennis players were becoming accustomed to making their living by winning prize money, but a paycheck whether they appeared or not, won or not, was compelling. So attendance wasn't so good? So what.

The money was in the bank, and they'd be back on the tournament circuit soon enough. Tom Okker was getting almost $150,000 for the sixteen weeks as player-coach of Buffalo-Toronto, and was still skittering here and there to fit in some tournament appearances, too.

It was a time of more craziness than usual in tennis, but a lot of fun, even if crowds didn't materialize. "Is not tennis, even if you use court, racket, and balls," surmised the Draculean Ion Tiriac, player-coach of the Boston Lobsters. "Is different category, different game."

It sure was—for one thing, very noisy. The format called for a match to be determined by cumulative games scored in five different sets: men's and women's singles and doubles, and mixed doubles. Clearly the women were in positions of true equality, as responsible as the men for victory and defeat. Presently, as Chris Evert, Martina Navratilova, and Virginia Wade joined up, females became the principal stars. The top women were solidly enlisted in WTT while some of the male names began to drift away.

Intent on breaking from practically all tennis traditions, the league's organizers encouraged a spiritual kinship with other professional team sports that was displayed in such forms as audience cheering for and against players and teams, bench-jockeying, tumult of any kind. Whenever the Freedoms scored a game, a replica of the Liberty Bell (painted blue) tolled for the home side. "Bong-bong—you're dead!"

A multicolored court, looking like a large patchwork quilt, was installed, along with Jimmy Van Alen's no-ad scoring that eliminated deuce games. Substitution was permitted, so that a savior might spring from the bench, although a man couldn't replace a woman, and vice versa. It Stolle wasn't serving too well, put in Gerulaitis.

It was a well-paid rest home for old-timers, who could manage to play one brisk set. One of them, thirty-nine-year-old Kenny Rosewall, Pittsburgh's player-coach, seemed the least likely to get carried away in the new boisterous atmosphere. But he was. "I've found myself clapping for the other team's double faults," admitted the paragon, looking as though he were confessing to an ax murder.

More shocking, Kenny actually considered assault and battery. Playing against Brian Fairlie of Philadelphia, Rosewall was absorbing a ferocious heckling from the Freedoms' bench. Kenny stopped playing and offered to punch the foremost heckler, Buster Mottram, twenty years younger and seven inches taller.

Coach Billie Jean stepped between them, snorting at Rosewall, "Grow up, you little punk!" He stared at her, gawking, until she smiled.

Most of the players got used to the sound and fury, and enjoyed the alien atmosphere, figuring this wasn't their real world anyway. They'd soon be back on the tournament circuit. But John Alexander said he feared for his life once in Buffalo, where the public-address announcer whipped up the crowd against him and his Los Angeles teammates. "We had to have a police escort to get out of the place."

Perhaps the most curious of American franchises showed up in WTT in 1977: the Soviets. The Soviets were strictly for export. WTT didn't include the USSR as a stopoff, or any other location beyond U.S. borders for that matter. Russia's best players—former Wimbledon finalists Olga Morozova and Alex Metreveli, plus Teimuraz Kakulia, Natasha Chmyreva, Vladimir Borisov, Marina Kroschina—were the ultimate road team. Forty-four matches, each and every one on somebody else's home court. But Metreveli shrugged that he didn't feel like that historic roamer, the Man without a Country. "We are always away from home anyway to play tournaments, so it doesn't make much difference."

It seemed a good deal both ways. WTT got an offbeat attraction, and publicity for the first Russian team in an American league. The Russian Tennis Federation got $200,000 for the use of the players, as well as expenses, from the franchise holder, Larry King, and could pay their so-called amateurs whatever. King needed to negotiate with only the Federation, paying a package price set by some bureaucratic Big Brother, instead of haggling with several agents to assemble an undoubtedly more costly team. He was also spared hiring a hall. Maybe Larry offered to pay off in bushels of wheat before the two-hundred-grand figure was reached.

The Soviet Federation could feel genuinely patriotic in sending their chattels to the States. They were contributing to the bankruptcy of a capitalist enterprise. While the Soviets sold some tickets, they weren't as boffo as the Bolshoi, and ended with a losing record. Like WTT itself. Andy Jick of the Boston

Lobsters PR staff, saying, "We want to make them feel at home," considered replacing the net with an iron curtain when the Russians visited.

Joe Zingale in Cleveland, who brought the Graebners together (and then parted them) continued as a romantic three years later in bagging Bjorn Borg for something like a million bucks. Joe put Bjorn's girlfriend, Mariana Simionescu, on the 1977 team, too, as designated roommate. Mariana, a fair player from Romania, was one-third of the Borgian odd trio, who shared championships, travel, lodgings, and room service meals. The other was the paternal coach-trainer Lennart Bergelin, a Swede three decades their elder, who had blended splendidly with his pupil for five straight Wimbledon titles.

After that, Bjorn and Mariana were married for a while. Nothing in the divorce proceedings stated that she held a summer in Cleveland against him.

However, WTT was indeed responsible for mental cruelty in the love affair of Kerry Melville of Melbourne, Australia, and Grover ("Raz") Reid of Greenville, South Carolina. It was love at first smite of the tennis ball when the luck of the organizational draft boxed them as colleagues on the Boston Lobsters of 1974. Having found bliss in one another's claws, they became engaged and then (curses!) were separated before they could be sacramentally joined together—scattered by a fiendish instrument of fate called the WTT redistribution draft. It was enough to wring tears from the eyes of a horseshoe crab.

Because of first-year financial troubles, the Lobsters had to leave their players open to pinching by other teams in 1975. Indiana grabbed the groom-to-be, Philadelphia the bride. Indiana also took the player-coach, Tiriac, who grumbled. "What is Indiana? I don't go to this Indiana for all the money in Albania!"

Melville, a far better catch than her man, a top-ten player ranked about 110 lengths ahead of him on respective computers, remained loyal. She refused to play unless they were reunited, preferably in Boston.

Love-and-marriage fans, not to mention Kerry and Raz, were rewarded. Not long after they wed, Lobsters general manager John Korff was determined that what the good Lord joins together WTT must not keep asunder. He swung a deal to bring them both back to Boston as teammates and roommates just before the 1975 season commenced.

"It's wrong for them to be in different cities," cried Korff, obviously a driven sentimentalist. "But playing for us as a married couple would be perfect. Especially for our expenses. They room together, share a car. We can have a lovers' night promotion, and they'll cut a big wedding cake."

So it happened. It should be said that Korff did spring for separate salaries and meal money. It should also be said that the Reids pulled probably the biggest upset in the history of tennis romances: They're still married, thus outlasting by more than a decade their matchmaker, dear departed WTT.

43

○

Hunting
"Dwight's Pot"

The chase for "Dwight's pot"—a.k.a. the Davis Cup—remains the most exciting, unpredictable form of tennis. And the most unwatched. It is an infrequent joy, one that I've traveled great distances to savor—sometimes even paying my own way, a shameful admission for a sportswriter.

A deprived majority are the tennis nuts who haven't sampled this zesty sideshow launched in 1900 by a do-gooder, rich kid out of St. Louis, twenty-one-year-old Dwight Filley Davis. From the original contest in Boston, in which donor Davis and a couple of Harvard chums were the United States (defeating Great Britain), it has expanded to a year-long, worldwide also-happening, woven in and around the Grand Prix schedule.

Called "Dwight's pot" in mock derision by his Longwood cronies, the silver tub, which cost him $750 from his walking-around money, was at first entitled the International Lawn Tennis Challenge Trophy. A mouthful—from which countless gullets full of victorious champagne have been gulped, mostly by Americans and Australians. The Davis Cup was easier. Three words and thirty letters shorter. Davis made an aw-shucks protest, but understood the common, linguistic sense dictating that it become the Davis Cup, whose pursuit embraces eighty-nine countries and six continents in 1989.

Some of those countries were nonexistent when Davis was swinging a mean, left-handed racket for his country. Believing that international friendship could be fostered by the competitive visits of national teams to other countries, he would be pleased at the spread of his tournament. Although he wasn't pleased at the 1932 Challenge Round in Paris. The French stole the Cup from the United States through an outrageous decision against Wilmer Allison by an extremely patriotic line judge. While a nationalistic crowd was delighted, Davis was momentarily rash, saying he was sorry he'd ever started the whole damned thing.

For such a pervasive enterprise, the broadest of annual international sporting championships, the Cup is, to the layfan, as comprehensible as the scoring of figure skating. In the United States the four principal TV networks contribute to the event's undercovered status by uniformly avoiding these often excruciating dramas, best-of-five match series over three days. For them, the time factor makes coverage of the Cup prohibitive: Best-of-five matches, without tiebreakers, consume hour after hour, with the possibility that the third day's matches will be meaningless, the outcome having been decided on the second.

But as pressure thicker than that of a Wimbledon or U.S. final settles like molasses on a flea circus, stranger things happen than in *Nightmare on Elm Street*. Champions have swooned to the occasion, coming apart like sawdust-stuffed dolls. Rod Laver and Mats Wilander, for instance. No-names like Spaniard Juan Gisbert or Colombian Jairo Velasco, to cite a couple of nightmares for the United States, have petrified their betters.

More often than not a Cup match is staged out of the mainstream, sometimes in a remote foreign location, pigeon-holed into the regular Grand Prix schedule. That adds to the appeal, but not to the public's understanding of where each match fits in the total global scheme. "How does it work?" is a question I hear all the time. A small collection of Davis Cup junkies know, and for us it's irresistible. The rest of the tennis crowd finds it highly resistible and unintelligible, particularly Americans.

In an earlier, simpler time of tennis confined to spring and summer, outdoors, it seemed that everybody was aware. All you had to know was that an American knight in white flannels named Big Bill Tilden was sequestering the grail from foreigners, and keeping it on his side of the Atlantic. He did that, with some help from teammates, for six straight Challenge Rounds after snatching the Cup from Australia in 1920. The Challenge Round system, abolished only as recently as 1972, provided that the champion nation sat back and waited at home for a challenger that was determined by an elimination tournament involving the rest. In his unequaled time of National Singles championships and Cup defenses, Tilden became a god of the magnitude of Babe Ruth, Red Grange, and Man o' War.

At last, France's thorough team effort by the Four Musketeers—Rene Lacoste, Jean Borotra, Henri Cochet, Jacques Brugnon—brought Tilden down in 1927 at Philadelphia's Germantown Cricket Club, a scene of American anguish and Gallic jubilation.

Before turning pro in 1931, Tilden led three futile assaults on Stade Roland Garros in Paris, trying to reclaim the Cup from the French. Still the crusade continued, and American yearning was rewarded in 1937 as Don Budge, Frank Parker, Bitsy Grant, and Gene Mako ended the longest U.S. drought, bringing the Cup home from Britain. A measure of public elation was the ticker-tape parade that hailed their arrival in New York with the Cup.

Those campaigns, in which only the United States, Australia, Britain, France, and Germany were serious contenders had been easy to follow. By 1988, with competition beginning the last weekend in January, and not ending until Sweden beat Germany in a mid-December indoor final at Göteborg, the number of Americans fathoming what had happened to their own team was limited.

The United States had lost before, to be sure, but never eliminated from the great pot chase altogether for two years within a single season as occurred in 1987, because of losses to both Paraguay and Germany. This was a first in Cup history for the Yanks, victimization by a double-defeat process, excluding them, in a sense, until 1989.

Paraguay? As tennis spread and developed, noticeably in the 1960s, American defeats such as would have been unthinkable in the days of Tilden, Budge, Kramer, and even Trabert, began to explode like terrorist attacks, in Italy, Mexico, Spain, Brazil, Ecuador, Colombia, Argentina. The world had become a dangerous place for the two preeminent rivals, Australia and the United States, who kept the Cup to themselves for the half-century between 1938 and 1958, with time out for World War II. They were antagonists in the grand finale, the Challenge Round, for sixteen successive years, and nineteen of twenty-five through 1968. Australia won sixteen Cups in that stretch, the United States nine, with the Aussies taking the head-to-head honors, barely, 10–9.

Yet the spirit of the annual Davis playoffs leading to the Challenge Round was obviously high among those others tapped, even if they were no-hopers. The attraction of playing for one's country outweighed the reality of a format so drastically tilted toward the Aussies and Americans, who already had an edge in talent.

The fun and unpredictability were turned up several notches in 1972 as the Challenge Round was scrapped, and everybody started equal. That year the United States, which had held the Cup since 1968, and won the next three Challenge Rounds, fought through to the uproarious final in Bucharest. As opponents, the Romanians Ilie Nastase and Ion Tiriac exemplified Dwight Davis's thesis that a country with as few as two good players could be a contender.

A further reorganization of the system in 1981 stipulated that only sixteen of the competing countries—the World Group— are certified to play for the Cup itself. The remainder are grouped according to zones, striving for a chance to win one of four zones (European A and B, Eastern, American) and thus be elevated to the World Group the following year. The eight first-round losers in the World Group are given a second chance to avoid demotion by playing off among themselves, with the four losers then descending to the boonies of zonal struggle. Losing the opening round of 1987 at Paraguay 3–2, the United States also flunked a last gasp opportunity against Germany at Hartford, 3–2.

Plunk! The trapdoor opened, and the Americans plummeted to the American Zone. For the first time since abstaining in 1919, the United States was ineligible to chase Dwight's pot. To find redemption in 1988, earning restoration to the big league for 1989, the United States needed to beat Peru and Ar-

gentina on the road. Captain Tom Gorman called on metro-
nomic Jay Berger, the brilliant kid, Andre Agassi, old Cup hand,
John McEnroe, and his undefeated doubles team Ken Flach and
Rob Seguso, and got it done.

Though embarrassing for the winner of the most Cups
(twenty-eight), the United States crash of '87 was just another
indication of increasing parity. Bomb throwers in sawed-off pants
lurked around every corner jeopardizing onetime super powers.
Won only by the Big Four—the United States, Australia, France,
Britain—until 1974, the Cup has since been claimed by South
Africa, Italy, Czechoslovakia, and Sweden.

From the first, pitfalls of the road have been part of the
fascination and frustration of Davis Cup, a departure from the
every-player-for-himself philosophy of customary tournaments
whose audiences are usually neutral. The more screaming and
flag-waving the better in some locales, where homers as line
judges add to the perils for visitors.

"There's no pressure in tennis like Davis Cup pressure,"
says Dennis Ralston, who represented the United States seven
years as a player and four more as captain, sometimes in prickly,
even frightening locales. "Those crowds can be tough in a foreign country. You feel like you're carrying your country on your
back. Your country may not even be aware that you're out there
somewhere with USA on your back, but you know it. It's a
very lonely feeling even if the natives aren't restless, yelling at
you, pounding on drums, or cheating you left and right. But
that's what makes Davis Cup such a great test."

Most champions, savoring that pressure, consider playing
for the Cup to be a career high. Even Pancho Gonzalez says so,
and he played only once, helping repel Australia in the Challenge Round of 1949.

Pressure was once defined by my broadcasting partner of
short, but amusing, duration, ex-quarterback Dandy Don Meredith: "the cold rush of shit to the heart." In tennis it also
rushes as concrete to the business elbow, with no regard for the
fame and accomplishments of that elbow's owner.

Nor, in 1967, did Ecuadorean nonentities Miguel Olvera
and Pancho Guzman have any regard for the fame and accomplishments of four of the world's finest (Arthur Ashe, Cliff Richey, Clark Graebner, Marty Riessen). Weekend warriors Guzman and Olvera won, 3–2; the ultimate shocker, Guzman
beating Ashe in the deciding match by the curious score of

0–6, 6–4, 7–5, 0–6, 6–3. Nobody can yet explain what happened to Ashe & Co. in that red-dirt rectangle in Guayaquil. Nor can Jimmy Arias in the twentieth anniversary gas-taking against Paraguay in Asunción, which started the United States's 1987 woes. Unlike Ashe, Arias reveled on clay, having won the Italian Open and other European tourneys. But when presented with 282-ranked Hugo (Who go?) Chapacu, practically an illusion, in the decisive encounter, Arias found a way to blow a 5–1 fifth-set lead and three match points.

That's Davis Cup for you.

Another Jimmy (Connors), whose competitiveness has never been questioned, was, nevertheless, an avoider—one of the oddest Davis Cup cases. He has probably the worst record, albeit a short one, among the genuinely great players. Uncomfortable in a team setting, perhaps because he was always a me-against-the-rest-of-the-world guy, Connors tried it only three years, and didn't lead a winning charge. He seemed disenchanted by losing to Raul Ramirez in the decisive 1976 match against Mexico, keeping his distance until a 1981 cameo.

In a 1984 reprise, convinced by his agent, Donald Dell, that a Davis Cup was the one gem missing from his tiara, Connors enlisted again. But he prepared carelessly (as did teammate John McEnroe) for the final in Sweden where the favored Americans were blotted, 4–1. After Jimmy lost the opening match to Mats Wilander, McEnroe, the winningest player in U.S. Cup annals, lost to another of those three-hour messiahs who have plagued the United States on clay, one Henrik Sundstrom.

Ugly Americanism was in full swing that day in Gothenberg. While Mac was merely snappishly disagreeable, Connors turned the full torrent of vitriol and vileness on umpire George Grime, who would have thrown him out if it hadn't been the Cup final. Handling it in print for the *Globe* wasn't as difficult as commenting for TV would have been. The readers couldn't hear Connors's remarks but viewers could.

A couple of weeks later at the Masters in New York, I was discussing Gothenberg with two friends, Dick Enberg, my NBC partner, and Gianni Clerici, who had done the match on Italian TV. "Thank goodness we didn't have that Connors match," Enberg was saying. "Wow, that audio. You were lucky, Gianni. Since all that lousy language was in English, you could sort of let it slide by—"

"Signor Enberg," Clerici raised his eyebrows. "I am a journalist. I understand English. It was my duty to inform my audience of what was taking place."

"Oh, my," Enberg was incredulous. "How'd you manage that?"

"Well, it is not easy. When Connors calls the umpire an 'asshole,' I have to explain because we do not have quite that expression. I say Connors is comparing him with a small posterior aperture."

"But . . ." Gianni paused, "when Connors calls him a fucking fag . . . that is very difficult. As you may know, the Italian slang for homosexual is *finocchio*. But *finocchio*, properly, means a plant that you call, in English, fennel. So I say Connors is accusing the umpire of making love to a vegetable."

When I began to notice Davis Cup, Australia seemed the eternal destination, the holy land for American crusaders intent on retaking the American-made treasure. That was the only constant about Davis Cup understood by American sports junkies: Can we beat the Aussies?

Since Challenge Rounds in Australia were traditionally played during the last week in December, the height of Southern Hemisphere summer and the holiday season, an American who joined the crusade knew he wouldn't be home for Christmas. He'd spend most of December training in Australian grass-court tourneys for the momentous three days that set the country afire and drew the largest crowds ever to watch tennis. In 1954 as many as 25,578 were stacked around Sydney's White City court where temporary grandstands rising above the stadium superstructure quivered scarily, but stayed up. All this when Wimbledon's daily 14,000 in Centre Court was the zenith of tennis attendance, and Forest Hills was fortunate to attract 10,000.

My dream was to cover one of those engagements, amounting to the world series of tennis, but, of course, I would have gotten a horselaugh from the Boss at the *Herald* if I'd even brought it up. Trip to Australia? Stop at the moon on the way home to pick up some cheese, junior.

There was no chance of even going to New York at those infrequent times that the Aussies showed up to retrieve the Cup, as they always did after losing it. But in November of 1963, as I made the move crosstown from *Herald* to *Globe*, I wondered if I mightn't keep moving to Adelaide for Christmas.

Secretly I considered a request to cover the 1963 Challenge Round outlandish. But I made it anyway when the *Globe*'s managing editor, Tom Winship, asked me what I'd like to do for my leadoff assignment. Asked me? Realizing I was in new territory, a solar system apart from the *Herald* where each subway token was accounted for, I bid for newer.

"How about the Challenge Round in Australia? Starts the day after Christmas," I replied.

His frown caused me to smile wryly. Oh well, nothing ventured, right? But it only meant that he didn't know what I was talking about. Listening to the explanation, Winship responded, "When do you want to leave?"

It isn't considered good form to kiss managing editors, so I refrained. Considering that my opening assignment for the *Herald* nine years before had involved a thirty-minute bus ride to a high school football game in Brookline, I really didn't mind the hours upon hours of flights, the last depositing me in the sunshine of Adelaide, South Australia.

Winship, who had begun to steer the *Globe* to clear primacy in New England, and recognition nationally and internationally, liked to make splashes with his new bylined acquisitions. He felt Globies should follow wherever the story line led, a policy continued by his successor, Jack Driscoll, and persevering sports editor Vince Doria.

Landing in Adelaide, I felt like a zoology major arriving in Africa, anxious to set aside impressions gathered at circuses, and to deal with the unfettered and fearsome creatures—Australian tennis players—in their own habitat. I was uplifted to be in the land from which these wandering warriors sprang, where "centuries" (100-degree days) came one after another, beaches and frontiers never ended, and "bloody Yanks" were considered blood brothers.

"G'dye, myte!" was the reassuring and welcoming salute from the leader of the pride, Roy Emerson, as I encountered him at the heart of the enemy camp, the beautifully landscaped Memorial Drive Grounds beside Lake Torrens. His black hair was slicked down, and his record was slicker, showing he'd played on four straight Cup winners. His greeting didn't sound as exotic as it had in America because everybody in Adelaide talked that way.

Emmo was pure delight. He trained harder, drank and danced

faster, and won more than anybody else in the amateur sphere he ruled. "You'll like our beer, Blue," he used his all-purpose nickname the way Babe Ruth called everybody "Kid." He was insightful. To my taste, Aussie beer was and is ambrosia in cans.

At once friendly and fun, Australia is the only country that still hasn't forgotten what happened in World War II. "You bloody Yanks saved us from the bloody Japs!" is still heard, possibly a sign of culture lag.

Tourism was minimal in 1963, the country much simpler and less frenetic than the United States, devoted to sport and outdoor life. Money didn't seem to mean a lot as long as there was a beach within reach, plenty of beer for the esky (portable cooler), and the barbecue in the backyard was in working order.

But the Davis Cup was reasonably serious business. Judging from the newspapers, radio and TV, and the talk in the pubs, the entire country was zeroed in on the showdown to be played out on the quick, emerald center court of Memorial Drive. This was a tennis atmosphere such as I had never encountered, and wouldn't again. I had never covered a tennis event so crowded with reporters, all looking for angles, each trying to outdo the other at drinking beer and divining "exclusives" from the suds. It was the last of the tremendous Aussie-Yank Challenge Rounds that engrossed the entire country even though one more was played, a perfunctory and inevitable United States win in 1968.

Although Emmo was an automatic starter, much suspense centered on Captain Harry Hopman's choice of the accompanying singles player. Would Hop use an old hero, Neale Fraser, thirty, whom he'd coaxed out of retirement? Or a guy whose fiery temper didn't please him, Fred Stolle? Or the dynamite new boy, nineteen-year-old John Newcombe?

U.S. captain Bob Kelleher, the lanky Los Angeles attorney who would skillfully rally U.S. support for open tennis as USTA president five years later, had only the problem of keeping his young, fixed lineup—Chuck McKinley and Dennis Ralston—in a good, relaxed mood.

McKinley, a peppery, combative teddy bear of twenty-two, wasn't your everyday American tennis player, country-club bred. Son of a roistering St. Louis construction laborer, he was a kid for challenges, a leaping, diving, squeaking attacker who would endear himself to TV cameras if he were playing today. "A pint-sized Boris Becker," recalls his partner, Ralston.

Grit was a prime asset, displayed even in his terminal days of 1986. Chuck stayed uncomplainingly cheerful, holding off a malignant brain tumor long enough to know he'd been inducted into the Hall of Fame. "Just playing the hand I've been dealt," he told me over the phone not long before he died. "The way I did in tennis."

Chuck's first big challenge of 1963, also against odds, was Wimbledon, where he'd been a first-round loser the year before. His college coach at Trinity University in San Antonio was lukewarm when Chuck asked permission to play in London. It meant missing the National Intercollegiates, which he was favored to win, thus living up to his scholarship as well as bringing honor to alma mater. The coach, Clarence Mabry, said the decision was up to the college president, Dr. James Laurie. Laurie said, "Chuck, what's good for the student is good for Trinity, so if your heart's set on Wimbledon . . ."

Chuck was out the door fast, but he heard prexy add, ". . . but you better win it!" Which he did.

Six inches taller and a year younger, Ralston, twenty-one, was moody, spoiled, battling himself and homesickness throughout his career. His was a Davis Cup boom-and-bust saga, more bust probably, even though he had a winning record as player and, later, U.S. captain. But it was tempering and strengthening, as he became an admirable man and fine coach. He, Chuck, and their squadmates, Frank Froehling, Marty Riessen, and Gene Scott, had been on the road forever, three months to prep for and beat Britain, India, and the Aussies. That sort of campaign is impossible today in the face of the demands of the pro circuit. If a captain has his team for three days prior to a match he's lucky.

Love of country is no longer enough incentive. Cup sponsorship has made it a prize-money endeavor, although this is seldom publicized. Prize money plus subsidies from national associations can amount to a not-so-insignificant amount for much less effort than was expended in 1963. John McEnroe and Peter Fleming, active in all four matches needed to win the Cup for the United States in 1982, received about $200,000 apiece plus first-class expenses, while teammates who played less were rewarded proportionately. Mainstays Connors, Fleming, and McEnroe got about $150,000 in 1984 when the Americans lost the final at Sweden. Patriotism has a price tag nowadays. Nathan Hale should have had it so good.

On Christmas morning in 1963, bright and warm, the teams lined up on the center court, sharing it with the perpetual star, the old crock itself, sixty-three-year-old Davis Cup. This was the ritual of the draw as conducted in Australia, and I was surprised to see that about two thousand fans were there, too, seated expectantly in the covered grandstand, to learn firsthand who Emerson's accomplice in singles would be—Fraser, Newcombe, or Stolle?

Newcombe, a tall, handsome kid, four years short of his first Wimbledon title, looked stunned when his name was plucked from the Cup along with Ralston's to play the opening match. That dissipated some of the suspense, but much more remained over the next three days before the United States carted off the Cup, 3–2.

Ralston did his part by slipping past Newcombe in five sets, and abetting McKinley in doubles for a 2–1 lead. But when he lost the fourth match to the unshakable Emerson, Memorial Drive became a bubbling caldron. At 2–2, it was up to McKinley and Newcombe to decide the fate of the Cup: back to the United States, or to its second home, a Melbourne bank vault.

McKinley was in his element, calm at the center of turbulence. He didn't mind that the customers were bellowing for Newcombe. He relished their feverish response. Not for twenty-four years had the fate of the Cup come down to a fifth match involving an American. "This is what I wanted, the way I figured it would be," said McKinley, who lost the tumultuous first set, 12–10.

Chuck won the second, but never had I heard such a clamor on a tennis court as the crowd raised up for Newcombe who banged ace after ace to go ahead, 4–1, in the third. "Come on, Johnny!" they were urging, pleading, and the new boy was responding. Less experienced than McKinley, he was nonetheless combative.

It was nearly 5:00 in the afternoon, but nobody moved from the grandstands toward the Queen's Head, the neighboring pub. It was a remarkably selfless tribute to these two men and their struggle. Thoughts of Australia's sacred "Five O'Clock Swill" entered innumerable heads, and were put aside, as McKinley and Newcombe slugged away.

Prospective swillers glanced longingly toward the Queen's

Head, but stood their ground in the Memorial Drive stands, dry and screaming martyrs to Newcombe and the homeland's cause.

Their sacrifice did no good. McKinley won the third set, 9–7, the fourth, 6–2, and with it the Cup. That set off the popping of corks for an American swill, champagne from the Cup itself, the punch bowl of champions. It was then that Ralston finally broke down. "I've lost my touch," he wailed, needing help from bystanders to get the cork out of the first bottle.

44

○

Bedlam in
Bucharest

The pillow talk was decidedly vulgar in the U.S. camp, but Real
Club de Tenis in Barcelona was so loudly jubilant that nobody
noticed. Five thousand Spaniards were too busy flinging their
red and green and plaid pillows toward the hot blue August
sky, and hollering "Olé!" and "Bravo!" over and over.

Oblivious to the rain (of seat cushions) in Spain that made
it plain which country had won, other Barcelonans were carrying Manolo Santana and Lis Arilla on happy shoulders, trotting
them around the crimson battleground as though they were
victorious bullfighters. Some sense of propriety was maintained, however, dissuading the celebrants from snipping the
ears of the defeated doubles partners, Dennis Ralston and Clark
Graebner, and presenting them to Arilla and Santana.

Did this 1965 victory over the United States make up for
the last Spanish-American War sixty-seven years before? Had
Arilla, Santana, and the unlikely Juan Gisbert expunged the
memories and deeds of Teddy Roosevelt, Admiral Dewey, and
William Randolph Hearst by assaulting this crop of Yankees?

It didn't matter at one of the more joyous celebrations I've experienced. Ralston's last shot into the net seemed to touch off a bomb in a bedding factory, hoisting colorful pillows like skyrockets. Spain had an insurmountable 3–0 lead. Though tennis ranked behind soccer, bullfighting, and basketball in Spanish sporting hearts, this Davis Cup triumph was unprecedentedly glorious because the 4–1 victim was mighty Los Estados Unidos. What goodwill ambassadors American tennis players were becoming through their collapses.

How long would this go on—the devouring of Stateside innocents abroad by red monsters disguised as clay courts? Where is a Yankee Doodling St. George who can pierce the beast with his racket by playing a waiting game so foreign to American men, cleverly plotting his charges on the slow terrain? Few have materialized in almost thirty years, although John McEnroe had the idea, and spearheaded the final-round triumph over France's dirt-plowing homesteaders in 1982. So did Stan Smith ten years before that in Bucharest—his the most spectacular triumph ever by an American tennis player. And now, young Andre Agassi may have the flair and firepower.

The 1965 model monster looked harmless enough lying there, a flat, rectangular dirt lot in Barcelona, purportedly the same dimensions as a court in Kalamazoo or Cuckamonga, Chicago or Brooklyn, belted with a net three feet in height. But when Americans in Davis Cup uniforms showed up to subdue the thing, it turned mean, seeming to expand to acres of quicksand with a net that became the Wailing Wall. Aroused by onlookers who taunted the monster's American prey, and abetted by the local boys making good, the resident red monsters, domiciled in such locales as Guayaquil and Göteborg, Hamburg and Buenos Aires, have swallowed red-white-and-blue tourists whole.

The dirt-kicking of America had commenced in 1961 in Rome, and the stomping hasn't stopped. Of the eighteen U.S. defeats between 1961 and 1987—an era of ten Cup-winning teams—a dozen were interments in overseas clay.

Ralston, a hero of Adelaide, came apart, inexplicably unraveling and losing a dominant grip on unheralded Juan Gisbert. From a 6–3, 4–1 lead, he clutched, and blew the leadoff match. There was no way out for the Americans in a series that had loomed tough but winnable. Nobodies would haunt the more-often-than-not-maligned Ralston. In 1966 it was Brazilian Edison Mandarino who ambushed him in the deciding contest, his last as a player, at São Paulo. Colombians Ivan Molina and Jairo Velasco and Mexican Vicente Zarazua would contribute to his surprise defeats as the captain. Still, in 1972, Dennis would be firm as Pike's Peak, an inspirational rock in the tremors of Bucharest, America's finest Davis Cup hour.

If Adelaide '63 was my Cup baptism, and exposure to boisterous galleries overseas, Barcelona '65 opened my eyes to the difficulties of playing in Europe and Latin America. The customers could be insulting and raucously partisan, and the line judges tinged with larceny in the exalted spirit of love of country.

Fortunately the galleries weren't hostile, as they would be in Guayaquil '67 or Asunción '87. But they were excitable, rabid, volatile, representing an incalculable ingredient in the home-court edge. I was familiar with this style of line judging because it resembled the infamous "Boston Decisions"—helpful scoring on behalf of a native pugilist. "Close enough to steal" was the cry. But that was boxing.

Yet boxing and tennis are close relations, closer than jock-strap cousins. Closer even than many of their fans would care to acknowledge. "What does the manly art have in common with that garden party game?" a prizefight purist could ask, feeling that his love was demeaned by the comparison. But a tennis devotee, possibly offended at the association, might report, "Boxing is uncivilized! Have you ever seen a punchy tennis player?"

All the time.

What I mean is that boxing and tennis are rare me-against-you games involving physical and mental skills, endurance, and a willingness to continue even though hurt. No bench, no substitutes. Two adversaries, alone in a confined space, head-to-head, trying to outsmart and pick each other apart, probing for weakness, setting up the knockout punch.

Tennis is boxing without bloodshed. Not always, however. Count Ludwig von Salm, an Austrian aristocrat who was one of the better European players after World War I, let his antipathy for opponents boil over a few times. So have others. The count was not averse to crossing into an opponent's territory and wrestling him to the court. Whether or not wounds were opened, grappling in that red clay sure made them look bloody.

"The count would shout at George Hillyard across the net,

'I'll have your balls for lunch!' " remembers Ted Tinling, who watched them at tournaments on the Riviera. "Hillyard would give it right back to him. But they were gentlemen, and gentlemen could talk to each other that way."

A few years ago a young Australian, Alan Haswell, was playing with a countryman in a tournament in Spain. They weren't getting along very well with their Spanish foes, particularly one of them, a constant irritant. So Haswell, once an amateur boxer, filed a grievance with one shot that ended the match—a right to a Spanish jaw that broke it.

He was subsequently suspended for a year by the Australian governing body, a penalty that hurt more—even before it was administered—when Haswell heard his partner say: "Crikey, mate, you hit the wrong bloody guy!"

The boxing analogy strikes me whenever I think back to the U.S. Open final of 1981, and the heavyweight title bout I covered at Kinshasa, Zaire, in 1974. Whether rumbled in the jungle or mugged in the Meadow of Flushing, George Foreman and Bjorn Borg were ruined the same way. Hardly kindred souls, though high school drop outs, the black Texan and the erstwhile Teen Angel of Sweden, were, nevertheless, champions of substantial worlds—until deposed with startling finality by left hands as cute and rapacious as any we've known.

Of course, those sinister weapons were attached to different frames. Muhammad Ali's put George Foreman on the scrap heap. Just as surely, seven years later, John Patrick McEnroe, Jr.'s, dumped Bjorn Borg among the remnants, similarly finished, though conscious. I am taken by the nearly identical way it all ended for them, with the sort of suddenness—short of death—that seldom terminates any career. Particularly at prime. So devastating, Borg and Foreman. Much too much for any of thousands of rivals—except that one with the career-razing left hand, the one with whom each had a last rendezvous in an amphitheater remembered as the end of their line.

For straight-arrow Stan Smith and Draculean Ion Tiriac the amphitheater of destiny was the dirt-floored, hastily carpentered stadium of the Progresul Club in Bucharest. Unlike Borg and Foreman, the American slugger and the Romanian counterpuncher would continue in the big league beyond 1972, but never so effectively.

To tennis traditionalists it was the amphitheater of the absurd for three cool, purplish days in October. Why not? Wasn't a leading playwright of bizarre dramas, Eugene Ionesco, a Romanian? And hadn't Ionesco created *The Rhinoceros*, a title that fit Tiriac's court presence and persona so aptly?

Self-proclaimed as "the brother of Dracula," Ion Tiriac had the credentials. Like the count, he is a Transylvanian, a Carpathian hillbilly whose evil eye could make Bela Lugosi—the movie Dracula—incontinent. Biting necks and sipping blood would have been simple nutrition for Tiriac, who reversed the order. After drinking a Bloody Mary he ate the glass—truly—although preferring fine crystal to ordinary tumblers. "I have taste standards," he said, always the straight-faced sardonic.

If Ion wished to cast an immobilizing spell, he clanged his head against that of his subject. Stan Smith said he had headaches for three weeks following an earlier such tête-à-tête, more concussive than discursive.

Tiriac was too quick and resourceful to get a stake pounded into his heart, as demonstrated in his hockey-playing days for the Romanian national team. Once, when the Czechoslovakian team approached him en masse—conceivably he had irritated all of them—with sticks raised and eyes raging, Ion turned the stake-sticking trick the other way. Breaking his hockey stick in half, he held the jagged remnants like daggers, and stared the Czechs down. He recalls the incident as an illustration of "old Transylvanian proverb: It is better to have his mother cry than my mother cry." The original Dracula, a.k.a. Vlad the Impaler, would have approved.

If Tiriac ever cries, it will be all the way to his safety deposit boxes, because the game of tennis has never known a shrewder operator. After devoting his youth to hockey, which led to the Olympic Games, he discovered tennis at fifteen, too late to become anything but "the best player in the world who cannot play tennis." That was his own appraisal of an ungainly, homemade style.

A hulking six-foot-two 210-pounder moving about the court in a Wolfmanly lope, Tiriac slashed his backhand like an assassin slitting a throat, and pushed his forehand as though slamming a door in the face of an obnoxious salesman. His unorthodoxy, however, was blended with a competitive heart wider than a vampire bat's wingspread, superb courtcraft and conditioning, plus intimidation. A self-critique: "When I win it is like making chicken salad out of chicken shit."

Glowering from behind a droopy mustache and thick black curls, though suavely groomed and tailored, he still seems a sinister figure out of a nonexistent Ian Fleming novel: the malevolent Eastern European who outdoes James Bond in every department, and finally subtracts 007 from the human race by fracturing Bond's skull with his own. A linguist, he dismisses that talent with, "All I can only say in fourteen languages is, 'I am innocent.' "

For the first seven years of a Davis Cup career that spanned nearly two decades, Tiriac was Romanian tennis. Before the mountain man from Brasov set aside his slap shot and volunteered his drop shot to his country in 1959, Romania had fielded no team in seventeen years, and recorded a grand total of one victory in the years before. Tiriac made the homeland a winner. The arrival of nineteen-year-old Ilie Nastase in 1966, completing the anomalous couple, made it a contender for the Cup itself.

Just as vampires wouldn't have made much of a name for themselves without Dracula, neither would Ilie Nastase. His own Big D, master of darkness, was Tiriac. Nastase, whose boyhood home stood near the courts of the Progresul Club, was an instinctive genius at the game, to be sure. Sleek and high-strung as a racehorse, he needed guidance, brushing up, a mentor. That was Tiriac, seven years his senior, showing him the world beyond Bucharest, beating the path for Nastase to win the Italian, French, and U.S. Opens, telling him about birds, bees, and bank accounts. Where Nastase was looney tunes, Tiriac was as deep as a Mahler symphony.

Nastase would go only as far as those magnificent legs carried him, but Tiriac's brain was the generator for a longer haul. He got more out of his body than the homeland had any right to expect, but who knows the extent of his business machinations within the game as player-manager, marketer, promoter? He has been Svengalian manager of three prospective Hall of Famers: Nastase, Guillermo Vilas, and young Baron Von Slam, the teenage Wimbledon champ, Boris Becker.

Pedagogue and protégé, Tiriac and Nastase were Beast and Beauty, Brainy and Batty. Romania hadn't put forth such a notorious pair since King Carol II and his blond roomie, Magda

Lupescu, were making the tabloids in the 1930s. Communism supplanted the monarchy; Romania was forgotten until Tiriac and Nastase became even more international and sensational than Carol and Magda. As popular traveling salesmen, whose capitalistic ways were winked at, they were granted rare privileges to roam. At home they hobnobbed with the Ceauşescus, the dictator and his family.

During their prime together, the five years between 1968 and 1972, Tiriac and Nastase combined to lug Romania to twenty-one wins in twenty-five Davis Cup starts. Three of those losses were in the championship matches to the United States, 1969, '71, '72, and they might have won the Cup the last two times if Nastase's nerves had held. At the same time their togetherness was such that they won twenty of twenty-four doubles, a daunting pair of defensive sharpers, who retrieved unceasingly and bounced lobs off the clouds until they drove opponents mad.

Their paperback autobiography was number one on the Romanian best-seller list for a couple of years, more than one hundred thousand peddled at 51 cents a copy. It was called *Ar Fi Fost Prea Frumos . . . (It Would Have Been Beautiful)*, referring to the painful 3–2 losses to the United States in 1971 and 1972. By Ion and Ilie's standards the profits were peanuts. But for their ghost, a genial Bucharest newspaperman named Radu Voia, his cut was a bonanza. He made enough to buy a new car, which is hitting it rich in economically depleted Romania. Voia will always remember those two, now gone to America, and the golden days they provided for a country dispirited by the harsh Ceauşescu reign.

But the most beautiful of would-have-beens, the magnum opus for which Tiriac drove himself so fiercely, connived so assiduously and orchestrated beyond belief—or any tenet of Anglo-American sportsmanship—crumbled in the gray pallor of the '72 final. Dwight's Pot, a prize known previously in name only to Romanians—an unimaginable vision pursued by Nastase and Tiriac for years—had journeyed farther east than ever before. It was there for the taking, in their midst.

Imagine the victory party? Tiriac guzzles champagne from the Cup in the acceptably decadent Western way, toasts the dethroned Yanks with, "Let them eat Twinkies!"—and then dines on the repast of champions, the empty goblets. Maybe, for dessert, he devours the Cup, too, so that nobody can take it away from Romania.

It is a Draculean reverie burst by the bane of Bucharest, Stan Smith, who waves his wooden racket in Tiriac's (and Nastase's) face as though it were a cross.

What was I doing in Bucharest again? But I didn't mind.

"What are we doing in Bucharest at all?" wondered the 1972 U.S. Davis Cup team. They minded a lot, since the regulations gave the Americans choice of location if they beat Spain in the semifinal at Barcelona. Little Harold Solomon, the human grindstone, took care of that. Wearing down Juan Gisbert in the critical match, Solly gave Captain Ralston delayed revenge over the Spaniard who had humiliated him on the same court seven years before.

However, USTA president Bob Colwell astounded, and enraged, his team by granting Romania the home-court advantage. We had only that chamber-of-commerce guy, Ion Tiriac, to thank. He came to New York to peddle a fairness doctrine, and Colwell and his first vice president, Walter Elcock, bought it. "Why we play three straight times in America? Is unfair," Tiriac pleaded eloquently, never believing the USTA would deed away a sure victory on a fast American court.

But Colwell and Elcock were sportingly correct in disregarding the sometimes unfathomable Cup formula. Since the United States had defeated Romania in the 1969 windup at Cleveland, it was logical that their next meeting should be in Romania. But, no. The formula gave home ground to the United States again in 1971, and, incredibly, 1972.

Naturally Captain Dennis Ralson and his lads thought Colwell and Elcock misguided. "No way they can win Bucharest," gloated Nastase, and everyone believed him. "Hell, no, we won't go!" was the team sentiment.

But Ralston, at thirty, had outgrown his rep as a fume-and-flop character, and was serene in guiding the most demanding of all U.S. seasons: each of five matches on the road, four of them on clay. Dennis talked his guys away from a mutinous stance, assuring them it wouldn't be as bad as they imagined. He was wrong; it was worse. But also sweeter, winning unthinkably in the bedlam of Bucharest.

Bucharest, once more. I had been there in June to watch Ilie and Ion dispose of Italy in a European zone match, recognizing this was as much their town as Beijing was Mao and Chou's. The Ceauşescus owned it, of course, but Nastase and Tiriac were the spiritual proprietors.

The plane from Paris came down in a wheat field transformed into an airport without interrupting farmers at their work on the edges. Biplanes and monoplanes were prominent at the military section of the airport, and ox carts were on the road into town.

Though lacking the ambience of Prague, the city was distinguished by broad boulevards, some well-designed buildings, cleanliness, pleasant parks, and legions of trees. The people, like those of Prague, did not seem very happy. Along the boulevards sped long black limos belonging to government officials, neither slowing nor stopping for anyone, disdainful of the man in the street.

During my first visit the atmosphere was entirely different. In June heat and greenery the Progresul Club was relaxed, the small concrete grandstand filled with people who took off their shirts, guzzled hard and soft drinks, kidded the Italians, and cheered Tiriac and Nastase. Journalists brought their girlfriends to sit in the press box, and you could wander in and out of the teams' dressing rooms. The wonder of the Romanian cubicle was the air-conditioning system: Vasilache, the trainer, standing on a table and flapping a towel.

We ate reasonably priced caviar from the Danube at Pescarus, an outdoor restaurant beside a lake, and danced beneath trees and stars to such avant-garde tunes as "Tea for Two" and "Softly as in a Morning Sunrise."

On Sunday, the only day the country's lone horse track was open, we did our bit toward improving the breed by attending. It was about an hour's drive, set in farmland outside of Ploesti, and we had to be up early. Post time was 9:00 A.M., beastly for the human breed, and probably the puritanical decree of some government official who thought everybody should be home for Sunday dinner. It was a primitive, shabby harness track, yet delightful—a place for families to gather in rural tranquillity, drink big bottles of 18-cent beer, and gamble madly at the five- and ten-lei windows (thirty and sixty cents). We picked mulberries from the trees, bought cherries from barefoot gypsy girls in brightly patterned skirts and blouses. I hit on a thirty-to-one shot called Inimos, and felt rich with wads worth nine dollars in lei in my pockets.

You probably could have gotten thirty-to-one on anybody against Tiriac and Nastase in Bucharest, where any of the minority of citizens who could identify the Davis Cup felt certain they'd win it.

Four months later everybody had heard of Cupa Davis, which was making a boffo personal appearance in a small hall on Boulevard Magheru. The seventy-two-year-old world-traveling pot seemed to gleam even brighter on its downtown pedestal of honor, received more respectfully than ever in its lifetime. Romanians stood in long lines, in rain and sun, for a glimpse of the Cup—as though it were Lenin's stiff—and actually paid for the privilege, twelve cents a visit. Photos and drawings of Nastase and Tiriac adorned store windows everywhere, along with good-luck messages. "Hai, Nastase!" [Go, Nastase!] and "Hai, Tiriac!" [Go Tiriac!] led the graffiti parade. Bakeries displayed huge cakes impersonating the Cup.

Adding to the tension of October for the Americans—as if Tiriac, Nastase, a clay court, and clamoring spectators weren't sufficient—ominous rumors of terrorists were making the rounds. One held that the Black September group, murderers of Israeli athletes at the recent Munich Olympics, would make a move during the Cup final. Two members of the U.S. squad were Jewish, Solomon and Brian Gottfried, and both teams were under heavy guard. The Romanian government was taking no chances, and it was impossible to talk to the players alone. They found it unbearably restrictive. The only action in town for normally free-spirited guys was holding hands with armed security guards. "These guys practically sleep with you," Tom Gorman said, nodding toward his personal chaperone, adding that it was the first time he could remember that room service meant eating alone.

But what a wonderful time it was, what a chance for a country with only two players (I must not overlook the enchanting, leggy Virginia Ruzici, who would win the French Open in 1978, and whose ground-stroking groans made Donna Summer's seem pristine). Here was the opportunity to overturn Uncle Sam, and every Romanian wanted this win. The tennis part was incidental. In mood Romanians resembled Czechoslovakians (I covered their team's match against Russia the year before in Prague), but with this exception: No hatred smeared those Bucharest-game faces. "This is going to be a very patriotic crowd," said Judith Elian, the charming and estimable tennis correspondent for *L'Equipe* in Paris. "Very noisy and one-sided. But you are lucky that they like Americans and won't be hostile."

The insignificant Progresul grandstand had been tripled in size to hold 7,200 customers, and those seats were sold quickly at the highest prices Romanians had ever paid to watch a game— eight dollars for three days (the series price was twenty dollars for foreigners).

What had happened to the homes on the club grounds I'd seen in June? Torn down to make way for the stadium, answered Alexandre Lasarescu, secretary of the Romanian federation. Just like that. The look of his new wooden stadium, a thirty-day wonder, did not fill this prospective occupant with confidence.

"Oh, it's quite safe," Lasarescu smiled.

Why was he so sure?

"We tested it."

How was that done?

"We called up the army and requested seventy-two hundred soldiers. They marched in, occupied every seat, and stamped very hard for a while. No problem."

Nice to have soldiers to burn, but what would the commanding general have done if the joint had collapsed, starting a run on purple hearts?

Lasarescu just smiled.

Could anybody in Bucharest doubt that their boys, Ilie and Ion, would topple the mighty Stati Uniti America? Who could beat them at home where they hadn't lost in five years? Not the Yankees, so clumsy on European soil, surely.

Hadn't the *baiat rau* (naughty boy), as they lovingly called Nastase, even infiltrated Forest Hills the previous month to steal the Americans' own championship? What wouldn't he do to them in his own backyard?

The sorrowful answer: Not much.

This was the saddest chapter in the rich Nastase saga, as mournful as Stan Smith's was glorious. Why did the maestro snap like a violin string during a solo, and fail so miserably in front of those most wanting to be pleased and whom he most wanted to please? Perhaps that was the answer—too much wanting. "They expect me to win all the time, everything," lamented Ilie. Or was it a blister on his racket hand, the unnat-

ural confinement with body guards, the majestic rise to un-
imagined heights of Smith?

The old lyric, "You call it madness, I call it love. . . ." is
evoked on many sporting occasions by crowds idolizing and
urging their heroes. In Bucharest, it could have been para-
phrased, "You call it larceny, we call it patriotism. . . ."

The patriotism of the 7,200 sound-barrier-busting patrons
and the judges on court centered on the man seemingly directing them—Tiriac—soon seen as their only hope. Ionesco would
have saluted him as rhinoceran. But lurching about the tile-red
stage belligerently, dangerously, and horning in when least expected, Tiriac trampled his rivals, the odds, and propriety and
protocol like a rogue rhino imagined by Hemingway.

The man was beloved. As Tiri Baby and the Thirteen
Thieves (the umpire and line judges), Ion nearly lifted the Cup,
even though Nastase fell at the outset, prolonging the contest
to late on the third day.

"A disgrace. He should be banned for life," Ralston hailed
Tiriac. A more objective, or pragmatic, observer might have
recognized Ion as the gamesman who invented Stephen Potter.
But Ralston kept his feelings to himself until the 3–2 victory
was over. He also kept his brood calm amid pandemonium, never
giving the crowd any reason to turn ugly despite Tiriac's twisting of the rules.

Because Smith, the crowd noise cracking his eardrums and
the homers on the lines cracking his innate equanimity, did
overcome both Nastase and Tiriac, as well as the terrain—their
element, certainly not his—Stan's victories have no equal among
those achieved by Americans abroad. He beat Nastase to lead
off, teamed with Erik van Dillen to quell the two Romanians
in the pivotal doubles, then overcame a supercharged Tiriac in
five sets to clinch the Cup.

When that sort of thing is discussed, the match generally
cited, and understandably so, is Don Budge's five-set comeback
in 1937 to beat Baron Gottfried von Cramm and Germany in
the deciding fifth match of the semifinal series at Wimbledon.
It keeps popping up in stories devoted to the "greatest matches
of all time." Budge lost the first two sets, won the next two,
but trailed 4–2 in the fifth, a set he won, 8–6, with a stupen-
dous diving, winning forehand on match point.

It was absolutely an all-time great match. However, Budge,

fresh from winning the Wimbledon title, confronted only the gentlemanly von Cramm. Don was playing on his surface, grass, in a neutral haunt whose patrons were as respectful as librarians. It was a pure, straightforward, highly competitive tennis match between the Nos. 1–2 players in the world under ideal conditions.

Of course, there was immense pressure. But there weren't the additional jagged elements of overzealous crowds, burglars on the lines, a clay court, and an overhanging threat by terrorists. With all this, Smith's accomplishments still never got the attention of Budge's. The pity of Bucharest was its more or less overlooked status in the outside world: No TV to the United States, where not much interest is shown an untelevised event, especially during football season. But in 1937 greater attention was paid to Davis Cup in the newspapers, and the decade-long crusade to retrieve it. Smith, after all, was powering the United States to a fifth successive Cup. A story existed only if Romania won. But the real story was: How could Smith and the Yanks possibly win?

It looked like another "mud-in-your-eyes" situation for the United States. Nastase had no equal as a clay-court player; Smith's record on dirt was unimpressive. And Tiriac, even at thirty-three, was surer on the footing than the other Yank, Tom Gorman.

Smith remembers, "I went onto the court against Nasty pessimistic for the first time in my life. I was preparing myself to lose, new for me, especially against him. I've always felt I could out-gut him in a big match, as I did in the fifth set of the Wimbledon final. . . . But with Nasty on clay, and the crowd, I was skeptical of my chances. . . . But when we got out there I noticed how nervous Ilie was, and I thought maybe the crowd is tougher on him. And it was. They helped Ion, but they put too much pressure on Ilie. In the first set my old confidence came back."

The seventy-two-minute first set shattered Nastase and Romania, although Tiriac refused to accept that. Premonitions of doom for the home team, and hope for Ralston's, radiated when Nastase served for the set at 9–8, and Smith broke his serve. That dispersed Stan's pessimism, at least for two days. Improvising a volleyed lob that kissed the baseline on set point, Stan had the first installment of an 11–9, 6–2, 6–3 win.

Consternation and gloom flooded Romania via the countrywide telecast. Was all lost before hardly begun?

Not yet. Bring on the man who described himself "best tennis player in the world who cannot play tennis." Ion Tiriac deepened Romanian sorrows by seeming to fulfill the second half of that advertisement. For two sets he looked clumsier and less refined than ever as Tom Gorman picked him apart, making Captain Ralston's thinking in selecting Gorman over Harold Solomon appear sound.

For two sets all was well for the Americans in the quiet stadium, and since Smith had beaten Nastase, a 2–0 lead seemed imminent at the conclusion of the first day. But night was approaching, and . . . then . . . Dracula raised the casket lid and came alive again, and so did his 7,200, raising their voices to the sullen sky. "TI-RI-AC!" they chanted as he began to win points in clusters. "TI-RI-AC! TI-RI-AC!"

His choristers couldn't be underestimated. Not only did they juice Dracula's morale, but they sapped Gorman's. Perhaps more importantly was the way Tiriac conducted them. They chanted to the rhythm he needed. If their man required rest, they might keep it up for as long as a minute while the umpire and referee ineffectually called for silence so the match could continue.

Sometimes an obliging line judge—ah, how obliging they were—would politely give Tiriac his chair for a mid-game breather, even supplying a towel as the chanting grew in length and strength. This delaying aid and comfort was strictly out-of-order, but what could the courtly referee, Argentine Enrique Morea, do? Nothing, though he tried, and was cursed and mocked by Tiriac. But, did anybody expect Morea to throw Dracula out of his own cellar?

Tiriac would nod when he was ready to play again, the hollering abated, and the next point commenced. The erosion of Gorman was under way. With the crowd uplifting Tiriac, the line judges started lifting a point here and there, and the cool, ebullient Gorman flushed and fretted, grew testy and lost his punch. He was certain that a Balkan coughing conspiracy was unfolding, that spectators were following instructions to clear their throats and jar the silence and his concentration whenever he served. At set point in the third, Tiriac performed a half-gainer into the dust to scoop a pitiful shot, and as he lay helplessly on his back, Gorman muffed it.

The rest was rejoiceful noise following Dracula like his cape. Gorman, the better player any other time, any other place, was a demoralized loser, 4–6, 3–6, 6–4, 6–3, 6–2, and Romania was even 1–1.

After the doubles win, spearheaded by van Dillen in the match of his career, U.S. Army Corporal Stanley Roger Smith was back in the caldron. He may have been the best player in the world, but this was Dracula's underworld. "I became afraid they wouldn't let me win no matter how well I played," said Smith. He showed signs of wavering in losing the fourth set, so the fifth commenced as a best-of-one test for the Cup.

Tiriac, his claque, and his line judges had just been rehearsing against Gorman. They were ready for their best/worst against Smith. As though trained by Fagan, the judges had their hands in Smith's pockets, extracting points with decisions as Tiriac needed them. "Doing their job for their country as they saw it," said one of a handful of American spectators, Jimmy Van Alen.

"TI-RI-AC! TI-RI-AC!" The vocal rain was acid to Smith, but he tried to block it out. "I concentrated so hard I had a headache for three days," he said later.

Ralston soothed him, and stayed placid himself, realizing, "If I started squawking the whole place would blow up." Ralston, the captain, was solid where Ralston, the player, had not been.

He must have come closest to exploding in the last game of Smith-Tiriac's third set, where I scrawled in my notebook "all-time screwing!" Tiriac was serving at 4–5, and three ridiculous hometown calls, two on one point, got him to 40–0. Smith countered with a rampage of winners for four points to ad-out— set point for Stan. Though the first serve on that point sailed a foot long, the line judge uttered no sound, an indication the ball was good, the point was on.

"By then," Smith said, "I was playing every ball no matter where it landed. I couldn't take a chance." So he cracked a mighty backhand return for a clear winner, well inside Tiriac's court. As the umpire was beginning to announce the game for Smith, the resourceful service-line judge sensed that he could keep Tiriac and the set alive. Hold everything. Of course that ball was long. "Fault!" he cried well after the fact that the point was over. Surely it was over, belonging to Smith?

Nope. Picking up on the belated judgment against Tiriac, the umpire halted in awarding the set to Smith. "Fault called . . . second serve," he declared, negating Smith's beautiful shot.

The point was still undecided. One fault? Even Tiriac looked startled at this reprieve, but shrugged his shoulders and prepared to serve again. Ralston squirmed. Smith responded with a broad smile that seemed to lighten the sooty clouds. "It was so unbelievable I had to smile."

Tiriac pushed another serve Smith's way, but the ball seemed believing, too. It lost momentum and plopped into the net. No way to reclaim that one. Double fault. Game and set to Smith for a 2-sets-to-1 lead. The umpire had no recourse but to state that as fact.

Justice at last? Hardly. In the fourth set Tiriac got better, the line judges worse, the chorus louder. Ion stalled, debated the referee, sat down whenever he pleased, beckoned the chanters, played to his own tempo, disorder's child. And he was spidery in spinning a web around Smith, 6–2.

One set to go for the bundle, because Gorman wasn't going to stop Nastase in the fifth match. Smith had to come to terms with his position: neck deep in a stormy sea. He was in a hanging judge's court, and the only way to escape was to shoot his way out. "I had to hit winners, and I had to hit them so far inside the lines that they couldn't take them away from me," was his conclusion.

On a slow clay court, against a hard-hearted retrieving specialist?

That's the way he did it as Smith became the incendiary innocent abroad. "Whap!" he opened with an ace, and just kept slugging for twenty devastating minutes without letup as Tiriac reached and reeled vainly. Now it was Smith as the sorcerer, casting a spell that transformed Tiriac into an aging hacker, muted the partisans, restored the eyesight of the judges. His irrefutable thunderbolt winners put them out of work. Point after unanswerable point, game after game rolled from his racket in a firestorming bagel. Tiriac got only eight of the thirty-three points in the 6–0 finale. The tensions of the weekend went up in the smoky overcast as Smith smacked outright winners for 76 percent of his points.

To Ralston and Smith's teammates, it was the Spirit of '76 with racket, Corporal Smith the impaler of Dracula. He had drained the hope from the crowd, but they applauded him generously at the end. Although made expectant by Nastase's boasts of victory, and wanting to believe, they may have known that in a country so beaten down by its own regime, there are no happy endings.

No Cupa Davis. On Monday morning, when all was dreary once more in Bucharest, the pictures of Nastase and Tiriac and the Cup coming down from store windows, a writer in one of the papers tried to console: "How can we have the Davis Cup when we don't really have tennis?"

But they almost had it.

The Cup was packed away, and vanished. So, too, the dream of the local deities, Nastase and Tiriac. Forever.

"Is nothing to play good, try hard if I don't win," said disgruntled Tiriac. "I do everything in my power to beat United States, but coming close is nothing. Forget 'great try' stuff. Is nothing." Not quite the spirit of Gottfried von Cramm, the mannerly German vanquished by a counterpart, Don Budge, in their titanic Cup struggle of 1937. Bucharest '72 was different. Stan Smith was in the Budge—von Cramm mold of competitive but considerate babes in toyland, but this hybrid Dracula was a tennis iconoclast, a realist in Pragmatic Park.

One man's nothing is another's everything. Without Tiriac's 1972 machinations off the court and on, the most delirious of all U.S. Davis Cup triumphs would not have been. Nor would Smith's feats of spitting in the eye of a hurricane for three days.

Those of us who had come from abroad to be crammed in with the hyper mob, shivering and thrilling, would always be grateful to the man who brought us this show: Tiriac.

Some of us would be furious with him, outraged at a despicable lack of sportsmanship and fostering of outright piracy. Others could appreciate his *carpe diem* thrusts at huge, rich America, fired by a "my country, right or wrong" philosophy. He was reaching for a once-in-a-millennium main chance— pygmy pauper waylays affluent giant?—where only the final score mattered. Surely Machiavelli and Kissinger would have embraced Tiriac as their brother.

Was the old Harvard, Dwight Davis, eavesdropping from the next world? Seventy-two years after the gentlemanly romp pitting English against his fellow Americans on the lawn of

Longwood Cricket Club, the Cup inaugural, did he tut-tut Tiriac as "a dreadful fellow"? Or did he wink at his Harvard teammates, Holcombe Ward and Malcolm Whitman, "You have to give the devil his due. Imagine the villain programming everyone to cough just as Gorman was serving?"

Afterward a Romanian smiled at Gorman's contention of clockwork catarrh attacks. "That's a good story, but we aren't well enough organized in this country for anything like that."

On their way out of town the American team stopped by his pale yellow palace for coffee with President Ceauşescu. During the conversation Ceauşescu happened to cough.

Gorman flinched, muttering, "Why'd he do that? I'm not serving."

45

○

One
Small Victory

If you were a Georgian—not the Jimmy Carter kind—named Alex Metreveli, weekending in Prague in June of 1971, you were about as popular as heart failure. So were your traveling companions who completed the Davis Cup team of the Soviet Union.

They were, specifically, as welcomed as Russian tanks had been only three years before. If looks could kill, Metreveli, the best tennis player to come out of the USSR, wouldn't have hit the first ball in a match that remains the most enthralling in my neural pantheon.

Czechoslovakia against Russia. A third rounder in European Zone A, it had no impact on the forty-six-country tournament that year, which was won by the United States over Romania. Yet to a subjugated people, the forlorn Czechoslovaks, it was one minuscule blow, but a heartening one, against the oppressor, as briefly gratifying as punching a bully in the nose. Nationalistic fervor—and sometimes excess—is inescapable in Davis Cup congregations. But did any of these international matches, dating back to the U.S.-Britain tiff in 1900, ever carry as much genuine meaning and feeling for the onlookers?

Had a country been gripped so strongly by a tennis match, whether the people were sweating it out in person at Stvanice Stadium, monitoring TV, or poring over the following day's newspapers?

This wasn't just national pride at stake for the home side and the home folks. Here were people concerned about their very national survival. Visiting teams are always "bad guys," but this one was a symbol of the brute threatening that survival. The true enemy had put on a games-playing face and short pants, a civilized disguise, but was nevertheless appearing at Stvanice with the intention of adding biting insult to deepest injury.

No one was more symbolic than Alex Metreveli, the dark young Russian champion from Tblisi, Joseph Stalin's hometown. In the hotel lobby following the first day's play, I remarked to him, "You aren't exactly beloved around here, Alex."

He smiled broadly, for an instant. "Oh, they hate me. I understand. But I'm just here to do a job, and get out as soon as possible. We're just athletes. We're not responsible . . ." He halted that thought, certainly not about to talk politics with a reporter. Then, "What are you doing here anyway? Nobody in America can be interested in this match."

"Wouldn't have missed it," I smiled. "There are things about this match that would interest anybody."

Alex returned the smile and nodded in agreement.

"Besides, I always wanted to see Prague."

Only a game of tennis, but the Czechs took more than a rooting interest. Czechs who didn't know a tennis ball from an Edam cheese would ache for a taste of victory here. They wanted it badly, even if they were more conversant with the more broadly compelling games, soccer and ice hockey. This was their homeland against the invader, no matter that the weapons were wooden clubs.

I sensed this in perusing the Davis Cup schedule for 1971, although I couldn't gauge the magnitude of emotion until enveloped in it. If these teams lasted in the tournament long enough for a collision in Prague, I'd try to go. Besides, as I told Metreveli, I'd always wanted to see Prague because it had the sound of old world mystique and intrigue, the brooding tone of Smetana's "Moldau," which flows through the city. I wasn't disappointed. Disheartened, yes, because through all these years somebody out there won't let the Czechs up. Then the Germans, now the Russians.

The wife of a local tennis official sighed, "Somebody is always trampling on us." Middle-aged, she had been a girl in the 1930s, and could remember the lilt of the cultivated city before the Nazi occupation, the intermittent sniffs of freedom, and the return of Russian tanks in 1968. She was showing me through the faded, unkempt gardens of Vrtba Palace, which remained fresh and romantic in some corner of her mind. Lines on her face softened for a moment. "We would dance in this garden before the war."

She was surviving, and so was her handsome city, the medieval spires and towers standing firm, and the saints lining the lovely Charles Bridge still holding their heads up. But Prague wasn't in a dancing mood in 1971, even though stomachs were full and goods filled shop windows. Miniskirts and hot pants were on the loose, the Beatles and Rolling Stones were on the jukeboxes, along with a local group called Prudy, imitating the Bee Gees (but in Czech) with "Massachusetts." Material prosperity, maybe, but not spiritual.

Gloom was the theme. The memory of the intruders' armament in St. Wenceslas Square was too vivid, the sight of Russian soldiers a reminder. When I asked a bookseller if she carried anything by the hometown boy, Franz Kafka, who used to write of repressive governments, she shook her head negatively. "No Kafka," she said, seeming not particularly disturbed that he was banned. "Life is enough sad here, we don't need anything worse."

Prague was framed in somber clouds for four days, damp and chill. It was the right atmosphere for what seemed time and again to be a lost, morose weekend. The match took more twistings and turnings than a snake in a maze, and Czechoslovakia despaired hour after hour, brightened, then despaired some more as the despised guests slithered within reach of victory.

They didn't reach it, though, because the least of the Czechs in reputation, though not physical stature, Jan Kukal, played over his six-foot, four-inch head to hold off the Russians in the doubles and begin turning the tide at nightfall of the second mournful day. Kukal came from Ostrava, the industrial town in Moravia where eleven-year-old Ivan Lendl was undoubtedly tied to the TV set. Figuratively. Not with a rope the way his mother, a very good player named Olga Lendlova, had leashed him to his baby-sitter, a net post, in his early days while she was playing. Kukal had first been noticed as a basketball player. After his and shell-shocked Jan Kodes's five-set resurrection to beat Metreveli and Sergei Likhaechev, Kukal said, "I like to play most when somebody cares."

He couldn't have asked for more caring from the five thousand townies bulging the old wooden grandstand, half of them standing, unfazed by their physical and mental discomfort, the interruptions by rain, and showers of soot and cinders from the adjoining railroad yard. Some had willingly paid scalpers one hundred crowns, a lot of money (six dollars) for a twenty-five-crown ticket. All would stay until nightfall each day, a Greek chorus of Czechs suffering and exulting throughout the drama being played out on the blood-red stage.

President Kennedy said he was a Berliner as he stood near the infamous wall. On joining that crowd I became a Czechoslovak, fast-clapping with the rest to encourage the natives on court, and chanting "*Doe-tuh-hoe! Doe-tuh-hoe!*" (Come on!) There was no neutrality in that press box, where I was scrunched in with a few Czech journalists. "Against the Russians we are all one people," a Czech newspaperman approved my collaboration. Even my friend and *Globe* colleague, John Powers, might not have maintained his celebrated journalistic objectivity, which manifested itself at the Lake Placid Olympics. Powers, a big man, cowed the shameless homers in the hockey press box at the celebrated United States victory over Russia, by rising balefully to enforce a basic First Amendment stricture: "You people know better than to cheer in the press box. I'll deck the next one of you who keeps it up."

But in Prague? I suspect Powers would have been clapping and *Doe-tuh-hoe*-ing! along with the rest of us.

If Jan Kukal drew strength from his single-minded compatriots, Jan Kodes found his own strength sapped by trying too hard for them. Despite his standing as the nonpareil of clay, having won the French Open for a second successive time a few days before, Kodes was pretzeled by the tensions and self-assumed responsibilities of the battle. Every Davis Cup player knows the feeling. To Americans it was no less a staggering weight even if they understood that the weight's existence was unknown to their countrymen. But Kodes was cast as Sisyphus in a public rerun of the Boulder Boogie. His entire country watched and pleaded for him to push, but the boulder, on which unflinching Metreveli's stony face was sculpted, kept rolling back on him.

Poor Kodes, Czechoslovakia's most loyal champion. In 1973 he would be the second of his countrymen to win Wimbledon, over his tormentor, Metreveli. But, unlike the first, Jaroslav Drobny, 1954, and the more illustrious champs to follow, Lendl, Martina Navratilova, Hana Mandlikova, he did not defect. Eventually rewarded with the Davis Cup captaincy that is his today, he had hung on long enough to realize the heady reverie of holding the Cup as a winner in his fifteenth and last playing campaign, 1980. He deserved it, a hard-working, competitive, intelligent guy whose gruff exterior masked an agreeable humor. Inserted for an early 1980 cameo, a winning doubles start in Romania, Kodes partnered Lendl, who powered their country's Cup seizure.

Though at his peak in 1971, Kodes was downright peaked, a palest pale, as shaky as the dancers named for St. Vitus, whose cathedral overlooked his trial by Metreveli. This was the court where he had grown up, but Metreveli lacked respect for the hero, who would mumble later, "I am so tired in the head—not the legs, the head. Pressure, pressure, pressure. It is not just a tennis match with all the politics things. We are trying too hard because the people want us to win so much."

Nevertheless, the day started well enough as a cutesy left-hander, Fratisek Pala, his style filled with curlicues, got rid of the Russian No. 2, stubby Vladimir Korotkov, in straight sets. Korotkov was a starter as the beneficiary of a capital crime. He replaced convicted Tom Lejus. Lejus, the first Soviet player of consequence, had been sent to jail for strangling his wife. Details were unavailable. Nobody knew if he'd used a western or continental grip.

Pala was glad to get off the court, wailing, "Such pressure! This is not sport. It's an extra category."

But he had given the home side a 1–0 lead in the best-of-five series, and by then the protocol for onlookers—the gallery and those closer at hand, the line judges—was established. Of course I expected a partisan crowd. But it was uniquely one-sided, altogether novel to me. Behavior was flat-out, 100 percent pure anti-Soviet, bathed in unmistakable vitriol, yet controlled and undisruptive. Even at my 1965 introduction to Davis Cup in Europe, Spain's beating of the United States in Barcelona, the crowd's patriotism hadn't been manifested in anti-Americanism. A modicum of applause saluted good shots by Americans. Not in Prague, not for the Russians. Wary of overt acts that might invite Soviet retaliation, the Czech government had laced the crowd with pacifiers, scores of plainclothesmen, and the legitimate customers knew it.

No insults were flung at the Russians, no anti-Soviet placards or demonstrations materialized. But neither were the tourists under any illusion that they were other than despised. "It is almost too much," a woman said. "This morning I saw some Russian soldiers as I was shopping, and to spend the afternoon watching Russian tennis players. . . ."

Naturally, the crowd was a gigantic noisemaker on their guy's behalf. Whenever a Czech scored, they generated more decibels by far than galleries three times the size at Wimbledon's Centre Court—either on his own shot or a Russian error. But the mood shift was eerie. A Russian point was received with the silence of a morgue, a threatening silence punctuated by ten thousand evil eyes cast at the offender. The silence followed an agonized groan if the point resulted from a Czech mistake. Any Russian run of points stretched the stillness so painfully that it seemed ready to burst in tears of outrage.

Happiness was a point won by a Czech, but there was nothing carefree here as I would encounter in Santiago at the final of 1976. Even though Chileans felt pretty nationalistic against Italy, they had fun, laughing and chanting to the beat of a tubby sixty-seven-year-old trumpeter, Jorge Juradini.

Juradini, waving his straw boater, would blow the charge as he toddled up the rows of Estadio Nacional. Then he led the cheer:

> Chee . . . lay!
> Chee-Chee-Chee . . . lay-lay-lay!
> Viva Chee . . . lay!

Even the Italians loved that guy, though they weren't very glad to be in Chile.

In Prague '71, however, the spirit was serious and earnest. No clowning horn players. No consideration for the foe. If any

Russian dared doubt a line call—there were ample reasons—he faced the music, all right, a scolding by hoots and piercing whistles. Only Metreveli was brassy enough to frequently summon that onslaught. I couldn't help but admire the way Alex, glaring back in the fangs surrounding him, fought off the entire ballpark as well as Kodes. Alex, the man as popular as heart failure, induced it from the start.

Quickly he, and a drizzle, dispelled the elation of Pala's victory. We had returned to our seats after a superb intermission repast of *pareks*—hot dogs—and Pilsener, both considerably superior to the American counterparts. Served on a paper plate with the large wiener alongside a blob of hot mustard and a roll, the *parek* is eaten differently from a hot dog. When in Prague . . . you dab the dog in mustard, munching it and the roll separately.

Metreveli began to mistreat Kodes like a dog, a haywire-haired terrier, while winning the first set in the rain. Umbrellas were up, hearts down, lamentations rife. It was the funeral scene from *Our Town*, and Kodes was being buried in the clay as it turned to a maroon goo.

Jan needed help, and got it from the line judges. All the balls that hit close to the lines were called his way, and some of those not so close. Russian disagreement provoked argumentative panoramas that looked like a back alley craps game with five or six men hunched over in a small space, concentrating and pointing at the ground where the ball was said to have landed. Quickly and excitedly assembling from their various locations were the competing players plus the two captains and the line judge, all debating the spot where each was certain the ball had struck.

Ball marks are distinct on clay—but which mark was the correct one? It depended on the eyes of the beholder, specifically the nationality of the eyes of the beholder. Sometimes the umpire hopped down from his chair to join the debating society, which became a mob in the doubles, adding two more players. Then the harried referee, the lone neutral, a Hungarian named Laszlo Gorodi, would have to unwillingly adjudicate.

Understandably, he upheld the Czechs most of the time, if only to stop the awful whistling and get on with the match. But a few times he bravely ruled for the Russians and flinched at the increased pitch of the whistles. Gorodi seemed convinced that the Russians were safe from bodily harm, but what were the chances of a stray Hungarian?

Many of those line decisions looked, well, curious, I ribbed Kodes when it was all over. "Oh, yes, we screwed them a little," he acknowledged matter-of-factly. "But not as bad as they screwed us last year in Moscow. They stole the last match for Metreveli against me, and we lost, 3–2."

But after he lost the first set, and got some official propping, Kodes seemed to relax and drive the ball like a champ. Was it possible that he was even receiving aid and comfort from the rail yard next door? Or was it coincidence that a steam locomotive chugged past several times just as Metreveli was serving an important point?

The rain stopped. It resumed, and their mudding continued. Smiles returned to the crowd as Kodes won the second and third sets, no longer hangdog. His back was characteristically straight again and his character firm. In mustache and best determined look, head extended forward, he looked like Dr. Zhivago peering through a snowstorm as he pumped to serve. The good soldier Kodes was back in charge. But it was getting dark, and the referee called curfew at 7:30 with Kodes ahead two sets to one.

Relieved, the crowd departed. Not bad. Czechoslovakia leads, 1–0, and Kodes has a winning lead on Metreveli. "Such a crowd," Metreveli rolled his eyes. "I never saw such a crowd except at a soccer game."

I had dinner at a jolly beer hall called Kalich with friends newly made at the matches, and we felt loose and confident for the next day. Optimism evaporated not long after breakfast. It was not a match to sleep on for Kodes, who was jangly again when they resumed, and lost the fourth set. Icier and more self-assured than ever, Metreveli bounded ahead in the fifth, 2–0. Kodes responded to the chants by catching up, and—hurrah!—breaking serve to go ahead, 3–2. That was his parting lunge. The rest was Metreveli and the furrows in Kodes's brow spread and deepened so, you could have planted an acre of corn above his eyes.

As Jan lost his serve to 3–5, Russian captain Sergei Andreev smiled for the first time in two days. His eyes fierce, Metreveli served through the closing game. Astoundingly some applause rent the violet stillness. Faintly. Who would have the nerve? Metreveli's three teammates in a courtside box were clapping. But only for an instant. Looking about, into ten thousand eyes drilling them, they sensed that they were disturbing a wake. And they abruptly stopped.

After a shower and rest, Kodes and Metreveli returned for doubles, and the Czech situation disintegrated further. Kodes had been within three games of a 2–0 Czech lead at 3–2 in the fifth. Instead, it was 1–1, with the Russians taking charge. Metreveli and the squat, fierce-looking doubles specialist, Sergei Likhaechev, grabbed the first set as Kodes continued to wobble. Disaster loomed, along with more rain.

Jan Kukal, the corn-haired basketball refugee, wasn't very mobile, but he began to hit winners, heartening Kodes and the crowd. The second set went to the Czechs, but the third to the Russians. Now the Russians were one set from a 2–1 lead with Metreveli a cinch to beat Pala in the concluding singles.

Woe is us! Help! Ah, those line judges will have some imaginative decisions.

Indeed. Petty theft here and there. Exceedingly resourceful were the baseline arbiters, who upset Likhaechev's rhythm by deciding he was footfaulting. He objected. The crowd subjected him to the shrillest barrages yet. As Likhaechev wilted, Kukal came on strong, dragging Kodes with him, smashing mighty overheads and dominating the match, standing as tall in the twilight as a St. Vitus steeple.

Within an hour, it had all changed for the better. At the nocturnal curfew, shutting down play, though suspense hung from the clouds, the Czechs were in good shape, ahead, 5–2 in the fifth. On the morrow, they had briskly completed the five-set victory as Kodes served it out for a 2–1 series lead. Kodes, stiff as the Tin Man at first, seemed years younger as he blew kisses to the ecstatic crowd. They returned the favor and pounded their hands together ecstatically for one minute. That's a ton of applause.

After these desperate hours and days, the match was now Kodes's to win. After taking a shower, he took Korotkov apart. With a full head of steam, Jan no longer needed locomotives or line judges. He was so dominant in baking a first set bagel, 6–0, that the crowd began laughing derisively at helpless Korotkov. Game after game, nothing could stop Kodes as the sharp-edged laughter mounted. Jan had the first eleven games. At 0–

6, 0–5, Korotkov managed to win his own serve, and heard the first applause for a Russian. Sarcastic applause. But after that, their ordeal dissipated, the mood lightened, they were sporting and gave Korotkov his due on good shots: light, polite applause.

More kisses were blown to and from Kodes at the conclusion of the 6–0, 6–3, 7–5, triumph, and his captain, Antonin Bolardt, embraced him. Jan had vindicated himself, he would be able to celebrate—and sleep. With Czechoslovakia holding a winning margin, 3–1, Pala and Metreveli were anticlimax. After Pala took a lead, Metreveli quit, complaining of an injured foot. For perhaps the only time in his exceptional career, Alex was booed as he walked from a court. His captain, Andreev, seemed to have inherited Kodes's brow-etching furrows, complemented by a Siberia's-not-so-bad-in-the-summer look.

The Russians, en route to London, were recalled home, withdrawn from Wimbledon. All but Metreveli.

At the hotel, the friendly diminutive hall porter had watched much of it on TV, understanding little except the essence. Like a fisherman describing a catch with his hands, he struggled with English to explain: "Leetle Czechoslovakia," his hands, close together, then spread back as far as possible, "beat beeeeg Russia!"

His grin was as wide as his wingspread.

46

○

Eureka!

Moments of discovery are sweet indeed. Maybe looking back on them is even better, remembering just where and when you spotted somebody as a nobody, and made a mental note: Watch that kid. They are freeze-frames still frying in the brain pan, picture puffs gone up in the smoke of time, yet lingering like a first kiss.

Of course it happens, too, that numerous discoveries stay undiscovered by everyone else because they never grow to the stature you imagine for them.

Not that it took genius to be captivated by plump sixteen-year-old Billie Jean Moffitt one August morning in 1960 as she romped across the lawn of Essex County Club, near Boston, fashioning a second-set bagel against the No. 1 American, Darlene Hard. What a kid! I thought, though she didn't win the match. But who could hallucinate that, down the road, she'd become Bully Jean King, turning Bobby Riggs into an Astrodome pumpkin? Or that teenagers named Tony Trabert, Rosie Casals, Martina Navratilova, Bjorn Borg, Ivan Lendl, John

McEnroe, Yannick Noah, Steffi Graf, and Boris Becker were on their way to the heights?

Twenty Wimbledon titles are one thing, but if Billie Jean is remembered by any member of the general populace it's for slaying His Piggishness, a puckish dirty old man named Bobby Riggs in 1973.

It took Houston's Astrodome to hold all the people (a record tennis congregation of 30,472) who wanted to pay, many at one hundred dollars ringside, to watch a meaningless engagement that somehow took on great meaning. The mixed singles championship of a soap operatic world—can the feminist broad beat the geriatric sex symbol?—may have been a schlockathon, but it gripped people who had never given tennis a thought. It divided households, inspired American bookmakers to make a line on tennis for the only time, and spurred the Tennis Epidemic of the 1970s. At its acme, a sabbath afternoon in August 1975, which I recall as Sadistic Sunday for couch potato heads, there was no way to avoid tennis: the game ran simultaneously on all four national channels (ABC, CBS, NBC, PBS). It was so bad that I ran head-to-bald-head against myself—a tournament on PBS live, another, taped, on NBC. A little of Collins went a short way that day.

Little Bobby Riggs, fifty-five, went a long way on amiable braggadocio in a remarkable resurrection thirty-four years after his own Wimbledon championship. "When I could really play, who the hell knew? Wimbledon 'thirty-nine? Just tennis people. Now I got one foot in the grave and everybody knows me."

True enough. Suddenly he was a name, after challenging and beating a nerves-stricken Margaret Court in a promotion for a California housing development. His Piggishness was squealing all the way to the interviews and commercial endorsements, the best known for a candy called Sugar Daddy.

Who would defend womankind against this crass skirt-buster, whose humiliation of all-time champ Court made the female tour look bad? "How good are they if the best can't beat an old guy like me?" he chortled, trying to egg on a bigger challenge for much more money and attention.

Who else but Mother Freedom, mouthpiece of the Virginia Slims? It was up to Billie Jean to shut him up and protect the integrity of the tour (only three years old then). Or something like that. Who cared? Everybody, as it turned out.

Bookmakers said it was 8-to-5, favoring the geezer, and did plenty of business. And Bobby, ever the hustler (he had won one hundred thousand 1939 dollars from a London bookie by furtively betting on his amateur self to sweep Wimbledon's singles, doubles, and mixed doubles) was wagering thousands on himself to zing King. Feminist writers Grace Lichtenstein and Nora Ephron took up a collection in New York and journeyed to Houston to personally take a piece of Bobby's action.

Would it be the lady or the wrinkled tiger? At zero hour they entered the Astrodome like potentates. Billie Jean rode high on a palanquin shouldered by a bare-chested beefcake brigade. Pulling Bobby in a rickshaw were his "bosom buddies," the greatest young collection of breastworks since the Colonists fortified Bunker Hill.

Riggs, born the same year as Billie Jean's father (1918) assured his son, "No broad can beat me."

With the world watching and rooting as never before or since for a game of tennis, Billie Jean came through—for her sex, her Slims sisters, not to mention her savings account ($200,000 or so)—in straight sets.

Bobby, she said, "played like a woman."

Obviously somebody else had been captivated before me, or these kids of my reveries wouldn't have been on view to be "discovered." All of them except one: Sri Hashan Anandan.

Now there was a discovery as likely as finding an IBM stockholder in the Kremlin. You don't bump into too many tennis players in Dar-es-Salaam, the capital of Tanzania, situated on the East African shore of the Indian Ocean. There are a few, but nothing to write recruiters at home about. Except for the improbable—though unstructurable—Sri Hashan Anandan, a lanky Indian youth who hit the ball like a paragon from a tennis textbook. Which he was.

We happened upon him during a State Department journey through Africa in 1970. The star attractions were Arthur Ashe and Stan Smith, obviously in that order, even though Stan stood above Arthur in the rankings as the No. 1 American. In fact Stan was only a semiattraction. Invariably they were introduced by the hosts as "world champion Arthur Ashe" and oh, yes, Smith—presented as an afterthought.

By the time we got to Lusaka, Zambia, the fourth stop, the usually placid Smith was ruffled. It was the only time I've ever heard him curse. "Jee-zus, Arthur!" he fumed over a beer. "I know you're black, and everything, but I am the number-one American, and today they barely acknowledged I was here."

Ashe seemed a little embarrassed until another of the small group, Frank Deford of *Sports Illustrated,* put it in perspective. "Stan, you ought to understand one thing: This is the Arthur Ashe Tour, and you are merely the Big O—for opponent. Like some nonentity Muhammad Ali would bring along to spar against. It's Ashe and Opponent. They aren't interested in the world rankings here—just Brother Ashe."

Made sense, and Smith, learning his place, cooled off with, "Okay. Okay, but Arthur, I can't wait to take you on my State Department tour of Mississippi."

Considerable anti-American sentiment was churning in Zambia at the time. Embassy officials, warning us that we might have to withdraw from the court immediately if demonstrators appeared, wondered if Arthur and Stan should even wear their Davis Cup jackets with USA on the back. (They did). In Dar es Salaam, a recent goodwill delegation of astronauts had been turned back, and an American theatrical troupe jeered and pelted with milk cartons.

However, sport seemed to make a difference. Even emblazoned USA, Ashe and Smith were cordially, enthusiastically received at their clinics and exhibition matches, though nobody regarded Stan as the better player. It was during an instructional session in Dar that a local, Sri Hashan Anandan, seventeen, stood out more than the USA logos or Smith's pale face. His father, a gas-station attendant who had never played tennis, brought him to see Ashe, and the kid was belting balls in wondrous style, looking like an old pro. Nobody could believe it. How? Why? In this tennis backwater? His father shyly explained that he had come across an old how-to book by Bill Tilden, and decided that it would be a good game for his son. Together they followed the text and photos, and practiced swings in front of a mirror. Eventually Sri had every stroke in the book down pat, and delivered each impressively in hitting with Smith and Ashe.

"Nobody learns tennis like that!" exclaimed Ashe. "At least not that well." So enthused was Arthur that he promised father and son he'd find the boy a college scholarship in the United States, preferably at his alma mater, University of California at Los Angeles.

Ashe followed through. We were all anxious to follow Sri's

progress through college and into the pros, but it wasn't forth-
coming. Arthur landed him at Southern Methodist University,
but it was all too alien for Sri. The studies coupled with homesickness were forbidding. And he couldn't beat anybody. Despite those sparkling strokes, he'd never competed, except for
some pickup stuff in Dar. Competition itself proved too stress-
ful. The miracle of Dar es Salaam was undeniable. Sri was picture
perfect—until they started keeping score. All that talent . . .

You might shake your head as people say and do when a can't-
miss prospect misses. But for me, a guy named Nikki Pilic had
the last, insightful word on "talent" a few years ago at a Stockholm tournament. Pilic, who now labors as Germany's national
coach and Davis Cup captain, was among a collection of players at a morning practice. Taking a turn on court and swatting
balls masterfully was an equipment salesman, an Englishman
named Dickie Dillon.

Answering the "Who's that?" queries, another Limey, Ger-
ald Battrick, said, "Dickie's from up North, same as Roger Taylor. He was better than any of us as a junior. Much more talent.
If he'd stuck with it, with all that talent, he'd be near the top
now, and—"

"Bullshit!" growled Pilic from a nearby bench.

Battrick and the rest of us looked askance at Nikki.

"I am so tired," Pilic said, "tired of hearing this everywhere, about how some talented guy would be so great if he
felt like it. Like hitting the ball great is what talent is all about.
I'll tell you what real talent is: Is working when you don't feel
like it. Is working harder than ever when you're losing. Is going
to America and eating the lousy food and being homesick to
play the toughest tournaments. Is wanting to keep improving
and making yourself doing everything you can, and hanging in
here when you're sick of travel and this tough life.

"Please don't give me bullshit about what some big-tal-
ented guy could do if he wanted to take the trouble. If somebody is really talented, then they're out here with us."

Tirade concluded, Niki had made his point. At least with
me, and probably Jimmy Connors, who wasn't there. Connors
frequently says, "Staying out here week after week, year after
year—and winning, or you can't stay—that's the test of a real
player." Jimmy has passed the test, wouldn't you say?

The last I heard of the memorably discovered Sri, he was working as a teaching pro in Texas. Considering how well he applied himself to the lessons of Bill Tilden, he's probably doing all right in imparting them. I hope so.

The following year, 1971, Ashe, on another African swing, made a more substantial find in Cameroon: eleven-year-old Yannick Noah, who a dozen years later would win the French Open. Yannick was batting balls with an oversized paddle, a slat carved to the shape of a racket. As the issue of a Cameroonian father and French mother, the patently athletic kid was a French citizen. This was helpful in Ashe's enlisting the aid of Philippe Chatrier, president of the FFT. "You ought to bring him to France for training. He has definite potential," was Ashe's recommendation.

It was done. Left in Yaounde, Noah would have improved little. Plucked from West Africa, he bloomed to fulfillment on that electrifying June afternoon in 1983 when he elated France as the first male citizen to win the national championship in thirty-six years.

Having heard about Yannick from Arthur, I was eager for a look. The wish was granted at Miami Beach six years after the discovery. He was still raw, but undeniably talented, as I believe Pilic would have confirmed, in leading France to victory in the Sunshine Cup, a worldwide team event for juniors.

Ivan Lendl was another I encountered at the Sunshine Cup. He was on a practice court, topless, treating his ashen eighteen-year-old frame to the winter rays of Florida. Laughing and smiling, this wasn't the Lendl persona to become ingrained with the public. I wasn't startled because I didn't know him. But his mammoth forehand was very startling. Identifying him for me, one of the Czech coaches said, "Why shouldn't he be happy—being here instead of Czechoslovakia in December?" Or any time? Maybe Lendl, like Martina Navratilova before him, was making plans already for American residency.

Seen purely by accident in 1947, Tony Trabert was my first "phenom." Only a burr-headed little high school sophomore from Cincinnati, he was beginning an eight-year ascent to one of the three best seasons ever put together by an American man.

I was in Columbus, watching a classmate compete in the state schoolboy track meet, and wandered outside of Ohio State Stadium to courts where the tennis tournament was taking place.

As a loser in a district qualifying tournament in Cleveland, I was curious to see how my conqueror, Joey Russell, was doing. I thought he'd win it, until I took a look at this kid, Trabert, who could barely see over the net.

Decked out in a big-time cable-stitched sweater with striped V neck and a white eyeshade, Trabert was bouncing with confidence and the kind of good-looking shots I'd seen only once before. That was in an obscure pro match between Welby Van Horn and Franc Kovacs in a Miami public park.

But Van Horn and Kovacs were seasoned campaigners, and Tony, crowned that weekend as the Ohio high school champ, was a little kid. I vowed to keep as close track of his career as I could. It was mainly through reading since I saw him play but two more times, once in an inconsequential doubles match, and a little later against Pancho Gonzalez on a pro one-nighter. But I still think, whenever I watch him as astute TV tennis commentator for CBS, "That's my boy!"

A personal record for discoveries is two in one morning, during a prowl of the back courts at the U.S. Open of 1983. I'd learned of Steffi Graf from my Italian crony, Clerici, who cooed, "You must see this little German monster!" Since neither he nor any other Italian male could be accused of interest in a female player, unless she were spectacularly conformed, this was quite an endorsement. There she was, a gem all right, skinny, fourteen years old, with blond tresses streaming down her spine, and a power game quite evident. "When I was a kid I played for fun," she told me, making it clear that she expected to get to the top.

After leaving Steffi I sought a look at Bill Stanley, a good American junior who was going to enter Harvard. Stanley was getting kicked around in a way that would never happen to him in the Ivy League, by a big, rugged-looking redhead. Because he was playing serve-and-volley, I took the redhead for an American, maybe an Iowa farm boy. Then I heard him swearing in German. German? Playing like this? Hello, Boris Becker, Wimbledon champ twenty-two months hence.

My next look at the poised Becker was profound, too, though he was flat on his back, severely wounded at his first Wimbledon the following June. He had just tumbled, tearing up an ankle, in the third round against Billy Scanlon. He had to surrender, but before departing on a stretcher, Boris insisted on getting to his feet long enough to shake Scanlon's hand.

Nancy Richey, one of the best clay-court players who ever lived, was as surprised as I was when an amply-waisted left-handed sixteen-year-old with an impossible name beat her in Paris by serve-and-volleying in 1973. Nobody could do that. Martina Navratilova did. I could see that I would have to learn to pronounce that eleven-letter jumble fast. Though it would be nine years before she and her game were finely tuned enough to go all the way in the French Open, Martina gave notice that day.

She came to Boston the next winter for an indoor tournament, wider and happier than ever, having made a discovery herself: her country-to-be, America, along with its trash cuisine. "Do you remember me? From Paris?" she bubbled.

I was not likely to forget such form, in every respect. Her English was already in pretty firm control.

"I'm going to get better," Martina promised, unboastfully.

Understatement. Better? Better than anyone before her, in my opinion. But Steffi Graf may add another gear to Martina's highest. Martina seldom does anything undramatically. The day in 1975 that Manolo Orantes pulled one of the great upsets by beating Jimmy Connors for the U.S. Open title, Martina upstaged him at Forest Hills by announcing her defection. Orantes made the sports pages all right, but Martina was on the front pages. A wonderful woman. And if she prefers the company of women, what of it. So do I. But I was jealous of her when she was seeing the witty, radiant writer, Rita Mae Brown.

As clever as Navratilova is, I don't believe that anyone of either sex had a greater gift for racket dexterity than the soulful mite Rosie Casals.

Oh-ho-ho? Who's this? Quickly I was beguiled by the Rosebud one 1965 afternoon at Phoenix when I sneaked away from the Red Sox spring training camp in Scottsdale to look in on the Thunderbird Championships. I had wanted to say hello to Karen Hantze Susman, the Wimbledon champ of 1962, who was a homemaker and withdrawing, but I was transfixed by the sixteen-year-old gamine across the net. Casals. Flying and flicking with abandon, five-foot Rosie briskly went at Karen, unawed, and nearly beat her in three sets. "Ah, these little kids are a trial," laughed Karen, indicating her baby daughter in a stroller—and Casals, who would never stroll when she could run.

Rosie, who won her share of singles titles but will be remembered as an all-time doubles virtuoso, particularly alongside Billy Jean King, is a little bit miffed whenever prodigies are discussed. "When Chris Evert, then Tracy Austin and Andrea Jaeger came along, people acted like there'd never been such sensational kids before. I could do more things at the same age." Correct. "And I wasn't the only one, in California anyway. But before open tennis, and prize money, there weren't the opportunities to get around, and develop. And there wasn't TV and press attention."

Another morning vigil in an empty grandstand was graced by another genius, this time John McEnroe. The court at Roland Garros in Paris was the same one on which Martina Navratilova had beaten Nancy Richey four years earlier. Like many teenagers, McEnroe was in his Bjorn Borg phase, though only in appearance. Streaming hair was kept moderately ruly by headband. But there was no aping of Bjorn's two-fisted backhand and exaggerated topspin as so many others were doing. McEnroe was unique among the current crowd, with a thoughtful style that coupled baseline strength with an innate feel for the net. "My God, here's an American who understands how to play on this stuff!" I said to myself, watching him during the French Open's junior tournament, which he won. "He can win and look good, too, without boring us to death." That was exciting.

"This stuff" was turgid European clay in which so many American males have been interred since Trabert won the French in 1954 and 1955.

It was 1977, the first time around for McEnroe, eighteen, a delicious time. He was having fun, winning his first major out of the blue, the French Mixed, with his hometown pal, Mary Carillo, and only days later illuminated Wimbledon by doing the unthinkable: Rising from the ruck of the qualifying tournament he penetrated the Big W all the way to the semis. His three qualifying wins plus five in the tournament proper are a Wimbledon record. No anonymous outsider has come close to that exploit, although seventeen-year-old Boris Becker, winning the title unseeded in 1985, outranks it.

I wonder if Mac has ever experienced such a joyous time in tennis since. The limelight, under which he has always squirmed in shy discomfort, had not yet found him, although its rays had the range. Everything was there for him, glittering, within the reach of his left hand.

Numerous other, and less desirable, unimaginable acts have also been committed by McEnroe at Wimbledon, and elsewhere. Everywhere. Had he not succumbed to tantrum against courtside photographers in the third set, I feel he wouldn't have squandered a two-set final-round lead against Ivan Lendl in Paris in 1984. He could have been the American finally to emulate Trabert, ending a twenty-nine-year French drought, following through on the promise I glimpsed on the outer courts of Roland Garros. And, since he would win Wimbledon and the U.S. Open in that, his zenith, year, John might well have concluded a Grand Slam at the Australian, on his turf, grass.

Unfortunately, his temperament has overshadowed accomplishment in the public mind. He is ever contrite, as his press conference confessionals attest, yet never self-corrective. Sportswriters, who have undergone innumerable such encounter sessions, would be justified in charging Mac $50 per hearing, or some suitable therapist's fee, for attending his recitals of sin and apology. Only a couch is missing.

Often, someone will say to me, having read of his mea culpas, "Sounds like he means it this time. Has he ever sounded like that to you before?"

"Why, yes," I answer each time with a practiced response, "and I can almost name the exact date. I remember it clearly. August in Boston. The U.S. Pro. He had nearly defeated Jimmy Connors, but wasn't experienced enough to realize he could win. And he had behaved badly. I found him alone in the locker room and decided that, just once, I would deliver a sermon on behavior. I liked him immensely, and was enamored of his game. I thought I owed him a friendly scolding.

"I told him that I thought he was going to be a champion, probably a great one, and that the great ones—Laver, Rosewall, Kramer, and the rest—didn't sully their reputations with bad-acting. For one thing, they thought too much of themselves and the game.

"He took it, nodding affirmatively, saying, 'Thank you. You're right. I'm working on it, and this will never happen again.'

"I left him, feeling good. That was 1977."

So much for good intentions and deeds.

At the other end of the spectrum, behaviorally, in the upper echelon of sportsmen are Roy Emerson, the rollicking Aussie, and Bjorn Borg, the reticent Swede. They are also 1–2 among the all-time champions: Emmo won twelve major singles, Bjorn eleven. But Borg, at sixteen, was still a dozen short of Emerson, age thirty-five, when I hung on a fence of an outside court at Forest Hills for their U.S. Open clash of 1972.

"What are you doing out here? Watching Emmo one more time?" a few of his fans inquired. It was his last major.

"Always good to see him," I replied, "but it's the Swedish kid who interests me."

Overflowing blond locks arrested by headband, two-handed backhand, and *beaucoup de* topspin—there he was, Teen Angel. And in deep trouble on alien footing, grass, that appeared as forbidding to him as swamp grass to an explorer in Africa. Out of it as he was, against a man born to lawns, Bjorn nevertheless showed good signs, and great determination in those cobalt eyes. He would persevere, all right, overcoming grass at Wimbledon.

What a neat historic panorama, Borg, coming, against Emerson, going. It wasn't until almost a decade later that I learned that another participant was there who made it three of a kind. John McEnroe, thirteen, who would topple Borg from the Wimbledon throne, and beat him twice in U.S. Open finals, was one of the ballboys.

47

○

Up and Away

Never missed a shot from the press box or the broadcast booth, or erred on a line call. Raised a sweat at Wimbledon only when the air-conditioning failed in the booth. The game's easy, playing from those positions. Took a few cheap shots, of course, and didn't always hit winners, but never lost a match.

However, lost my job at the Sunshine Cup in Miami Beach, after five years of telecasting that tournament. Carelessly I happened to mention the fact that the temperature was thirty-six degrees in explaining why the players didn't take off their warm-up suits and my Floridian partner, Donna Fales, sounded like Fred Astaire tapdancing when she attempted talking. The underwriter, the Miami Beach tourist bureau, considering me a traitor to their cause, insisted that the producer, the local PBS station, dump me.

Lost a few on-air arguments with my longest-term partner, Donald Dell, who, benefiting from legal training and degree, was able to speak louder and longer. But not the one concerning the argument a client of his, Eddie Dibbs, was having with an umpire during a Canadian Open semifinal in 1978. As Dibbs

349

complained about a line call against him, Donald was supportive, "Eddie's right. His shot was definitely good."

This was a low-budget, not-exactly-straightforward production of a match in Toronto at which Donald and I were not present. Instead we were watching the feed on a small monitor in a cramped studio in New York, and providing commentary with the air of guys at courtside. "Donald," I ventured, "don't you think we're a little far from that line to be making judgments?" He acceded to that with silence.

Donald wasn't silent often, although I felt for him on an ostensibly happy occasion in 1974 at Chicago. His personable kid brother, Dick Dell, an eager but ordinary player, was having the high-water tournament of a brief pro career. Reaching the semis against Marty Riessen, Dick was in one of two matches on that day's telecast. And Donald felt himself on the spot. Since both his brother and Riessen were clients, he sensed no conflict there. But he wanted Dick to win so badly that he could hardly talk—an upset in itself—and was afraid he'd sound biased. Dauntless Donald has never been so inhibited.

Eddie Dibbs, the remarkable and irrepressible little scuffler, was in the other semi against Stan Smith, and I assumed it was his first televised bit. "Not really," he told me. "One time in Miami I'm playing a junior match, and a station sends a camera crew to cover it. They get there just in time to film me rolling in the dirt with my opponent, a kid named Hershey. We were having a disagreement over a line call."

A feisty retriever who never won an easy point, Eddie nevertheless won over a million dollars in prize money, but had no illusions or conceit. After progressing to the quarters of the French Open in 1979, he said, "I'm not kidding myself. If I wasn't playing tennis, I'd be a bag boy at Safeway."

Eddie had a clearer outlook than most, especially after his vision was tested and they fitted him for contact lenses at the University of Miami, where he held a tennis scholarship and was an honors student in math at the nearby dog track. "The doc says to me, 'God, how could you even see the ball with these eyes?' And I say I couldn't. But I sort of knew where it was."

A right-handed hustler, he would offer to play you left-handed if the stakes were right, neglecting to mention that he was born left-handed. Many a bagel did he hang on professional foes with his right hand (and on suckers with his left), but Eddie's lasting contribution may have been in neology.

It was Dibbs who coined "bagel" as noun or verb applied to a shutout, a love set—bagel, bagel job, bageled. Just as it was Fred Stolle who came up with "hackers," a term of endearment for those of us constituting the vast tennis-playing majority.

"They must think I'm just an old hacker," snorted Stolle after reporting to Forest Hills in 1966. We hadn't heard that usage before. Fresh from winning the German title and certainly one of the world's best, Stolle was grousing justifiably about being put down without a seeding at the Nationals. Disregarding the official disdain, Fred, twenty-seven, won the championship. He smiled then, "Reckon the old hacker can still play a little."

How old is the old hackerly diversion anyway? There are differing counts. You could date tennis from 1874 when the patenting papa, Major Walter Clopton Wingfield, staked his founding claim in London. Or 1877, the first Wimbledon. Maybe 1926, when the flamboyant American promoter C. C. ("Cash-and-Carry") Pyle established a new occupation, professional tennis, by signing up Suzanne Lenglen, Vinnie Richards, and others for his traveling squad.

For me, the game came of age in 1989, celebrating a twenty-first birthday on the April anniversary of open tennis. From Bournemouth '68, first of a dozen open tournaments that year whose total prize money fell short of a half-million, to the present bonanza has been a breathtaking leap. Sometimes it seemed a suicidal leap as the game burst all the old constricting seams like a slob gorging on fast foods with no concern or responsibility for the consequences.

Money unlimited appeared to be the rule as the unending season—the thirteen-month year some years—offered about fifty million dollars annually in prize money for men and women on the legit circuits, the Grand Prix and Virginia Slims. Nobody knew how much there was in the make-believe whirl of exhibitions where, in their heyday, Borg, McEnroe, Connors, Lendl, Becker could command $50,000 nightly, and Evert, Navratilova, and Graf could come pretty close.

The exo pot, stirred and supervised by the Vultures, the agents, has made the playing personages, particularly the men, careless. They neglect their obligations to the side of their profession that matters: the matches and tournaments whose results enter the records and are registered by the remorseless computers. Too often the exhibitions and accompanying easy money up front seemed to take precedence over the labors of substance.

Take Ivan Lendl in 1988. As No. 1 at a time in his career when he'd become a great player, an attraction whose presence enhanced tournaments wherever he went, he chose to do less to uphold the game that needs all the help possible from the leading lights. Lendl, who became fabulously wealthy through tennis, received permission from the MTC to reduce his schedule from the minimum of fourteen tournaments—hardly an imposition—to twelve. In return, Lendl agreed to slim his exhibition time from fourteen weeks to ten, "averaging four exos a week," by his count. That means forty of them at fifty-grand per pop, or a cool two million dollars for showing his scowling face. Winning or losing mattered not at all. In his legitimate 1988 life, the Grand Prix, Ivan played not many more matches for less in prize money, though enough added in rules-flouting guarantees to keep him above the poverty level.

That's the absurd proposition in men's tennis: Exhibitions mean more to the upper crust than the tournaments that are the lifeblood of their profession, and where they make names to cash in on at make-believe. It's as though big league ball players were better recompensed for their spring training games than the championship season. Something's haywire.

Lendl isn't alone in going for the minimum workload where it counts, and moaning that he's overworked on the Grand Prix circuit. It's the exos that are the overworking factor, requiring time and energy even if there's no pressure to win, offering the chance of injury or aggravating an injury when a player might otherwise be resting up for genuine competition. When Boris Becker lost disappointingly in an early round in the 1988 U.S. Open, he blamed foot injuries of some duration. Nevertheless, he had kept his exo appointments the weekend prior to the Open. Where were his priorities? And wasn't he cheating himself and the public?

No other sport offers similar temptations, a situation where "let's pretend" is more lucrative than the real, hard thing. This is dangerous for the credibility of a game whose elite are perceived, accurately, to be coddled and avaricious beyond belief.

Why did the MTC cave in to Lendl, giving him most-favored treatment? "Otherwise," Ivan himself answers, "I would play even less tournaments. I would get automatically into the French and U.S. opens as a former champion. The Australian would give me a wild card, and even if Wimbledon made me qualify that would just give me more grass-court practice."

That statement says it all for the concept of responsibility to the game where he was nurtured. Lendl isn't alone in giving back more and more nothing of the championship something he has become, but it is especially disheartening to hear and see it from a leader, a man who had been No. 1 for so long, and worked so hard to get there.

It's unimaginable that open tennis pioneers such as Arthur Ashe, John Newcombe, Rod Laver, Ken Rosewall, and Stan Smith would think or talk that way. And certainly not the noblest pro of them all, whose like we'll never see again. He was a Limey, Major J. C. S. Rendall, whose motto might have been liberty, equality, and fraternity if somebody else hadn't used it first. After winning the pro tourney at Menton, France, in 1923, Rendall cut up first prize—the only prize offered, by the way—with his seven fellow competitors. Sure it was only four hundred dollars, but fifty bucks apiece wasn't too bad in 1923. A similar deed today would probably brand Rendall a socialist or a fool.

But maybe I romanticize the guys who kept the game going in the early years. Maybe, if they came along now, amid all the undreamed-of financial scams, they'd be just as thoughtless and greedy. I choose not to think so. I choose to believe the good old Aussies, as a group, would be true to themselves and the game at any period.

Lendl and his agents—all the agents—have got it figured wrong for tennis, if not for their bank accounts. So, unfortunately for the game and its devotees, did Bjorn Borg and John McEnroe, finished as champs too soon. Those two precious beings were gutted more by heavy exo itineraries than anything else. How many times millionaires did they need to be?

To thrive, the game needs to see more of the exceptionals in championship arenas, not less. Wouldn't it be ironic if the pros, who arrived at the dawn of open tennis as one-nighting nomads, were to be returned to that existence as tournaments declined and exos became the rule for the select few?

But it's very difficult for the Wise Old Owls of the MTC

and WIPTC, the Badgers of the ITF and the Beavers of the ATP and WITA, to hold off the Vultures, and break their talons gripping the game and spreading the exos like manure.

What is needed is a sensible nine-month season (at most), concluding shortly after the U.S. Open. That would provide an off-season, a relief from the grind such as existed during the days of the Lost Civilization of summer game amateurism. The sport cries out for a time to heal mind and body, refresh, reflect, and recharge batteries. A time for self-improvement and practice that is virtually impossible now as the computer calls the pressurized tune. And, yes, a separate time for all the exos that almost anybody could desire. Detracting and distracting from the circuits, they should be banned during a regulation season, that would ideally run from January through September.

But will agents, players, and administrators ever come together in true long-term concern for the game to agree on such a beneficial reduction of the bloated calendar?

It's hard to believe they would in a game so fragmented and opposed to change that even the usually level-headed heads of Wimbledon and the French Open can't see the self-preserving wisdom of moving the Big W back one week on the calendar, and the French forward by one week. Thereby they'd open a month's gap (instead of the all too brief fortnight) between themselves and the French Open. For the good of the players, and their play, those two demanding major tournaments in Paris and London should be further apart. That would put rain-dogged Wimbledon in a period of more favorable weather, and the players in more favorable condition, readier physically and artistically. If Wimbledon hopes to maintain its grass cachet—as it should—there must be more opportunity for prior play on this surface so alien to today's players.

When I get discouraged, though, I try to put tennis in the perspective of two decades—the phenomenal rise from Lost Civilization's secret sport to eminence and acceptance as a profession with worldwide following and TV coverage. As Billy Talbert says, "The game will go on in spite of itself."

A welcome addition to that "going on" was the restoration of tennis to the Olympics in Seoul. Although the players were out-and-out, unapologetic pros, as was fitting at a playground where the world's best gathered in the autumn of 1988, they indulged in a refreshing departure from money for two weeks.

"There was a purity in playing just for the sake of playing," silver medalist Tim Mayotte of the United States summed it up well.

The tableau of incongruous new doubles partners, Garrison and Shriver, hugging each other and weeping for joy on winning their gold medals would not be forgotten. Zina Garrison, the black from Houston, exulted, "This means more where I come from than my beating Martina [Navratilova] at the U.S. Open." Pam Shriver, the preppy from Lutherville, Maryland, eight inches taller at six-feet, and holder of nineteen major doubles titles, including the 1984 Grand Slam, sobbed, "None of it comes close to this."

Completing the first ever Quintessential Quintuple—attaching a gold medal to her Grand Slam—Steffi Graf was considerably more emotional than she had been in closing the Slam at Flushing Meadows not long before. "Well, an Olympic gold medal is something everybody understands."

While some of the better players didn't care to neglect breadwinning long enough to take part, it was their loss.

Another welcome arrival in 1988 was Andre Agassi, at eighteen the youngest ever to hold the No. 1 American ranking. His rip-roaring style and his manner were the embodiment of fun, a quality too often submerged or forgotten. Andre has a good time playing, and transmits it to the witnesses. Some colleagues gave him jaundiced looks, as though the kid were breaking a law. He wasn't going at tennis in the right spirit, making it seem like coal mining or assembly-lining. Dangerous guy—having fun out there. Jimmy Connors and John McEnroe thought Agassi might be showboating, and questioned his carefree behavior. Imagine those two criticizing anybody's deportment?

Change does come, however, as we've seen in the twenty-one years since cataclysmic Bournemouth. Most good. Some bad, as in the very implements of the game.

Everybody laughed, of course, when Ion Tiriac and Valerie Ziegenfuss stood up to play with Howard Head's huge-headed green monsters, which were called the "Prince." It was 1977, and the game began to get out of hand with what they held—oversized rackets of zingier metallic compositions. Soon enough everyone would have them, of one make or another.

Brief laughter, then grave concern, was voiced about another weird racket that year, gripped by a reborn Rumpel-stiltskin, a bearded gnome from the Vermont hills, Michael Fishbach. His was a shaggy racket story that amused before turning worried heads at Forest Hills. After this nonentity, Fishbach, slaughtered ex-champ Stan Smith in the second round of the Open, his homespun club, quickly dubbed the "spaghetti racket," became a hot, fearful topic. Since Fishbach had to win three qualifying matches to get in, Smith was the fifth victim throttled by spaghetti.

"It's not against the rules," laughed Fishbach, whose racket seemed a platter of blending pastas in its stringing. Doubled-up nylon, twine, fishing line, adhesive tape were ingredients that produced fiendish, unpredictable spin and soaring bounce, while emitting no sound. The magical *Puh! Puh! Puh!* was gone.

"That's what got me," said Stan Smith. "If you can't hear the ball hit the other guy's racket you're disoriented."

Fishbach, who had pinched the idea from Aussie Barry Phillips-Moore, was a mediocre player, gone in the next round despite what the players termed an unfair edge. Brian Teacher wondered what would happen if one of the really good players got his hands on a spaghetti wand.

Shortly one did. Ilie Nastase. With his wizardry, the game was over. A new game of aberrational spin was being ushered in, dictated more by the racket's stringing than the talent of its user. Guillermo Vilas, who had won the U.S. Open, and run a record string of fifty successive match wins to the final of Aix-en-Provence, was strung up there by Nastase-wielded spaghetti. So unstrung was Vilas by the unnatural acts-of-spin Nastase was committing that he quit after the second set. Here was Vilas, who, with Bjorn Borg, was creating an abominable base-line style of exaggerated topspin that is with us yet—the Swedish disease?—and he was being done in by swirls that made his stuff look like faint ripples.

Fishbach was correct. No rules governed size, shape, weight, substance of rackets, or methods and materials of their stringing. Alarmed at this pronounced change, the ITF, reacting with uncharacteristic rapidity, prudently barred spaghetti and placed limits on stringing and racket size. But, unfortunately, not the composition of rackets for male pros.

It was a mistake to allow wood to be superceded as the weaponry for the strongest of pros, the men. Alas, it wasn't perceived—by me or anybody else—that baseball had a lesson to offer and to be followed. Despite the introduction of livelier, high-tech bats, used widely, even in college, administrators of professional baseball decreed that old-fashioned bats would not go the way of wooden rackets. Baseball players themselves have gotten stronger and better, as have tennis players. But the guardians of baseball have maintained a certain continuity in the level of play by not permitting equipment to overpower their game as it has tennis.

A return to wooden rackets—for male pros—would be as wise as the continued use of wooden bats at the top.

Fiberglass, aluminum, kevlar, graphite, boron, kryptonite, and the other newfangled materials and compositions are wonderful for you and me—and the female pros, whose game is improved. But they've knocked the men's game out of whack. Subtlety and balance have been lost in a binge of overhitting and hyped-up topspin. Tediously protracted points result because everybody can stand on the baseline, hitting the ball a ton, knowing topspin will keep it in. Can another artist, a McEnroe, appear in this climate?

A young man, Bjorn Borg, thirty-three, who introduced the dominant style of today, but with wood, agrees. At the Hall of Fame, where he accepted his induction medal in 1988, he told me, "The move from wood was a mistake that I see now. The game is more powerful, but it isn't as good to watch."

They say you can't hold back progress, but baseball leaders recognized that high tech didn't mean progress for their game. I hope the MTC and ATP soon see through the glisten of false modernity, and bring back wood, a greater measuring stick for a man's skills.

High-tech high-flying, a tribute to an extraordinary woman's skills, was, I like to believe, testimony that once in a while I've done something worthwhile. Even patriotic, although I don't mean the time during the Korean War that Private First Class Arthur Kaplan and I, a corporal, won the Fourth Army Ping-Pong championship, doing-not-dying for dear old Camp Polk, Louisiana. Did that send shivers through the distant enemies in North Korea? Why else did peace talks begin soon thereafter, sparing the North Koreans the wrath of our sharpshooting paddles? Also, thank God, sparing Kaplan and me.

Possibly more in the national interest was an even less likely victory in California in 1975. This time no championship was at stake, or so-called chauvinistic honor such as Bobby Riggs had vainly promised to uphold against Billie Jean King two years before. My partner, Barry ("Orso") Lorge, and I were just trying to survive against a couple of female pros who were kind enough to give us the time of day on a concrete court in Palm Springs.

Lorge, the loveably bearish sports editor and thoughtful columnist for the *San Diego Union*, was then a bachelor reporter for the *Washington Post*. They had better things to do, but he charmed the young women named O'Shaughnessy and Ride into a game of doubles during a women's tournament we were covering.

He and I were thrilled to be on the same court. They were gracious, even when Orso and I inexplicably got hot in our shotmaking, threw in a few outrageous line calls—and beat them.

But as Tam O'Shaughnessy and Sally Ride shook hands with their hackerly conquerors, the sweaty, newspapering million-to-one shots, they must have realized that Lorge and I represented destiny. We were the message: If anybody, even on an off day, could beat them, they deserved liberation from the pro tour.

Tam O'Shaughnessy got a straight job, and seemed happy the last time I saw her. So did Sally Ride, a government position with the National Aeronautical and Space Agency. Sally went higher on her job than any woman, and only a few men, before her—as America's first female astronaut.

Do the two of them mention us nightly in their prayers for giving direction to their lives? Isn't it reasonable to say that Orso and I sent Sally Ride into outer space? It was the least we could do for our country.

Index